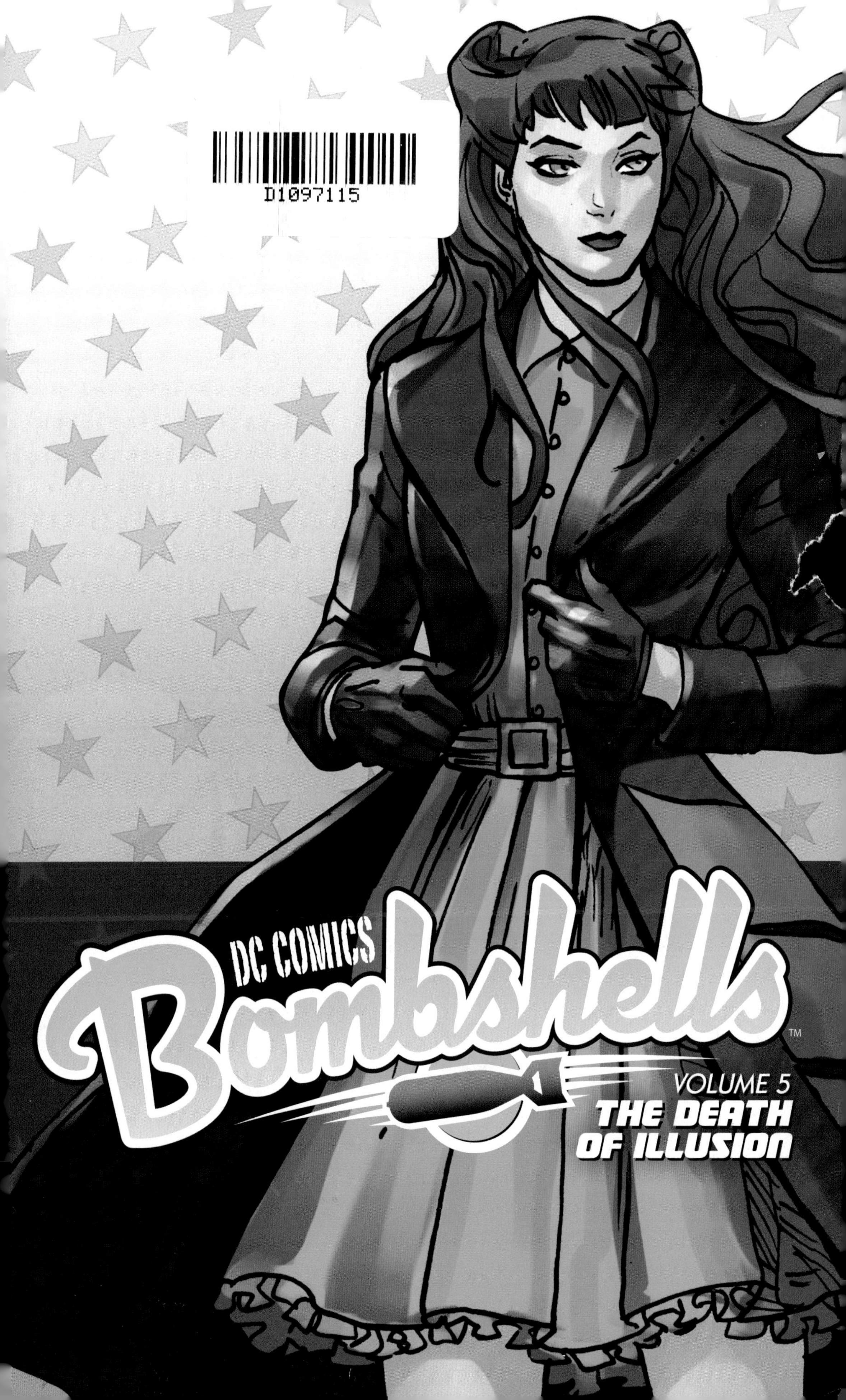
DC COMICS
Bombshells
TM
VOLUME 5
THE DEATH
OF ILLUSION

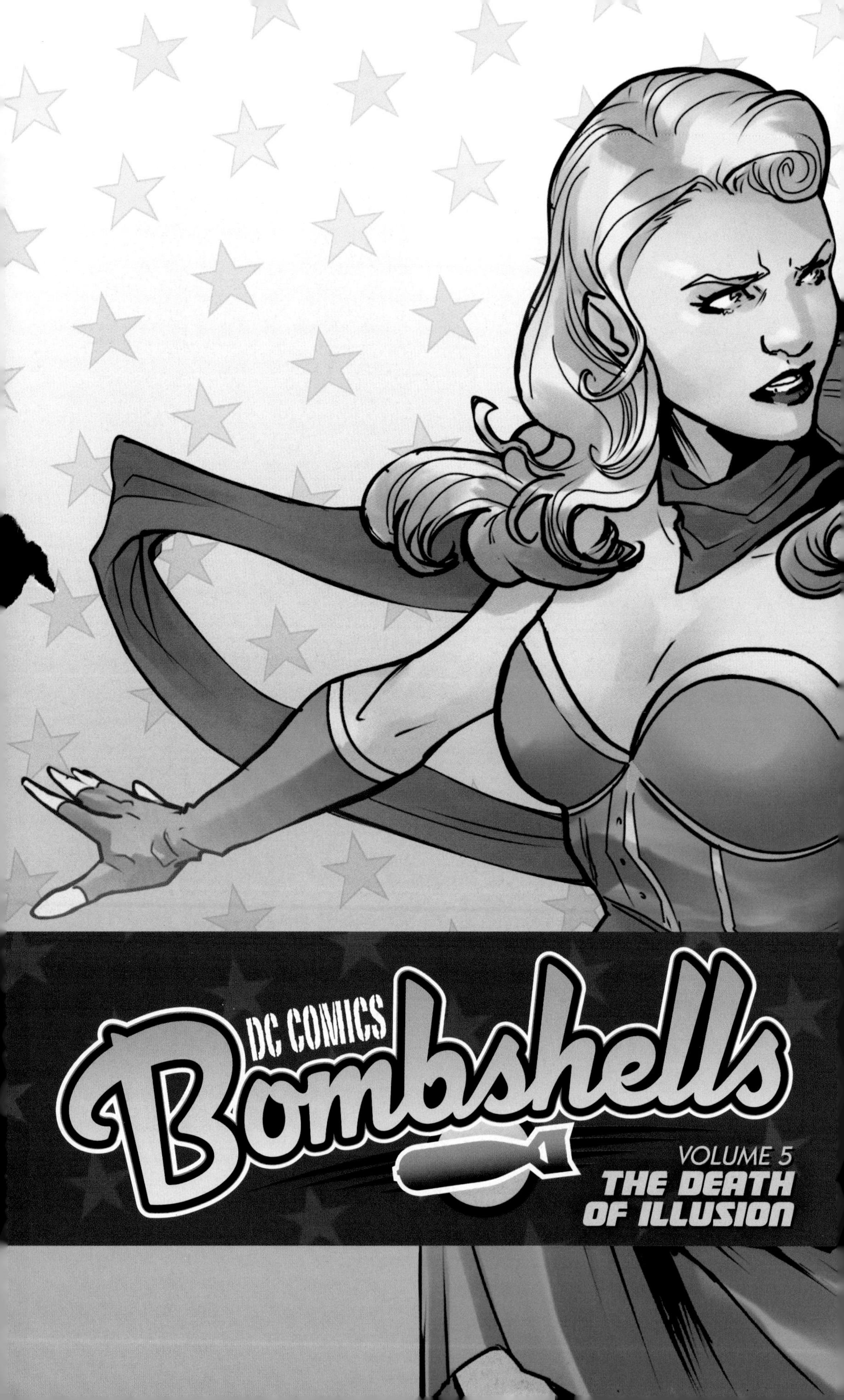
DC COMICS
Bombshells
VOLUME 5
THE DEATH
OF ILLUSION

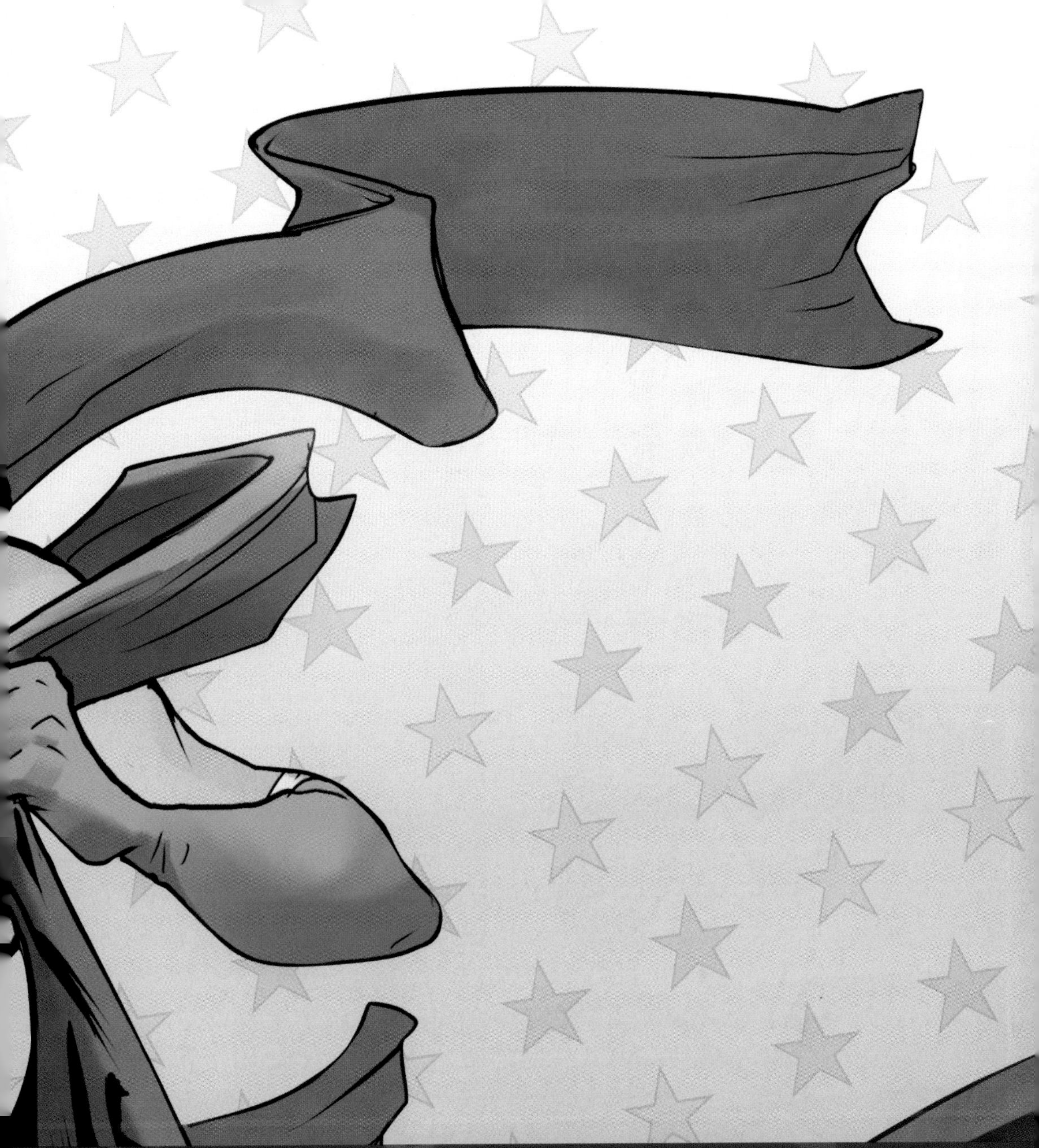

Written by
MARGUERITE BENNETT
Art by
MIRKA ANDOLFO
LAURA BRAGA
ELSA CHARRETIER
CARMEN CARNERO
RICHARD ORTIZ
RACHAEL STOTT
ANEKE

Color by
J. NANJAN
WENDY BROOME
SANDRA MOLINA
HI-FI
Letters by
WES ABBOTT

Collection Cover Art by
ANT LUCIA

SUPERMAN created by
Jerry Siegel and Joe Shuster
SUPERGIRL based on the characters created by
Jerry Siegel and Joe Shuster
By special arrangement with the Jerry Siegel family

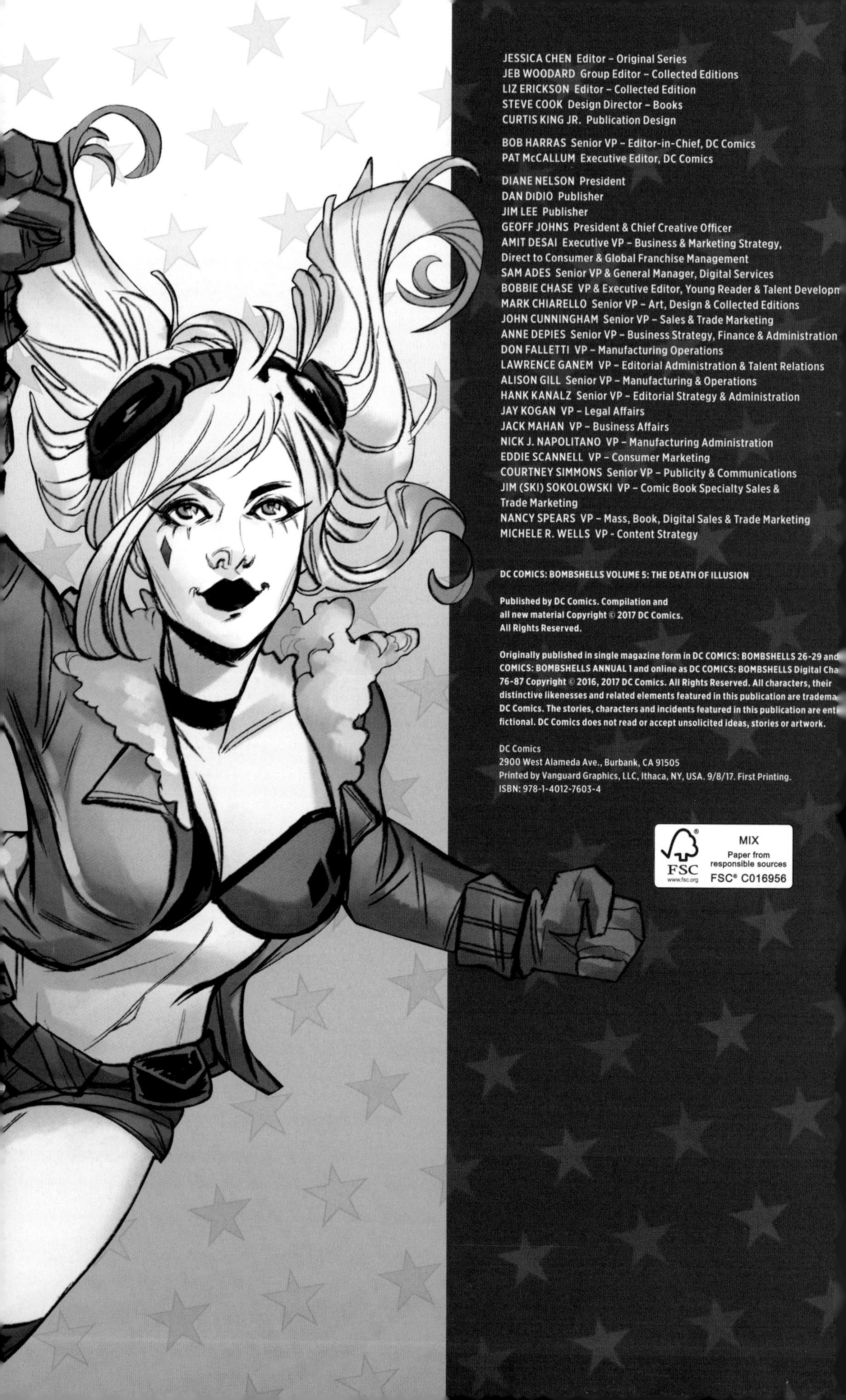

JESSICA CHEN Editor – Original Series
JEB WOODARD Group Editor – Collected Editions
LIZ ERICKSON Editor – Collected Edition
STEVE COOK Design Director – Books
CURTIS KING JR. Publication Design

BOB HARRAS Senior VP – Editor-in-Chief, DC Comics
PAT McCALLUM Executive Editor, DC Comics

DIANE NELSON President
DAN DIDIO Publisher
JIM LEE Publisher
GEOFF JOHNS President & Chief Creative Officer
AMIT DESAI Executive VP – Business & Marketing Strategy, Direct to Consumer & Global Franchise Management
SAM ADES Senior VP & General Manager, Digital Services
BOBBIE CHASE VP & Executive Editor, Young Reader & Talent Developm
MARK CHIARELLO Senior VP – Art, Design & Collected Editions
JOHN CUNNINGHAM Senior VP – Sales & Trade Marketing
ANNE DEPIES Senior VP – Business Strategy, Finance & Administration
DON FALLETTI VP – Manufacturing Operations
LAWRENCE GANEM VP – Editorial Administration & Talent Relations
ALISON GILL Senior VP – Manufacturing & Operations
HANK KANALZ Senior VP – Editorial Strategy & Administration
JAY KOGAN VP – Legal Affairs
JACK MAHAN VP – Business Affairs
NICK J. NAPOLITANO VP – Manufacturing Administration
EDDIE SCANNELL VP – Consumer Marketing
COURTNEY SIMMONS Senior VP – Publicity & Communications
JIM (SKI) SOKOLOWSKI VP – Comic Book Specialty Sales & Trade Marketing
NANCY SPEARS VP – Mass, Book, Digital Sales & Trade Marketing
MICHELE R. WELLS VP - Content Strategy

DC COMICS: BOMBSHELLS VOLUME 5: THE DEATH OF ILLUSION

DC Comics
2900 West Alameda Ave., Burbank, CA 91505
Printed by Vanguard Graphics, LLC, Ithaca, NY, USA. 9/8/17. First Printing.
ISBN: 978-1-4012-7603-4

FSC www.fsc.org MIX Paper from responsible sources FSC® C016956

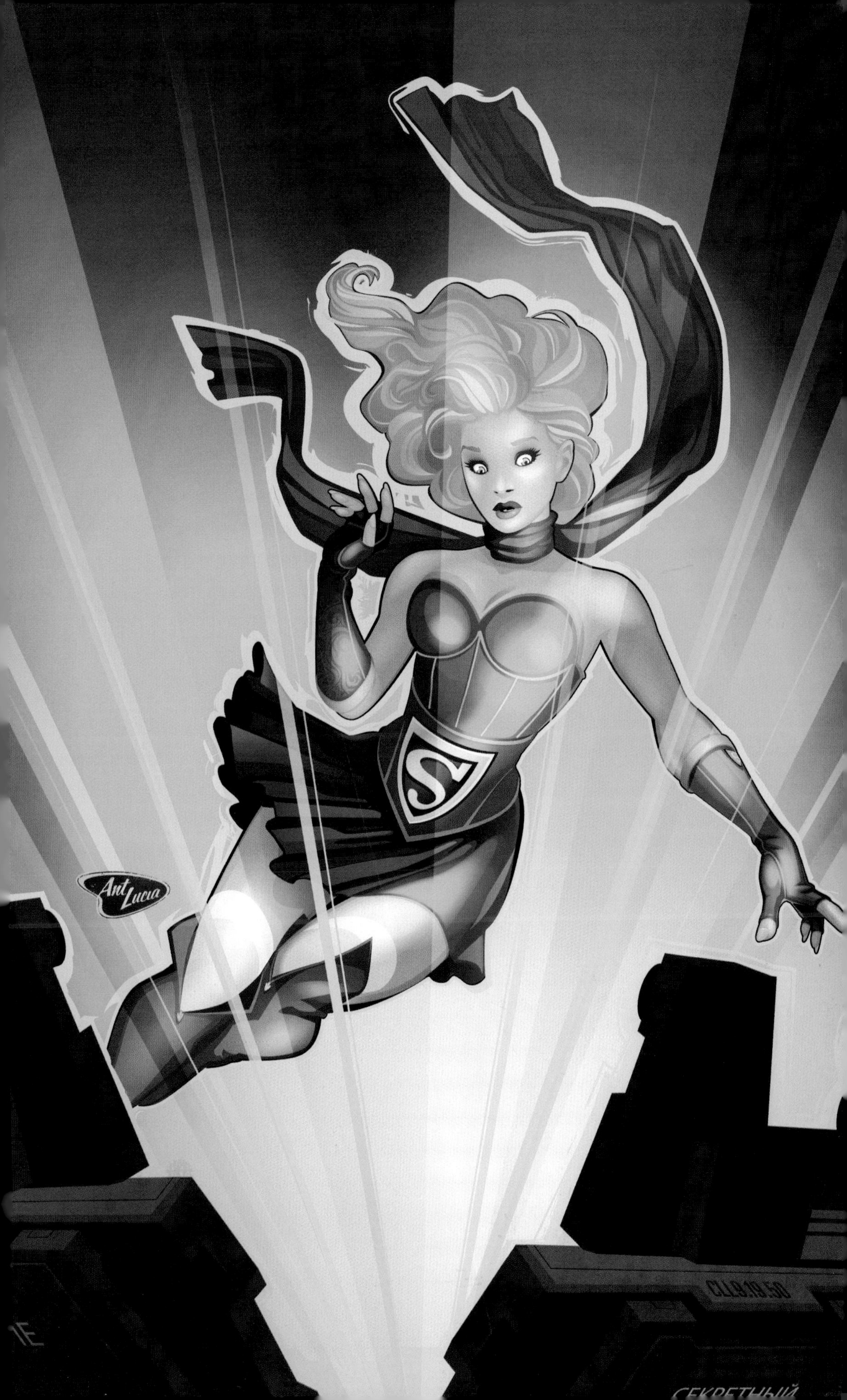
Ant Lucia
СЕКРЕТНЫЙ

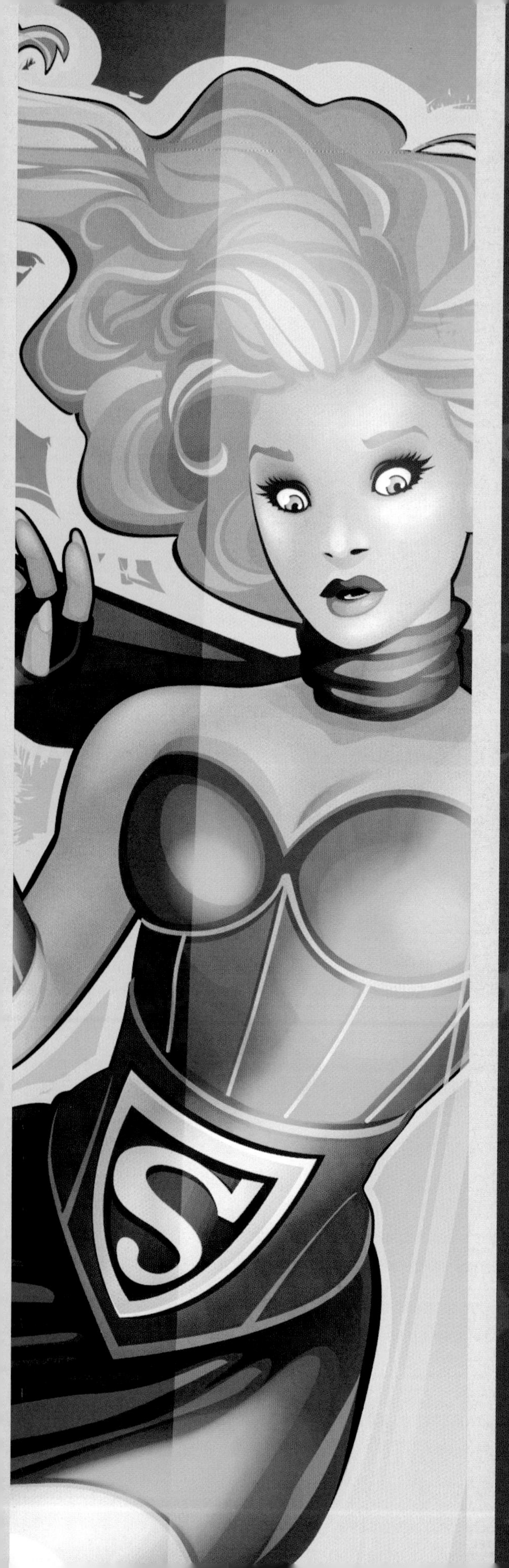

ALL GOOD THINGS

MARGUERITE BENNETT
Writer

CARMEN CARNERO
RICHARD ORTIZ
RACHAEL STOTT
MIRKA ANDOLFO
Artists

J. NANJAN
Colorist

Cover by
ANT LUCIA

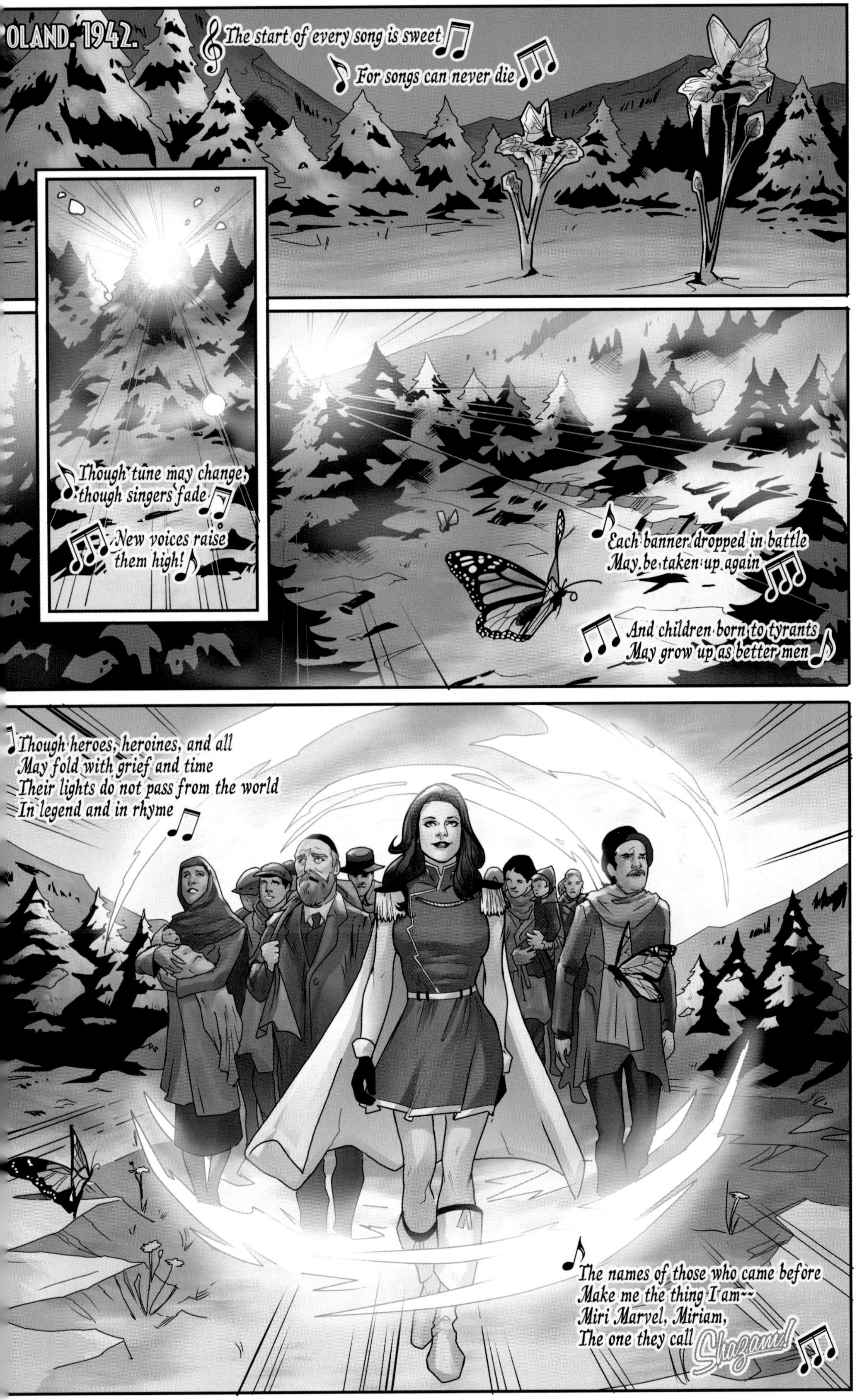
OLAND. 1942.
The start of every song is sweet
For songs can never die
Though tune may change, though singers fade
New voices raise them high!
Each banner dropped in battle
May be taken up again
And children born to tyrants
May grow up as better men
Though heroes, heroines, and all
May fold with grief and time
Their lights do not pass from the world
In legend and in rhyme
The names of those who came before
Make me the thing I am--
Miri Marvel, Miriam,
The one they call
Shazam!

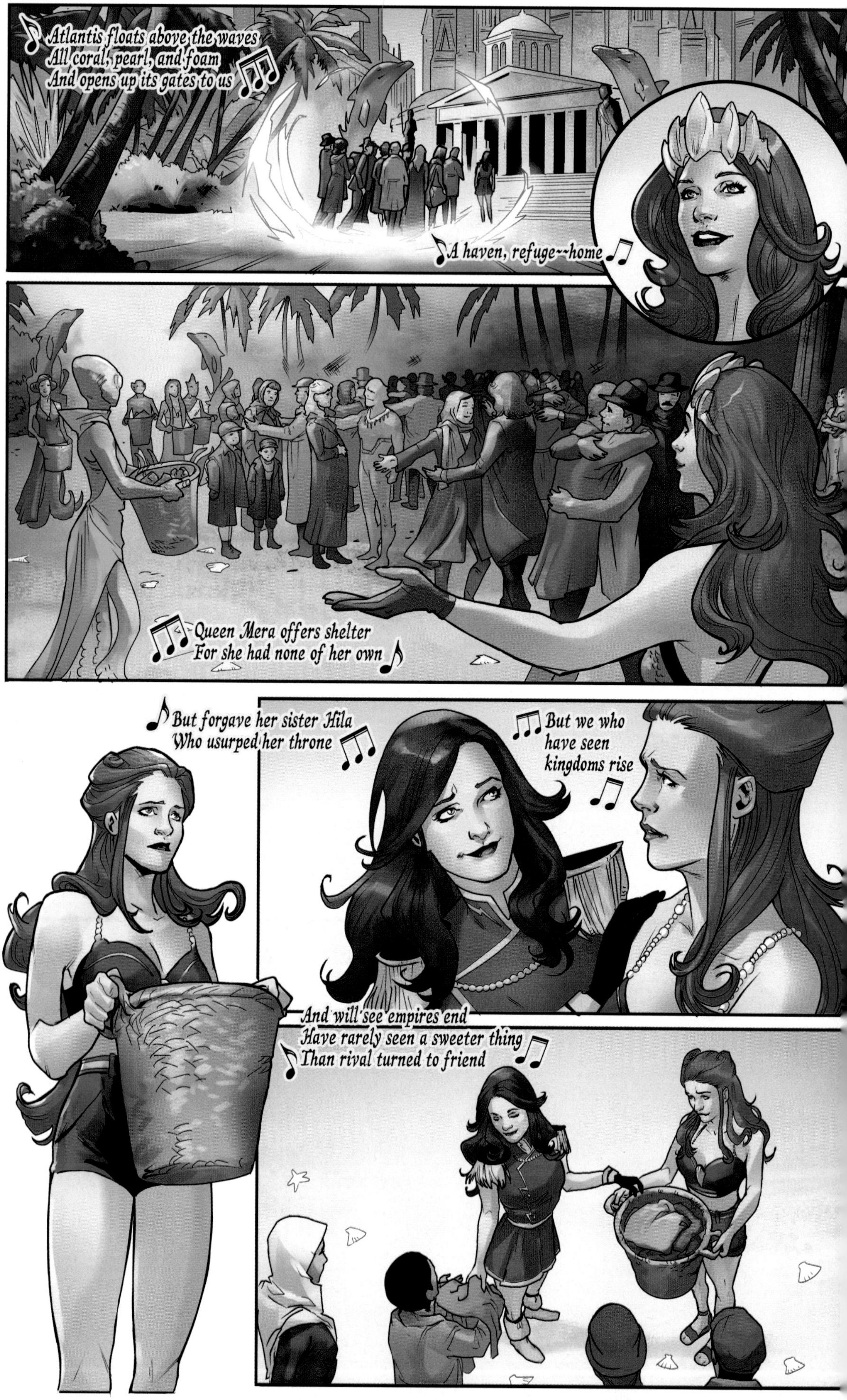
Atlantis floats above the waves
All coral, pearl, and foam
And opens up its gates to us
A haven, refuge--home
Queen Mera offers shelter
For she had none of her own
But forgave her sister Hila
Who usurped her throne
But we who have seen kingdoms rise
And will see empires end
Have rarely seen a sweeter thing
Than rival turned to friend

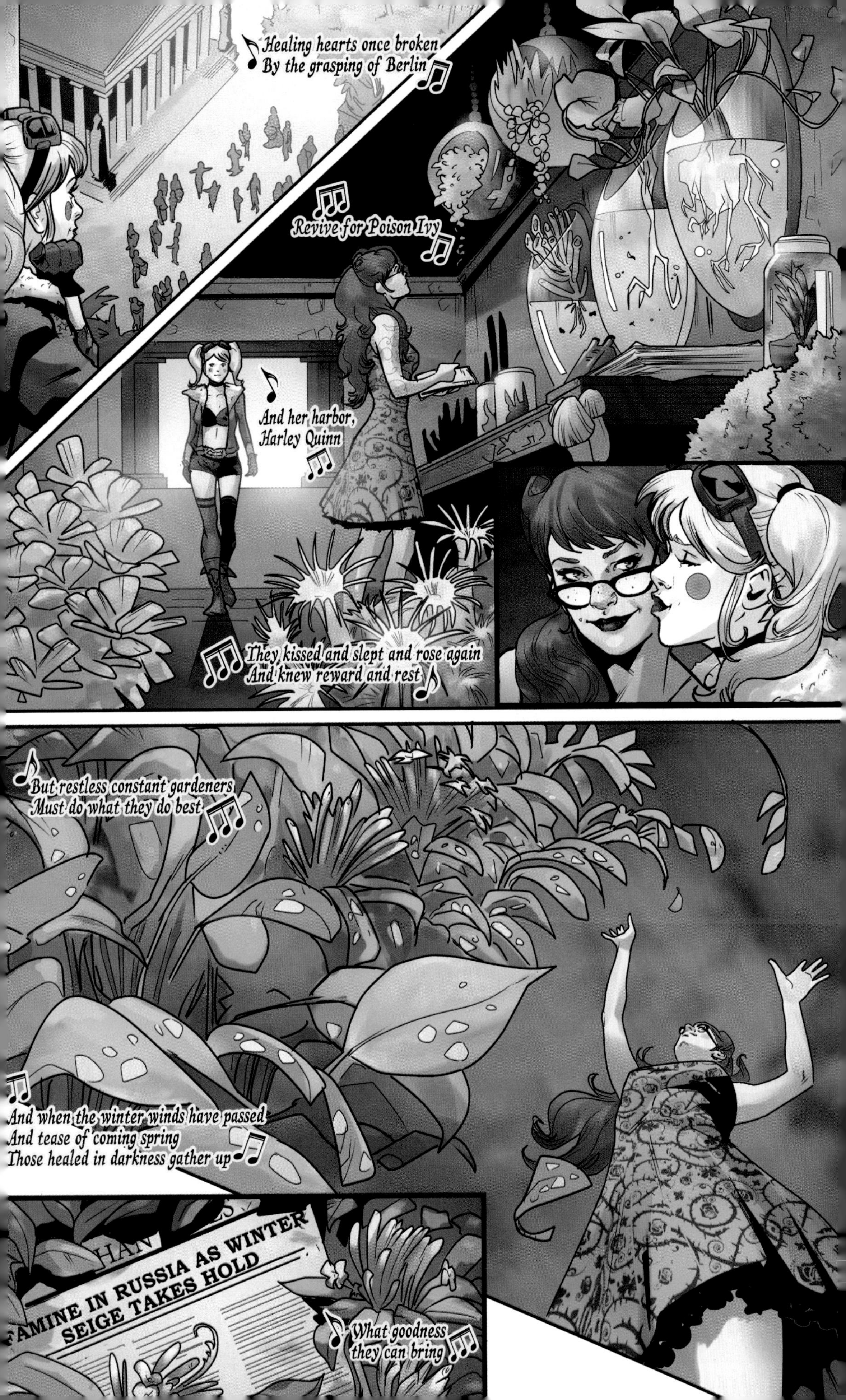
Healing hearts once broken
By the grasping of Berlin
Revive for Poison Ivy
And her harbor, Harley Quinn
They kissed and slept and rose again
And knew reward and rest
But restless constant gardeners
Must do what they do best
And when the winter winds have passed
And tease of coming spring
Those healed in darkness gather up
FAMINE IN RUSSIA AS WINTER SEIGE TAKES HOLD
What goodness they can bring

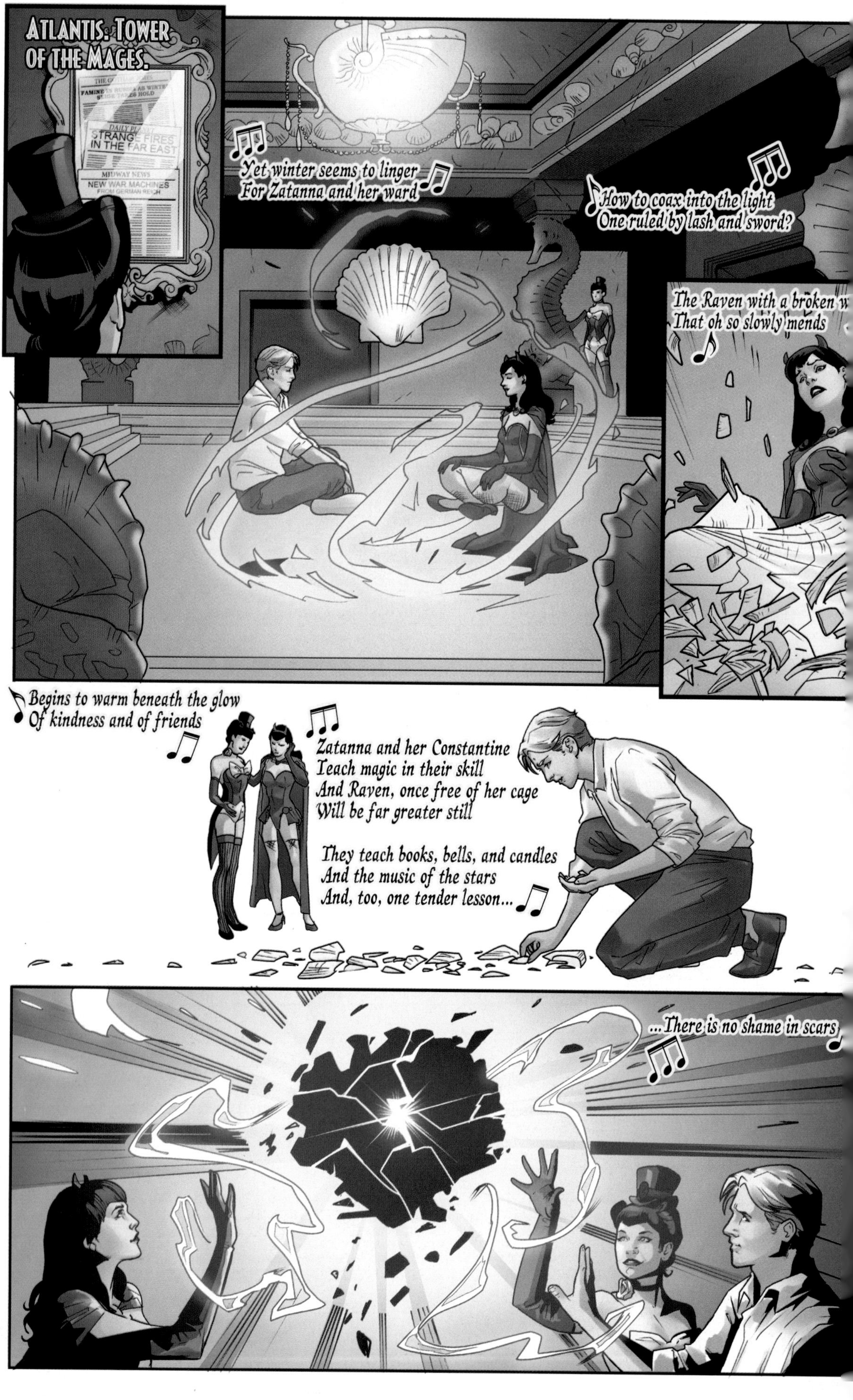

ATLANTIS: TOWER OF THE MAGES.
DAILY PLANET
STRANGE FIRES IN THE FAR EAST
MIDWAY NEWS
NEW WAR MACHINES
FROM GERMAN REICH
Yet winter seems to linger
For Zatanna and her ward
How to coax into the light
One ruled by lash and sword?
The Raven with a broken w
That oh so slowly mends
Begins to warm beneath the glow
Of kindness and of friends
Zatanna and her Constantine
Teach magic in their skill
And Raven, once free of her cage
Will be far greater still
They teach books, bells, and candles
And the music of the stars
And, too, one tender lesson...
...There is no shame in scars

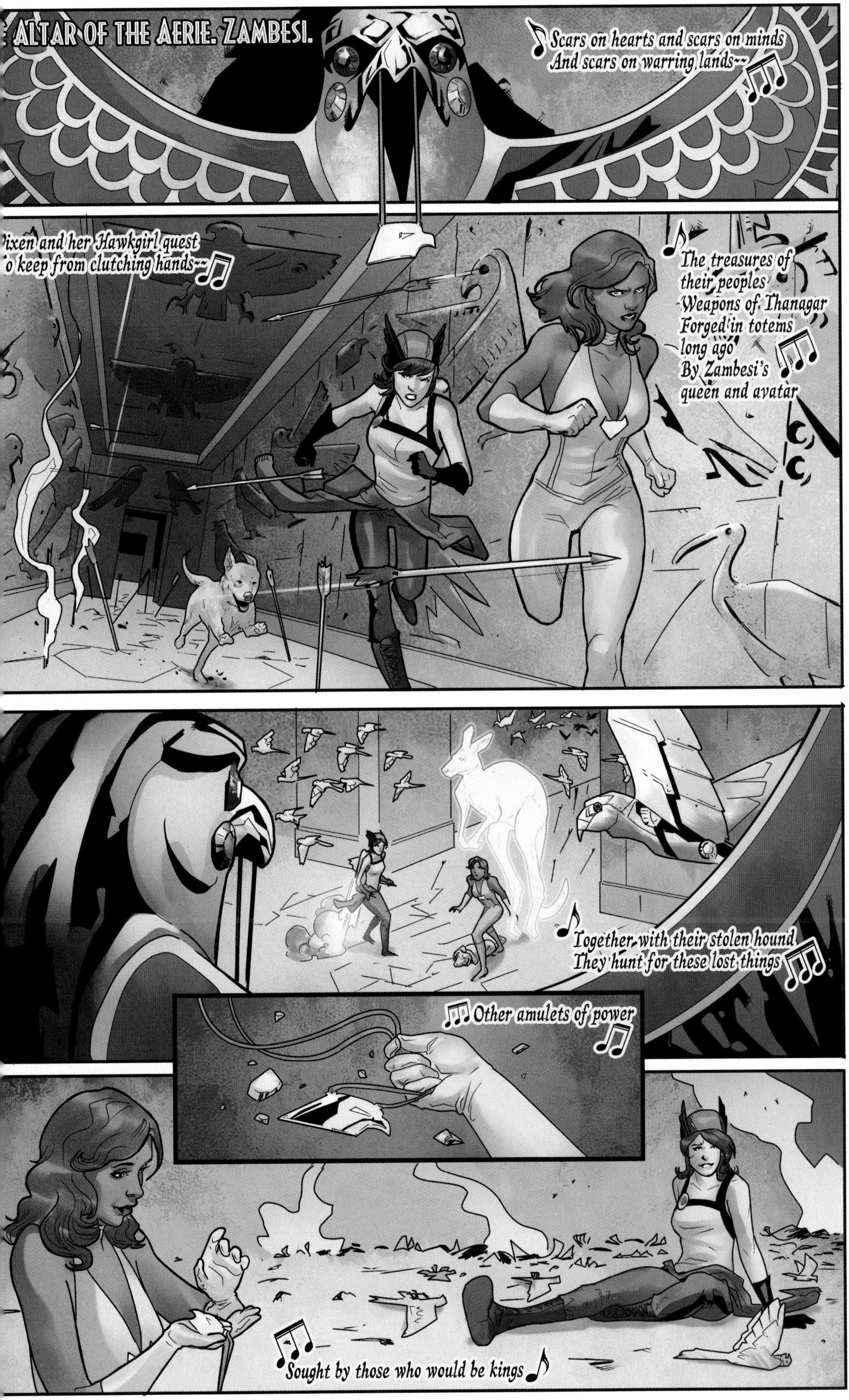
ALTAR OF THE AERIE. ZAMBESI.
Scars on hearts and scars on minds
And scars on warring lands~~
Vixen and her Hawkgirl quest
To keep from clutching hands~~
The treasures of their peoples
Weapons of Thanagar
Forged in totems long ago
By Zambesi's queen and avatar
Together with their stolen hound
They hunt for these lost things
Other amulets of power
Sought by those who would be kings

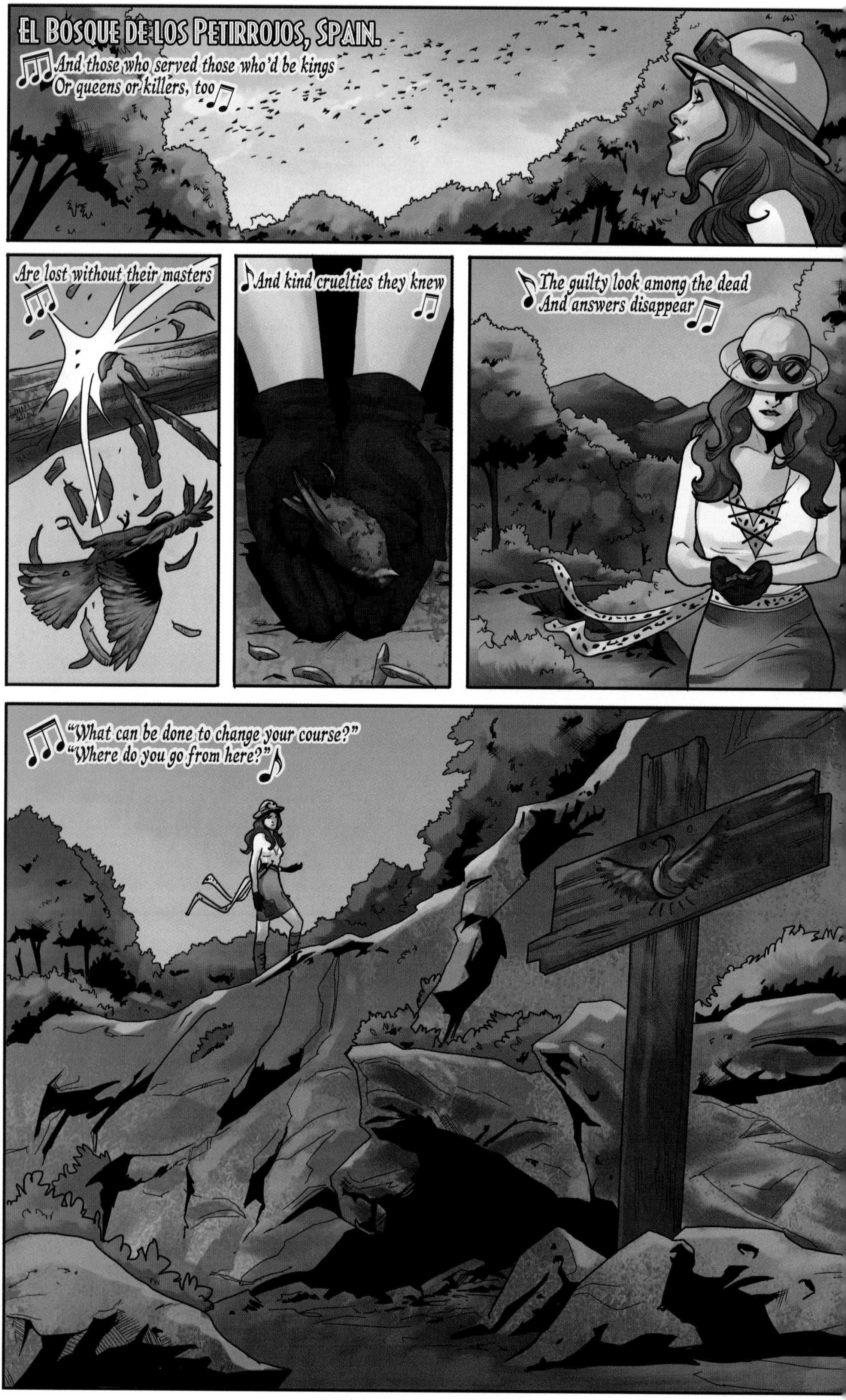
El Bosque de los Petirrojos, Spain.
And those who served those who'd be kings
Or queens or killers, too
Are lost without their masters
And kind cruelties they knew
The guilty look among the dead
And answers disappear
"What can be done to change your course?"
"Where do you go from here?"

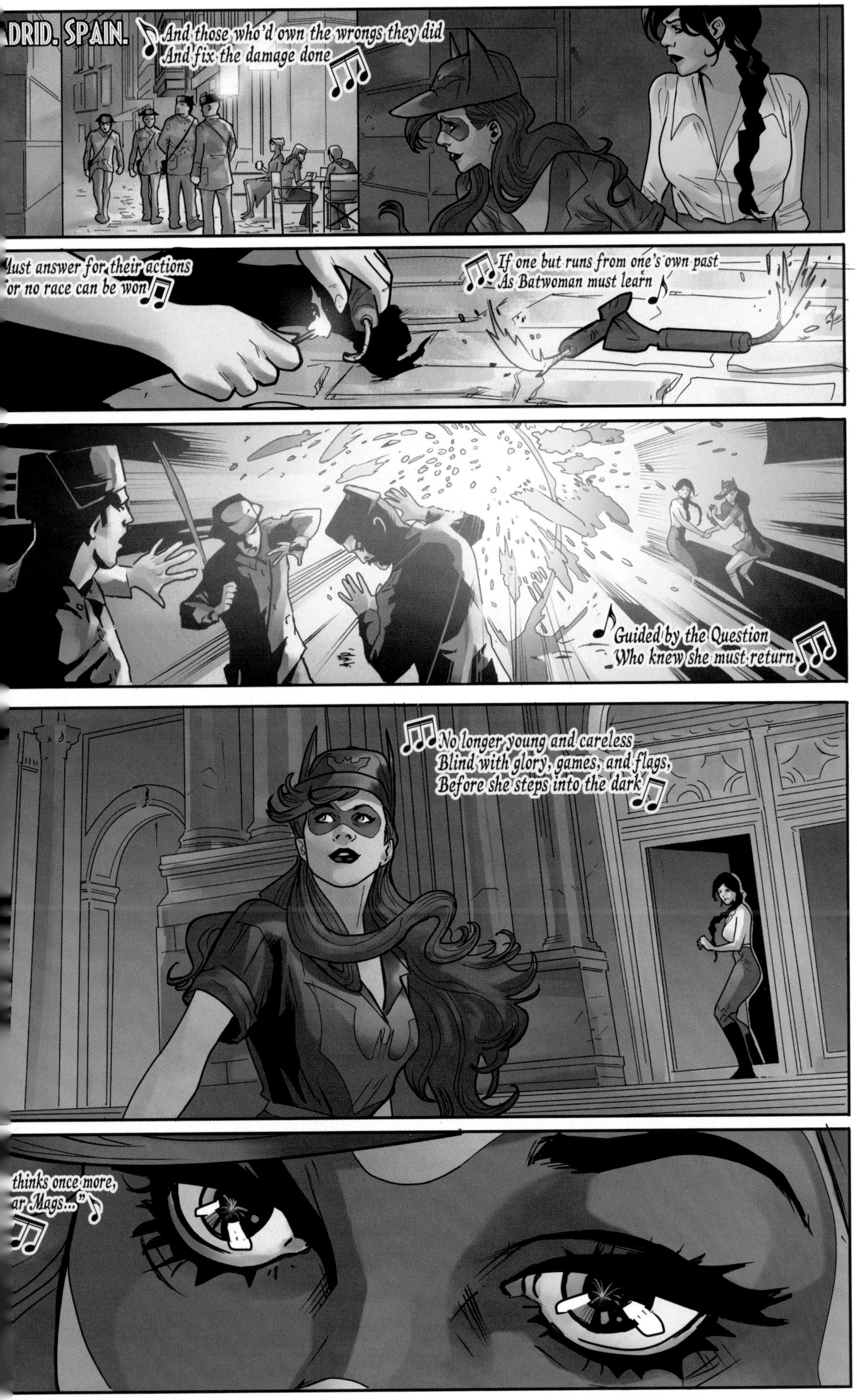
DRID. SPAIN.
And those who'd own the wrongs they did
And fix the damage done
Must answer for their actions
or no race can be won
If one but runs from one's own past
As Batwoman must learn
Guided by the Question
Who knew she must return
No longer young and careless
Blind with glory, games, and flags,
Before she steps into the dark
thinks once more,
ar Mags..."

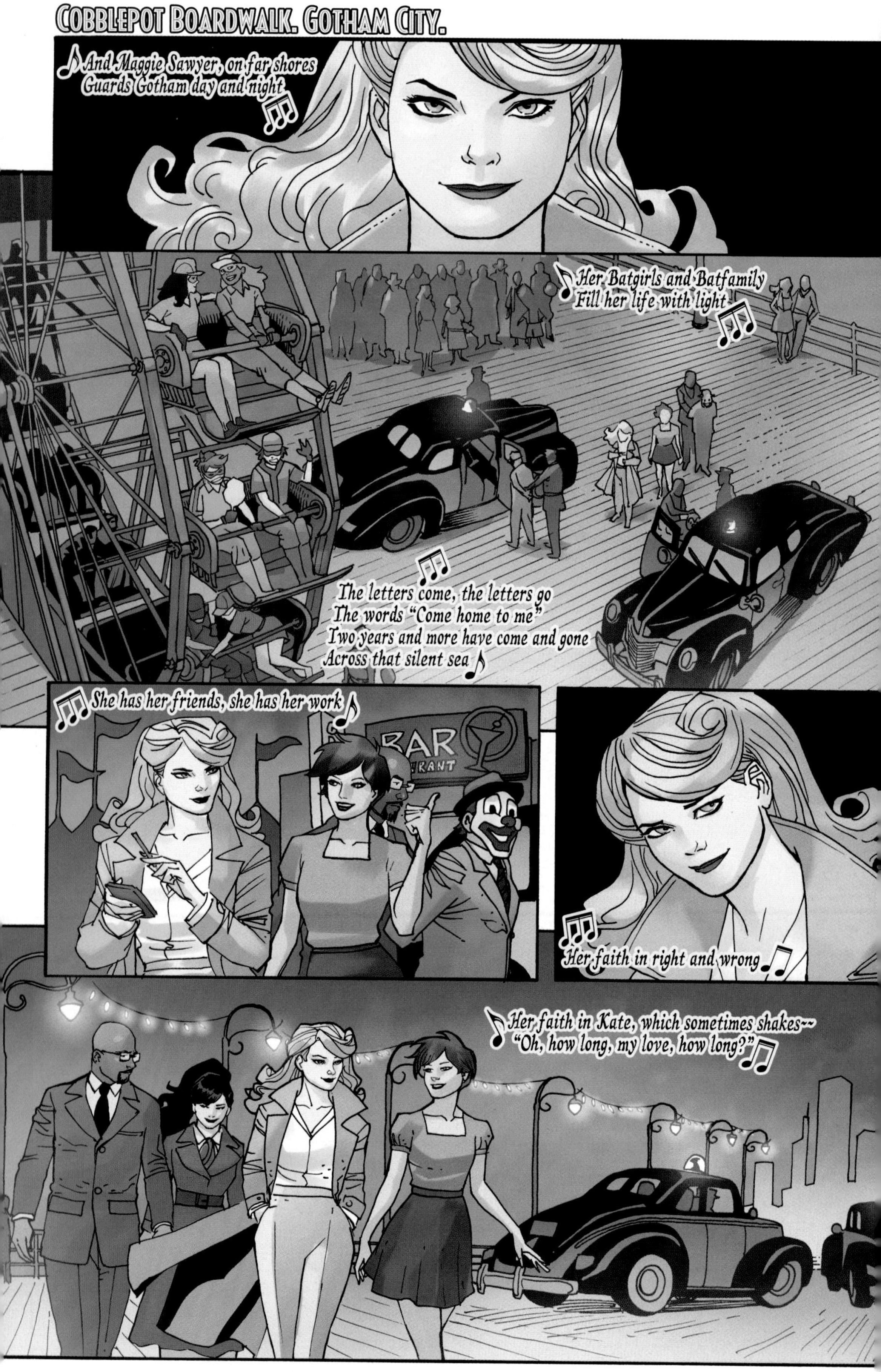
COBBLEPOT BOARDWALK. GOTHAM CITY.
And Maggie Sawyer, on far shores
Guards Gotham day and night
Her Batgirls and Batfamily
Fill her life with light
The letters come, the letters go
The words "Come home to me"
Two years and more have come and gone
Across that silent sea
She has her friends, she has her work
BAR
Her faith in right and wrong
Her faith in Kate, which sometimes shakes--
"Oh, how long, my love, how long?"

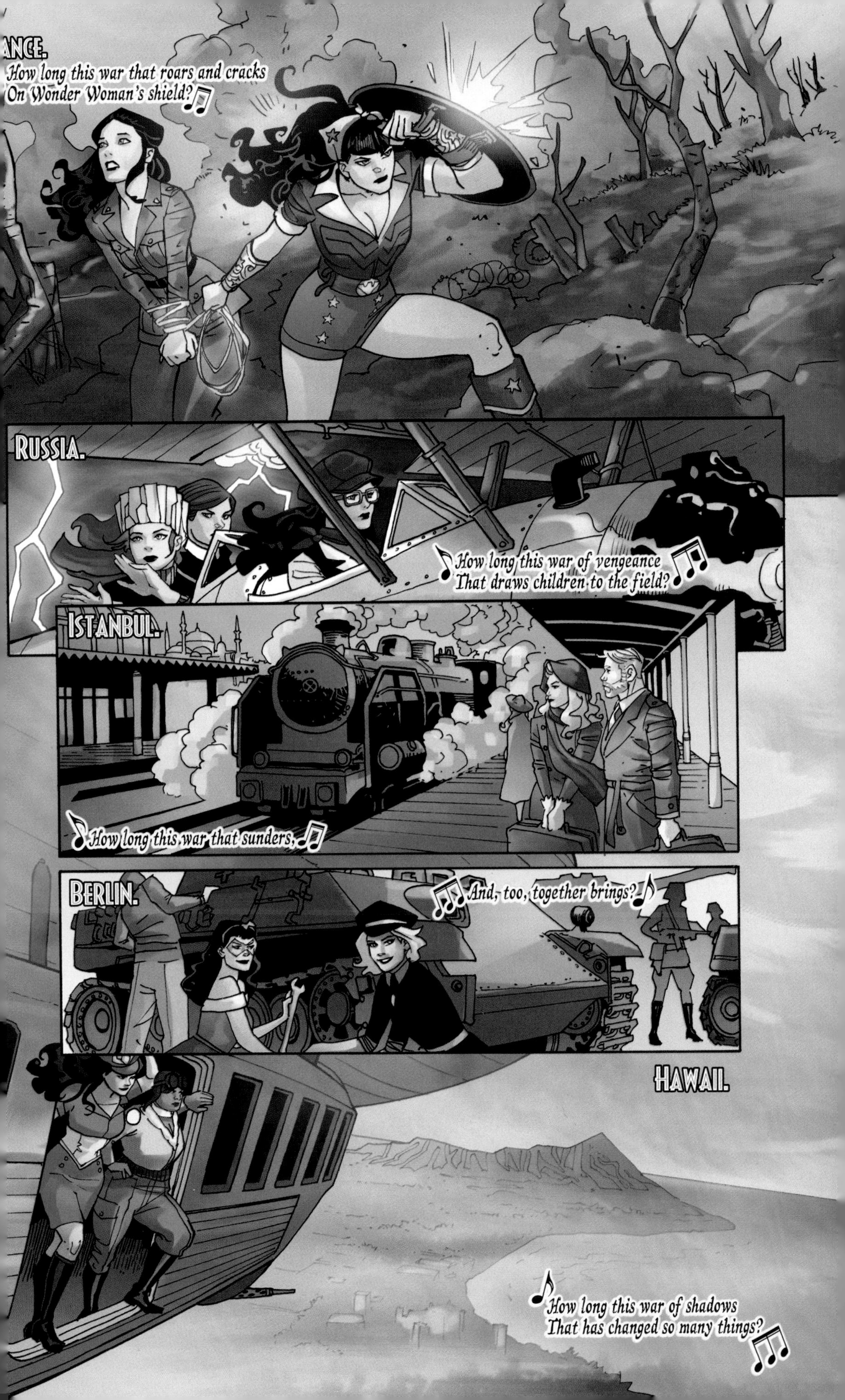
ANCE.
How long this war that roars and cracks
On Wonder Woman's shield?
RUSSIA.
How long this war of vengeance
That draws children to the field?
ISTANBUL.
How long this war that sunders,
BERLIN.
And, too, together brings?
HAWAII.
How long this war of shadows
That has changed so many things?

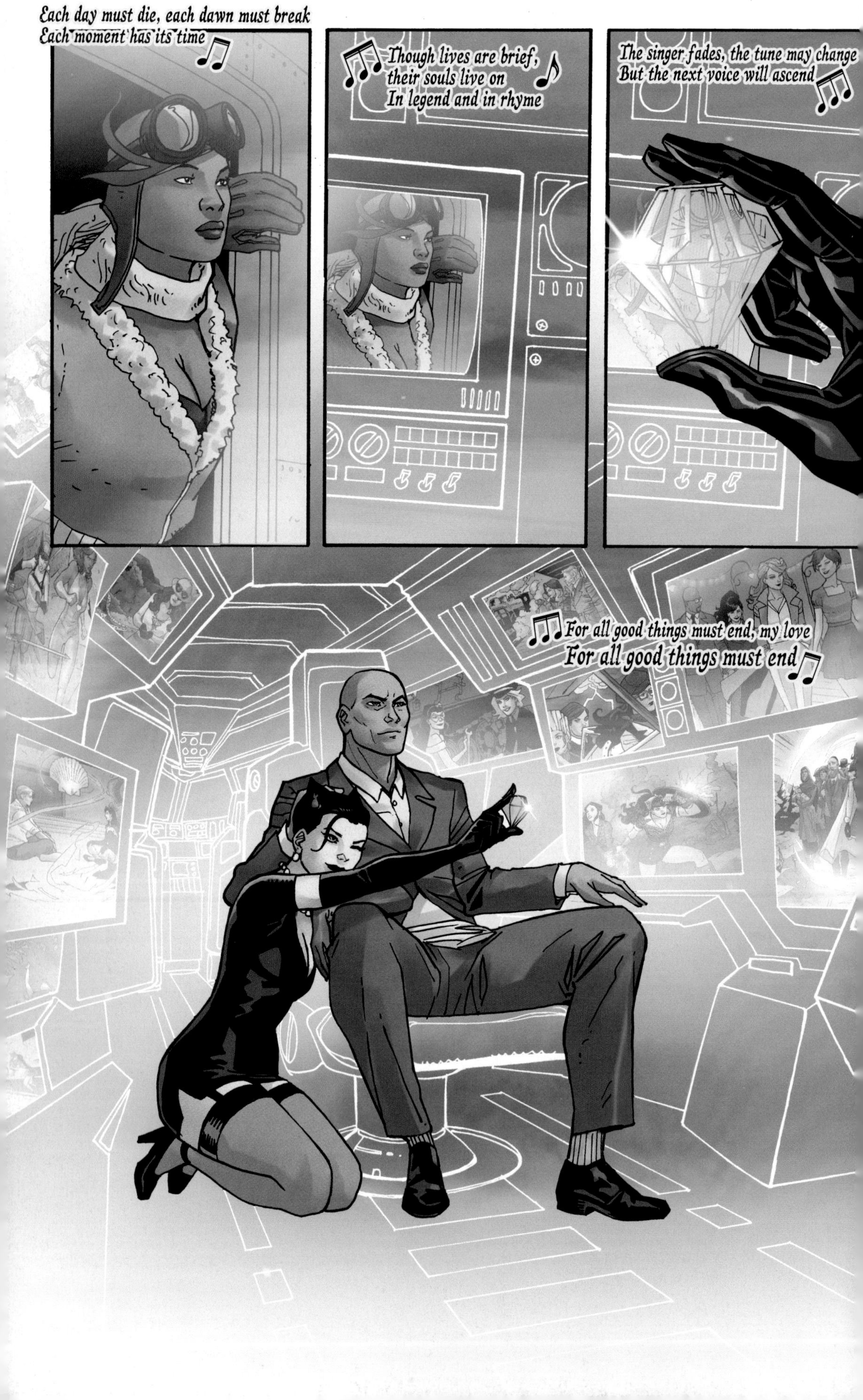
Each day must die, each dawn must break
Each moment has its time
Though lives are brief, their souls live on
In legend and in rhyme
The singer fades, the tune may change
But the next voice will ascend
For all good things must end, my love
For all good things must end

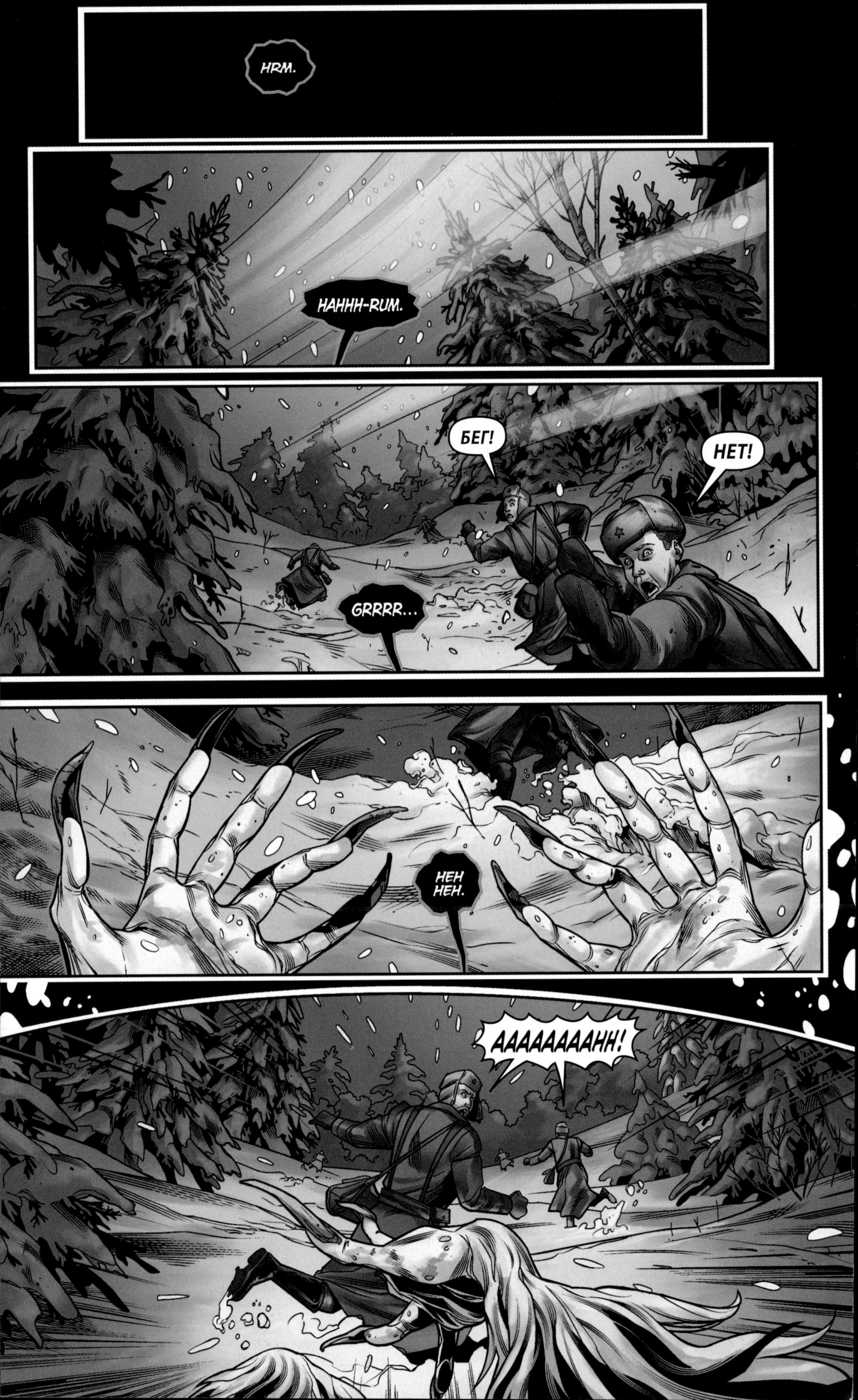

HRM.
HAHHH-RUM.
БЕГ!
НЕТ!
GRRRR...
HEH HEH.
AAAAAAAAAHH!

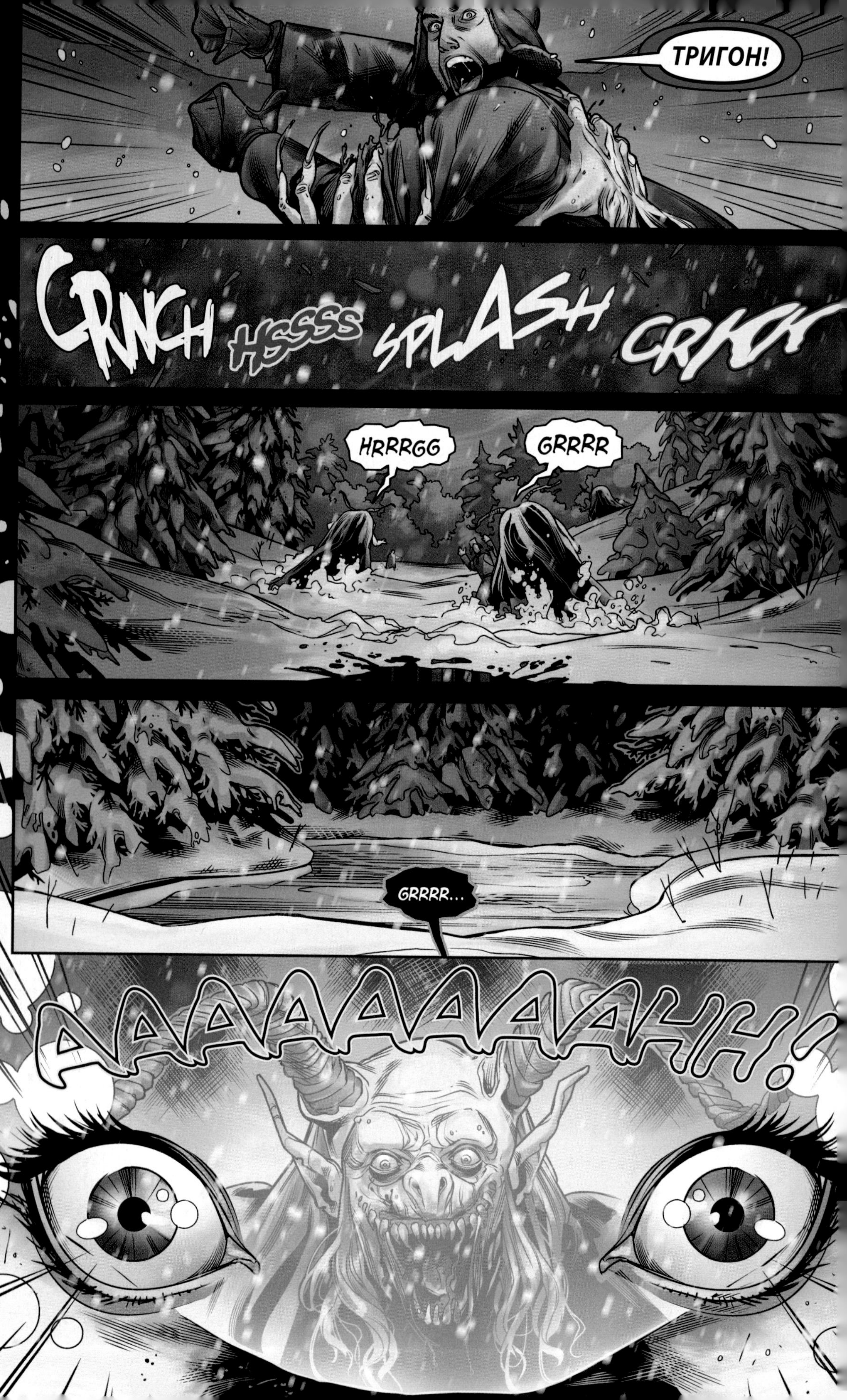
ТРИГОН!
CRNCH
HSSSS
SPLASH
HRRRGG
GRRRR
GRRRR...
AAAAAAAAAHH!

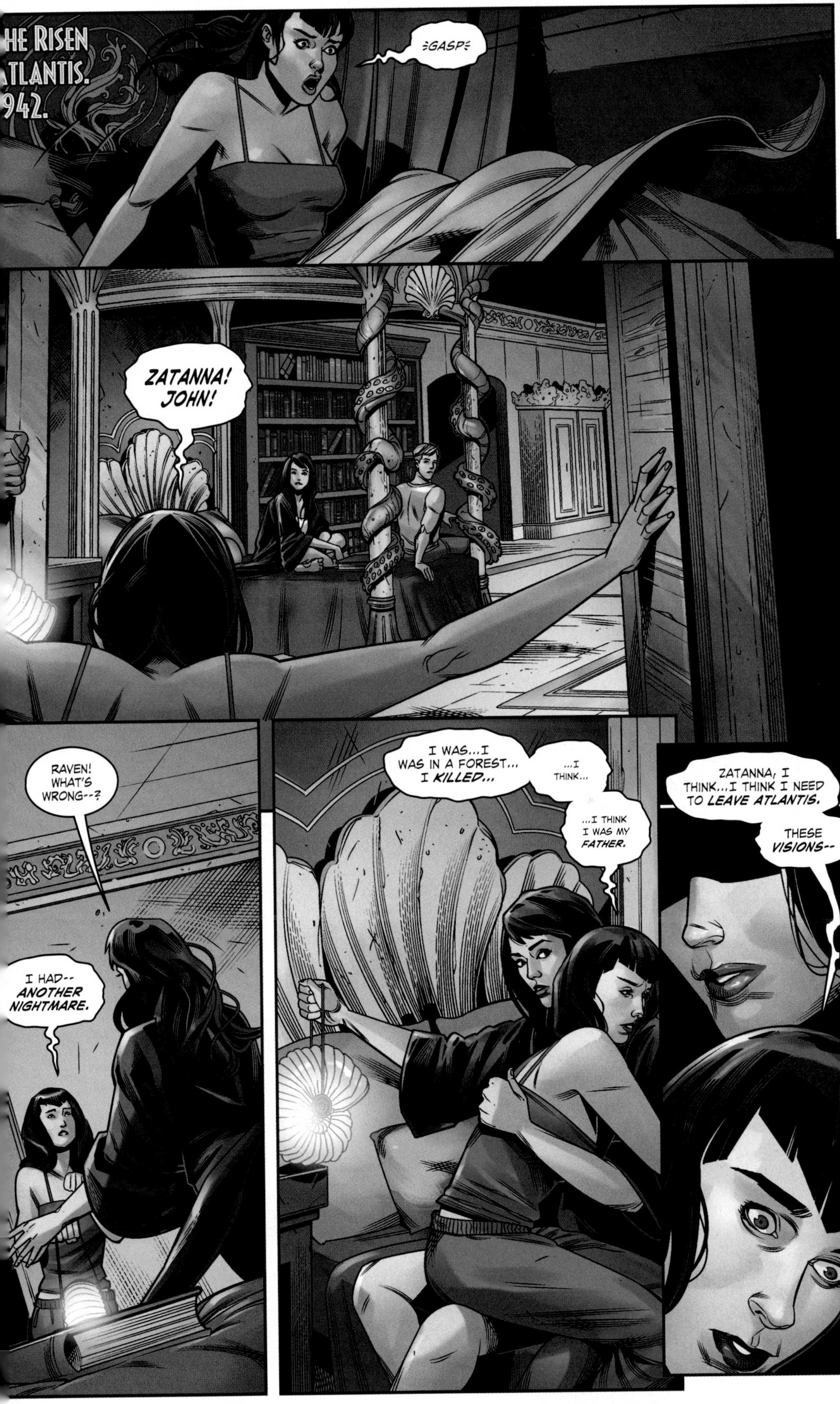

HE RISEN
TLANTIS.
942.
GASP
ZATANNA! JOHN!
RAVEN! WHAT'S WRONG--?
I HAD-- ANOTHER NIGHTMARE.
I WAS...I WAS IN A FOREST... I KILLED...
...I THINK...
...I THINK I WAS MY FATHER.
ZATANNA, I THINK...I THINK I NEED TO LEAVE ATLANTIS.
THESE VISIONS--

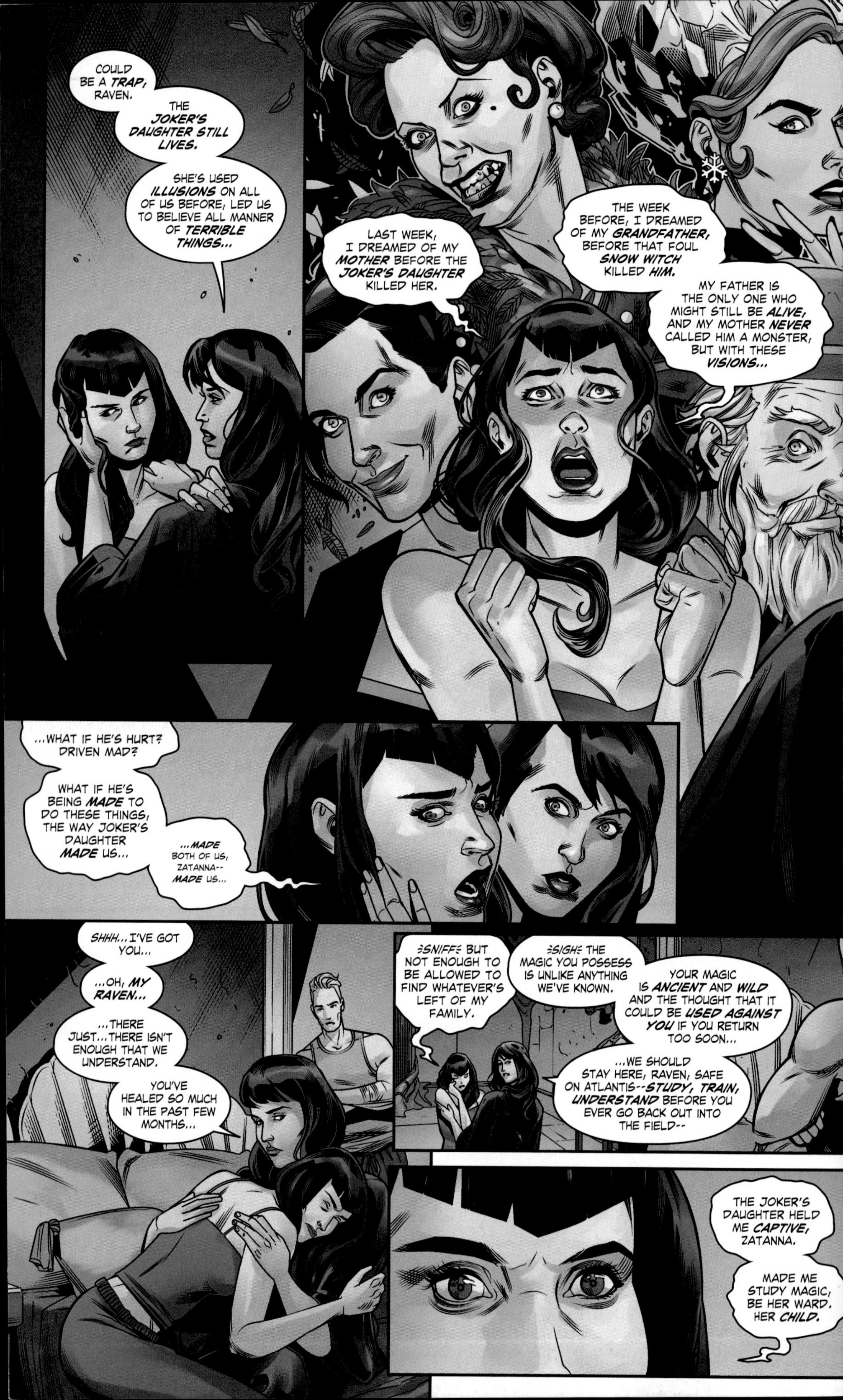

COULD BE A TRAP, RAVEN.
THE JOKER'S DAUGHTER STILL LIVES.
SHE'S USED ILLUSIONS ON ALL OF US BEFORE, LED US TO BELIEVE ALL MANNER OF TERRIBLE THINGS...
LAST WEEK, I DREAMED OF MY MOTHER BEFORE THE JOKER'S DAUGHTER KILLED HER.
THE WEEK BEFORE, I DREAMED OF MY GRANDFATHER, BEFORE THAT FOUL SNOW WITCH KILLED HIM.
MY FATHER IS THE ONLY ONE WHO MIGHT STILL BE ALIVE, AND MY MOTHER NEVER CALLED HIM A MONSTER, BUT WITH THESE VISIONS...
...WHAT IF HE'S HURT? DRIVEN MAD?
WHAT IF HE'S BEING MADE TO DO THESE THINGS, THE WAY JOKER'S DAUGHTER MADE US...
...MADE BOTH OF US, ZATANNA-- MADE US...
SHHH... I'VE GOT YOU...
...OH, MY RAVEN...
...THERE JUST... THERE ISN'T ENOUGH THAT WE UNDERSTAND.
YOU'VE HEALED SO MUCH IN THE PAST FEW MONTHS...
SNIFF BUT NOT ENOUGH TO BE ALLOWED TO FIND WHATEVER'S LEFT OF MY FAMILY.
SIGH THE MAGIC YOU POSSESS IS UNLIKE ANYTHING WE'VE KNOWN.
YOUR MAGIC IS ANCIENT AND WILD AND THE THOUGHT THAT IT COULD BE USED AGAINST YOU IF YOU RETURN TOO SOON...
...WE SHOULD STAY HERE, RAVEN, SAFE ON ATLANTIS--STUDY, TRAIN, UNDERSTAND BEFORE YOU EVER GO BACK OUT INTO THE FIELD--
THE JOKER'S DAUGHTER HELD ME CAPTIVE, ZATANNA.
MADE ME STUDY MAGIC, BE HER WARD. HER CHILD.

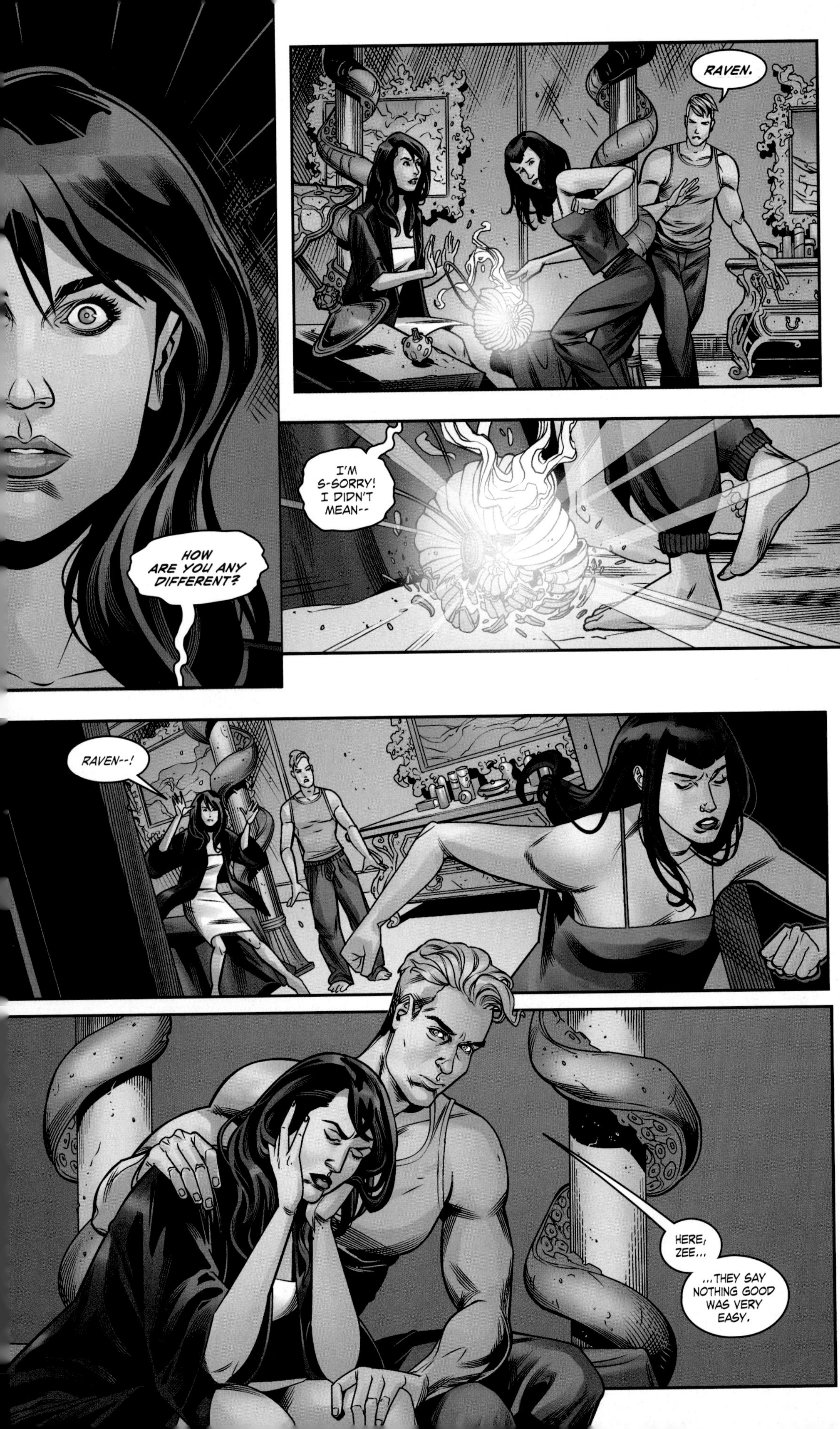
RAVEN.
HOW ARE YOU ANY DIFFERENT?
I'M S-SORRY! I DIDN'T MEAN--
RAVEN--!
HERE, ZEE...
...THEY SAY NOTHING GOOD WAS VERY EASY.

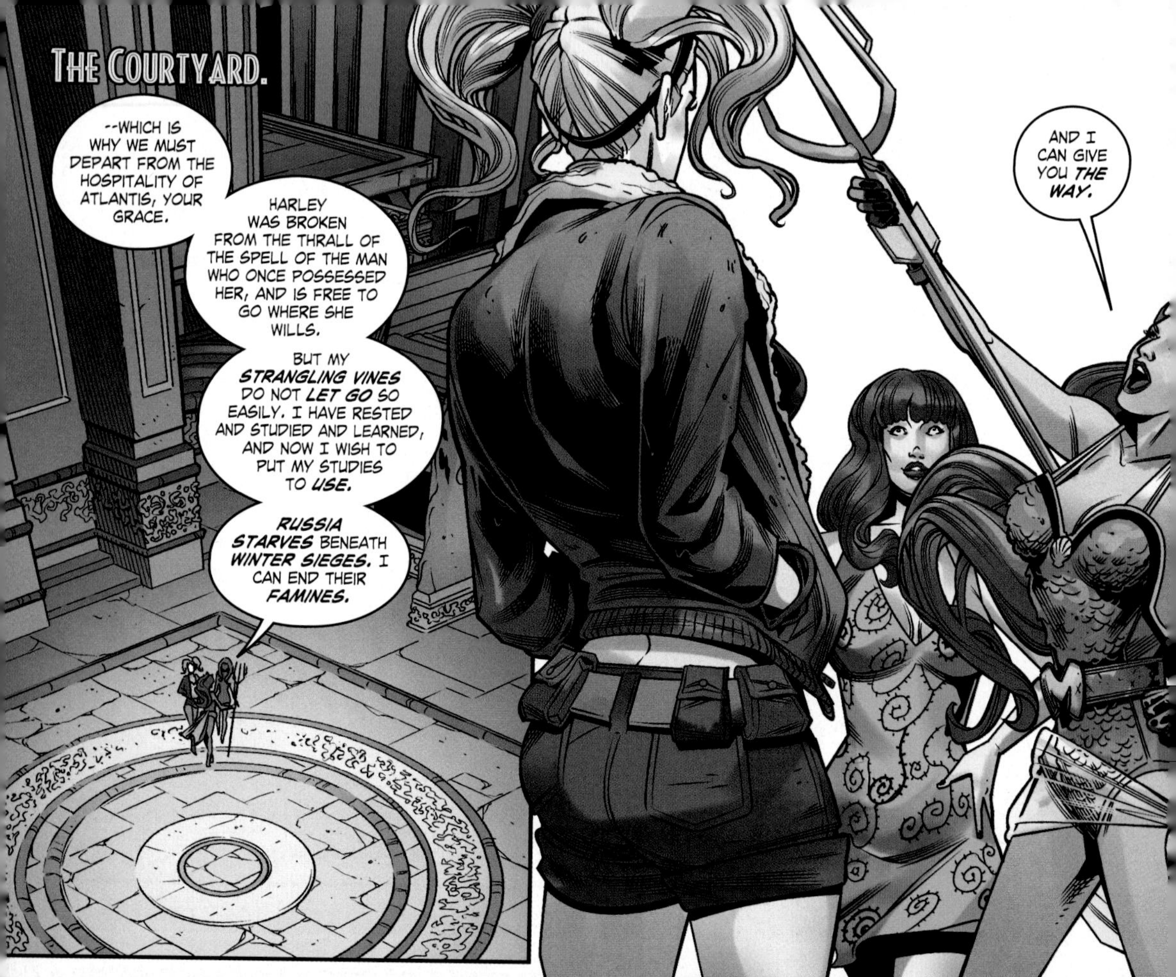
THE COURTYARD.
--WHICH IS WHY WE MUST DEPART FROM THE HOSPITALITY OF ATLANTIS, YOUR GRACE.
HARLEY WAS BROKEN FROM THE THRALL OF THE SPELL OF THE MAN WHO ONCE POSSESSED HER, AND IS FREE TO GO WHERE SHE WILLS.
BUT MY STRANGLING VINES DO NOT LET GO SO EASILY. I HAVE RESTED AND STUDIED AND LEARNED, AND NOW I WISH TO PUT MY STUDIES TO USE.
RUSSIA STARVES BENEATH WINTER SIEGES. I CAN END THEIR FAMINES.
AND I CAN GIVE YOU THE WAY.

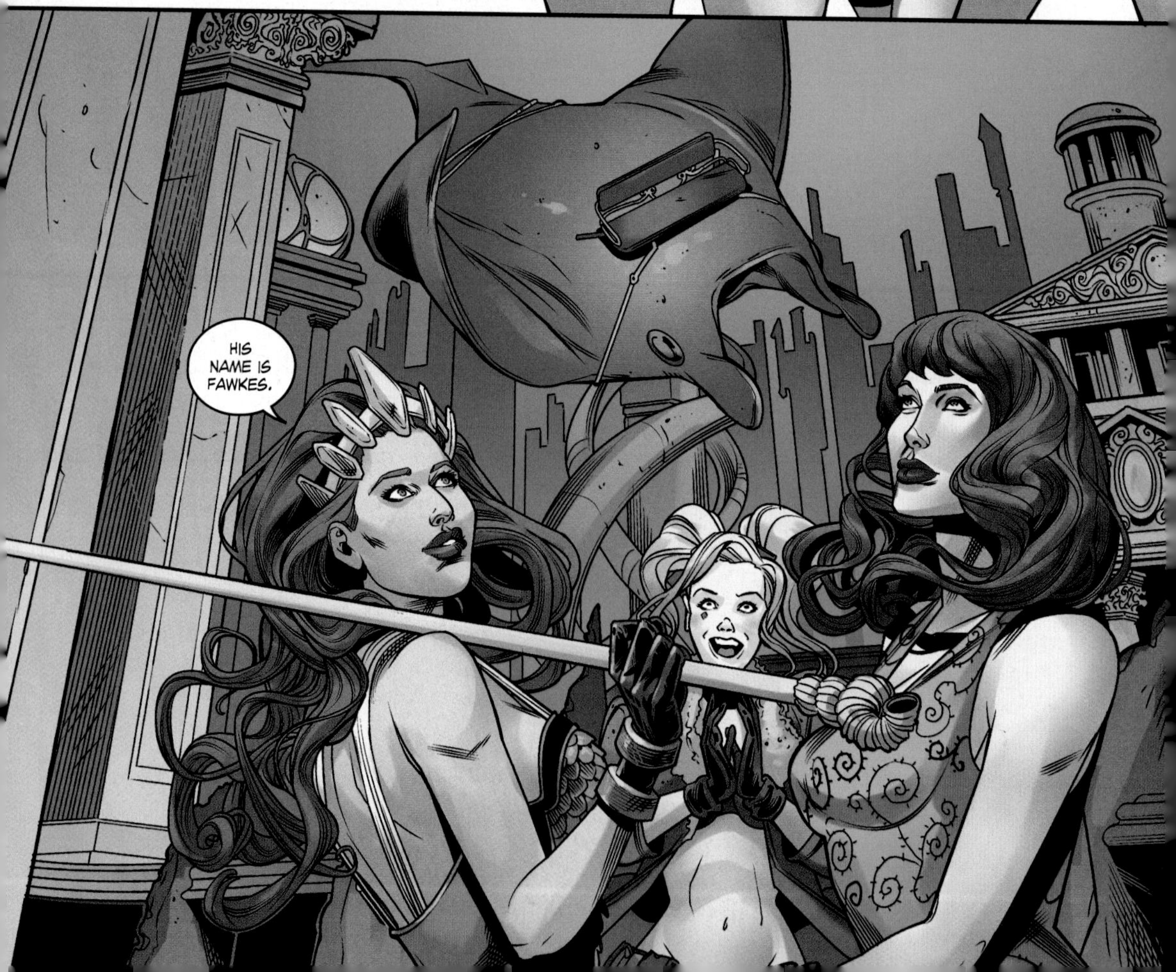
HIS NAME IS FAWKES.

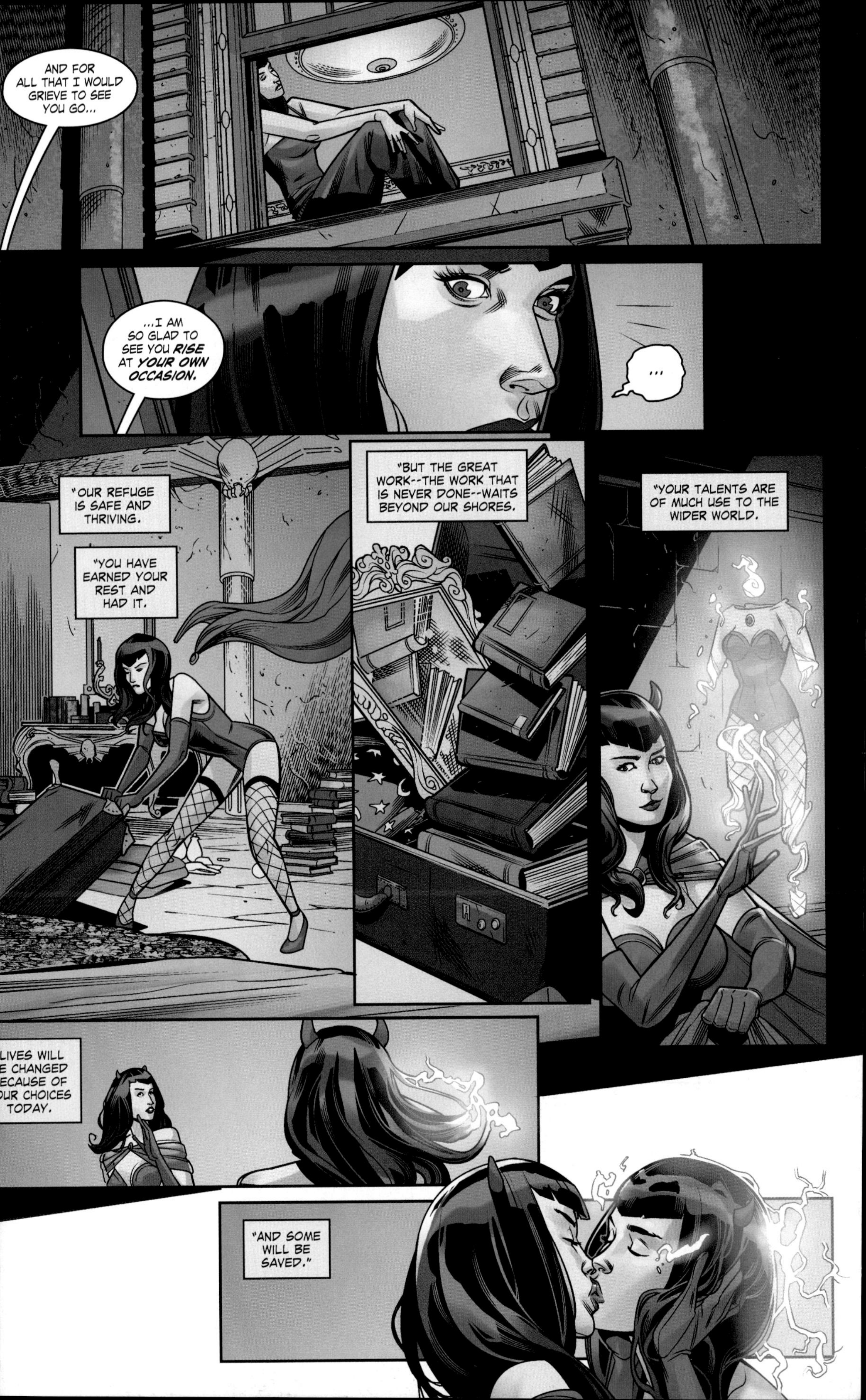
AND FOR ALL THAT I WOULD GRIEVE TO SEE YOU GO...
...I AM SO GLAD TO SEE YOU RISE AT YOUR OWN OCCASION.
...
"OUR REFUGE IS SAFE AND THRIVING.
"YOU HAVE EARNED YOUR REST AND HAD IT.
"BUT THE GREAT WORK--THE WORK THAT IS NEVER DONE--WAITS BEYOND OUR SHORES.
"YOUR TALENTS ARE OF MUCH USE TO THE WIDER WORLD.
LIVES WILL E CHANGED ECAUSE OF OUR CHOICES TODAY.
"AND SOME WILL BE SAVED."

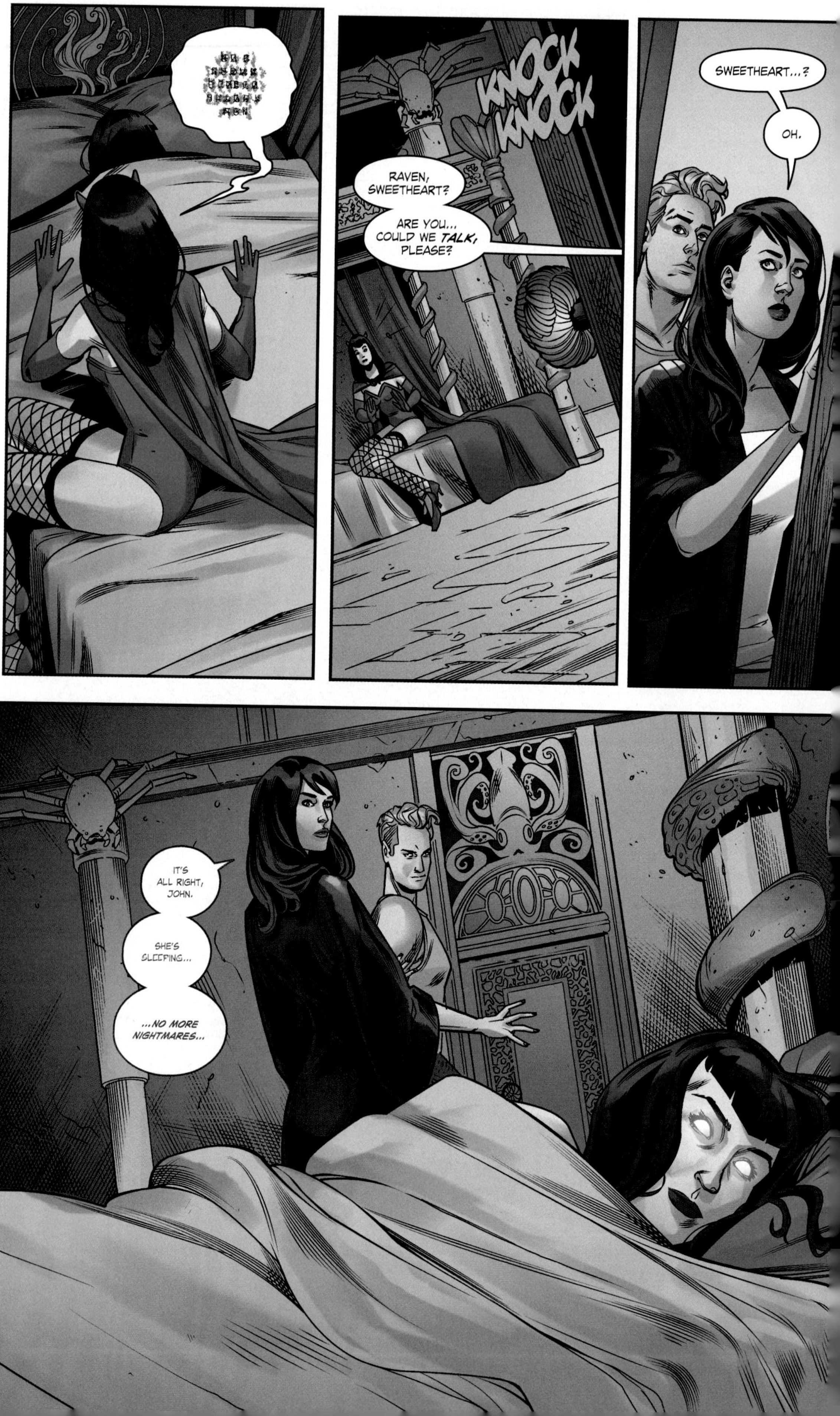
KNOCK KNOCK
RAVEN, SWEETHEART?
ARE YOU... COULD WE TALK, PLEASE?
SWEETHEART...?
OH.
IT'S ALL RIGHT, JOHN.
SHE'S SLEEPING...
...NO MORE NIGHTMARES...

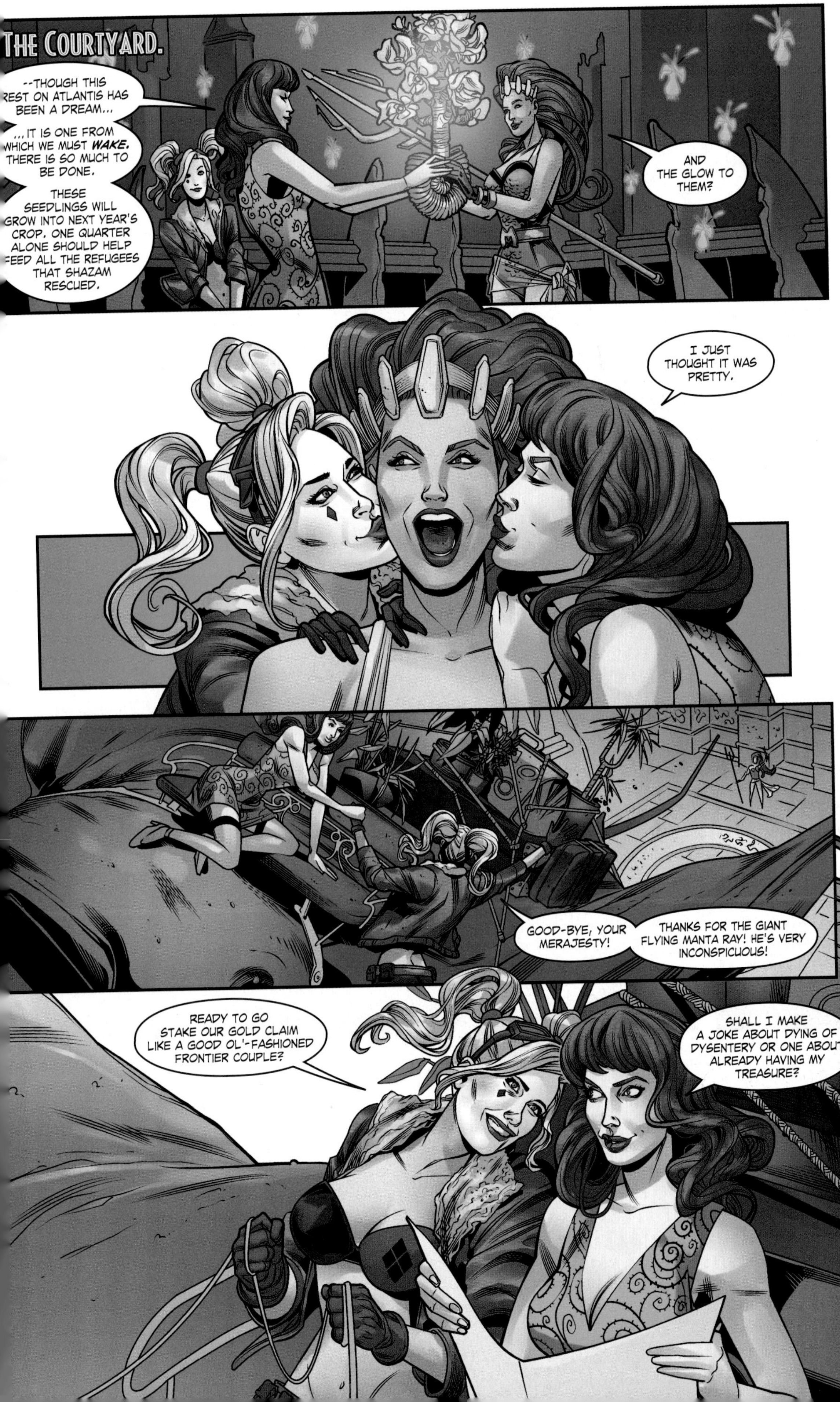
THE COURTYARD.
--THOUGH THIS REST ON ATLANTIS HAS BEEN A DREAM...
...IT IS ONE FROM WHICH WE MUST WAKE. THERE IS SO MUCH TO BE DONE.
THESE SEEDLINGS WILL GROW INTO NEXT YEAR'S CROP. ONE QUARTER ALONE SHOULD HELP FEED ALL THE REFUGEES THAT SHAZAM RESCUED.
AND THE GLOW TO THEM?
I JUST THOUGHT IT WAS PRETTY.
GOOD-BYE, YOUR MERAJESTY!
THANKS FOR THE GIANT FLYING MANTA RAY! HE'S VERY INCONSPICUOUS!
READY TO GO STAKE OUR GOLD CLAIM LIKE A GOOD OL'-FASHIONED FRONTIER COUPLE?
SHALL I MAKE A JOKE ABOUT DYING OF DYSENTERY OR ONE ABOUT ALREADY HAVING MY TREASURE?

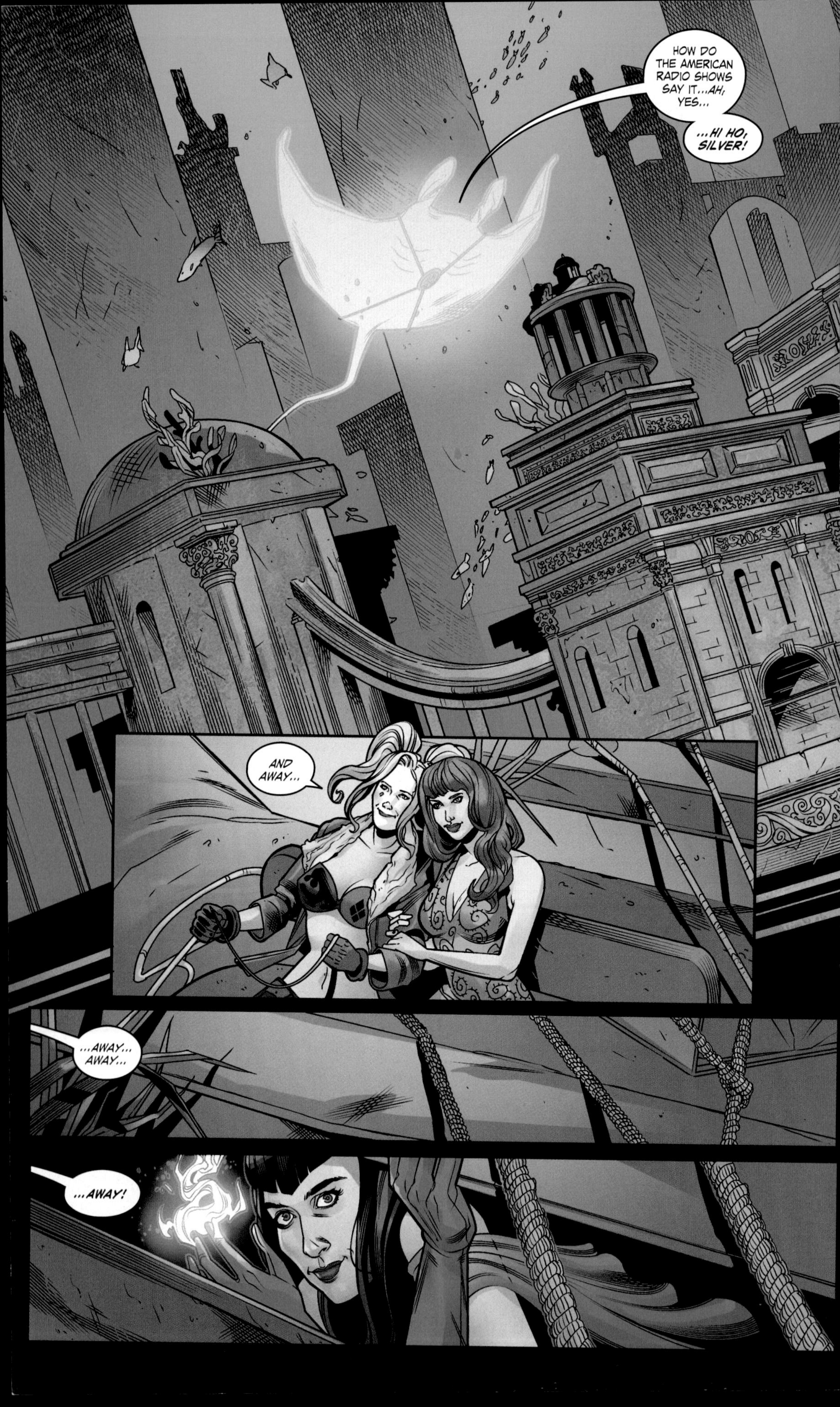
HOW DO THE AMERICAN RADIO SHOWS SAY IT...AH, YES...
...HI HO, SILVER!
AND AWAY...
...AWAY... AWAY...
...AWAY!

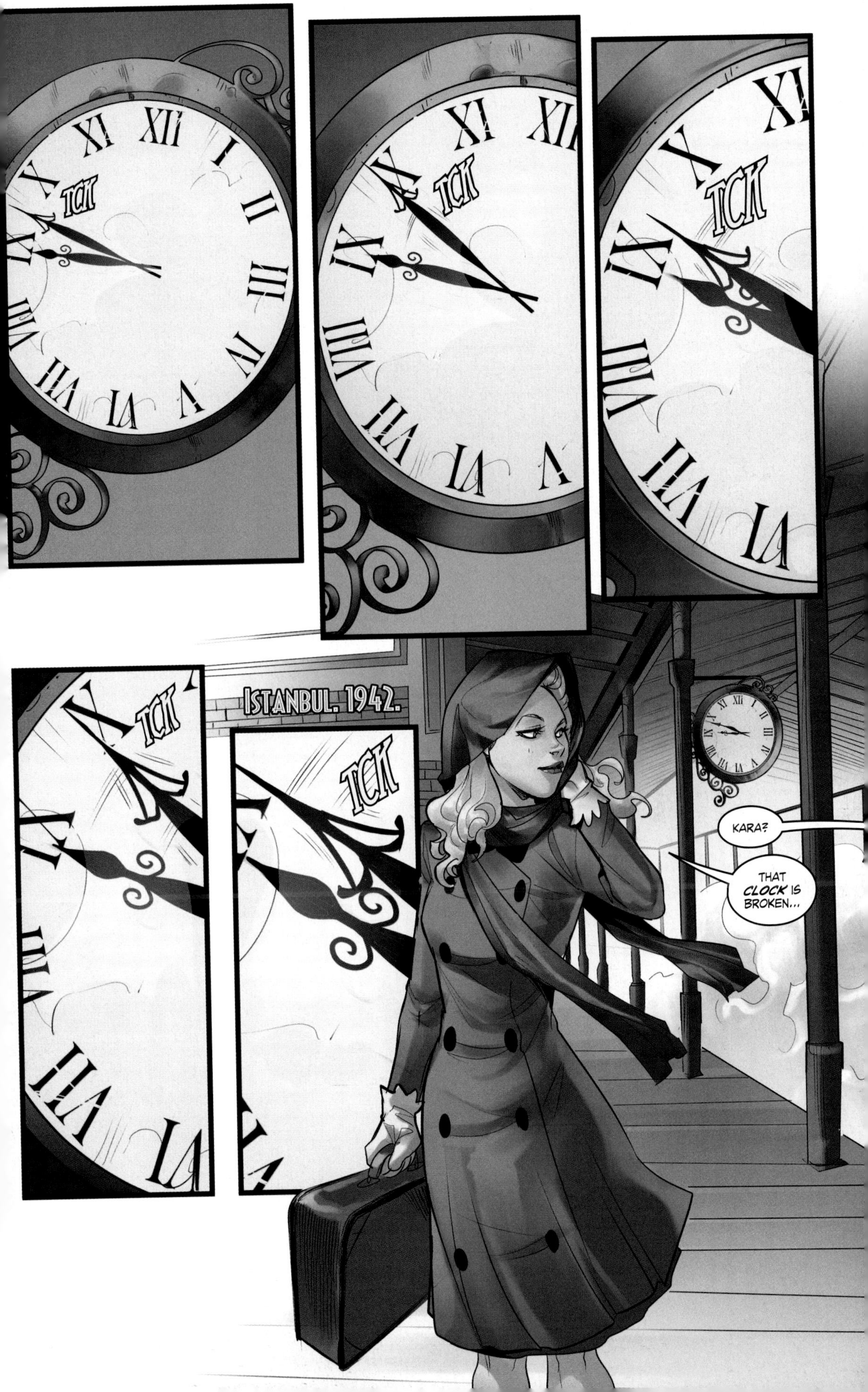
TCK
TCK
TCK
TCK
ISTANBUL. 1942.
TCK
KARA?
THAT CLOCK IS BROKEN...

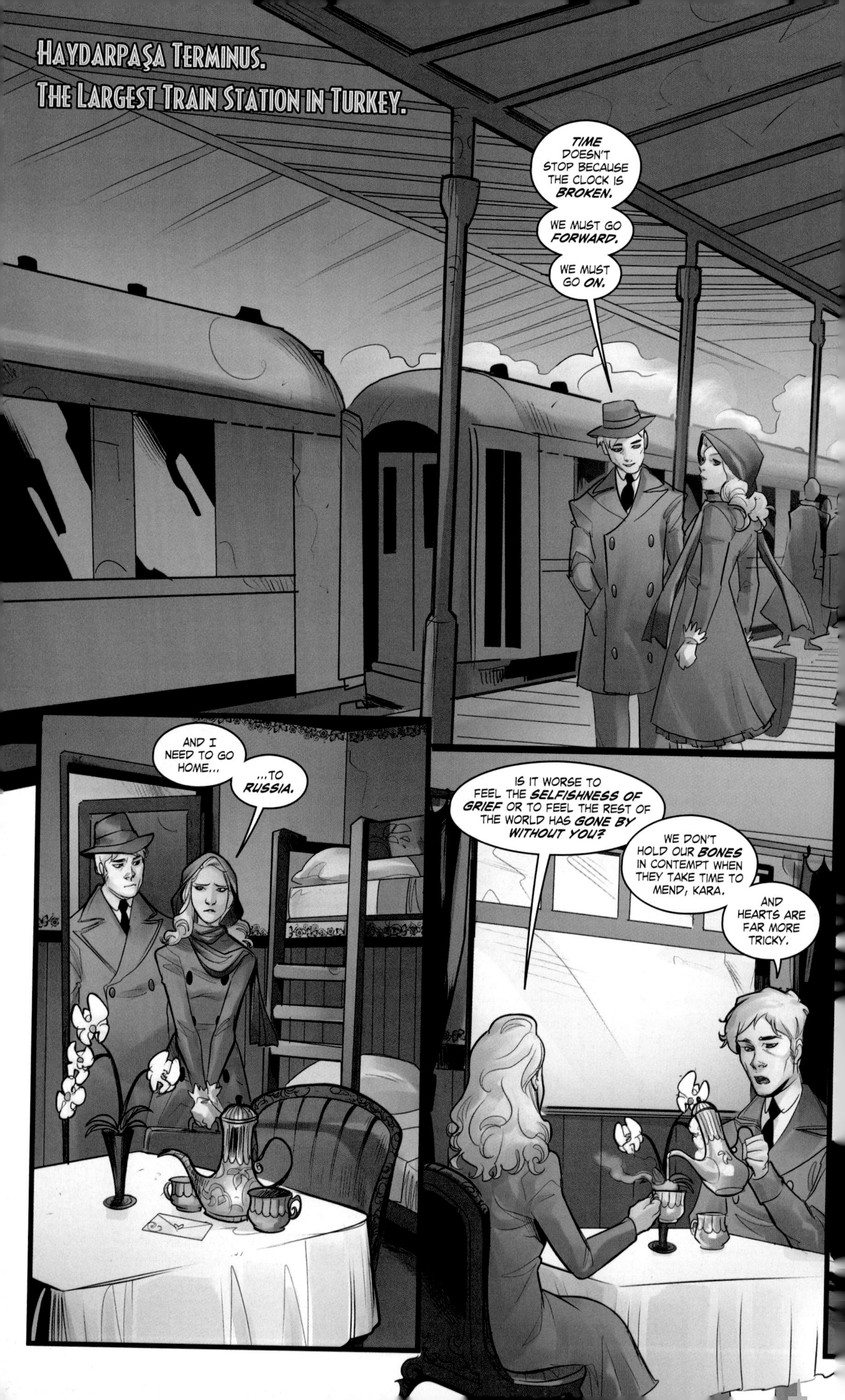

Haydarpaşa Terminus.
The Largest Train Station in Turkey.
TIME DOESN'T STOP BECAUSE THE CLOCK IS BROKEN.
WE MUST GO FORWARD.
WE MUST GO ON.
AND I NEED TO GO HOME...
...TO RUSSIA.
IS IT WORSE TO FEEL THE SELFISHNESS OF GRIEF OR TO FEEL THE REST OF THE WORLD HAS GONE BY WITHOUT YOU?
WE DON'T HOLD OUR BONES IN CONTEMPT WHEN THEY TAKE TIME TO MEND, KARA.
AND HEARTS ARE FAR MORE TRICKY.

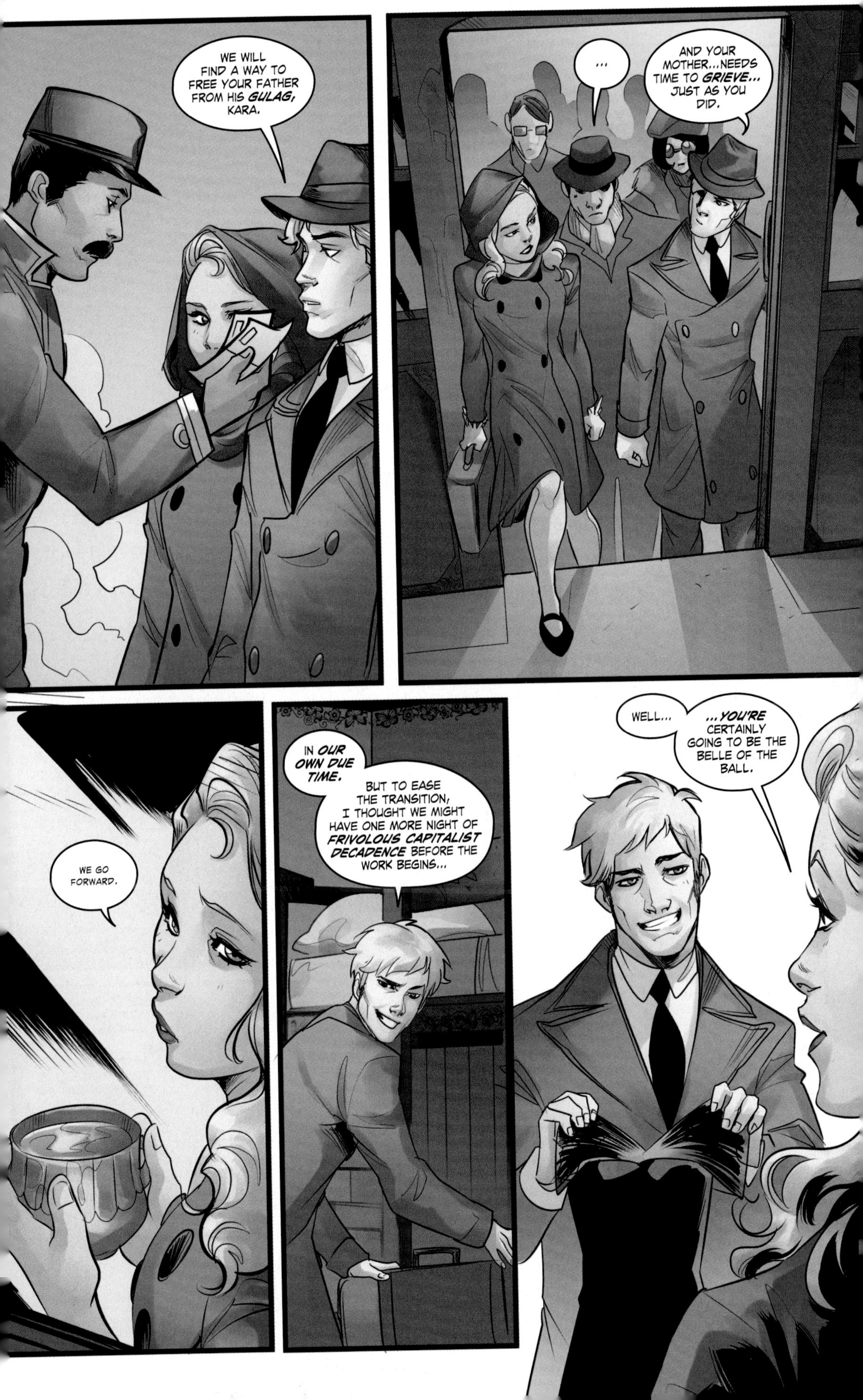

WE WILL FIND A WAY TO FREE YOUR FATHER FROM HIS GULAG, KARA.
...
AND YOUR MOTHER...NEEDS TIME TO GRIEVE... JUST AS YOU DID.
WE GO FORWARD.
IN OUR OWN DUE TIME.
BUT TO EASE THE TRANSITION, I THOUGHT WE MIGHT HAVE ONE MORE NIGHT OF FRIVOLOUS CAPITALIST DECADENCE BEFORE THE WORK BEGINS...
WELL...
...YOU'RE CERTAINLY GOING TO BE THE BELLE OF THE BALL.

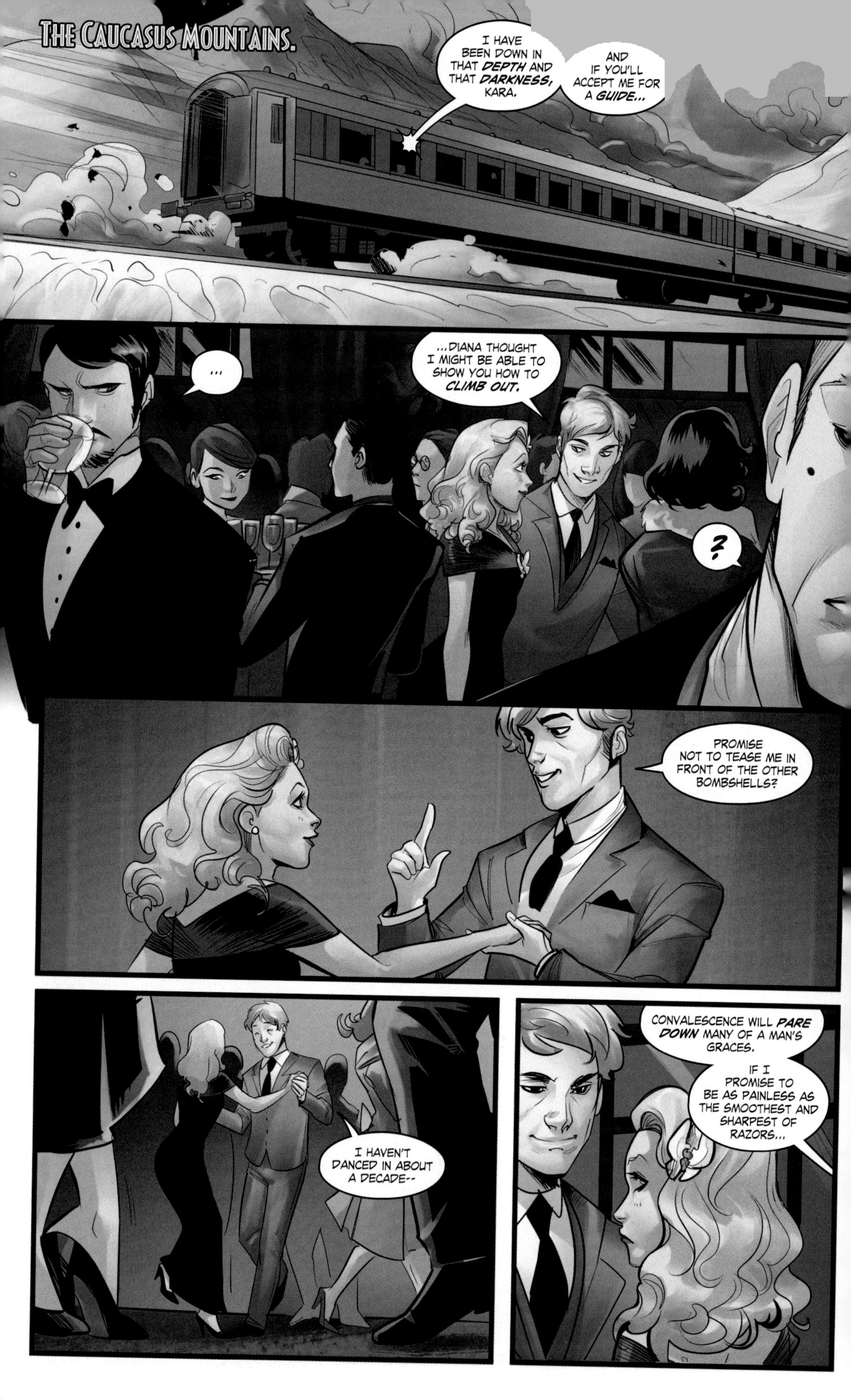
THE CAUCASUS MOUNTAINS.
I HAVE BEEN DOWN IN THAT DEPTH AND THAT DARKNESS, KARA.
AND IF YOU'LL ACCEPT ME FOR A GUIDE...
...
...DIANA THOUGHT I MIGHT BE ABLE TO SHOW YOU HOW TO CLIMB OUT.
?
PROMISE NOT TO TEASE ME IN FRONT OF THE OTHER BOMBSHELLS?
I HAVEN'T DANCED IN ABOUT A DECADE--
CONVALESCENCE WILL PARE DOWN MANY OF A MAN'S GRACES.
IF I PROMISE TO BE AS PAINLESS AS THE SMOOTHEST AND SHARPEST OF RAZORS...

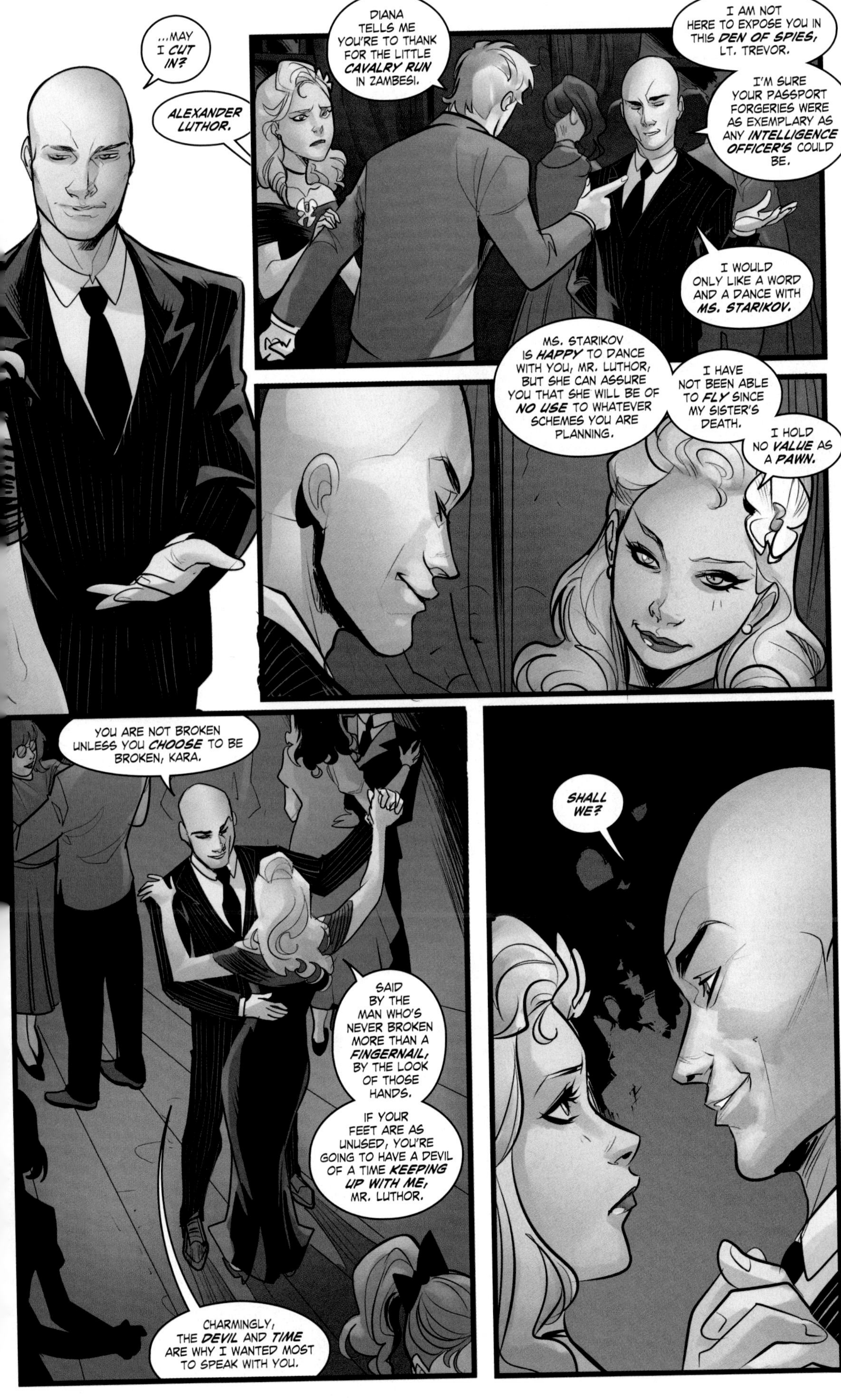
...MAY I CUT IN?
ALEXANDER LUTHOR.
DIANA TELLS ME YOU'RE TO THANK FOR THE LITTLE CAVALRY RUN IN ZAMBESI.
I AM NOT HERE TO EXPOSE YOU IN THIS DEN OF SPIES, LT. TREVOR.
I'M SURE YOUR PASSPORT FORGERIES WERE AS EXEMPLARY AS ANY INTELLIGENCE OFFICER'S COULD BE.
I WOULD ONLY LIKE A WORD AND A DANCE WITH MS. STARIKOV.
MS. STARIKOV IS HAPPY TO DANCE WITH YOU, MR. LUTHOR, BUT SHE CAN ASSURE YOU THAT SHE WILL BE OF NO USE TO WHATEVER SCHEMES YOU ARE PLANNING.
I HAVE NOT BEEN ABLE TO FLY SINCE MY SISTER'S DEATH.
I HOLD NO VALUE AS A PAWN.
YOU ARE NOT BROKEN UNLESS YOU CHOOSE TO BE BROKEN, KARA.
SAID BY THE MAN WHO'S NEVER BROKEN MORE THAN A FINGERNAIL, BY THE LOOK OF THOSE HANDS.
IF YOUR FEET ARE AS UNUSED, YOU'RE GOING TO HAVE A DEVIL OF A TIME KEEPING UP WITH ME, MR. LUTHOR.
CHARMINGLY, THE DEVIL AND TIME ARE WHY I WANTED MOST TO SPEAK WITH YOU.
SHALL WE?

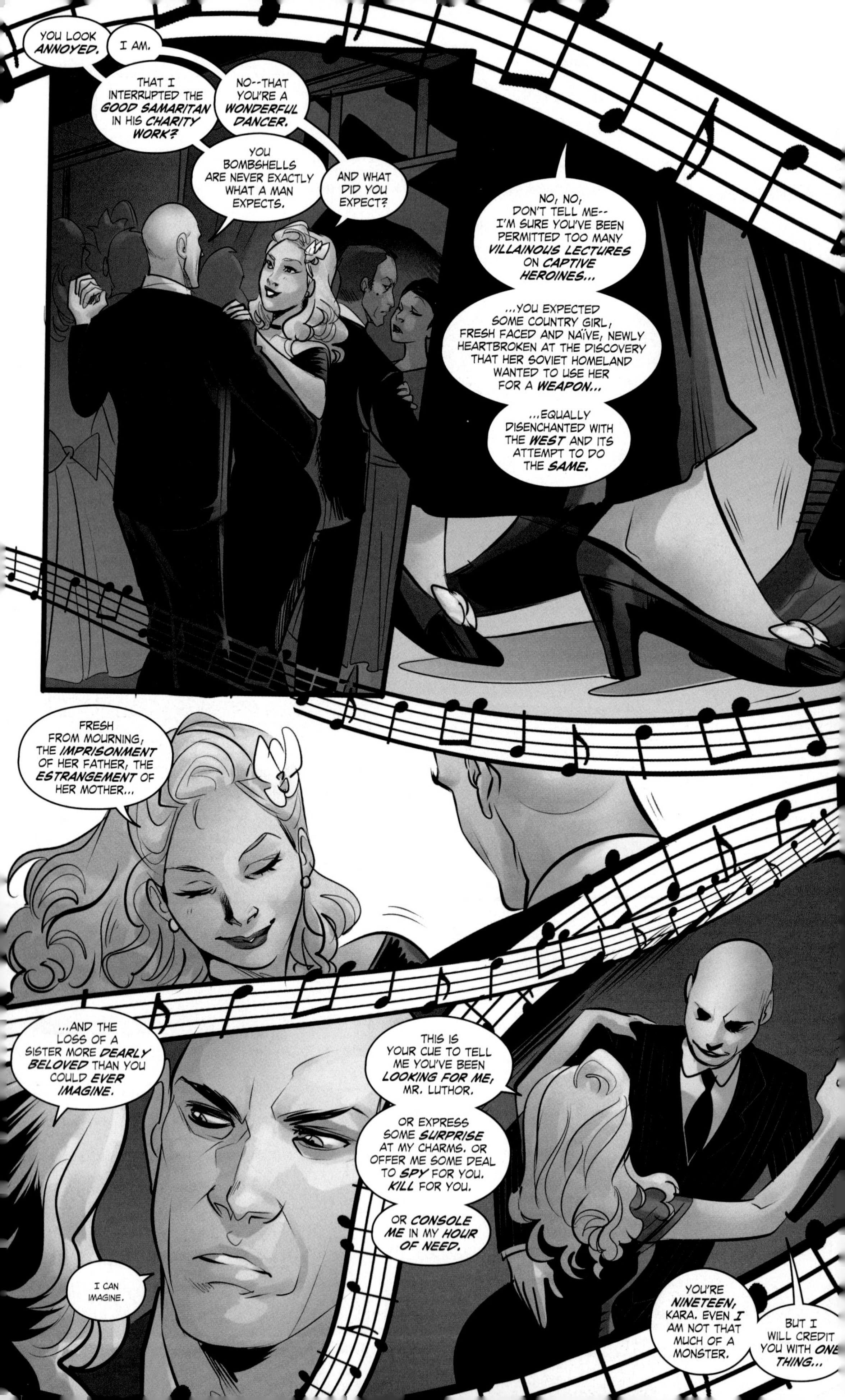
YOU LOOK ANNOYED.
I AM.
THAT I INTERRUPTED THE GOOD SAMARITAN IN HIS CHARITY WORK?
NO--THAT YOU'RE A WONDERFUL DANCER.
YOU BOMBSHELLS ARE NEVER EXACTLY WHAT A MAN EXPECTS.
AND WHAT DID YOU EXPECT?
NO, NO, DON'T TELL ME-- I'M SURE YOU'VE BEEN PERMITTED TOO MANY VILLAINOUS LECTURES ON CAPTIVE HEROINES...
...YOU EXPECTED SOME COUNTRY GIRL, FRESH FACED AND NAÏVE, NEWLY HEARTBROKEN AT THE DISCOVERY THAT HER SOVIET HOMELAND WANTED TO USE HER FOR A WEAPON...
...EQUALLY DISENCHANTED WITH THE WEST AND ITS ATTEMPT TO DO THE SAME.
FRESH FROM MOURNING, THE IMPRISONMENT OF HER FATHER, THE ESTRANGEMENT OF HER MOTHER...
...AND THE LOSS OF A SISTER MORE DEARLY BELOVED THAN YOU COULD EVER IMAGINE.
I CAN IMAGINE.
THIS IS YOUR CUE TO TELL ME YOU'VE BEEN LOOKING FOR ME, MR. LUTHOR.
OR EXPRESS SOME SURPRISE AT MY CHARMS. OR OFFER ME SOME DEAL TO SPY FOR YOU. KILL FOR YOU.
OR CONSOLE ME IN MY HOUR OF NEED.
YOU'RE NINETEEN, KARA. EVEN I AM NOT THAT MUCH OF A MONSTER.
BUT I WILL CREDIT YOU WITH ONE THING...

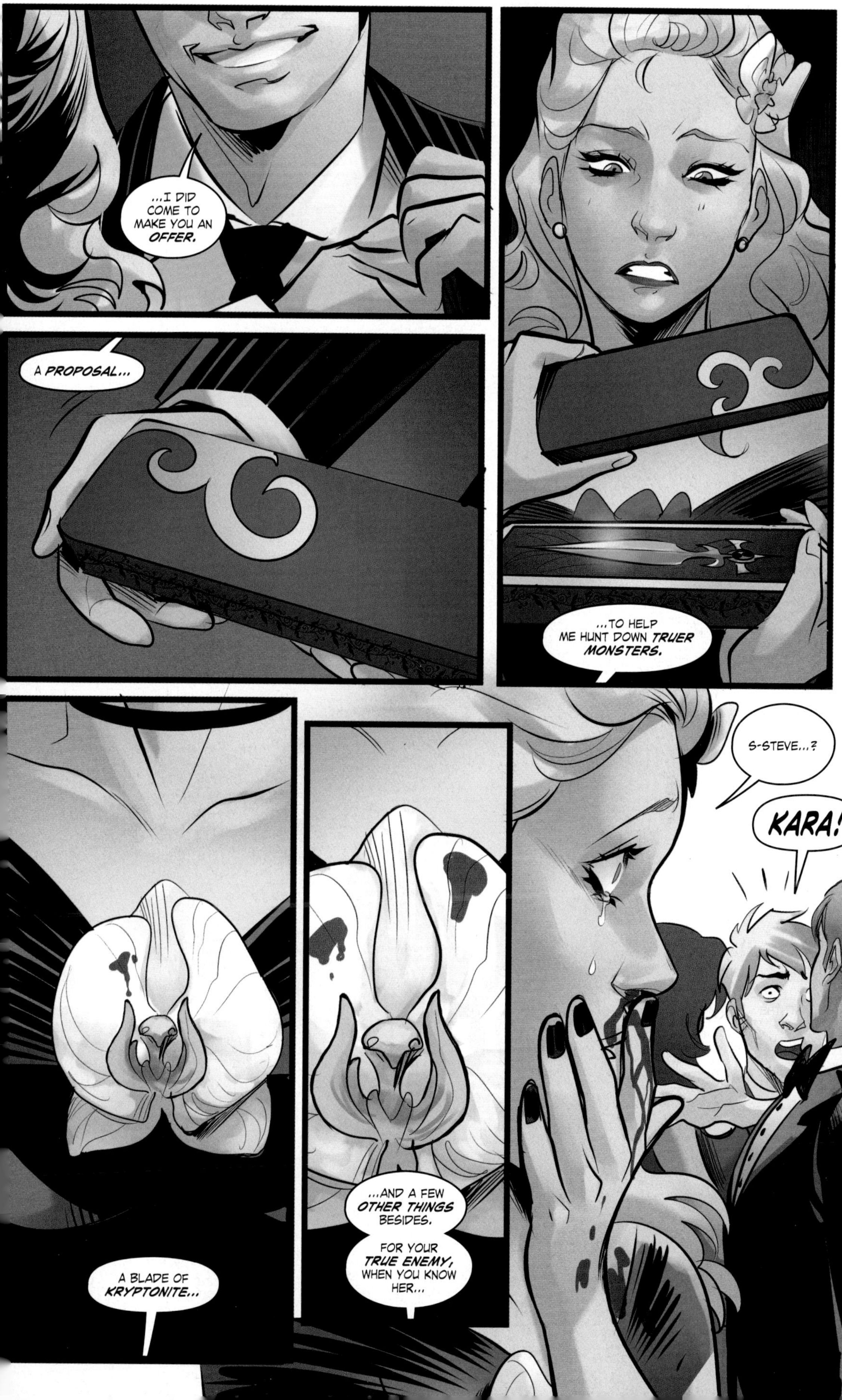

...I DID COME TO MAKE YOU AN OFFER.
A PROPOSAL...
...TO HELP ME HUNT DOWN TRUER MONSTERS.
A BLADE OF KRYPTONITE...
...AND A FEW OTHER THINGS BESIDES.
FOR YOUR TRUE ENEMY, WHEN YOU KNOW HER...
S-STEVE...?
KARA!

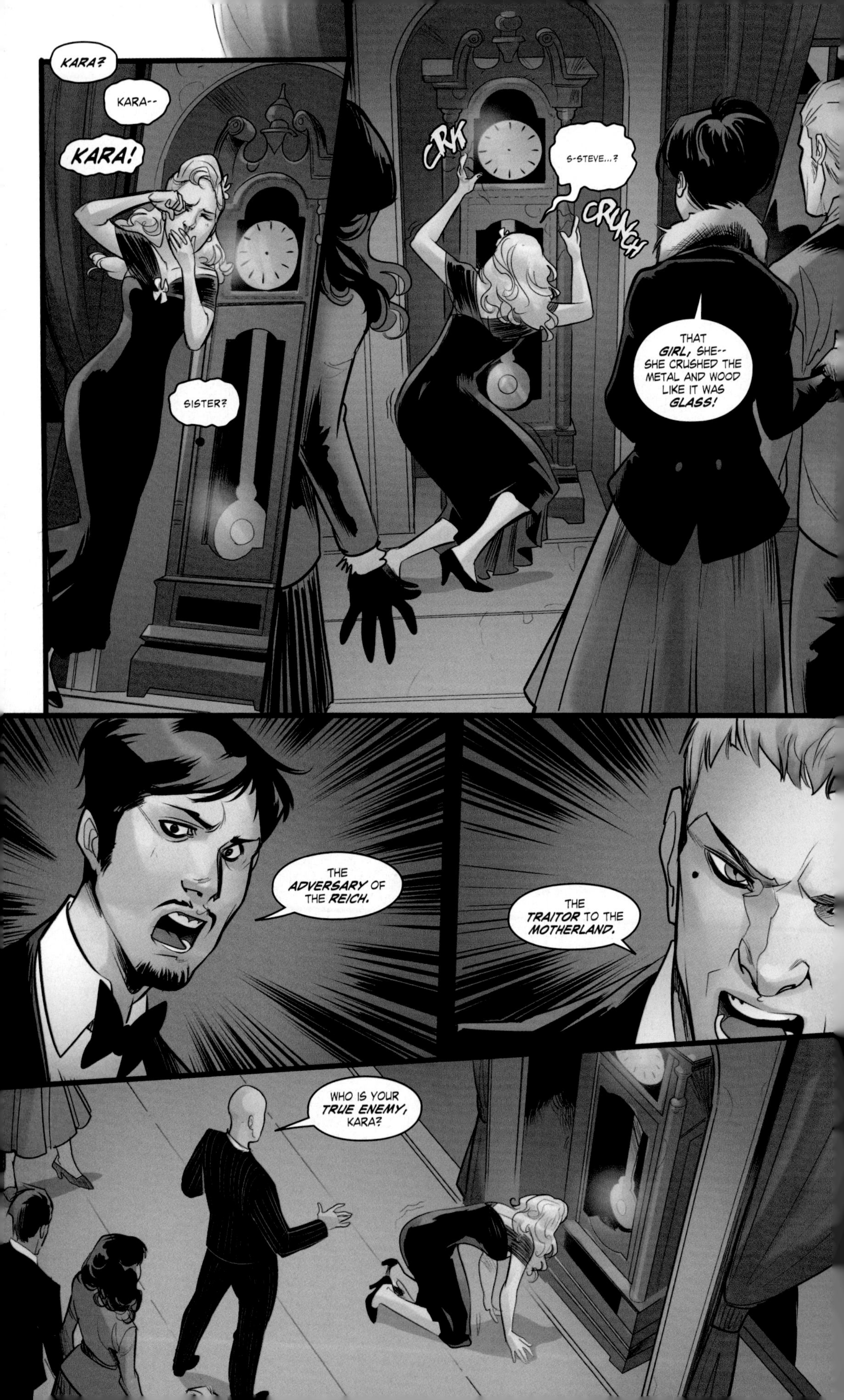
KARA?
KARA--
KARA!
SISTER?
CRK
S-STEVE...?
CRUNCH
THAT GIRL, SHE-- SHE CRUSHED THE METAL AND WOOD LIKE IT WAS GLASS!
THE ADVERSARY OF THE REICH.
THE TRAITOR TO THE MOTHERLAND.
WHO IS YOUR TRUE ENEMY, KARA?

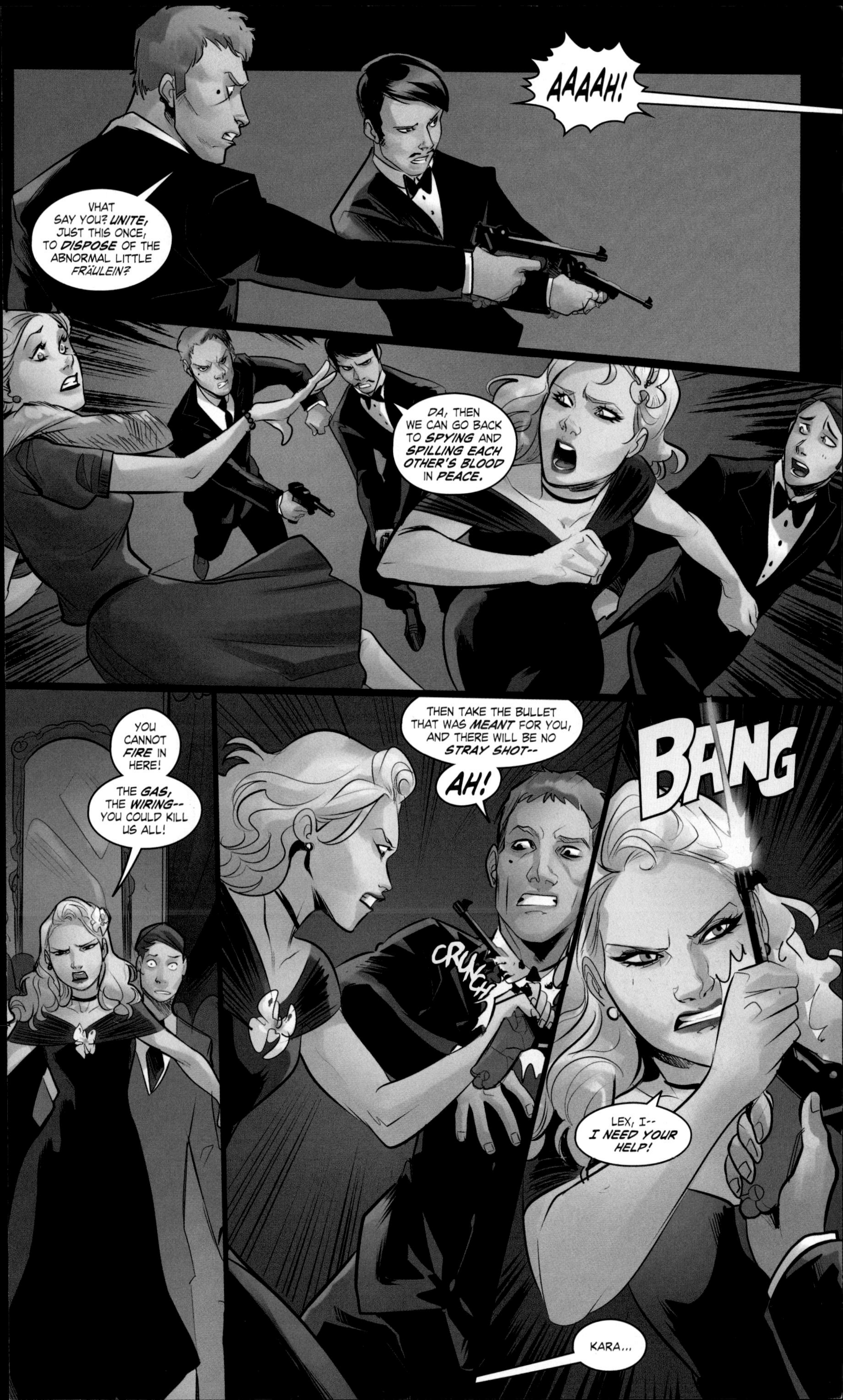
AAAAH!
VHAT SAY YOU? UNITE, JUST THIS ONCE, TO DISPOSE OF THE ABNORMAL LITTLE FRÄULEIN?
DA, THEN WE CAN GO BACK TO SPYING AND SPILLING EACH OTHER'S BLOOD IN PEACE.
YOU CANNOT FIRE IN HERE!
THE GAS, THE WIRING-- YOU COULD KILL US ALL!
THEN TAKE THE BULLET THAT WAS MEANT FOR YOU, AND THERE WILL BE NO STRAY SHOT--
AH!
CRUNCH
BANG
LEX, I-- I NEED YOUR HELP!
KARA...

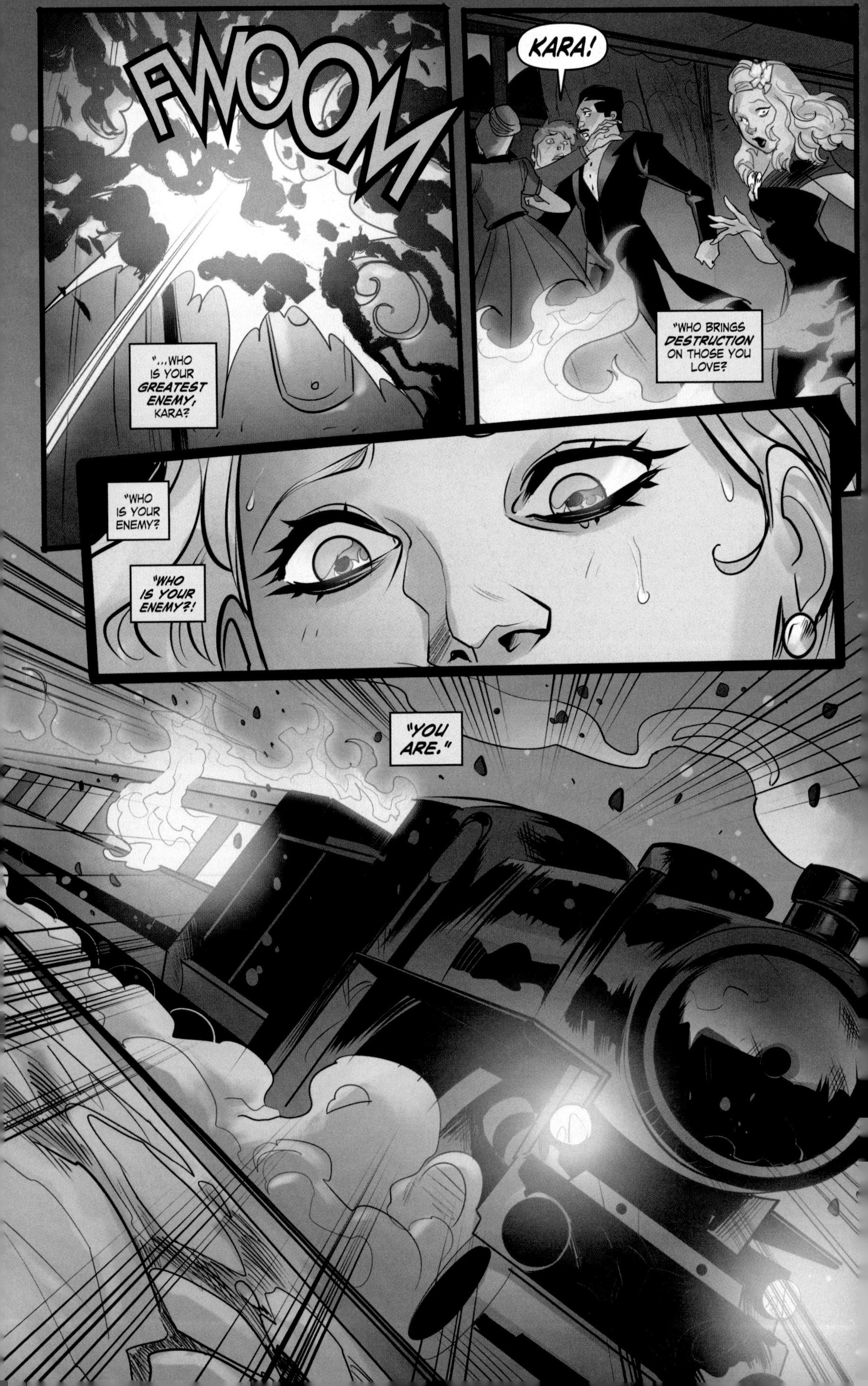
FWOOM
"...WHO IS YOUR GREATEST ENEMY, KARA?
KARA!
"WHO BRINGS DESTRUCTION ON THOSE YOU LOVE?
"WHO IS YOUR ENEMY?
"WHO IS YOUR ENEMY?!
"YOU ARE."

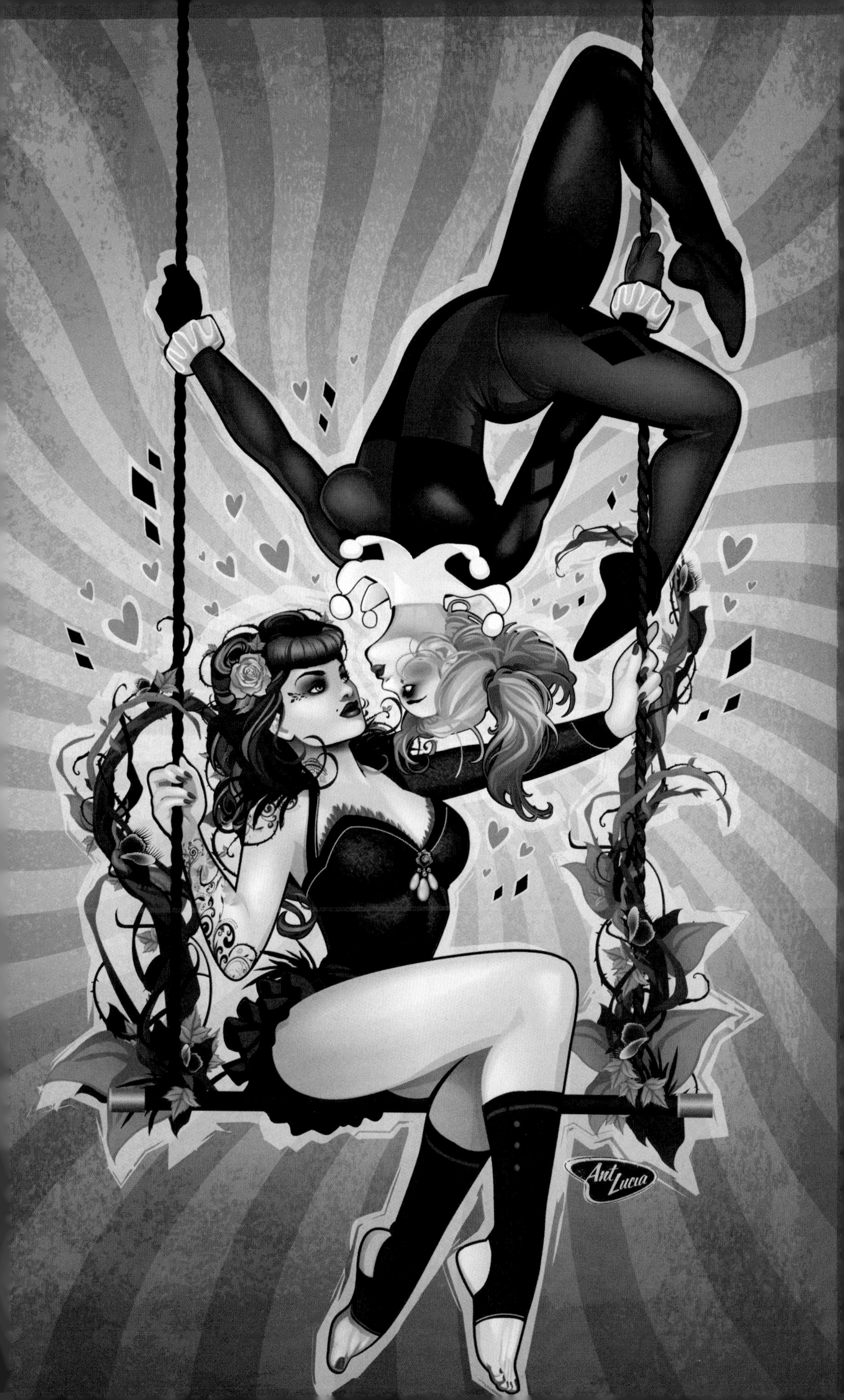
Ant Lucia

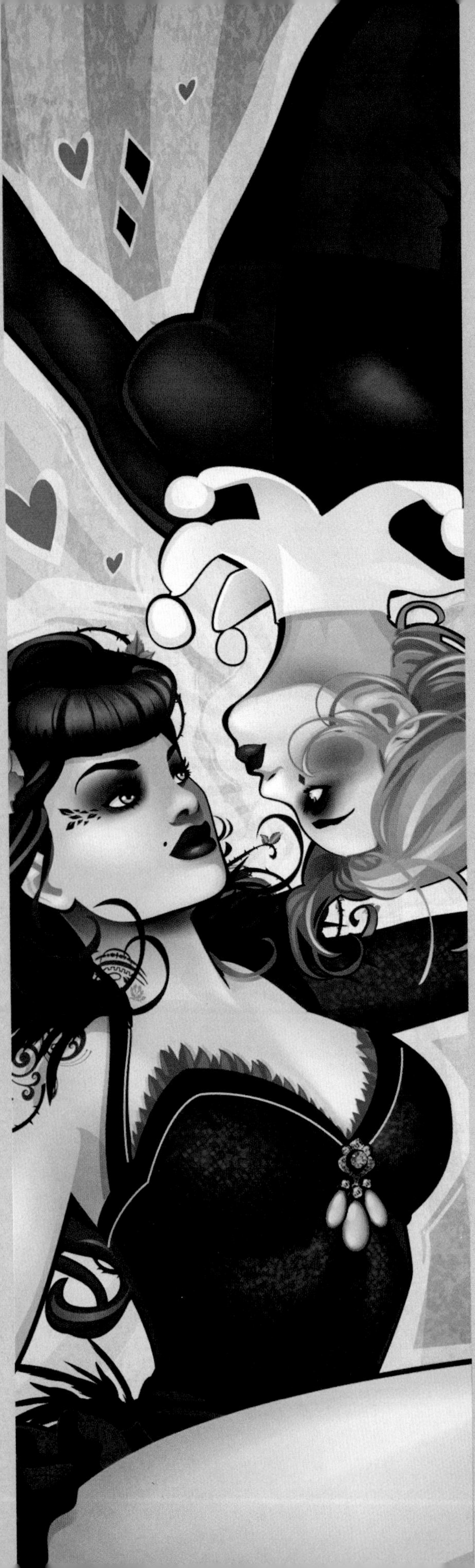

THE DEATH OF ILLUSION

MARGUERITE BENNETT
Writer

MIRKA ANDOLFO
LAURA BRAGA
CARMEN CARNERO
Artists

J. NANJAN
Colorist

Cover by
ANT LUCIA

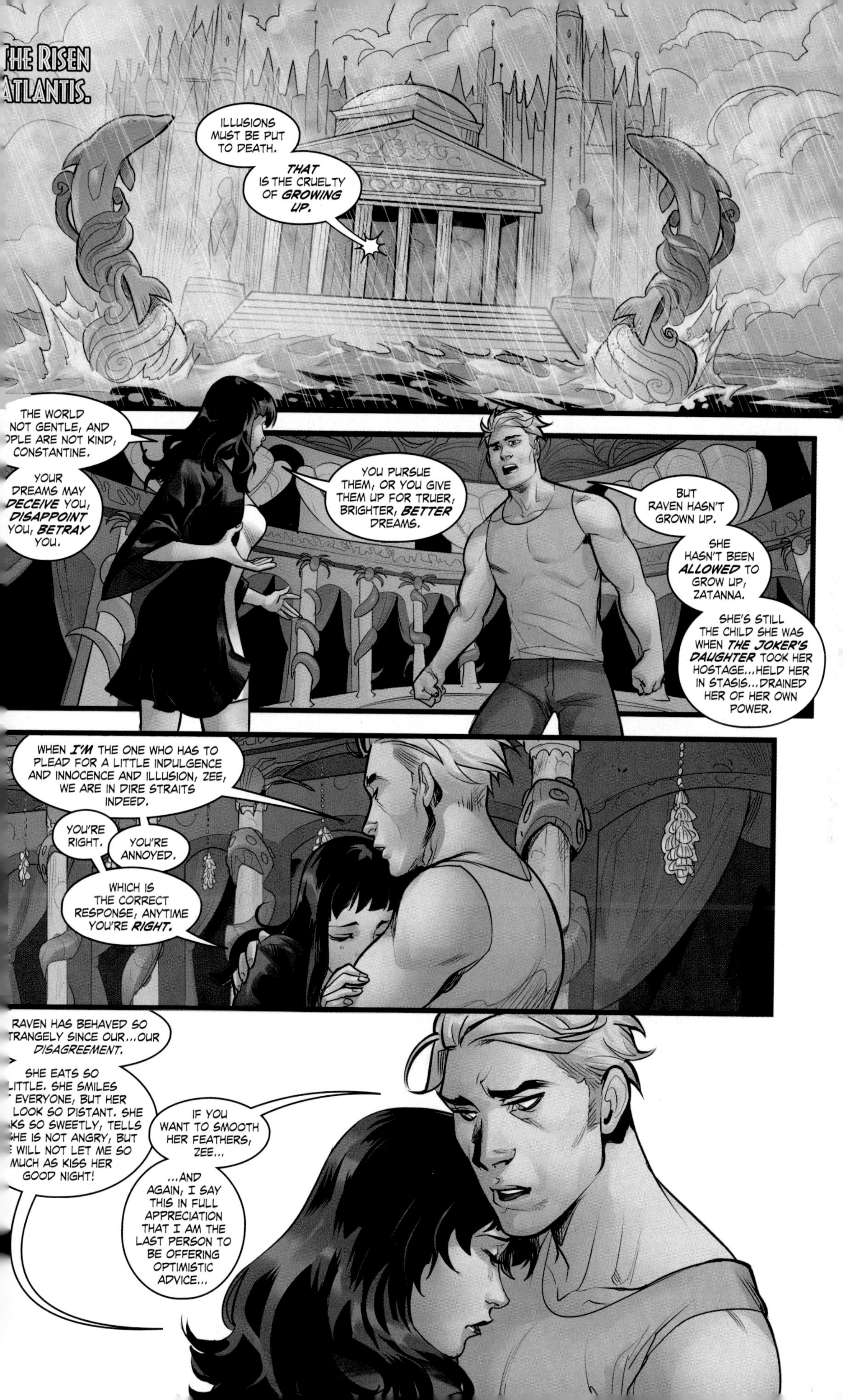

HE RISEN ATLANTIS.
ILLUSIONS MUST BE PUT TO DEATH.
THAT IS THE CRUELTY OF GROWING UP.
THE WORLD NOT GENTLE, AND OPLE ARE NOT KIND, CONSTANTINE.
YOUR DREAMS MAY DECEIVE YOU, DISAPPOINT YOU, BETRAY YOU.
YOU PURSUE THEM, OR YOU GIVE THEM UP FOR TRUER, BRIGHTER, BETTER DREAMS.
BUT RAVEN HASN'T GROWN UP.
SHE HASN'T BEEN ALLOWED TO GROW UP, ZATANNA.
SHE'S STILL THE CHILD SHE WAS WHEN THE JOKER'S DAUGHTER TOOK HER HOSTAGE...HELD HER IN STASIS...DRAINED HER OF HER OWN POWER.
WHEN I'M THE ONE WHO HAS TO PLEAD FOR A LITTLE INDULGENCE AND INNOCENCE AND ILLUSION, ZEE, WE ARE IN DIRE STRAITS INDEED.
YOU'RE RIGHT.
YOU'RE ANNOYED.
WHICH IS THE CORRECT RESPONSE, ANYTIME YOU'RE RIGHT.
RAVEN HAS BEHAVED SO TRANGELY SINCE OUR...OUR DISAGREEMENT.
SHE EATS SO LITTLE. SHE SMILES EVERYONE, BUT HER LOOK SO DISTANT. SHE KS SO SWEETLY, TELLS HE IS NOT ANGRY, BUT WILL NOT LET ME SO MUCH AS KISS HER GOOD NIGHT!
IF YOU WANT TO SMOOTH HER FEATHERS, ZEE...
...AND AGAIN, I SAY THIS IN FULL APPRECIATION THAT I AM THE LAST PERSON TO BE OFFERING OPTIMISTIC ADVICE...

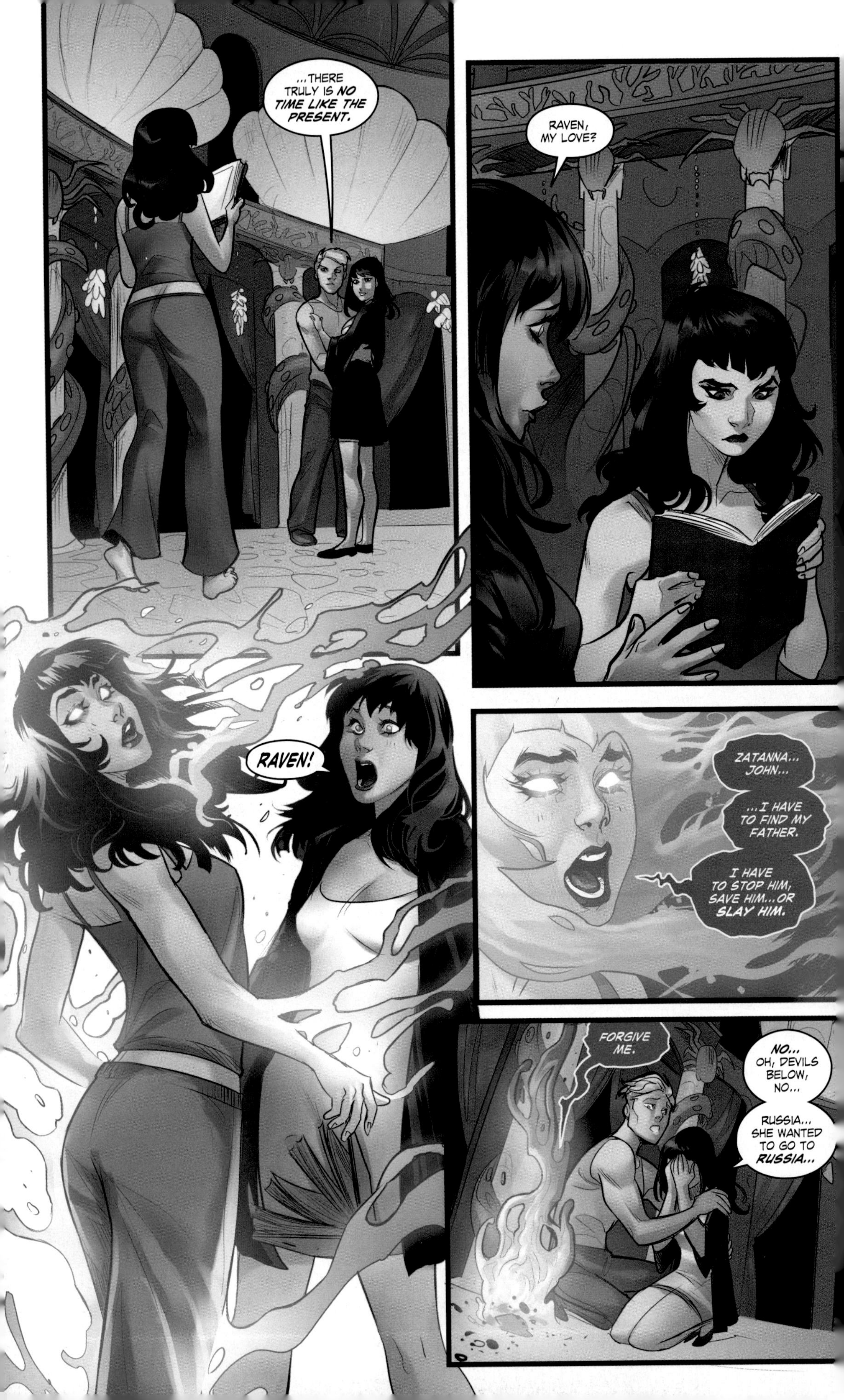
...THERE TRULY IS NO TIME LIKE THE PRESENT.
RAVEN, MY LOVE?
RAVEN!
ZATANNA... JOHN...
...I HAVE TO FIND MY FATHER.
I HAVE TO STOP HIM, SAVE HIM...OR SLAY HIM.
FORGIVE ME.
NO... OH, DEVILS BELOW, NO...
RUSSIA... SHE WANTED TO GO TO RUSSIA...

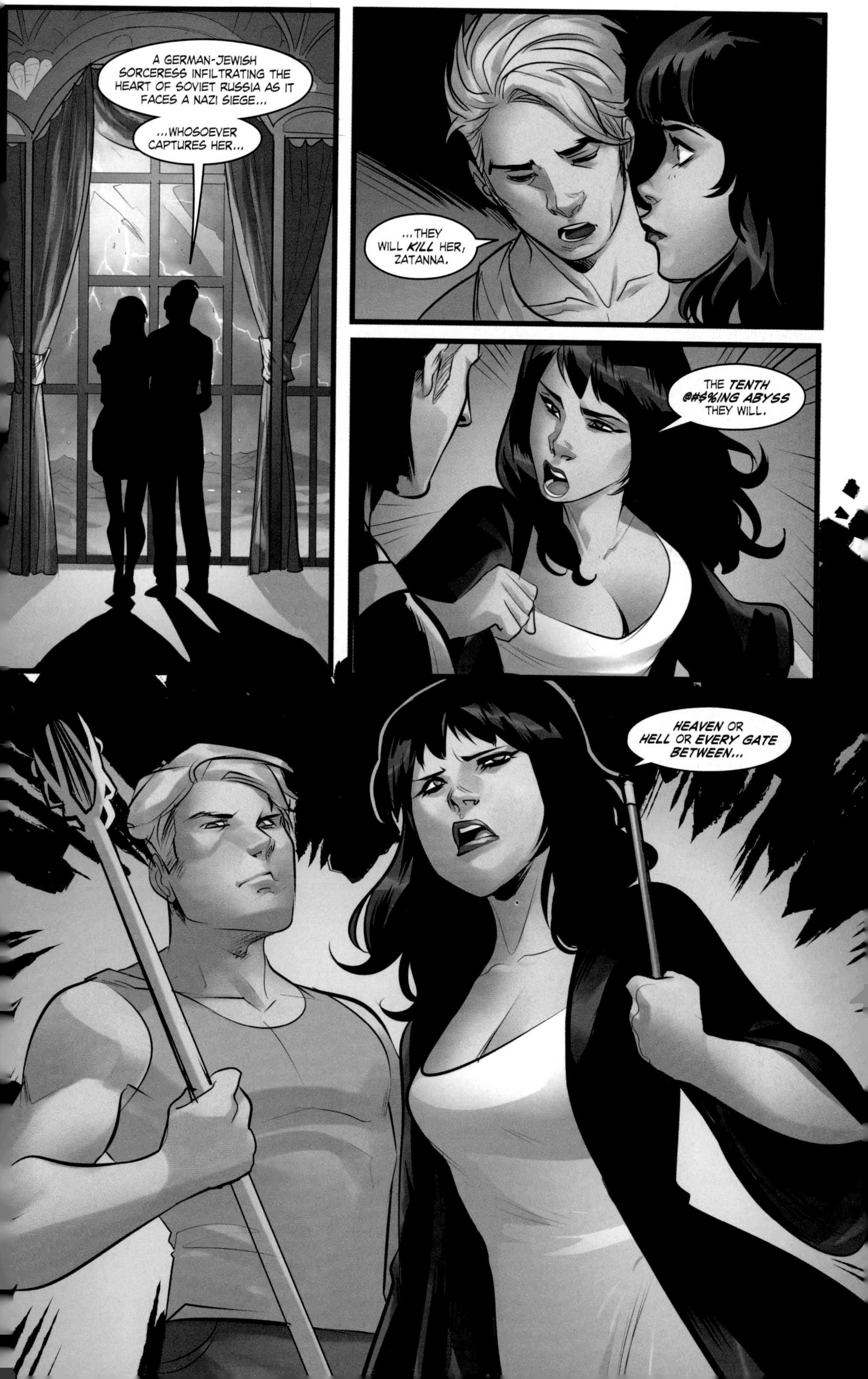
A GERMAN-JEWISH SORCERESS INFILTRATING THE HEART OF SOVIET RUSSIA AS IT FACES A NAZI SIEGE...
...WHOSOEVER CAPTURES HER...
...THEY WILL KILL HER, ZATANNA.
THE TENTH @#$%ING ABYSS THEY WILL.
HEAVEN OR HELL OR EVERY GATE BETWEEN...

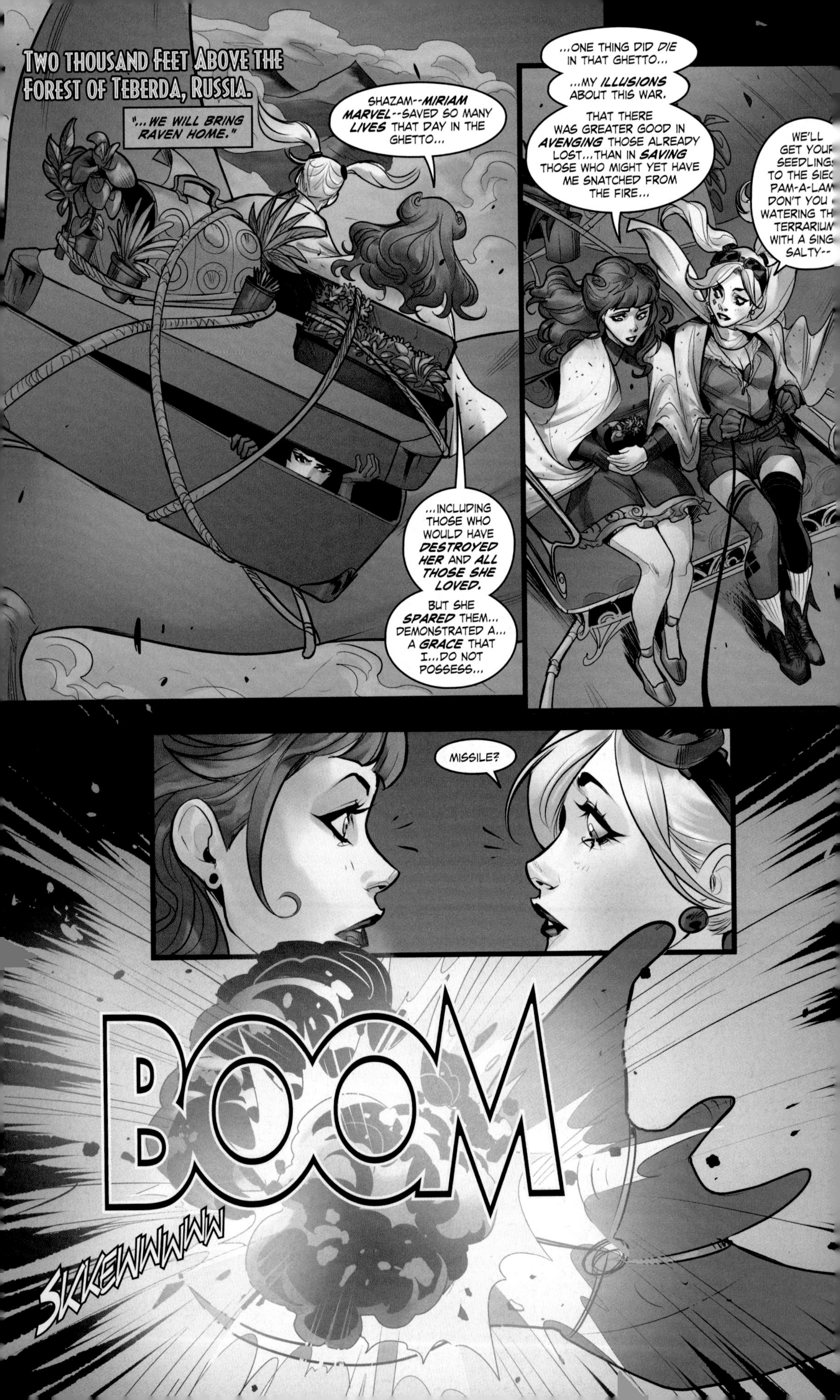

TWO THOUSAND FEET ABOVE THE FOREST OF TEBERDA, RUSSIA.
"...WE WILL BRING RAVEN HOME."
SHAZAM--MIRIAM MARVEL--SAVED SO MANY LIVES THAT DAY IN THE GHETTO...
...INCLUDING THOSE WHO WOULD HAVE DESTROYED HER AND ALL THOSE SHE LOVED.
BUT SHE SPARED THEM... DEMONSTRATED A... A GRACE THAT I...DO NOT POSSESS...
...ONE THING DID DIE IN THAT GHETTO...
...MY ILLUSIONS ABOUT THIS WAR.
THAT THERE WAS GREATER GOOD IN AVENGING THOSE ALREADY LOST...THAN IN SAVING THOSE WHO MIGHT YET HAVE ME SNATCHED FROM THE FIRE...
WE'LL GET YOUR SEEDLINGS TO THE SIEG PAM-A-LAM DON'T YOU WATERING TH TERRARIUM WITH A SING SALTY--
MISSILE?
BOOM
SKKEWWWWWW

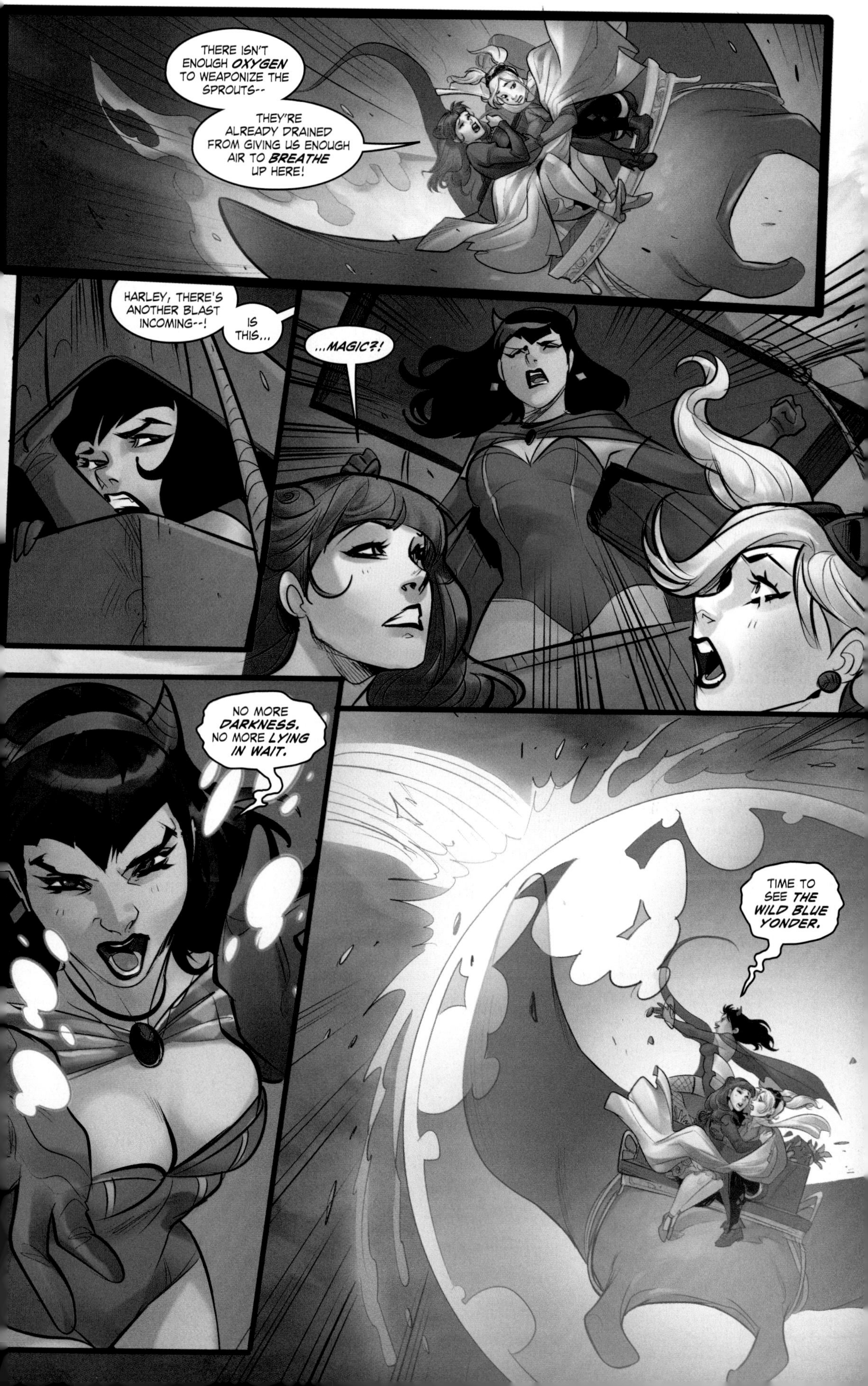
THERE ISN'T ENOUGH OXYGEN TO WEAPONIZE THE SPROUTS--
THEY'RE ALREADY DRAINED FROM GIVING US ENOUGH AIR TO BREATHE UP HERE!
HARLEY, THERE'S ANOTHER BLAST INCOMING--!
IS THIS...
...MAGIC?!
NO MORE DARKNESS. NO MORE LYING IN WAIT.
TIME TO SEE THE WILD BLUE YONDER.

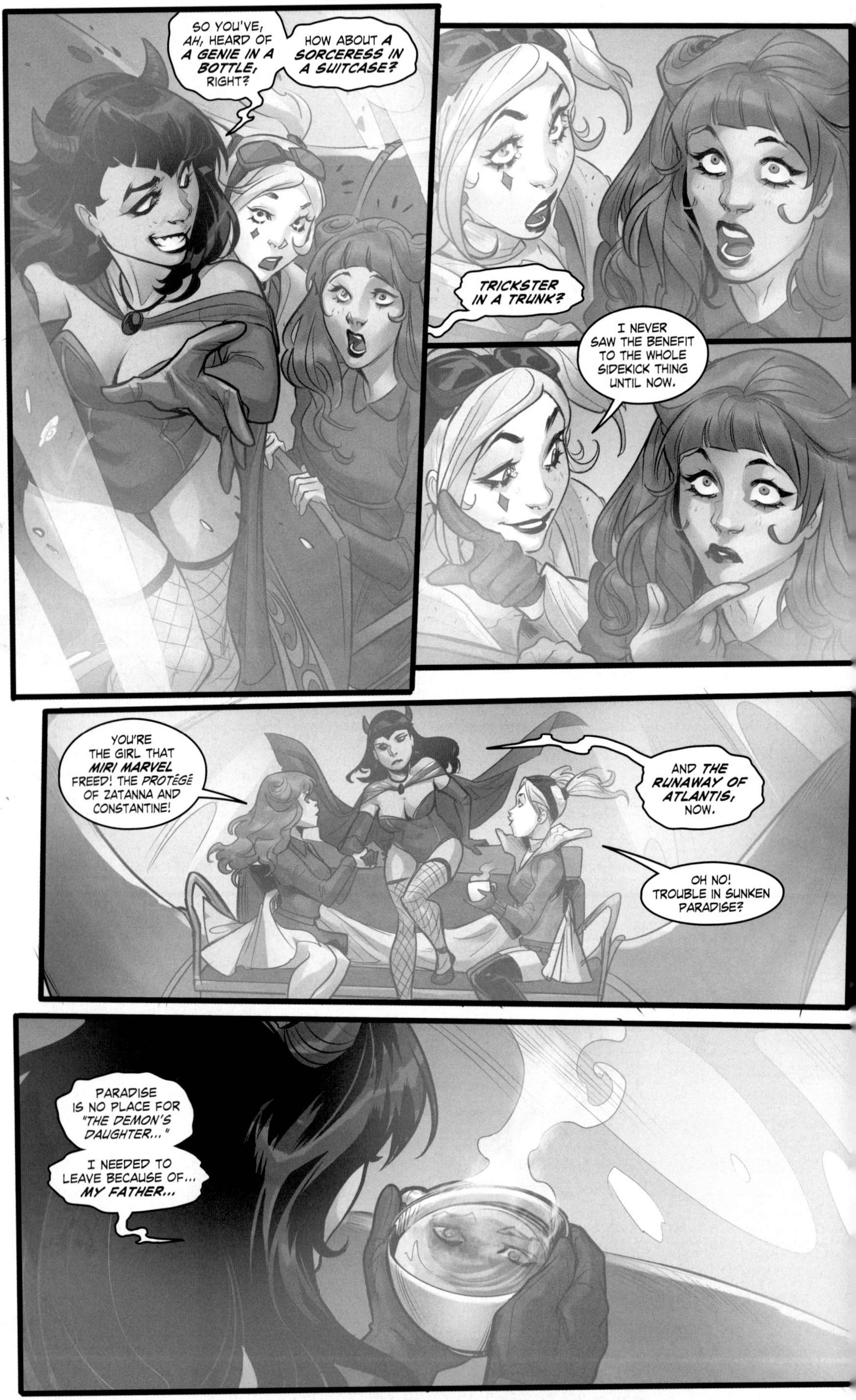

SO YOU'VE, AH, HEARD OF A GENIE IN A BOTTLE, RIGHT?
HOW ABOUT A SORCERESS IN A SUITCASE?
TRICKSTER IN A TRUNK?
I NEVER SAW THE BENEFIT TO THE WHOLE SIDEKICK THING UNTIL NOW.
YOU'RE THE GIRL THAT MIRI MARVEL FREED! THE PROTÉGÉ OF ZATANNA AND CONSTANTINE!
AND THE RUNAWAY OF ATLANTIS, NOW.
OH NO! TROUBLE IN SUNKEN PARADISE?
PARADISE IS NO PLACE FOR "THE DEMON'S DAUGHTER..."
I NEEDED TO LEAVE BECAUSE OF... MY FATHER...

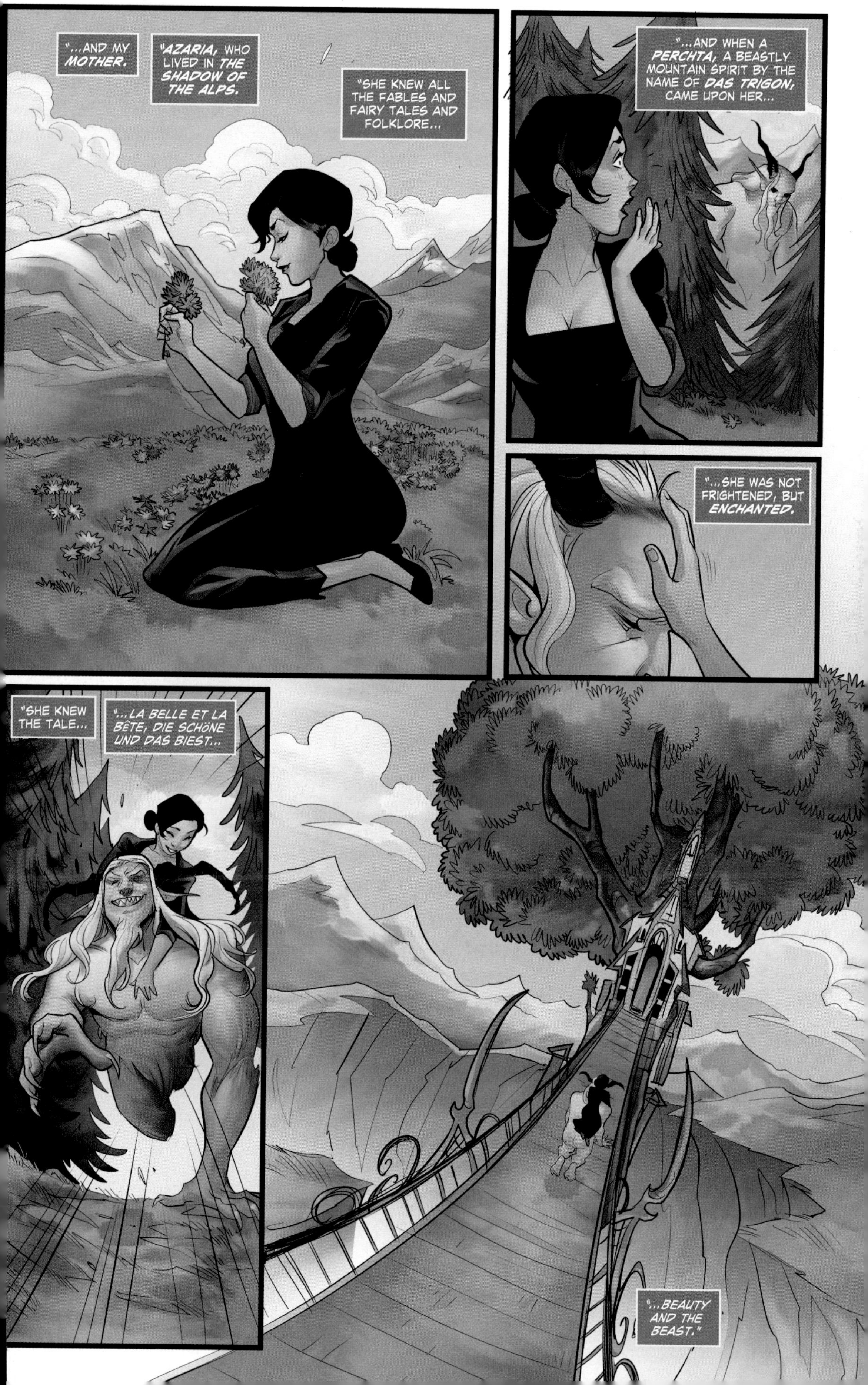
"...AND MY *MOTHER.*
"*AZARIA,* WHO LIVED IN *THE SHADOW OF THE ALPS.*
"SHE KNEW ALL THE FABLES AND FAIRY TALES AND FOLKLORE...
"...AND WHEN A *PERCHTA,* A BEASTLY MOUNTAIN SPIRIT BY THE NAME OF *DAS TRIGON,* CAME UPON HER...
"...SHE WAS NOT FRIGHTENED, BUT *ENCHANTED.*
"SHE KNEW THE TALE...
"...*LA BELLE ET LA BÊTE, DIE SCHÖNE UND DAS BIEST...*
"...*BEAUTY AND THE BEAST.*"

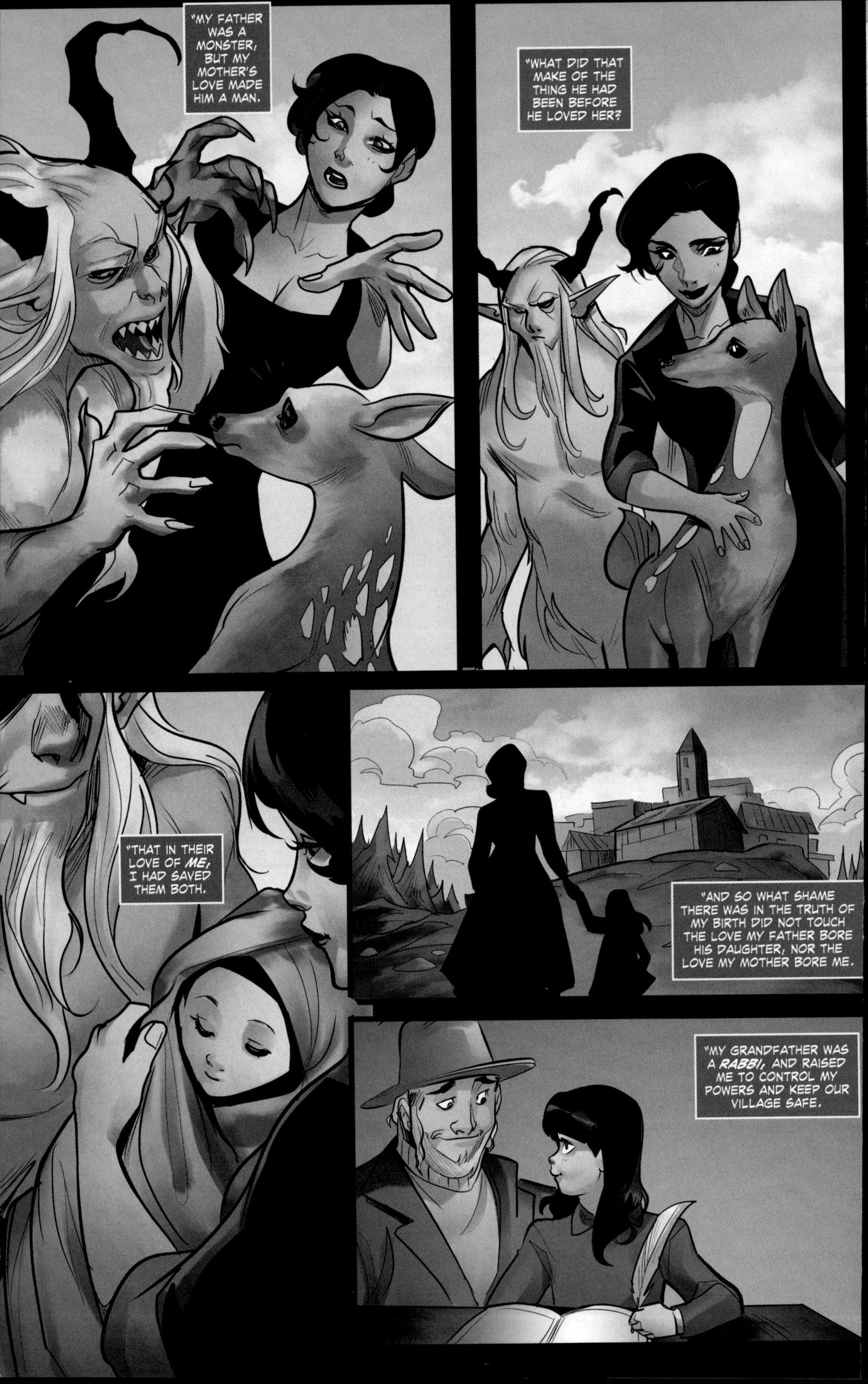
"MY FATHER WAS A MONSTER, BUT MY MOTHER'S LOVE MADE HIM A MAN.
"WHAT DID THAT MAKE OF THE THING HE HAD BEEN BEFORE HE LOVED HER?
"THAT IN THEIR LOVE OF *ME*, I HAD SAVED THEM BOTH.
"AND SO WHAT SHAME THERE WAS IN THE TRUTH OF MY BIRTH DID NOT TOUCH THE LOVE MY FATHER BORE HIS DAUGHTER, NOR THE LOVE MY MOTHER BORE ME.
"MY GRANDFATHER WAS A *RABBI*, AND RAISED ME TO CONTROL MY POWERS AND KEEP OUR VILLAGE SAFE.

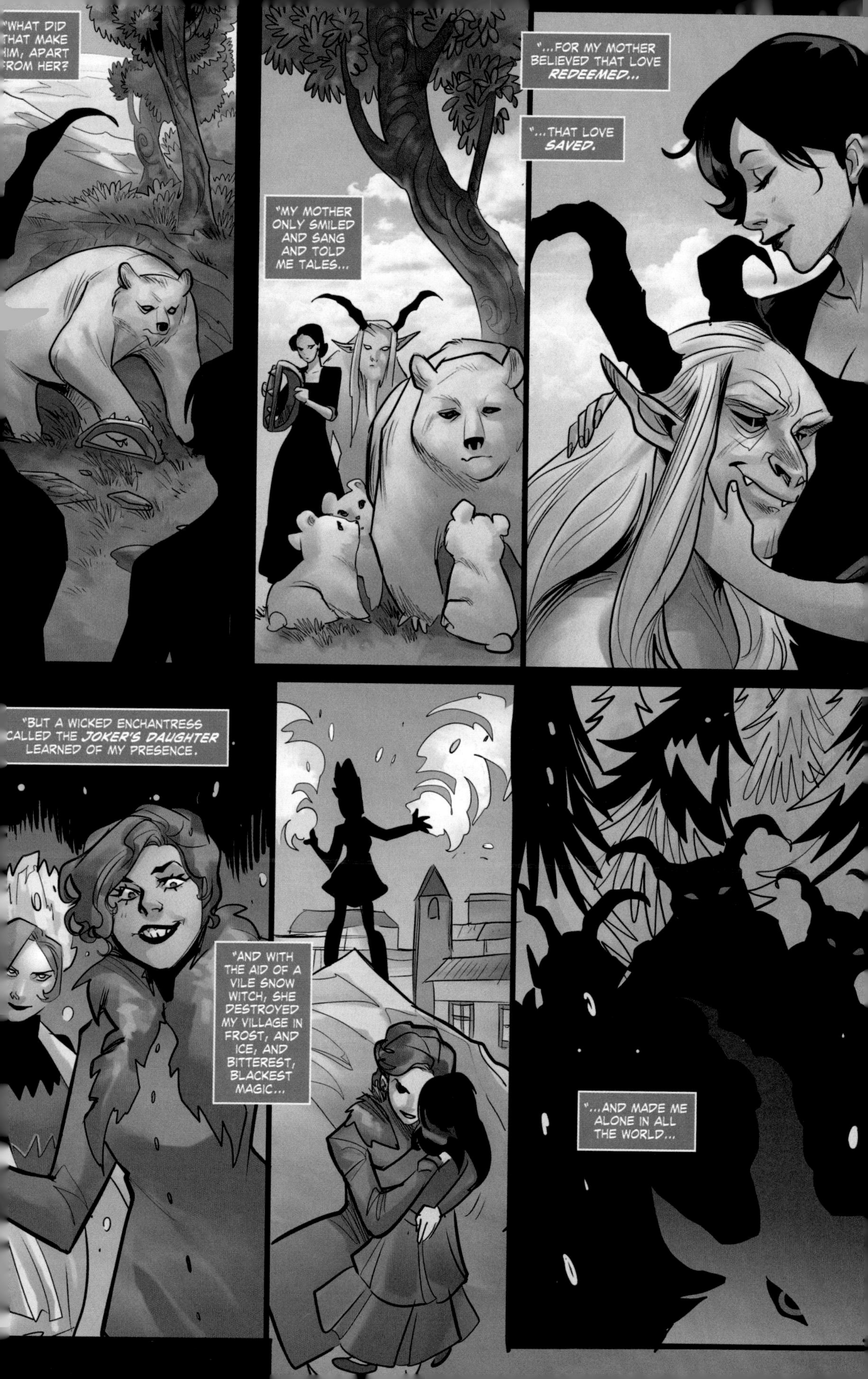
"WHAT DID THAT MAKE HIM, APART FROM HER?
"MY MOTHER ONLY SMILED AND SANG AND TOLD ME TALES...
"...FOR MY MOTHER BELIEVED THAT LOVE REDEEMED...
"...THAT LOVE SAVED.
"BUT A WICKED ENCHANTRESS CALLED THE JOKER'S DAUGHTER LEARNED OF MY PRESENCE.
"AND WITH THE AID OF A VILE SNOW WITCH, SHE DESTROYED MY VILLAGE IN FROST, AND ICE, AND BITTEREST, BLACKEST MAGIC...
"...AND MADE ME ALONE IN ALL THE WORLD...

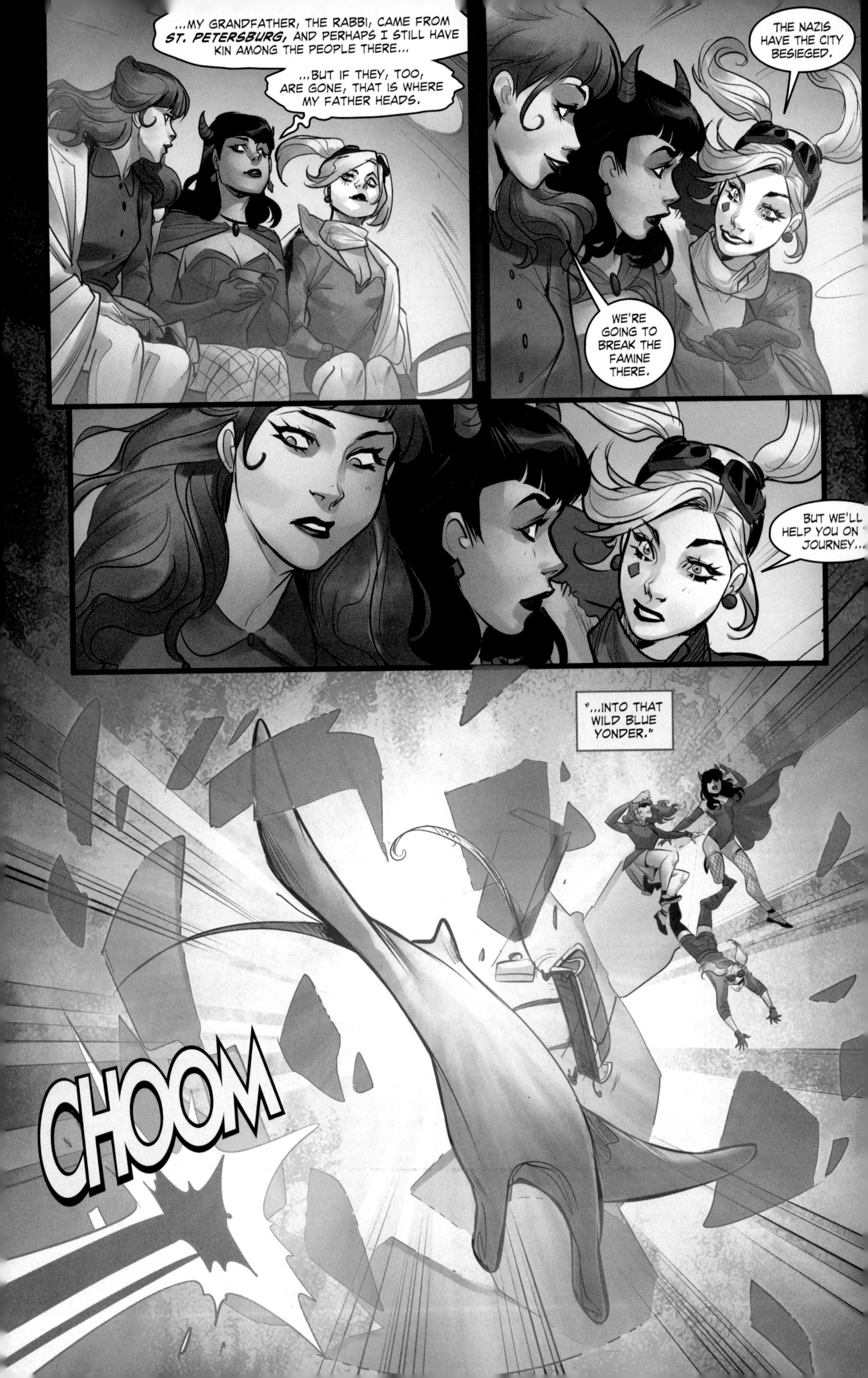

...MY GRANDFATHER, THE RABBI, CAME FROM ST. PETERSBURG, AND PERHAPS I STILL HAVE KIN AMONG THE PEOPLE THERE...
...BUT IF THEY, TOO, ARE GONE, THAT IS WHERE MY FATHER HEADS.
THE NAZIS HAVE THE CITY BESIEGED.
WE'RE GOING TO BREAK THE FAMINE THERE.
BUT WE'LL HELP YOU ON JOURNEY...
"...INTO THAT WILD BLUE YONDER."
CHOOM

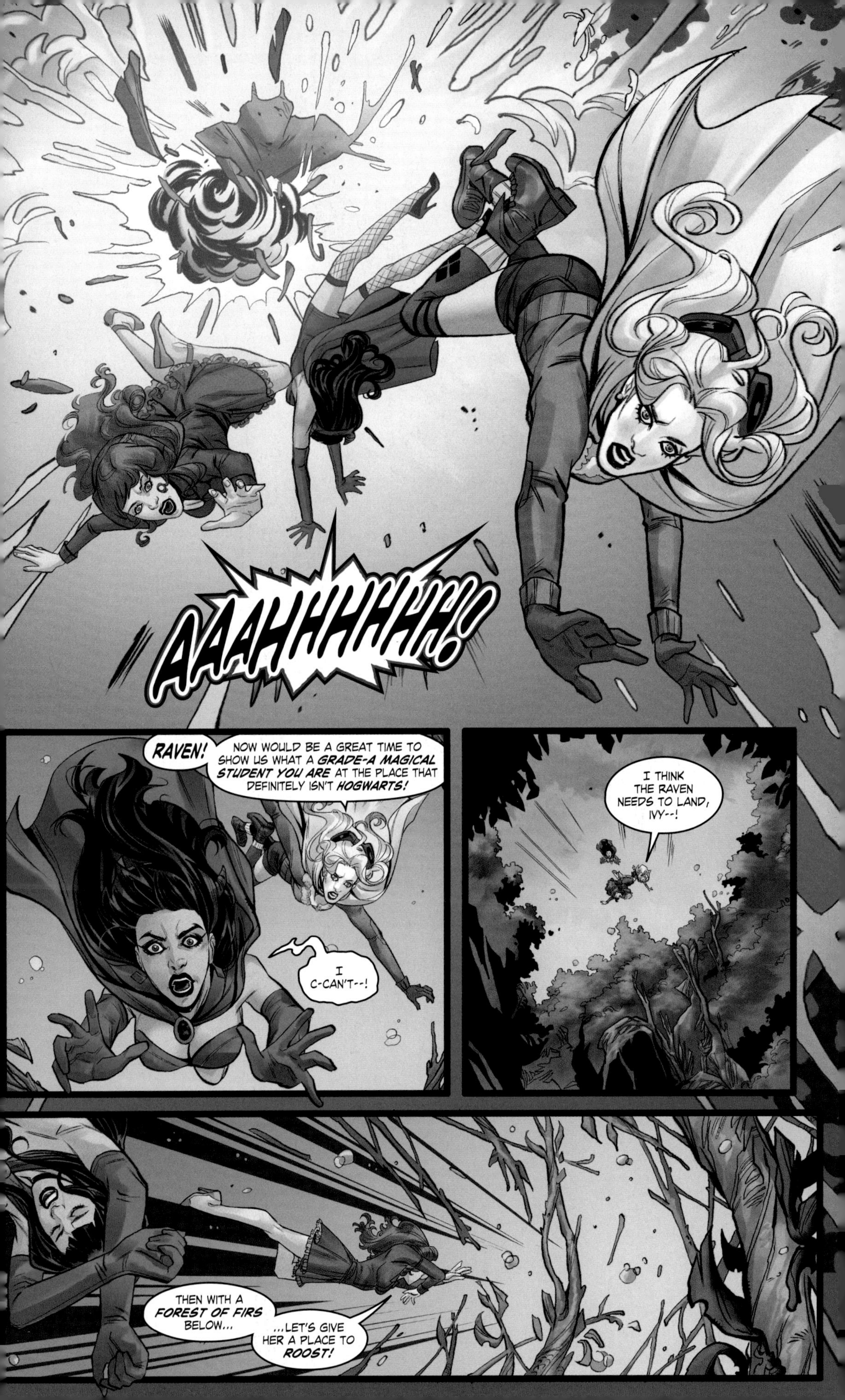
AAAHHHHHH!
RAVEN!
NOW WOULD BE A GREAT TIME TO SHOW US WHAT A GRADE-A MAGICAL STUDENT YOU ARE AT THE PLACE THAT DEFINITELY ISN'T HOGWARTS!
I C-CAN'T--!
I THINK THE RAVEN NEEDS TO LAND, IVY--!
THEN WITH A FOREST OF FIRS BELOW...
...LET'S GIVE HER A PLACE TO ROOST!

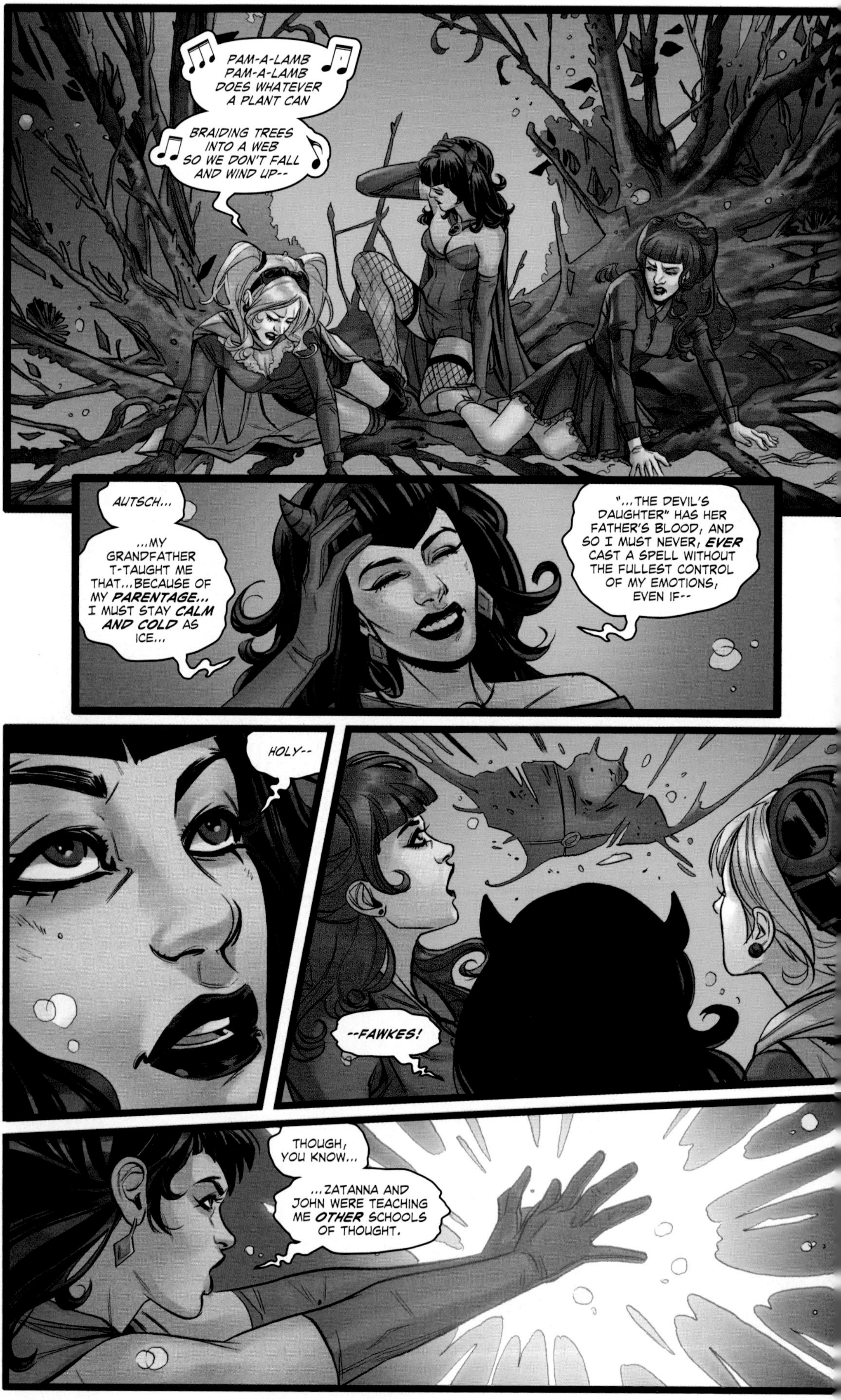
PAM-A-LAMB PAM-A-LAMB DOES WHATEVER A PLANT CAN
BRAIDING TREES INTO A WEB SO WE DON'T FALL AND WIND UP--
AUTSCH...
...MY GRANDFATHER T-TAUGHT ME THAT...BECAUSE OF MY PARENTAGE... I MUST STAY CALM AND COLD AS ICE...
"...THE DEVIL'S DAUGHTER" HAS HER FATHER'S BLOOD, AND SO I MUST NEVER, EVER CAST A SPELL WITHOUT THE FULLEST CONTROL OF MY EMOTIONS, EVEN IF--
HOLY--
--FAWKES!
THOUGH, YOU KNOW...
...ZATANNA AND JOHN WERE TEACHING ME OTHER SCHOOLS OF THOUGHT.

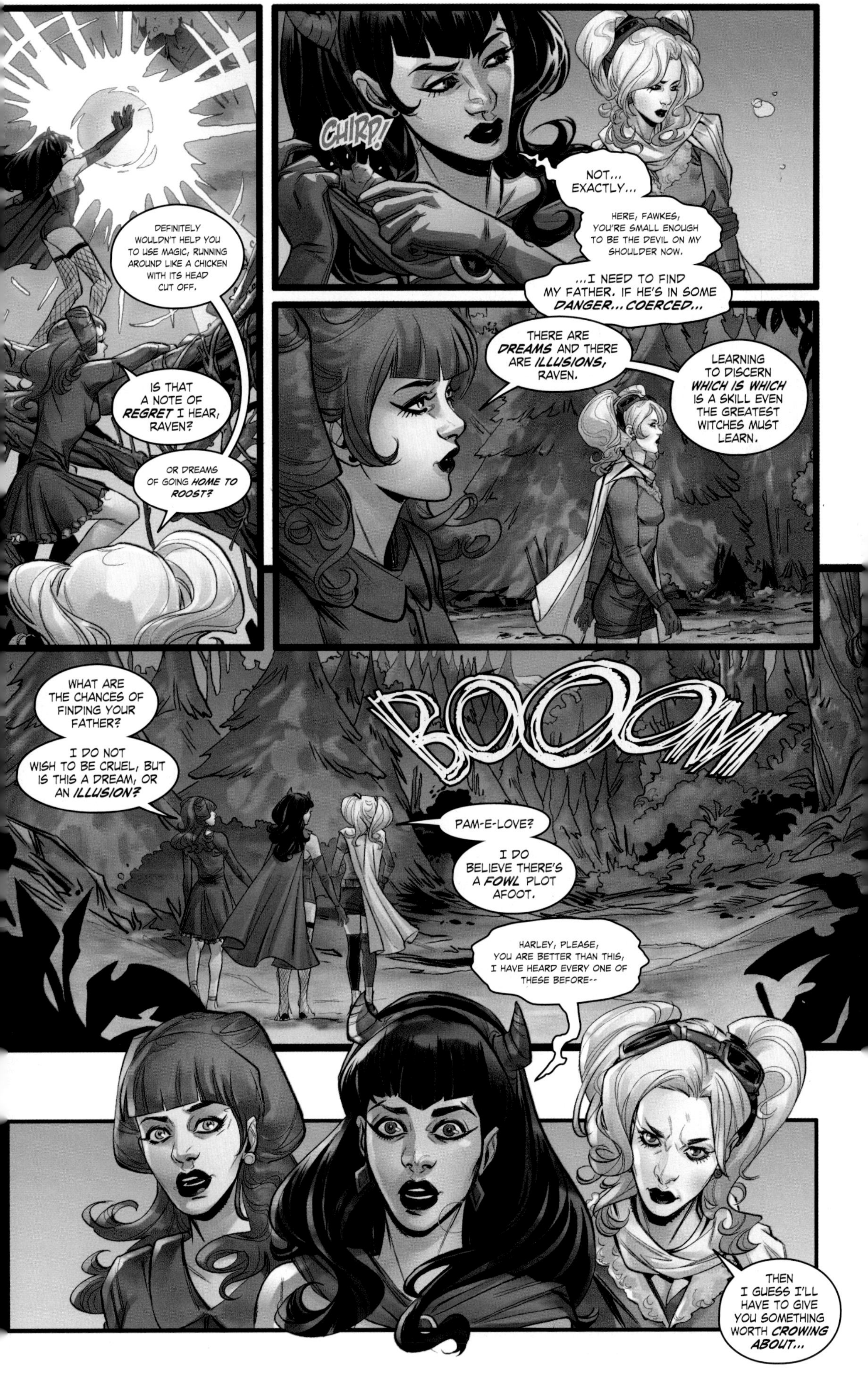
DEFINITELY WOULDN'T HELP YOU TO USE MAGIC, RUNNING AROUND LIKE A CHICKEN WITH ITS HEAD CUT OFF.
IS THAT A NOTE OF REGRET I HEAR, RAVEN?
OR DREAMS OF GOING HOME TO ROOST?
CHIRP!
NOT... EXACTLY...
HERE, FAWKES, YOU'RE SMALL ENOUGH TO BE THE DEVIL ON MY SHOULDER NOW.
...I NEED TO FIND MY FATHER. IF HE'S IN SOME DANGER...COERCED...
THERE ARE DREAMS AND THERE ARE ILLUSIONS, RAVEN.
LEARNING TO DISCERN WHICH IS WHICH IS A SKILL EVEN THE GREATEST WITCHES MUST LEARN.
WHAT ARE THE CHANCES OF FINDING YOUR FATHER?
I DO NOT WISH TO BE CRUEL, BUT IS THIS A DREAM, OR AN ILLUSION?
BOOOOM
PAM-E-LOVE?
I DO BELIEVE THERE'S A FOWL PLOT AFOOT.
HARLEY, PLEASE, YOU ARE BETTER THAN THIS, I HAVE HEARD EVERY ONE OF THESE BEFORE--
THEN I GUESS I'LL HAVE TO GIVE YOU SOMETHING WORTH CROWING ABOUT...

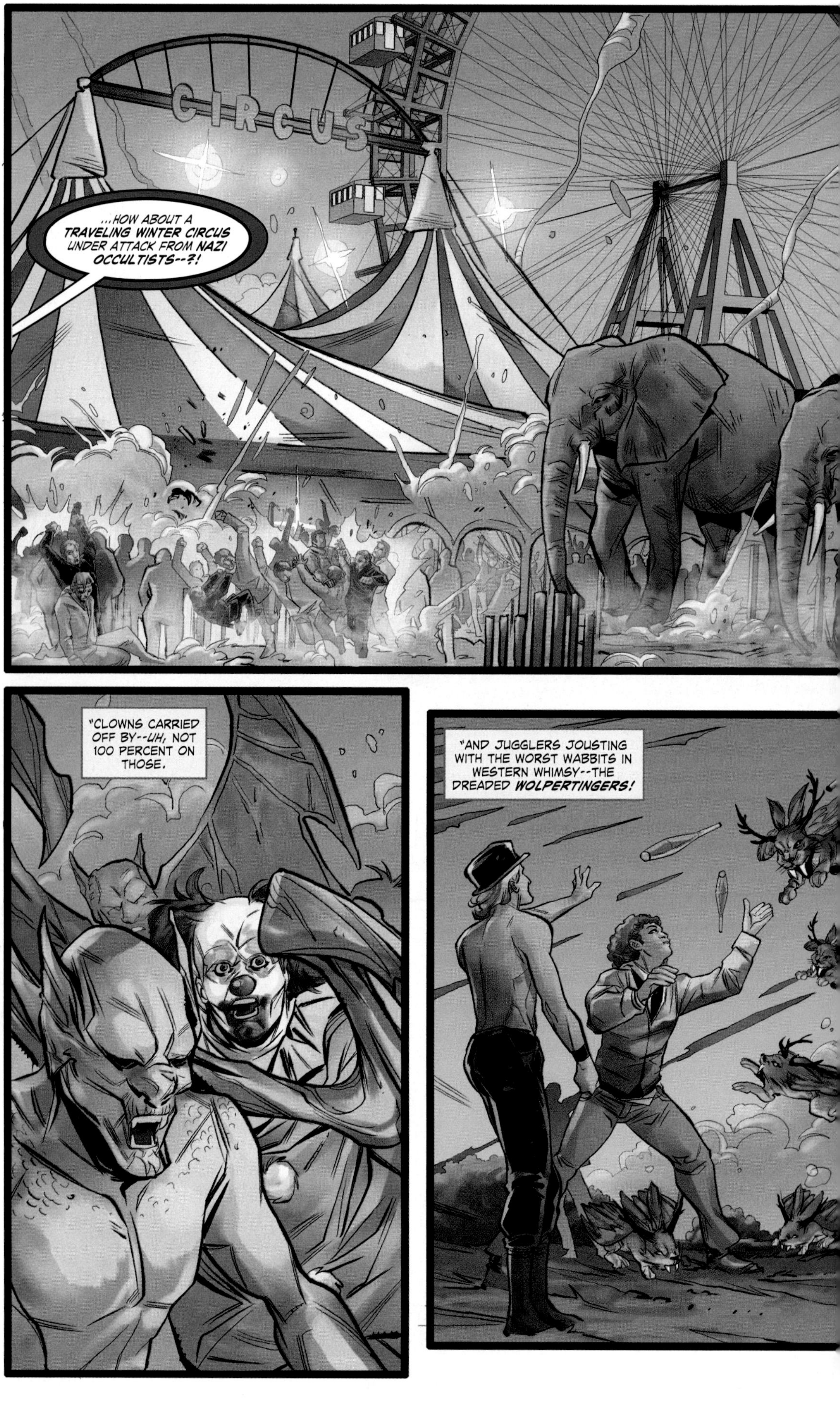
...HOW ABOUT A TRAVELING WINTER CIRCUS UNDER ATTACK FROM NAZI OCCULTISTS--?!
"CLOWNS CARRIED OFF BY--UH, NOT 100 PERCENT ON THOSE.
"AND JUGGLERS JOUSTING WITH THE WORST WABBITS IN WESTERN WHIMSY--THE DREADED WOLPERTINGERS!

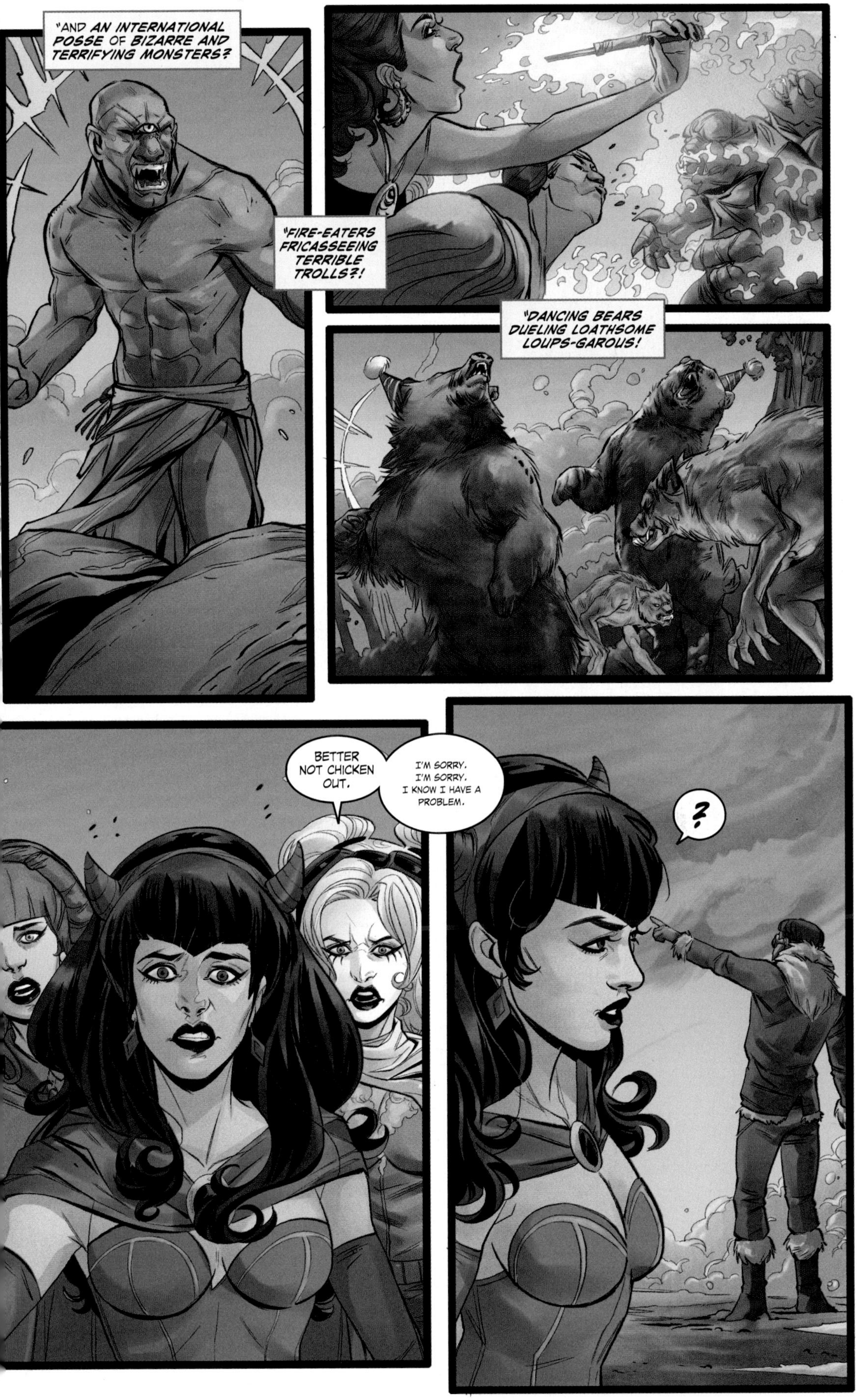
"AND AN INTERNATIONAL POSSE OF BIZARRE AND TERRIFYING MONSTERS?
"FIRE-EATERS FRICASSEEING TERRIBLE TROLLS?!
"DANCING BEARS DUELING LOATHSOME LOUPS-GAROUS!
BETTER NOT CHICKEN OUT.
I'M SORRY. I'M SORRY. I KNOW I HAVE A PROBLEM.
?

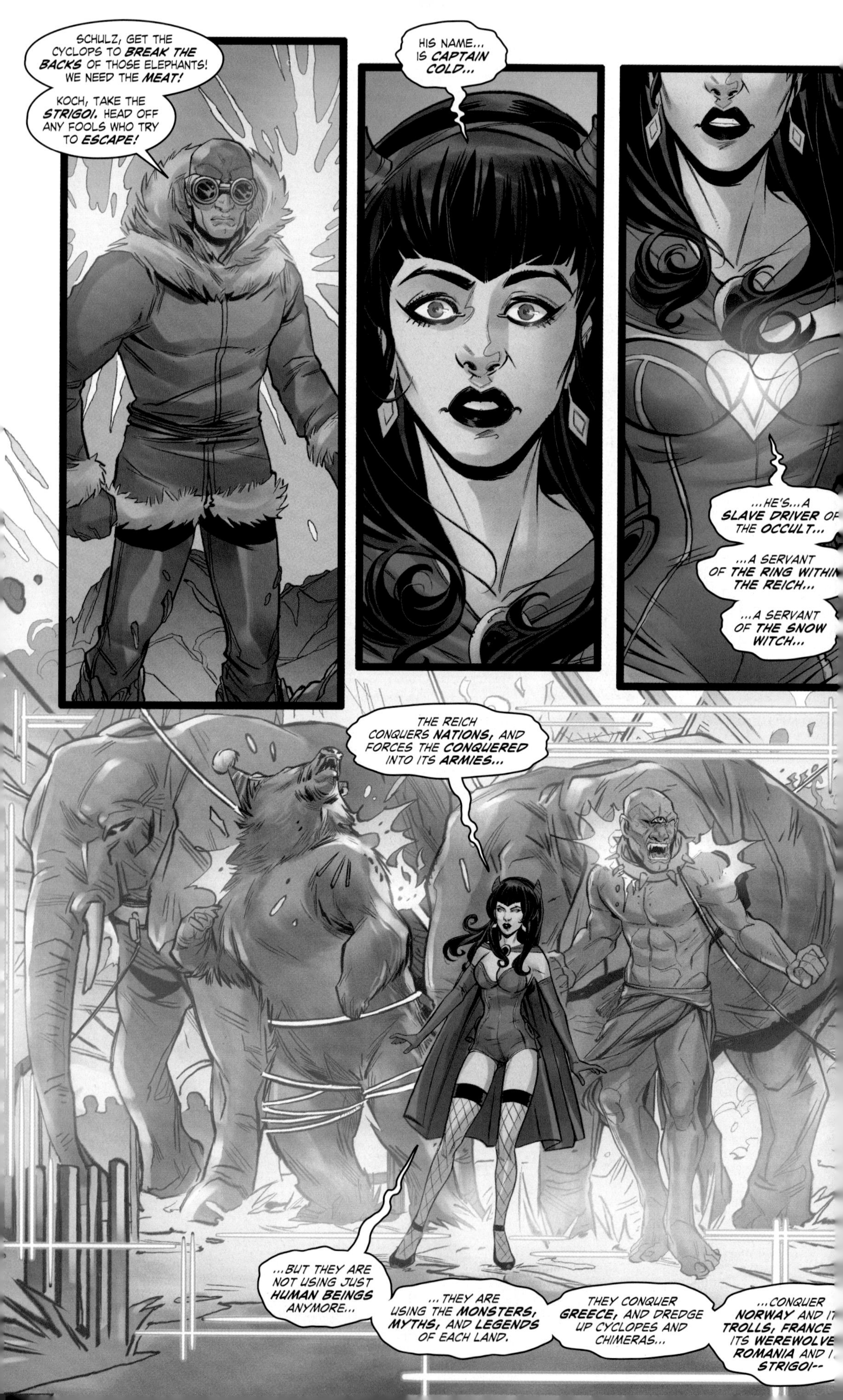
SCHULZ, GET THE CYCLOPS TO BREAK THE BACKS OF THOSE ELEPHANTS! WE NEED THE MEAT!
KOCH, TAKE THE STRIGOI. HEAD OFF ANY FOOLS WHO TRY TO ESCAPE!
HIS NAME... IS CAPTAIN COLD...
...HE'S...A SLAVE DRIVER OF THE OCCULT...
...A SERVANT OF THE RING WITHIN THE REICH...
...A SERVANT OF THE SNOW WITCH...
THE REICH CONQUERS NATIONS, AND FORCES THE CONQUERED INTO ITS ARMIES...
...BUT THEY ARE NOT USING JUST HUMAN BEINGS ANYMORE...
...THEY ARE USING THE MONSTERS, MYTHS, AND LEGENDS OF EACH LAND.
THEY CONQUER GREECE, AND DREDGE UP CYCLOPES AND CHIMERAS...
...CONQUER NORWAY AND IT TROLLS, FRANCE ITS WEREWOLVE ROMANIA AND I STRIGOI--

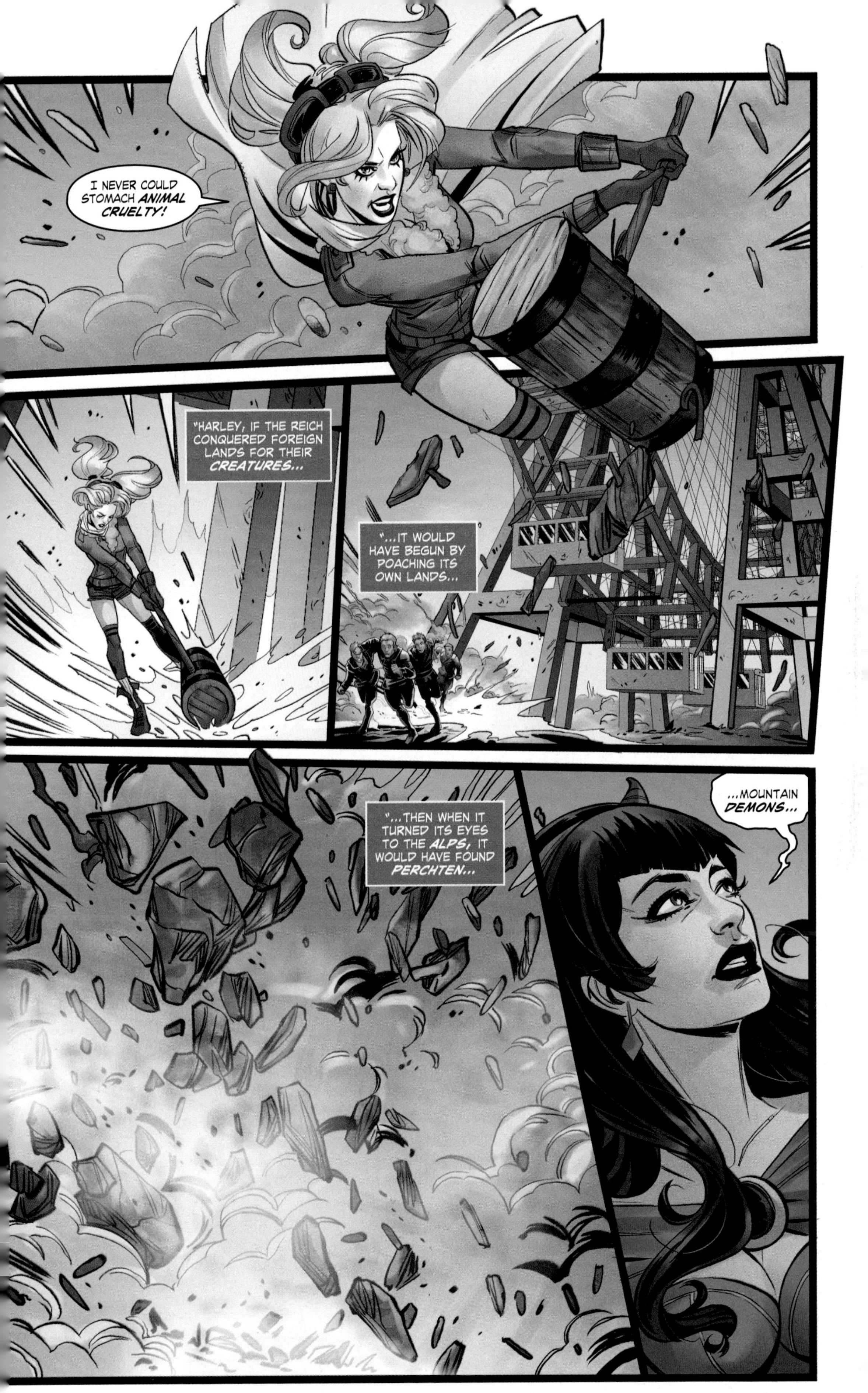
I NEVER COULD STOMACH ANIMAL CRUELTY!
"HARLEY, IF THE REICH CONQUERED FOREIGN LANDS FOR THEIR CREATURES...
"...IT WOULD HAVE BEGUN BY POACHING ITS OWN LANDS...
"...THEN WHEN IT TURNED ITS EYES TO THE ALPS, IT WOULD HAVE FOUND PERCHTEN...
...MOUNTAIN DEMONS...

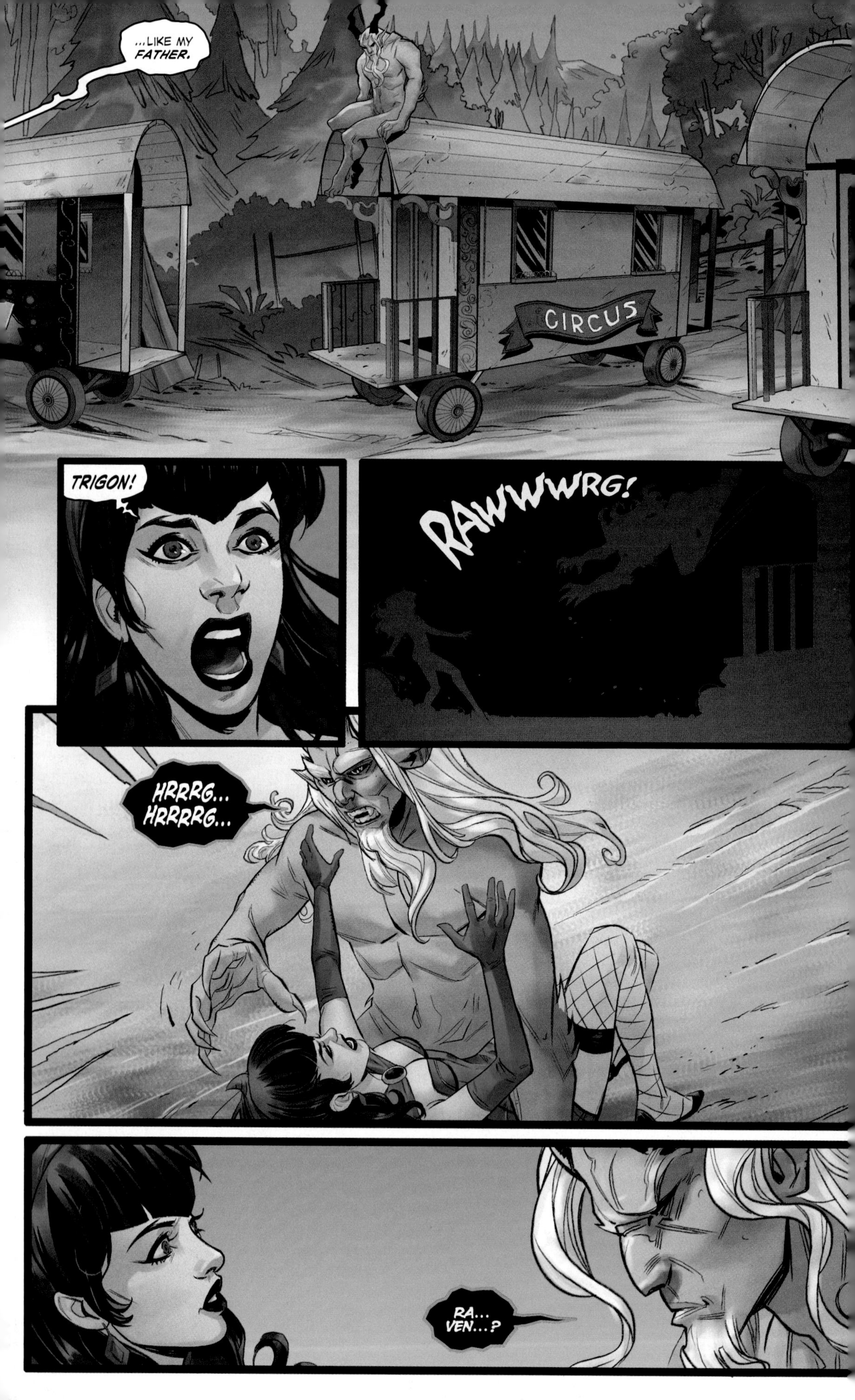
...LIKE MY FATHER.
TRIGON!
RAWWWRG!
HRRRG... HRRRRG...
RA... VEN...?

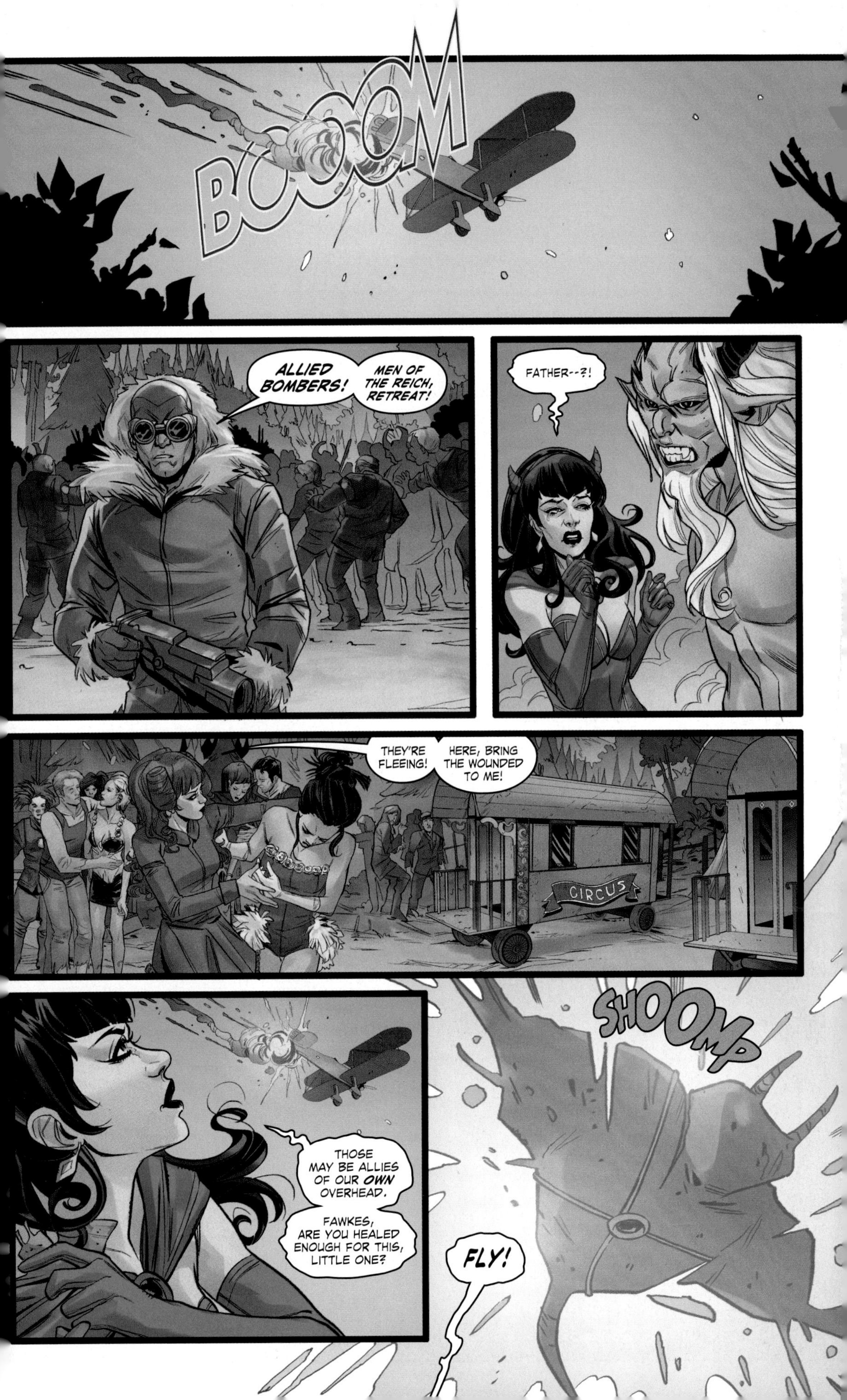
BOOOOM
ALLIED BOMBERS!
MEN OF THE REICH, RETREAT!
FATHER--?!
THEY'RE FLEEING!
HERE, BRING THE WOUNDED TO ME!
SHOOMP
THOSE MAY BE ALLIES OF OUR OWN OVERHEAD.
FAWKES, ARE YOU HEALED ENOUGH FOR THIS, LITTLE ONE?
FLY!

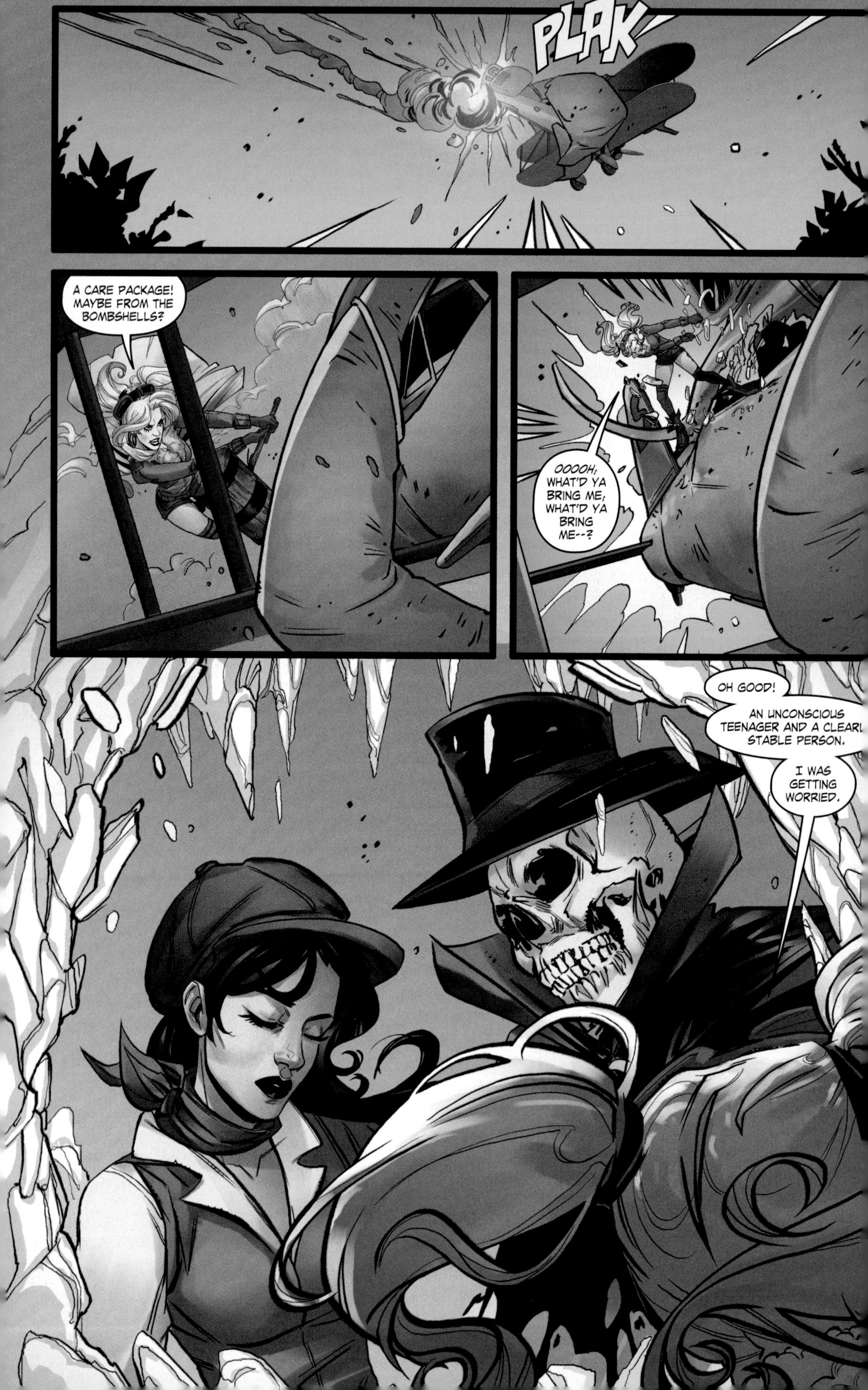
PLAK
A CARE PACKAGE! MAYBE FROM THE BOMBSHELLS?
OOOOH; WHAT'D YA BRING ME, WHAT'D YA BRING ME--?
OH GOOD!
AN UNCONSCIOUS TEENAGER AND A CLEARL STABLE PERSON.
I WAS GETTING WORRIED.

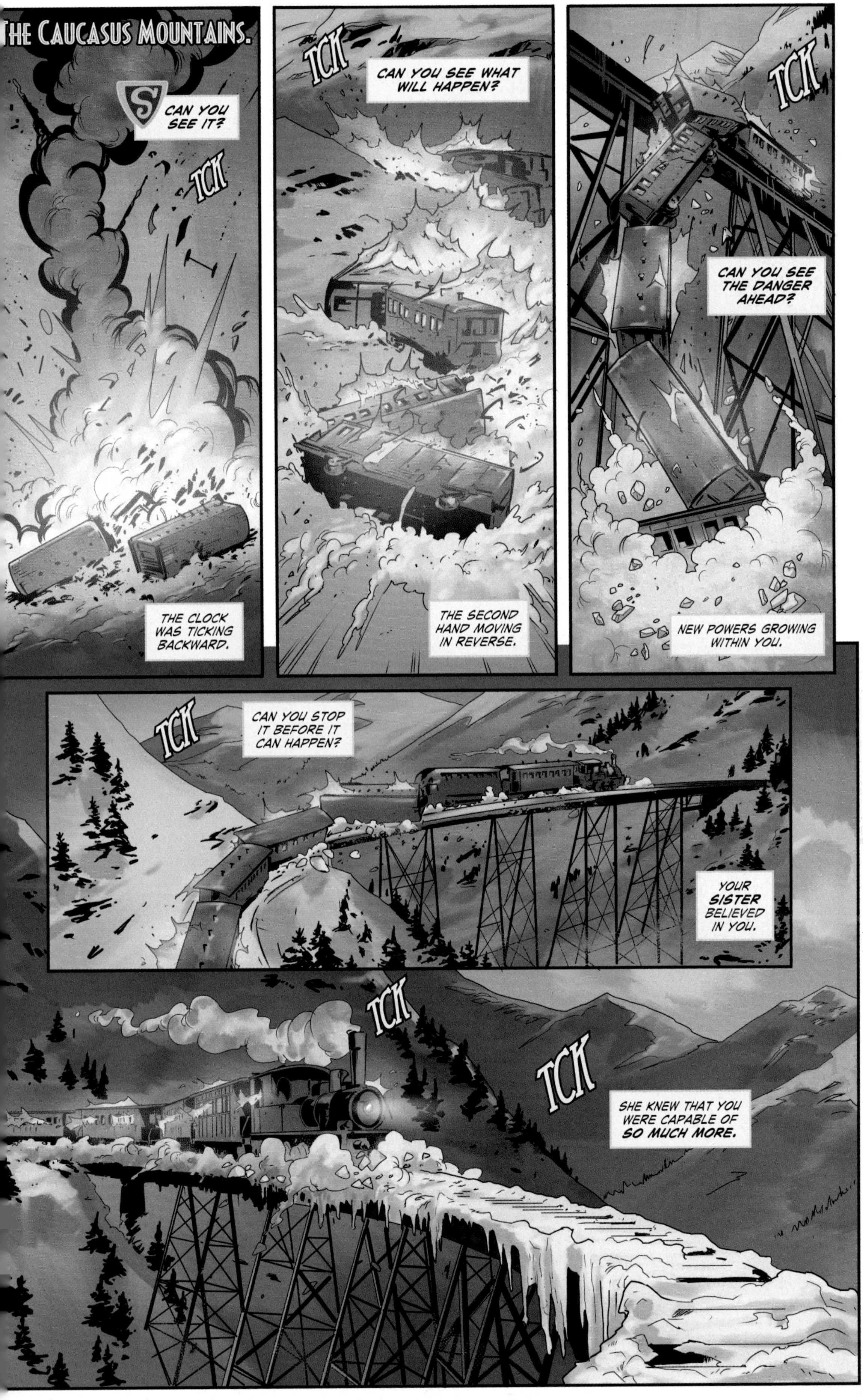
THE CAUCASUS MOUNTAINS.
CAN YOU SEE IT?
TCK
THE CLOCK WAS TICKING BACKWARD.
TCK
CAN YOU SEE WHAT WILL HAPPEN?
THE SECOND HAND MOVING IN REVERSE.
TCK
CAN YOU SEE THE DANGER AHEAD?
NEW POWERS GROWING WITHIN YOU.
TCK
CAN YOU STOP IT BEFORE IT CAN HAPPEN?
YOUR SISTER BELIEVED IN YOU.
TCK
TCK
SHE KNEW THAT YOU WERE CAPABLE OF SO MUCH MORE.

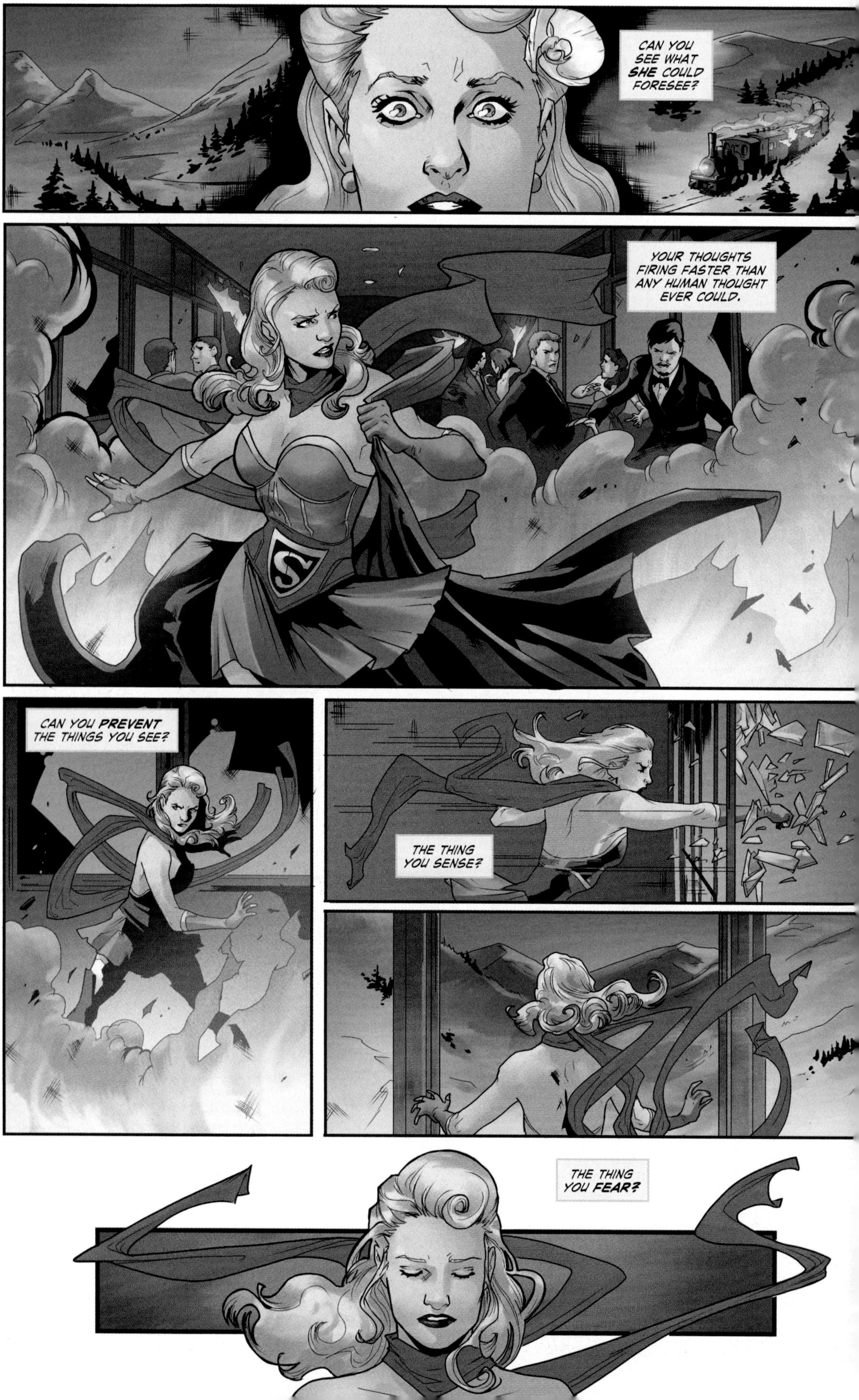
CAN YOU SEE WHAT SHE COULD FORESEE?
YOUR THOUGHTS FIRING FASTER THAN ANY HUMAN THOUGHT EVER COULD.
CAN YOU PREVENT THE THINGS YOU SEE?
THE THING YOU SENSE?
THE THING YOU FEAR?

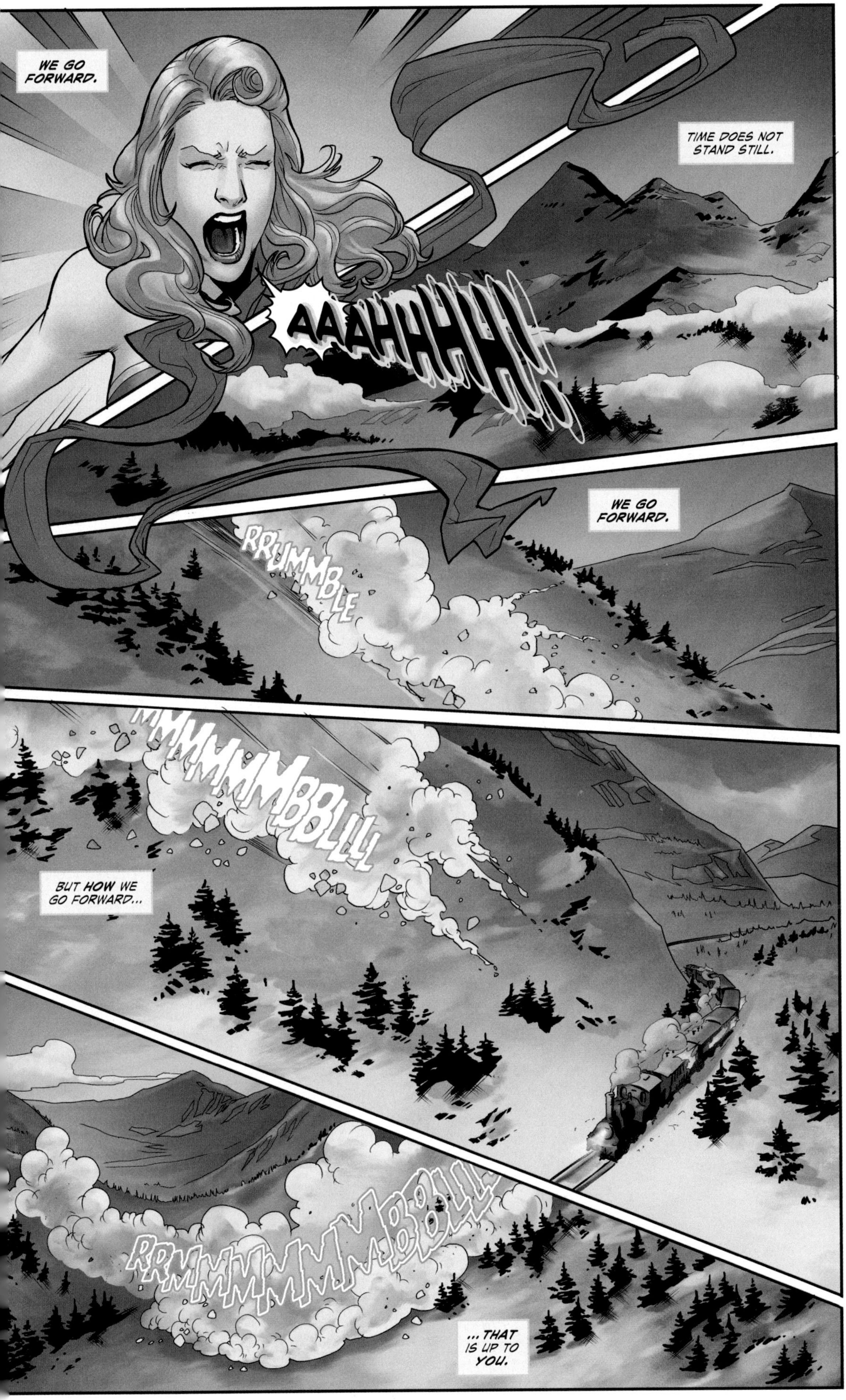
WE GO FORWARD.
TIME DOES NOT STAND STILL.
AAAHHHHH!!
WE GO FORWARD.
RRUMMBLE
MMMMMBBLLL
BUT HOW WE GO FORWARD...
RRMMMMMMMBBLLL
...THAT IS UP TO YOU.

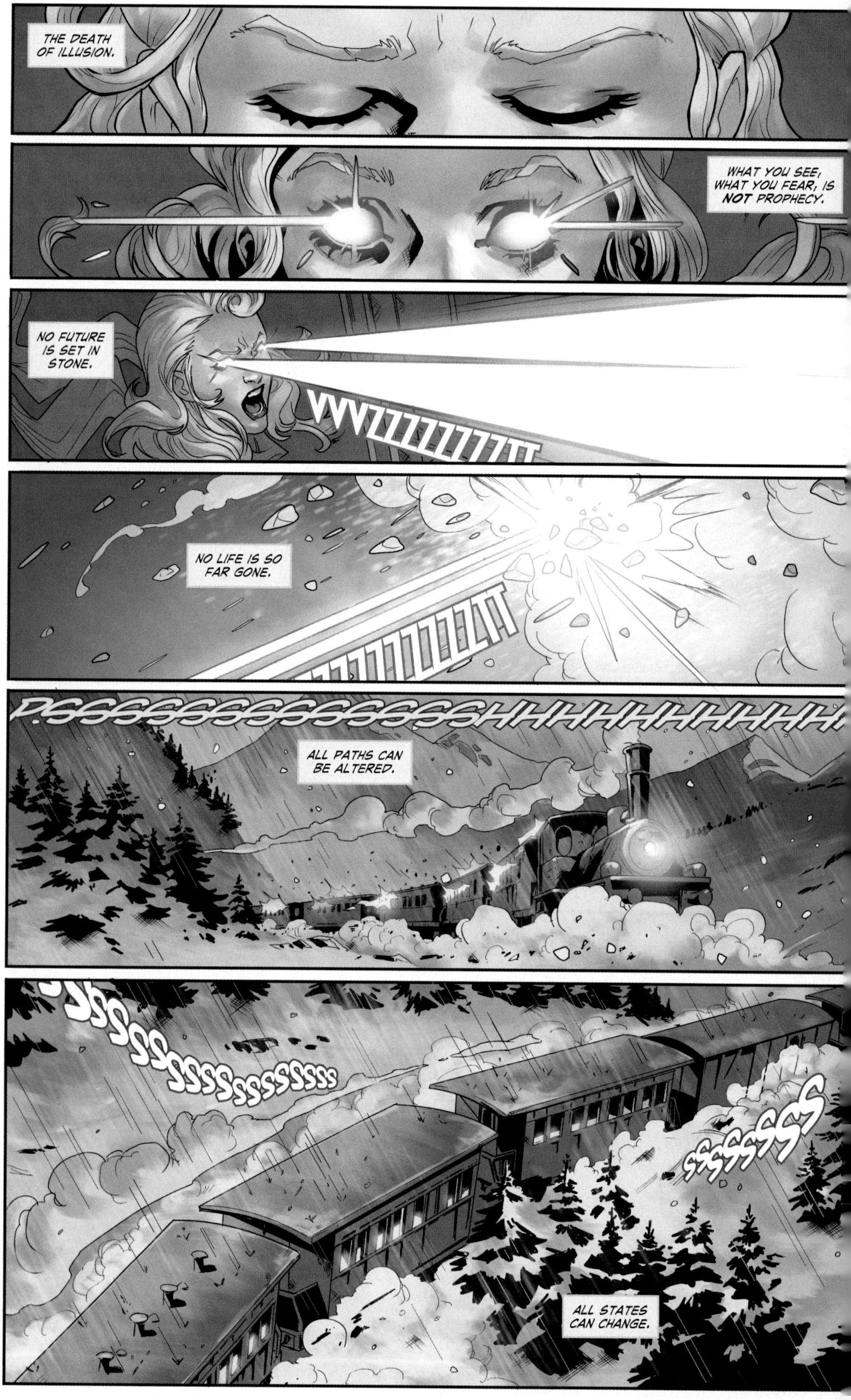
THE DEATH OF ILLUSION.
WHAT YOU SEE, WHAT YOU FEAR, IS NOT PROPHECY.
NO FUTURE IS SET IN STONE.
VVVZZZZZZZZZTT
NO LIFE IS SO FAR GONE.
ZZZZZZZZZZZTT
PSSSSSSSSSSSSSSSSSHHHHHHHHHHH
ALL PATHS CAN BE ALTERED.
SSSSSSSSSSSSSSSSSS
SSSSSSSSS
ALL STATES CAN CHANGE.

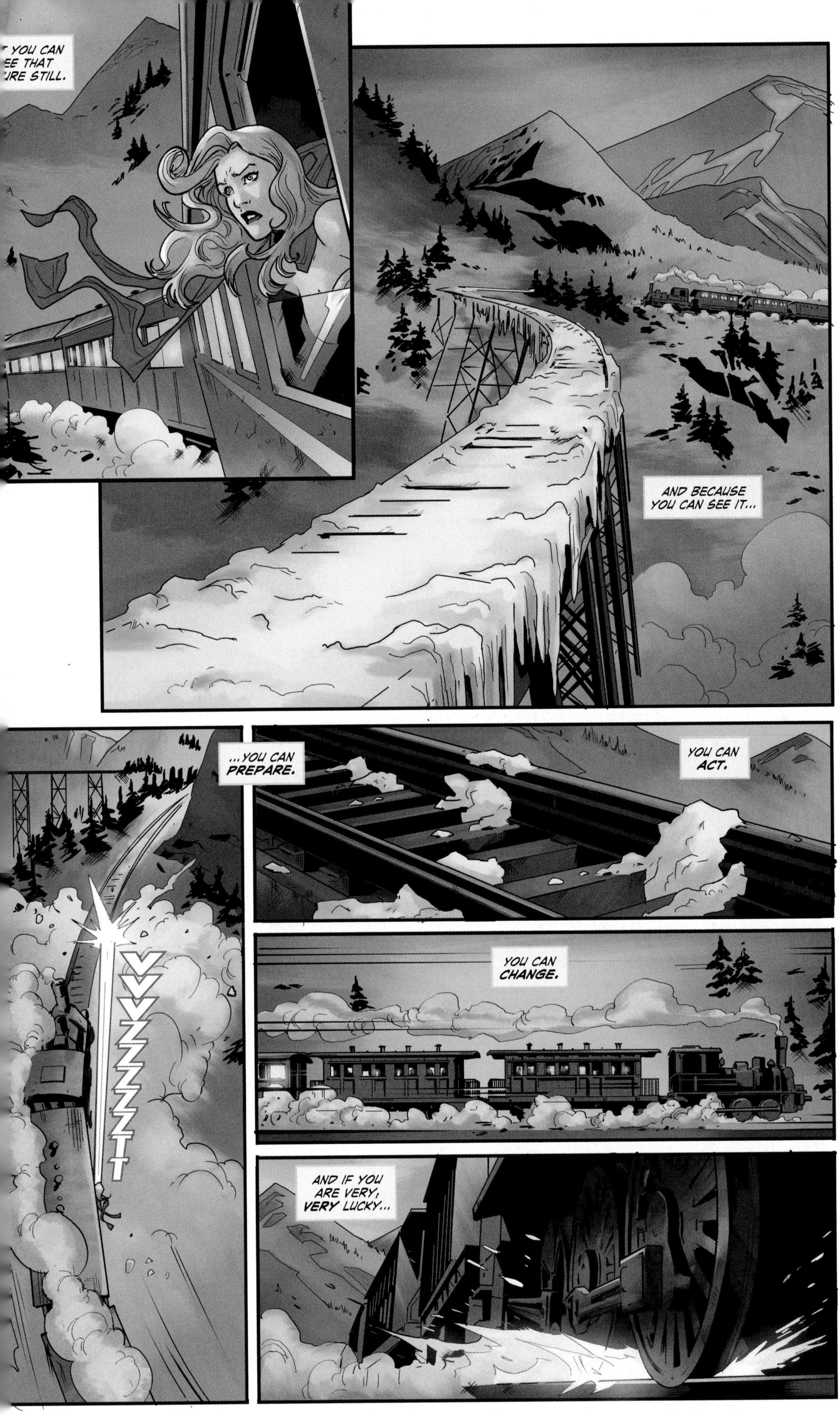
T YOU CAN
EE THAT
URE STILL.
AND BECAUSE YOU CAN SEE IT...
...YOU CAN PREPARE.
YOU CAN ACT.
VVVZZZZZTT
YOU CAN CHANGE.
AND IF YOU ARE VERY, VERY LUCKY...

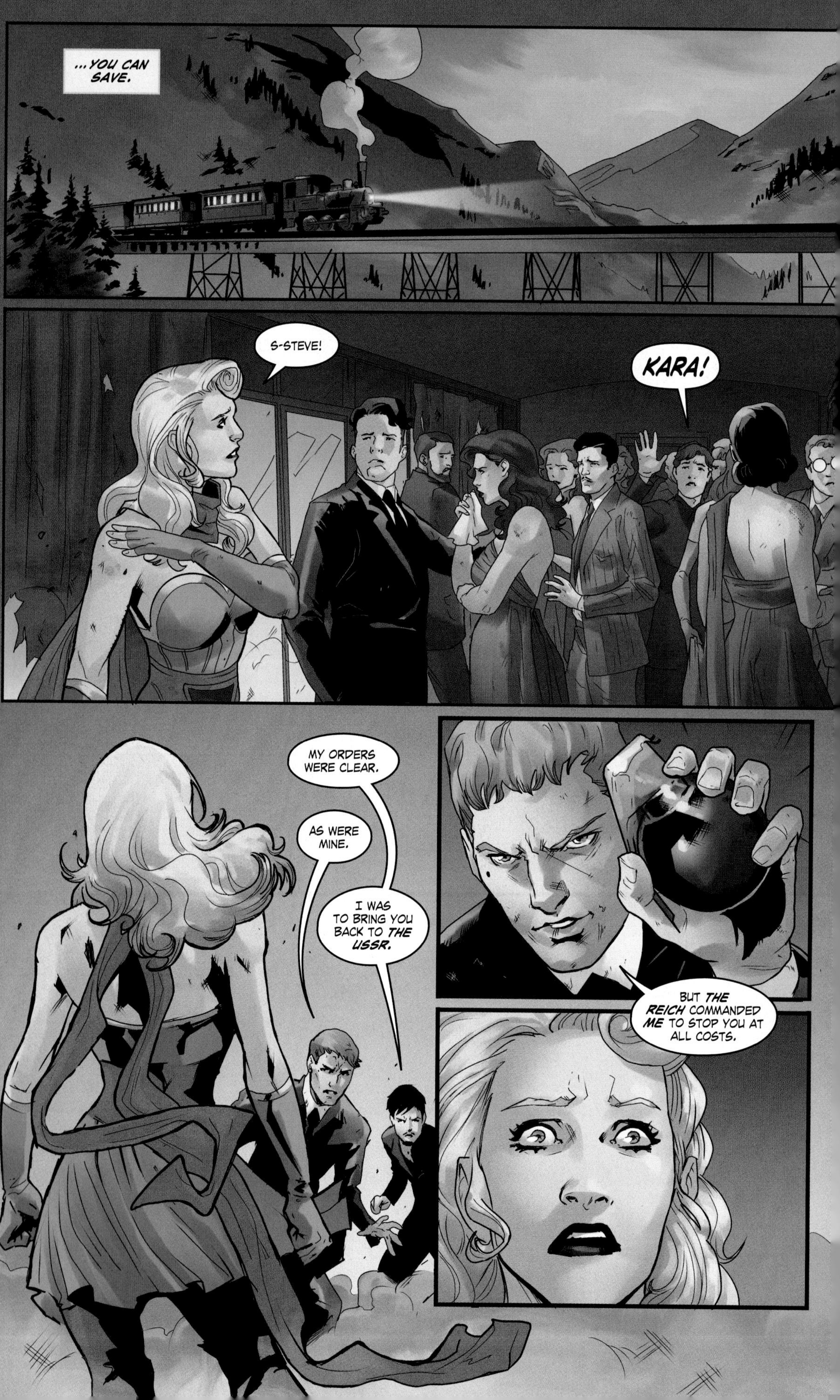
...YOU CAN SAVE.
S-STEVE!
KARA!
MY ORDERS WERE CLEAR.
AS WERE MINE.
I WAS TO BRING YOU BACK TO THE USSR.
BUT THE REICH COMMANDED ME TO STOP YOU AT ALL COSTS.

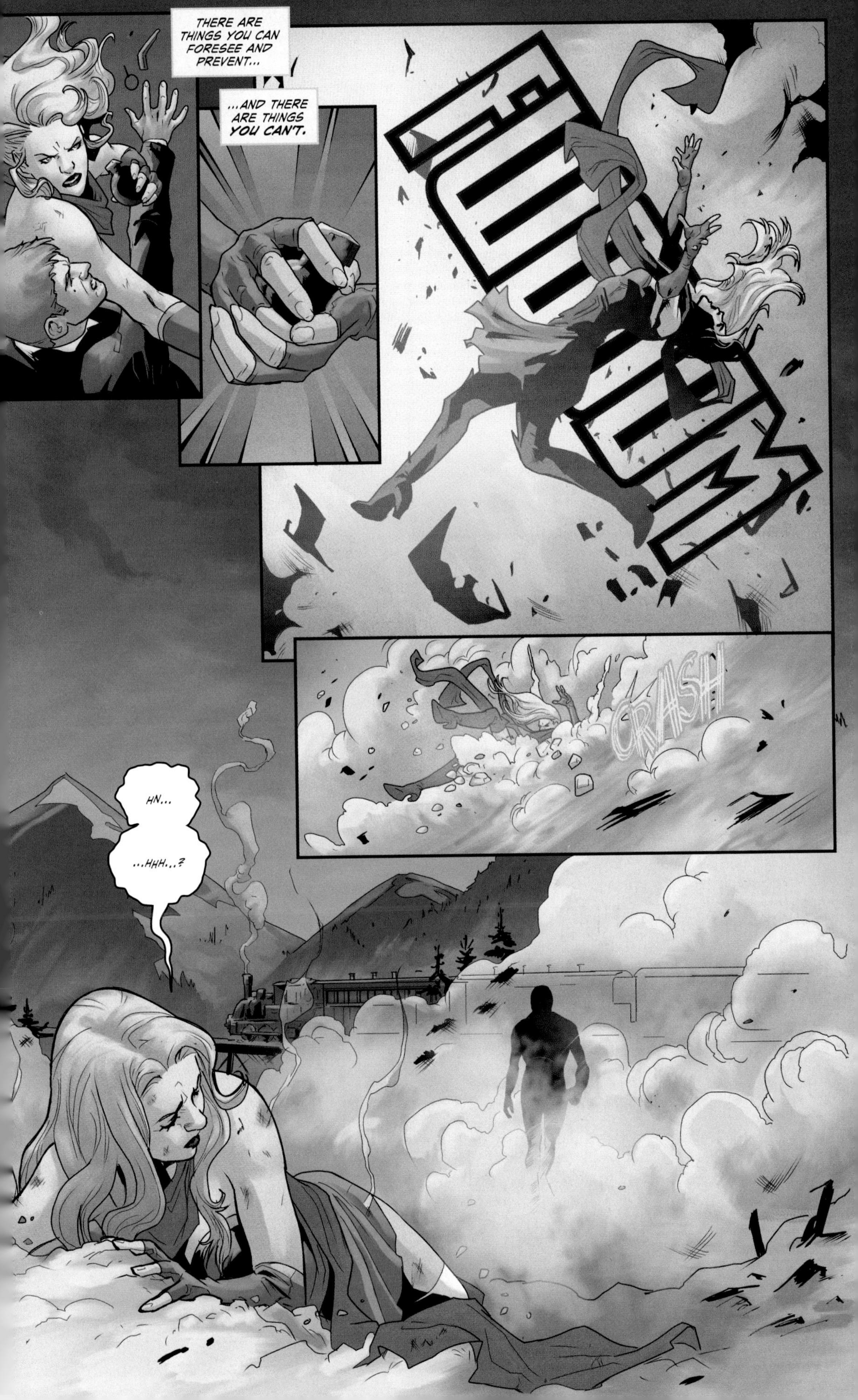
THERE ARE THINGS YOU CAN FORESEE AND PREVENT...
...AND THERE ARE THINGS YOU CAN'T.
BOOM!
CRASH
HN...
...HHH...?

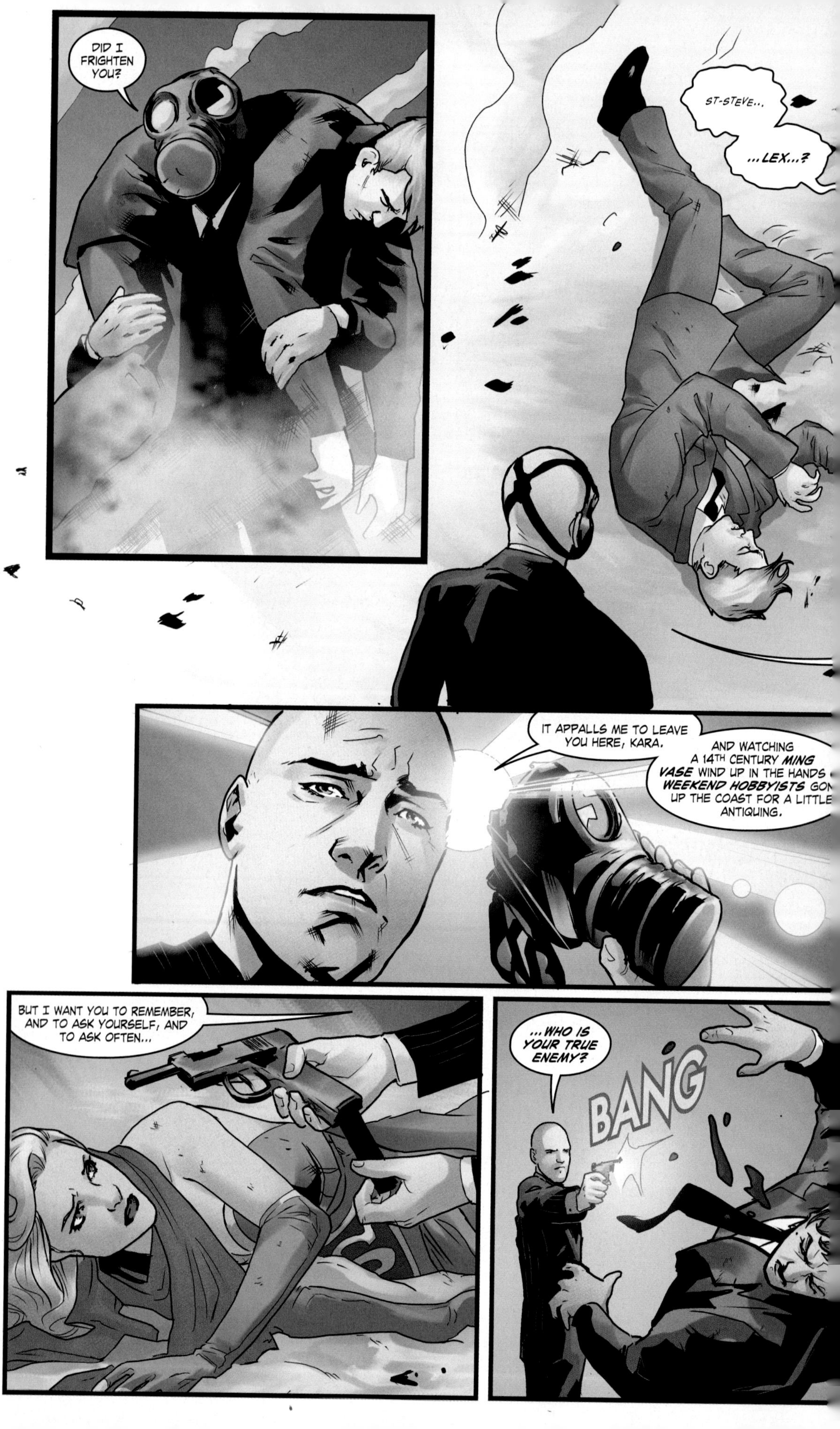
DID I FRIGHTEN YOU?
ST-STEVE...
...LEX...?
IT APPALLS ME TO LEAVE YOU HERE, KARA.
AND WATCHING A 14TH CENTURY MING VASE WIND UP IN THE HANDS
WEEKEND HOBBYISTS GON
UP THE COAST FOR A LITTLE ANTIQUING.
BUT I WANT YOU TO REMEMBER, AND TO ASK YOURSELF, AND TO ASK OFTEN...
...WHO IS YOUR TRUE ENEMY?
BANG

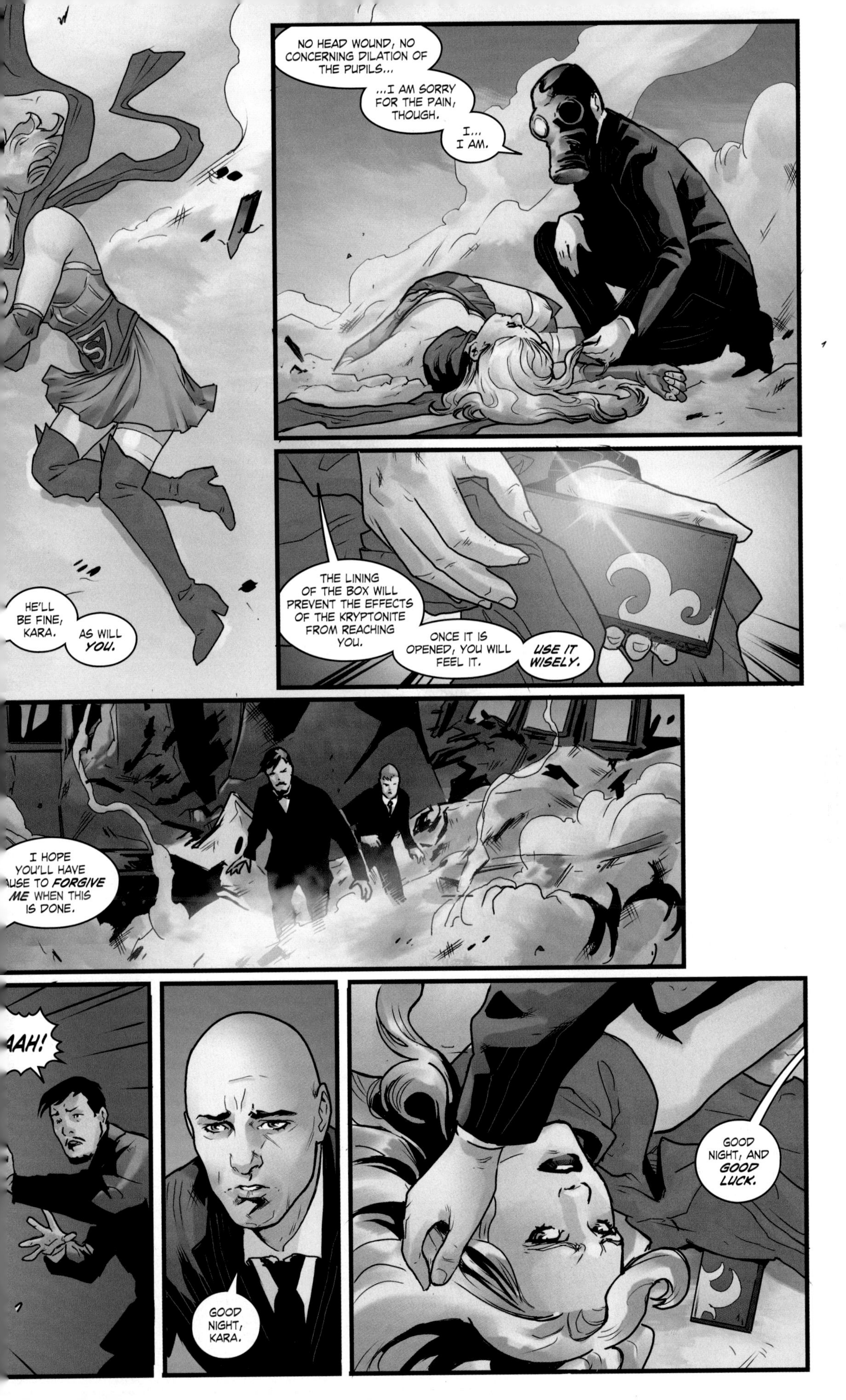
NO HEAD WOUND, NO CONCERNING DILATION OF THE PUPILS...
...I AM SORRY FOR THE PAIN, THOUGH.
I... I AM.
THE LINING OF THE BOX WILL PREVENT THE EFFECTS OF THE KRYPTONITE FROM REACHING YOU.
ONCE IT IS OPENED, YOU WILL FEEL IT.
USE IT WISELY.
HE'LL BE FINE, KARA.
AS WILL *YOU.*
I HOPE YOU'LL HAVE AUSE TO *FORGIVE ME* WHEN THIS IS DONE.
AAH!
GOOD NIGHT, KARA.
GOOD NIGHT, AND *GOOD LUCK.*

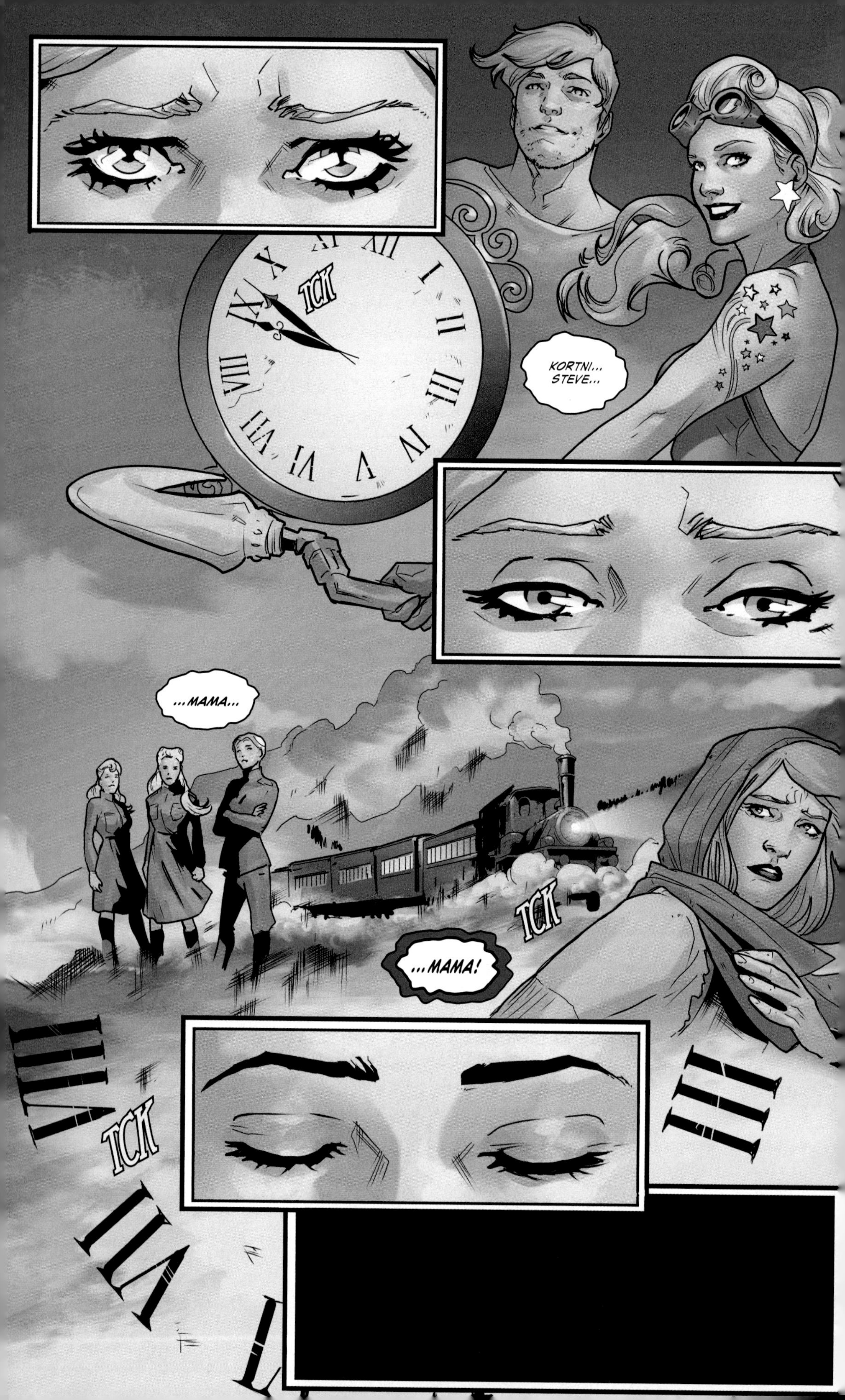
TCK
KORTNI... STEVE...
...MAMA...
TCK
...MAMA!
TCK

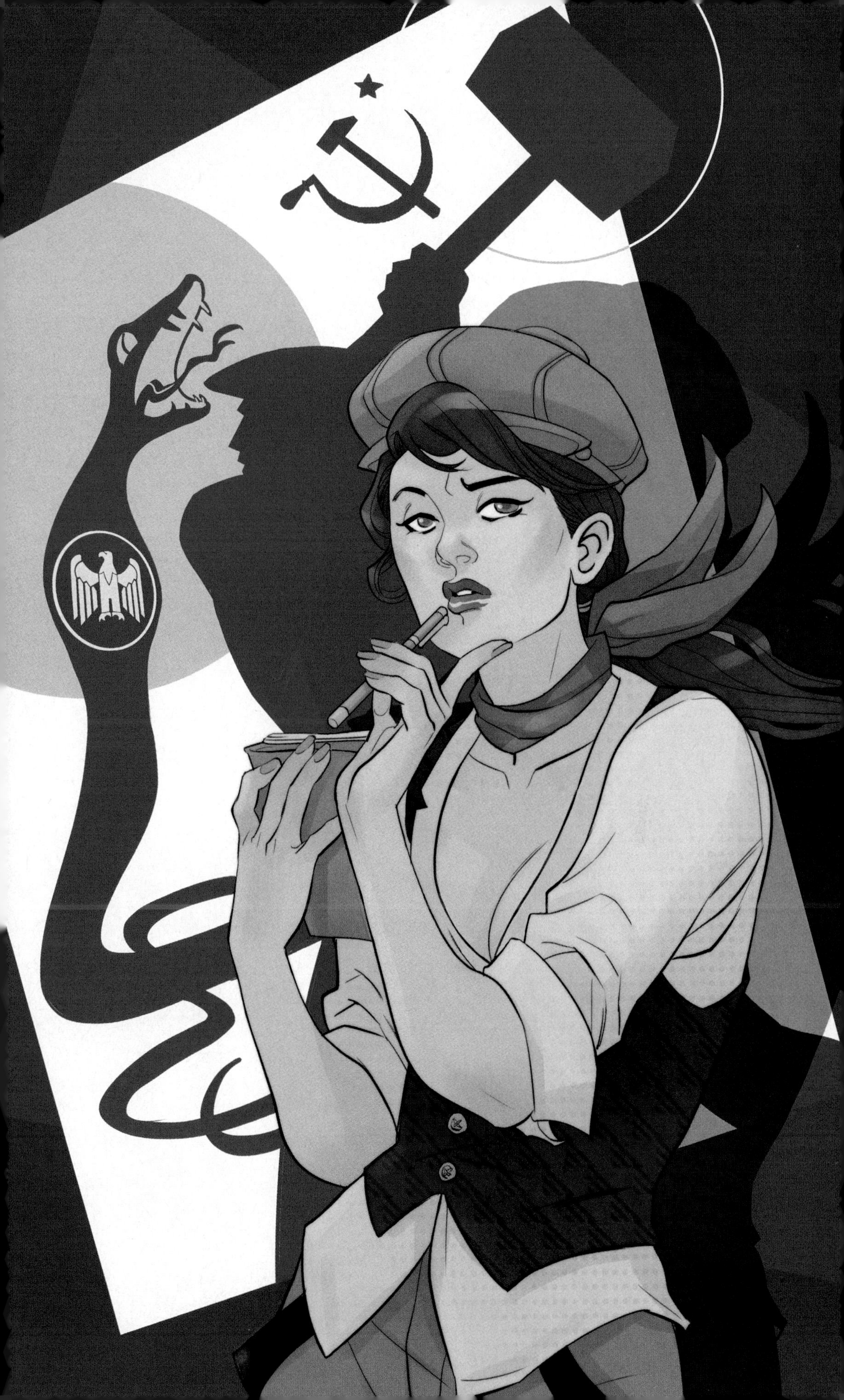

LENINGRAD

MARGUERITE BENNETT
Writer

MIRKA ANDOLFO
RICHARD ORTIZ
CARMEN CARNERO
Artists

WENDY BROOME
J. NANJAN
SANDRA MOLINA
Colorists

Cover by
MARGUERITE SAUVAGE

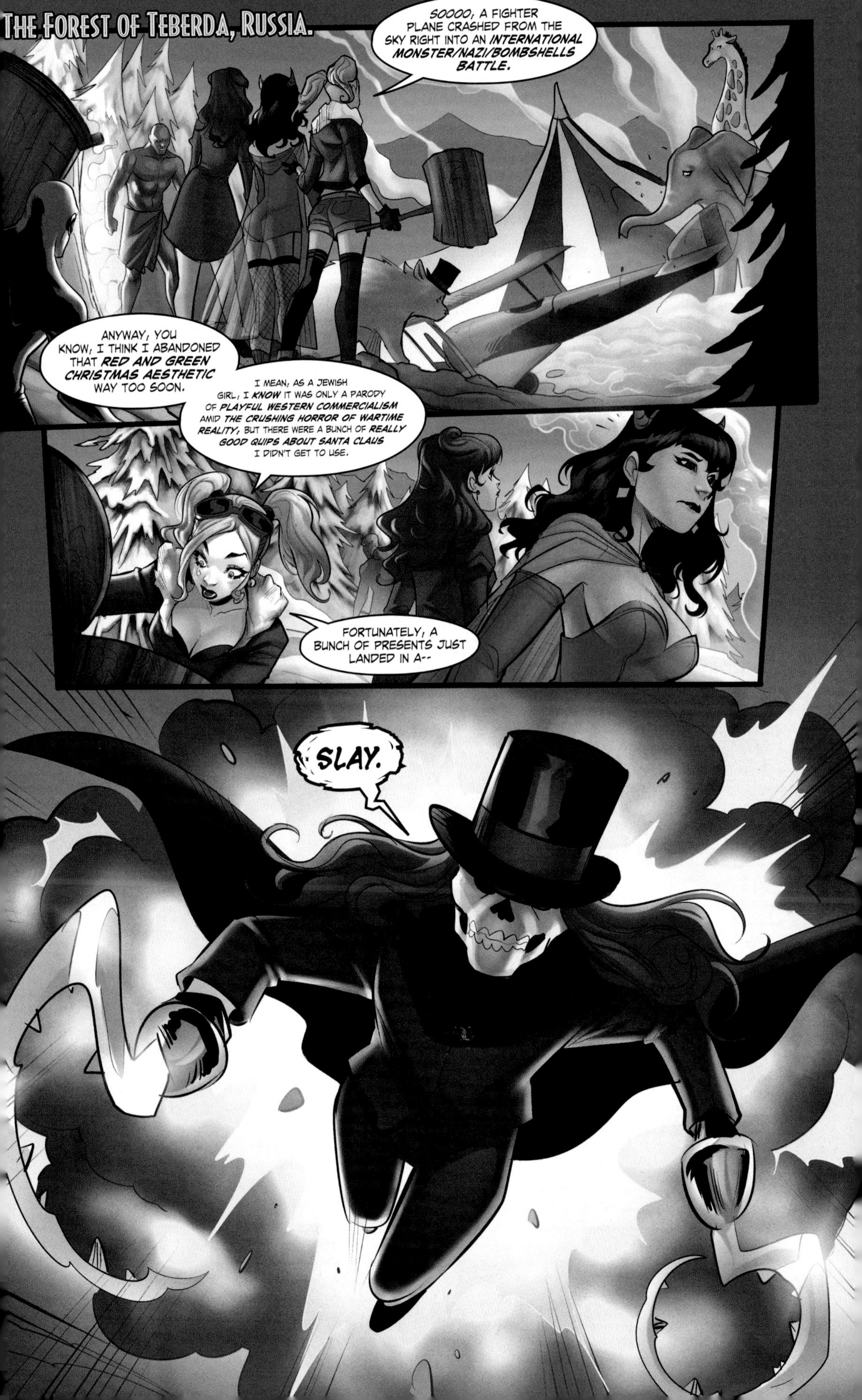
THE FOREST OF TEBERDA, RUSSIA.
SOOOO, A FIGHTER PLANE CRASHED FROM THE SKY RIGHT INTO AN INTERNATIONAL MONSTER/NAZI/BOMBSHELLS BATTLE.
ANYWAY, YOU KNOW, I THINK I ABANDONED THAT RED AND GREEN CHRISTMAS AESTHETIC WAY TOO SOON.
I MEAN, AS A JEWISH GIRL, I KNOW IT WAS ONLY A PARODY OF PLAYFUL WESTERN COMMERCIALISM AMID THE CRUSHING HORROR OF WARTIME REALITY, BUT THERE WERE A BUNCH OF REALLY GOOD QUIPS ABOUT SANTA CLAUS I DIDN'T GET TO USE.
FORTUNATELY, A BUNCH OF PRESENTS JUST LANDED IN A--
SLAY.

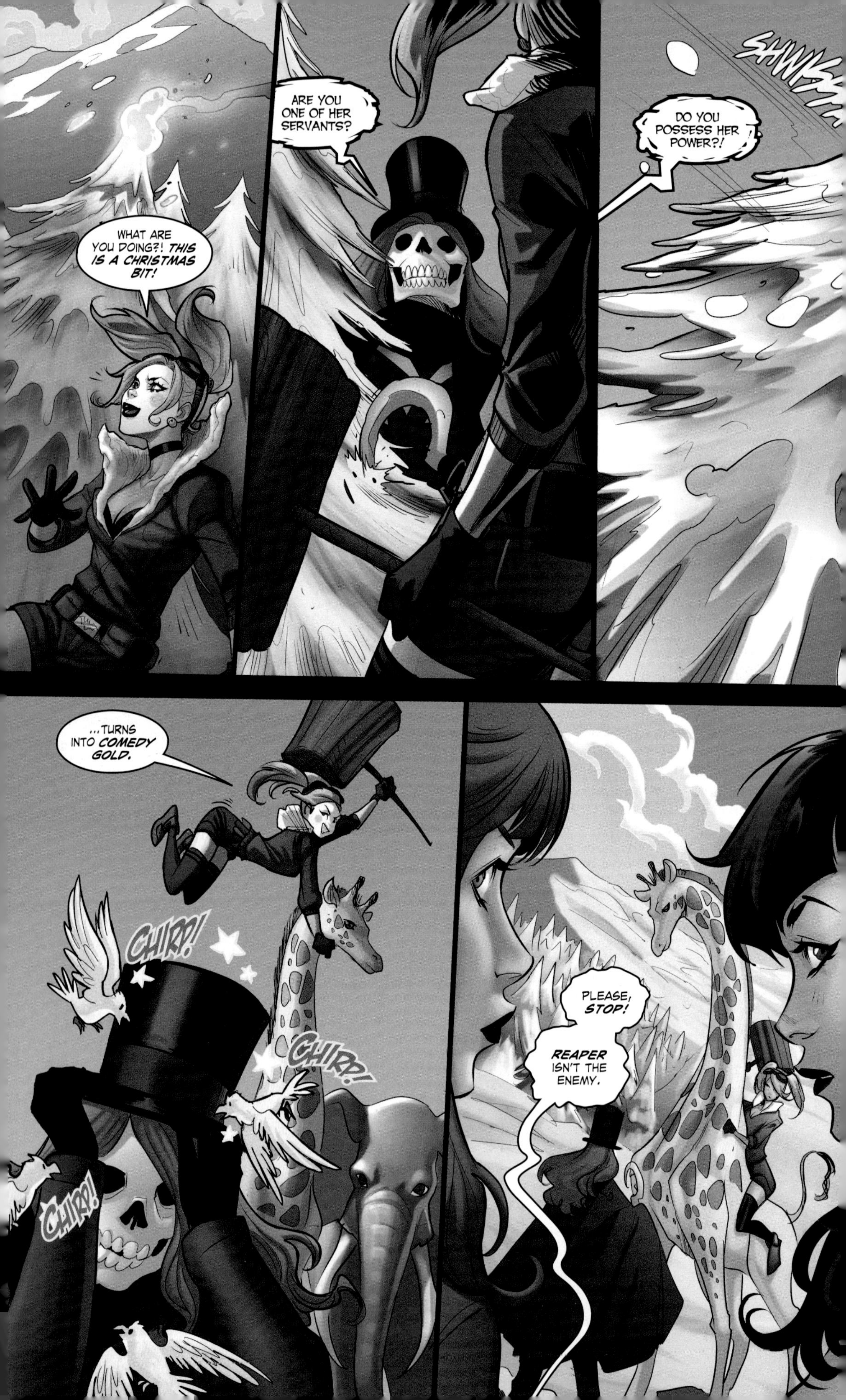
WHAT ARE YOU DOING?! *THIS IS A CHRISTMAS BIT!*
ARE YOU ONE OF HER SERVANTS?
DO YOU POSSESS HER POWER?!
SHWISH
...TURNS INTO *COMEDY GOLD.*
CHIRP!
CHIRP!
CHIRP!
PLEASE, *STOP!*
REAPER ISN'T THE ENEMY.

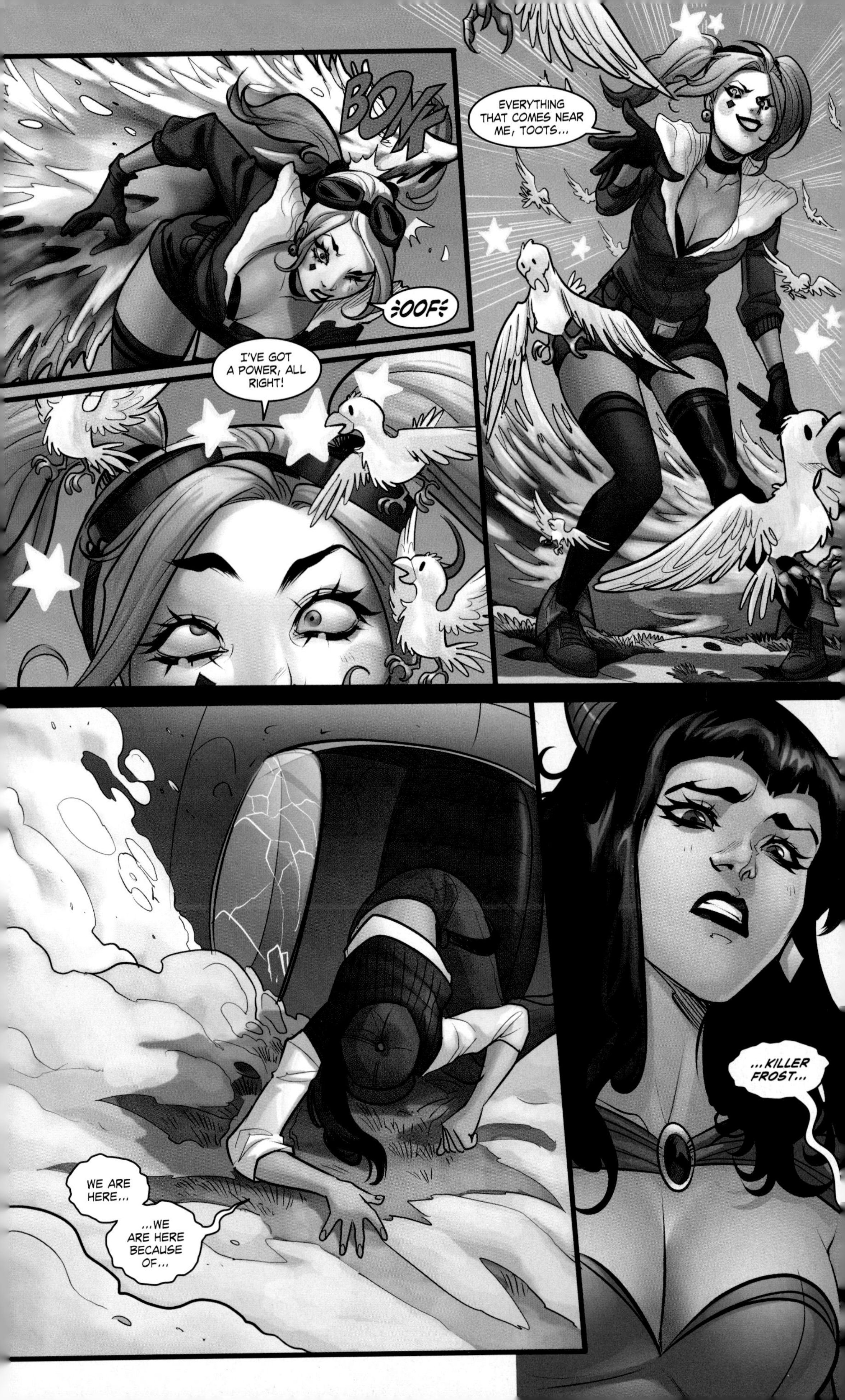
BONK
OOF
I'VE GOT A POWER, ALL RIGHT!
EVERYTHING THAT COMES NEAR ME, TOOTS...
WE ARE HERE...
...WE ARE HERE BECAUSE OF...
...KILLER FROST...

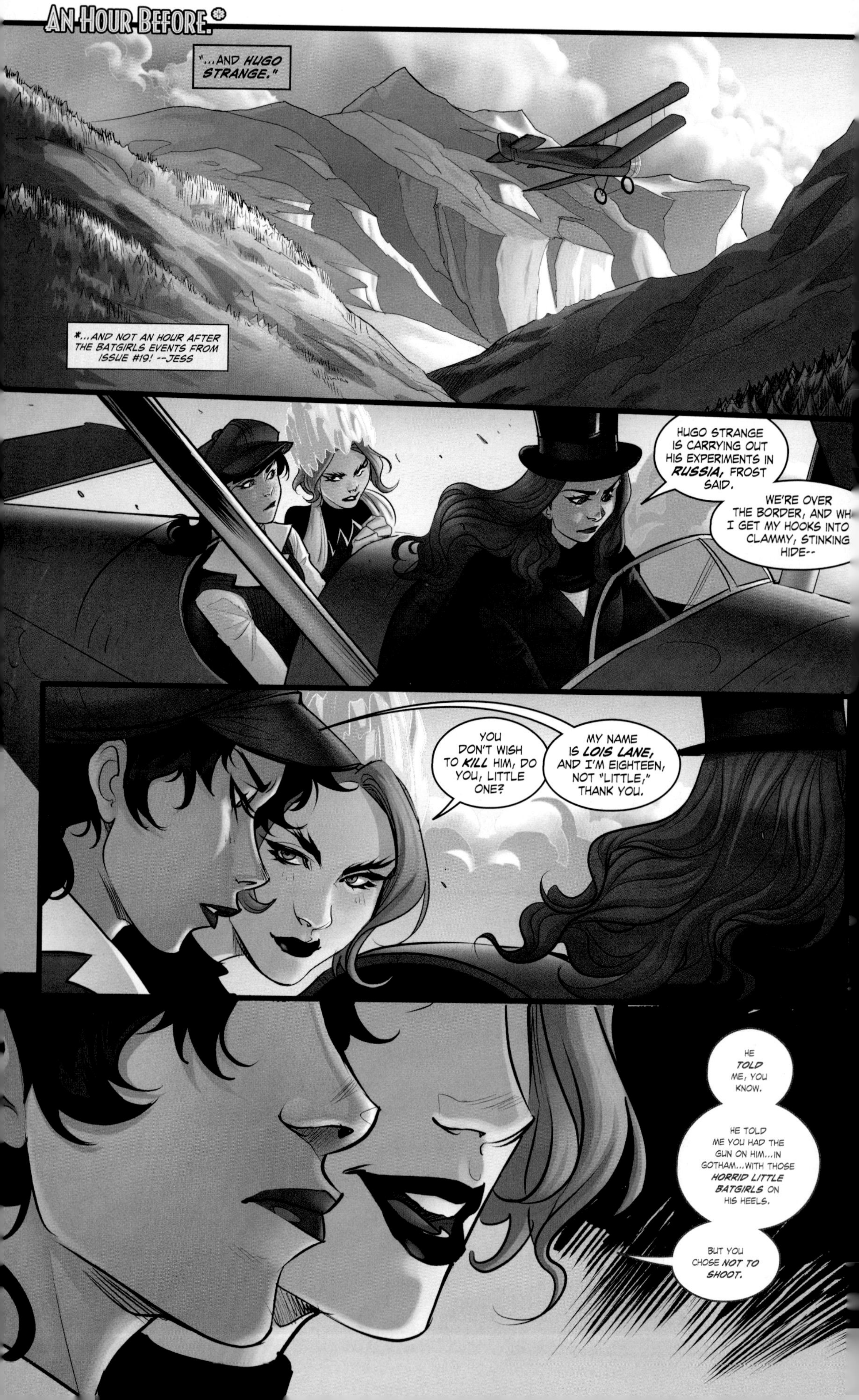
AN HOUR BEFORE.*
"...AND HUGO STRANGE."
*...AND NOT AN HOUR AFTER THE BATGIRLS EVENTS FROM ISSUE #19! --JESS
HUGO STRANGE IS CARRYING OUT HIS EXPERIMENTS IN RUSSIA, FROST SAID.
WE'RE OVER THE BORDER, AND WH I GET MY HOOKS INTO CLAMMY, STINKING HIDE--
YOU DON'T WISH TO KILL HIM, DO YOU, LITTLE ONE?
MY NAME IS LOIS LANE, AND I'M EIGHTEEN, NOT "LITTLE," THANK YOU.
HE TOLD ME, YOU KNOW.
HE TOLD ME YOU HAD THE GUN ON HIM...IN GOTHAM...WITH THOSE HORRID LITTLE BATGIRLS ON HIS HEELS.
BUT YOU CHOSE NOT TO SHOOT.

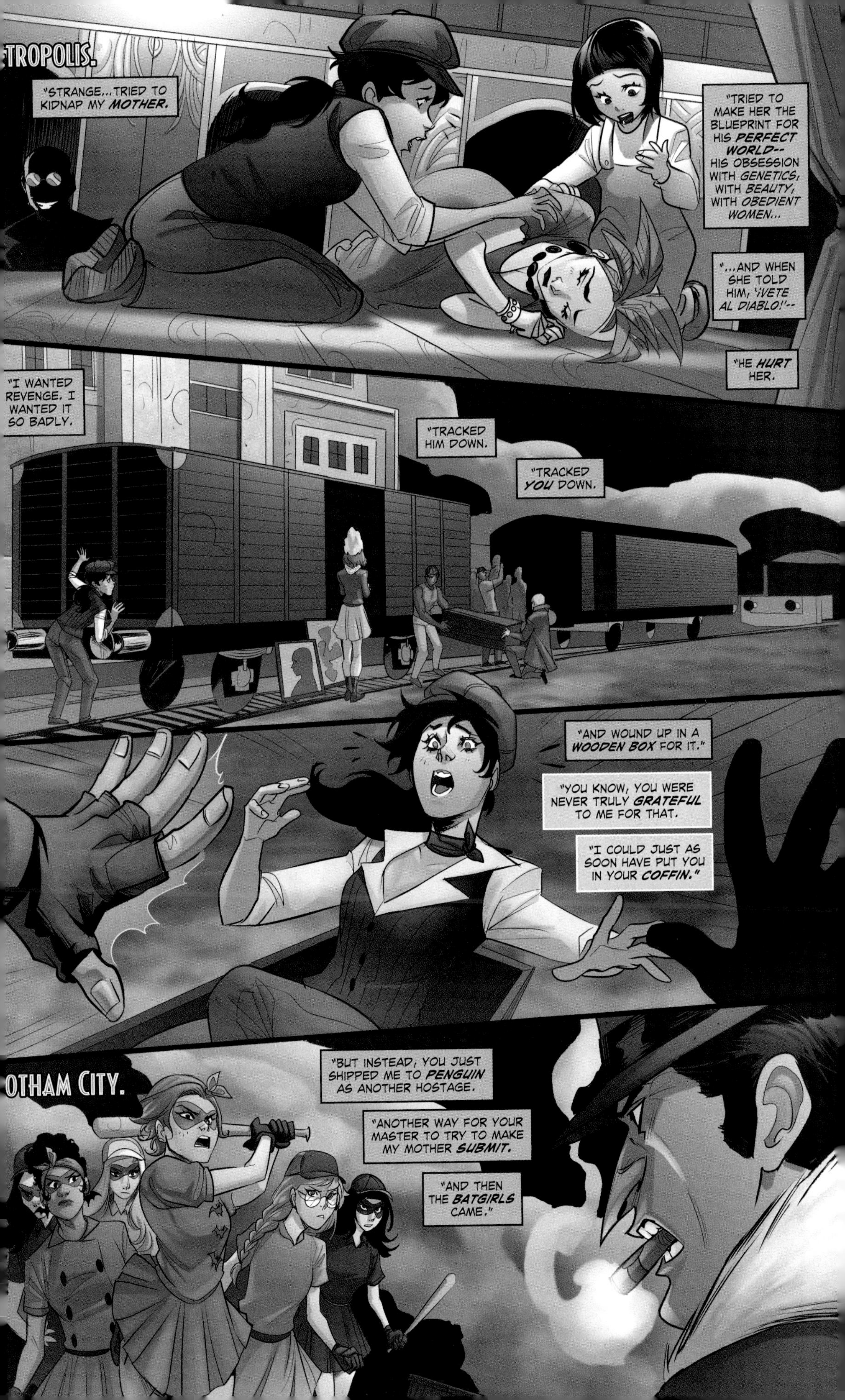
TROPOLIS.
"STRANGE...TRIED TO KIDNAP MY MOTHER.
"TRIED TO MAKE HER THE BLUEPRINT FOR HIS PERFECT WORLD-- HIS OBSESSION WITH GENETICS, WITH BEAUTY, WITH OBEDIENT WOMEN...
"...AND WHEN SHE TOLD HIM, '¡VETE AL DIABLO!'--
"HE HURT HER.
"I WANTED REVENGE. I WANTED IT SO BADLY.
"TRACKED HIM DOWN.
"TRACKED YOU DOWN.
"AND WOUND UP IN A WOODEN BOX FOR IT."
"YOU KNOW, YOU WERE NEVER TRULY GRATEFUL TO ME FOR THAT.
"I COULD JUST AS SOON HAVE PUT YOU IN YOUR COFFIN."
OTHAM CITY.
"BUT INSTEAD, YOU JUST SHIPPED ME TO PENGUIN AS ANOTHER HOSTAGE.
"ANOTHER WAY FOR YOUR MASTER TO TRY TO MAKE MY MOTHER SUBMIT.
"AND THEN THE BATGIRLS CAME."

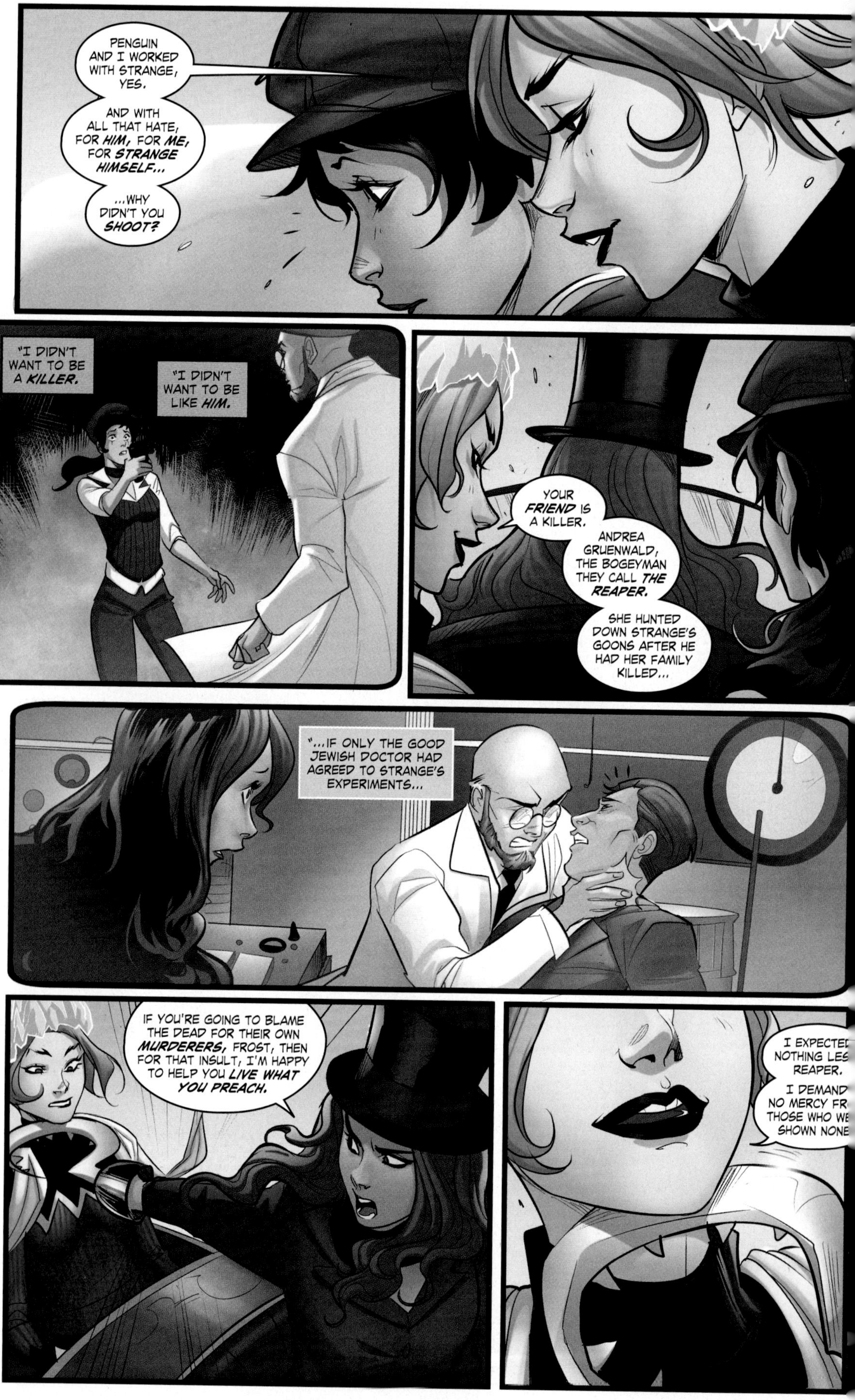
PENGUIN AND I WORKED WITH STRANGE, YES.
AND WITH ALL THAT HATE, FOR HIM, FOR ME, FOR STRANGE HIMSELF...
...WHY DIDN'T YOU SHOOT?
"I DIDN'T WANT TO BE A KILLER.
"I DIDN'T WANT TO BE LIKE HIM.
YOUR FRIEND IS A KILLER.
ANDREA GRUENWALD, THE BOGEYMAN THEY CALL THE REAPER.
SHE HUNTED DOWN STRANGE'S GOONS AFTER HE HAD HER FAMILY KILLED...
"...IF ONLY THE GOOD JEWISH DOCTOR HAD AGREED TO STRANGE'S EXPERIMENTS...
IF YOU'RE GOING TO BLAME THE DEAD FOR THEIR OWN MURDERERS, FROST, THEN FOR THAT INSULT, I'M HAPPY TO HELP YOU LIVE WHAT YOU PREACH.
I EXPECTED NOTHING LES REAPER.
I DEMAND NO MERCY FR THOSE WHO WE SHOWN NONE

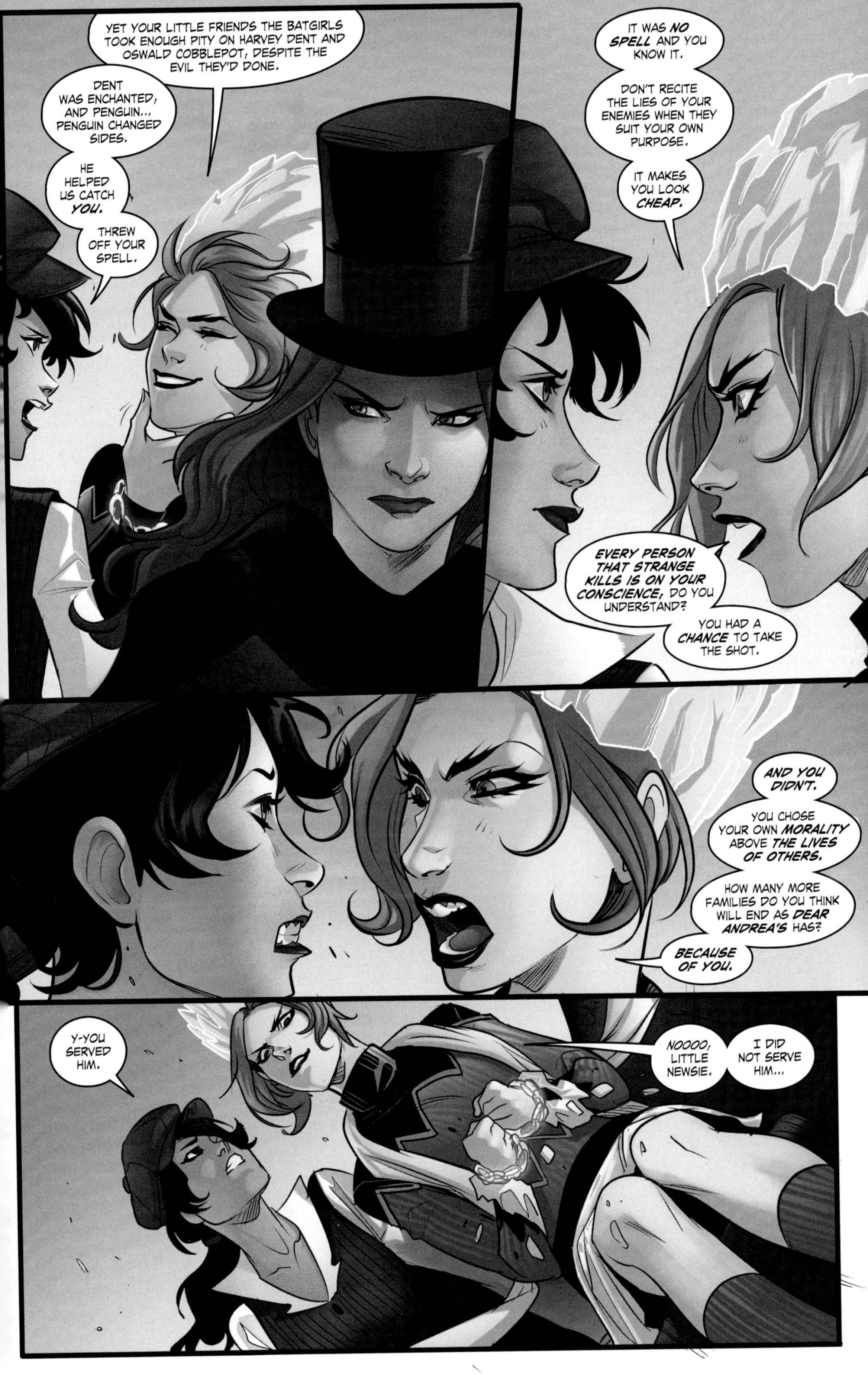
YET YOUR LITTLE FRIENDS THE BATGIRLS TOOK ENOUGH PITY ON HARVEY DENT AND OSWALD COBBLEPOT, DESPITE THE EVIL THEY'D DONE.
DENT WAS ENCHANTED, AND PENGUIN... PENGUIN CHANGED SIDES.
HE HELPED US CATCH YOU.
THREW OFF YOUR SPELL.
IT WAS NO SPELL AND YOU KNOW IT.
DON'T RECITE THE LIES OF YOUR ENEMIES WHEN THEY SUIT YOUR OWN PURPOSE.
IT MAKES YOU LOOK CHEAP.
EVERY PERSON THAT STRANGE KILLS IS ON YOUR CONSCIENCE, DO YOU UNDERSTAND?
YOU HAD A CHANCE TO TAKE THE SHOT.
AND YOU DIDN'T.
YOU CHOSE YOUR OWN MORALITY ABOVE THE LIVES OF OTHERS.
HOW MANY MORE FAMILIES DO YOU THINK WILL END AS DEAR ANDREA'S HAS?
BECAUSE OF YOU.
Y-YOU SERVED HIM.
NOOOO, LITTLE NEWSIE.
I DID NOT SERVE HIM...

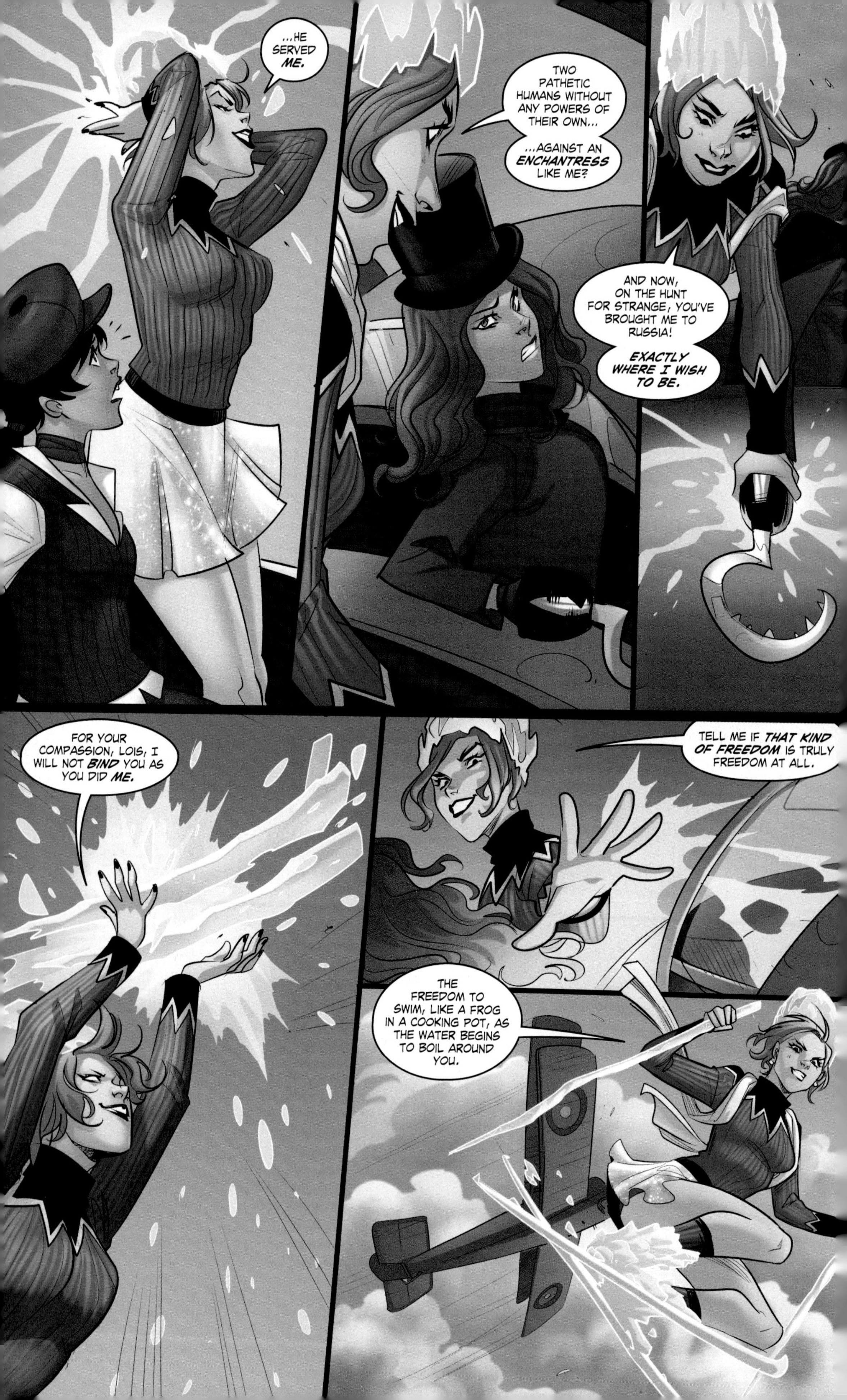
...HE SERVED *ME.*
TWO PATHETIC HUMANS WITHOUT ANY POWERS OF THEIR OWN...
...AGAINST AN *ENCHANTRESS* LIKE ME?
AND NOW, ON THE HUNT FOR STRANGE, YOU'VE BROUGHT ME TO RUSSIA!
EXACTLY WHERE I WISH TO BE.
FOR YOUR COMPASSION, LOIS, I WILL NOT *BIND* YOU AS YOU DID *ME.*
TELL ME IF *THAT KIND OF FREEDOM* IS TRULY FREEDOM AT ALL.
THE FREEDOM TO SWIM, LIKE A FROG IN A COOKING POT, AS THE WATER BEGINS TO BOIL AROUND YOU.

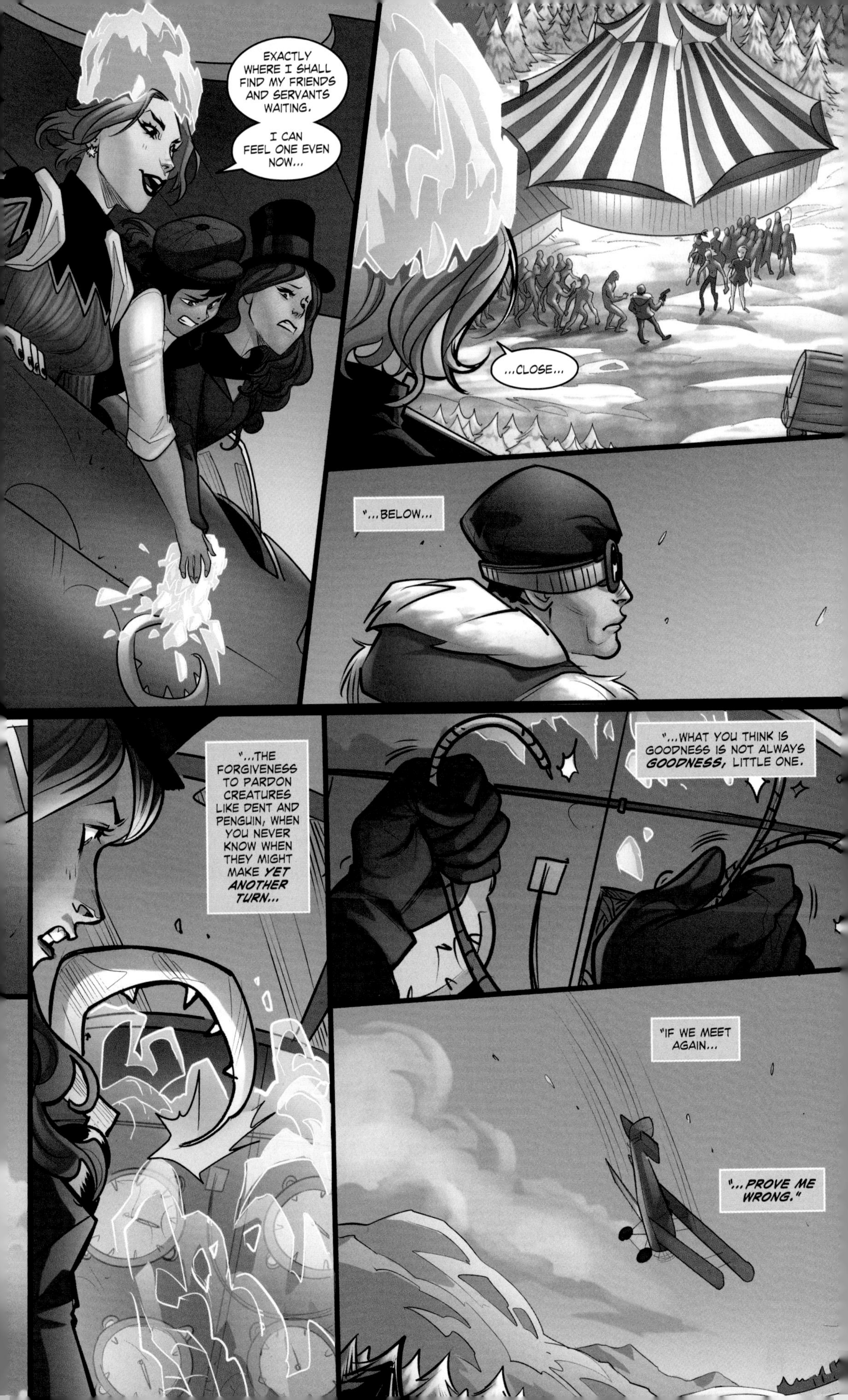
EXACTLY WHERE I SHALL FIND MY FRIENDS AND SERVANTS WAITING.
I CAN FEEL ONE EVEN NOW...
...CLOSE...
"...BELOW...
"...THE FORGIVENESS TO PARDON CREATURES LIKE DENT AND PENGUIN, WHEN YOU NEVER KNOW WHEN THEY MIGHT MAKE YET ANOTHER TURN...
"...WHAT YOU THINK IS GOODNESS IS NOT ALWAYS GOODNESS, LITTLE ONE.
"IF WE MEET AGAIN...
"...PROVE ME WRONG."

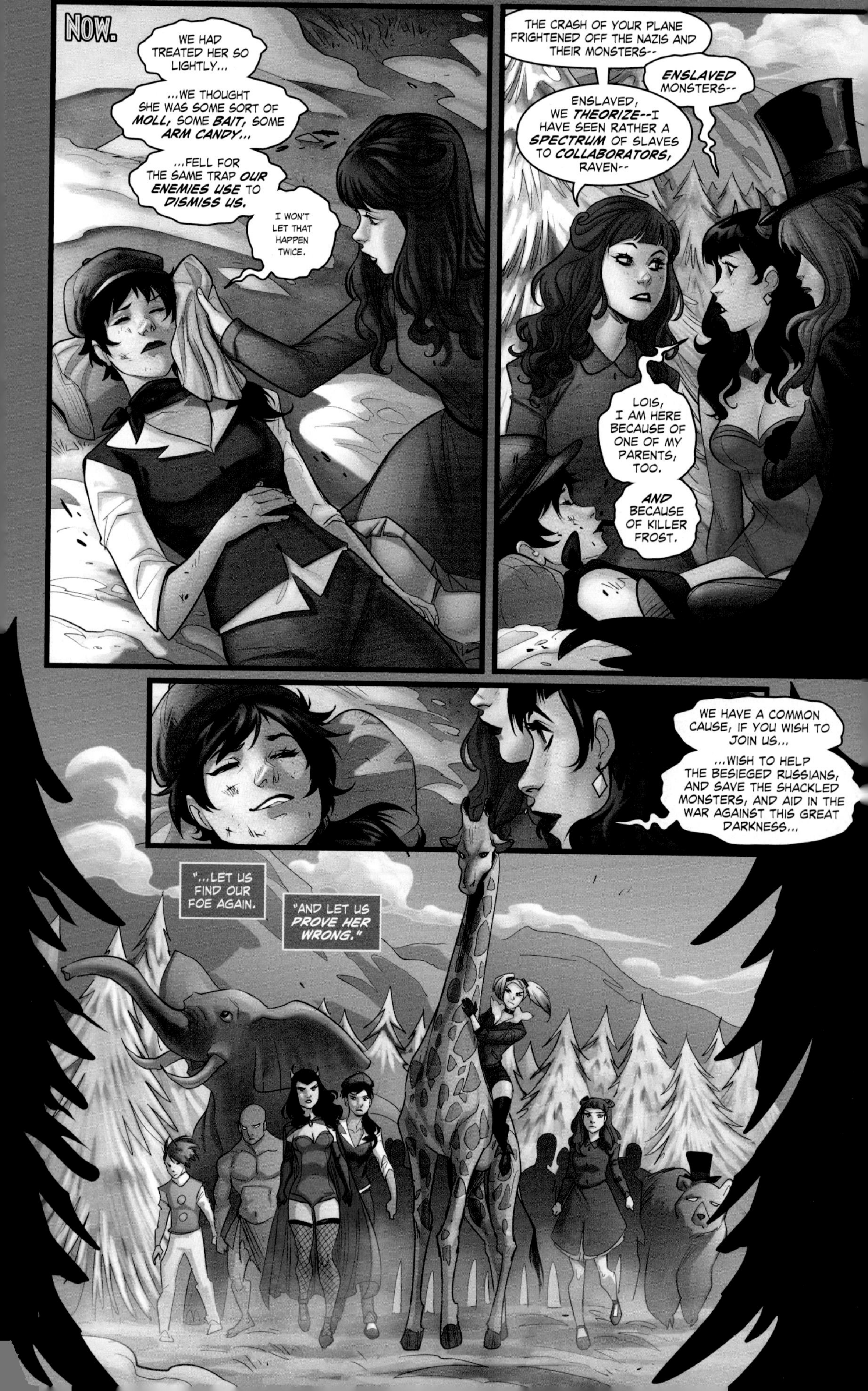
NOW.
WE HAD TREATED HER SO LIGHTLY...
...WE THOUGHT SHE WAS SOME SORT OF MOLL, SOME BAIT, SOME ARM CANDY...
...FELL FOR THE SAME TRAP OUR ENEMIES USE TO DISMISS US.
I WON'T LET THAT HAPPEN TWICE.
THE CRASH OF YOUR PLANE FRIGHTENED OFF THE NAZIS AND THEIR MONSTERS--
ENSLAVED MONSTERS--
ENSLAVED, WE THEORIZE--I HAVE SEEN RATHER A SPECTRUM OF SLAVES TO COLLABORATORS, RAVEN--
LOIS, I AM HERE BECAUSE OF ONE OF MY PARENTS, TOO.
AND BECAUSE OF KILLER FROST.
WE HAVE A COMMON CAUSE, IF YOU WISH TO JOIN US...
...WISH TO HELP THE BESIEGED RUSSIANS, AND SAVE THE SHACKLED MONSTERS, AND AID IN THE WAR AGAINST THIS GREAT DARKNESS...
"...LET US FIND OUR FOE AGAIN.
"AND LET US PROVE HER WRONG."

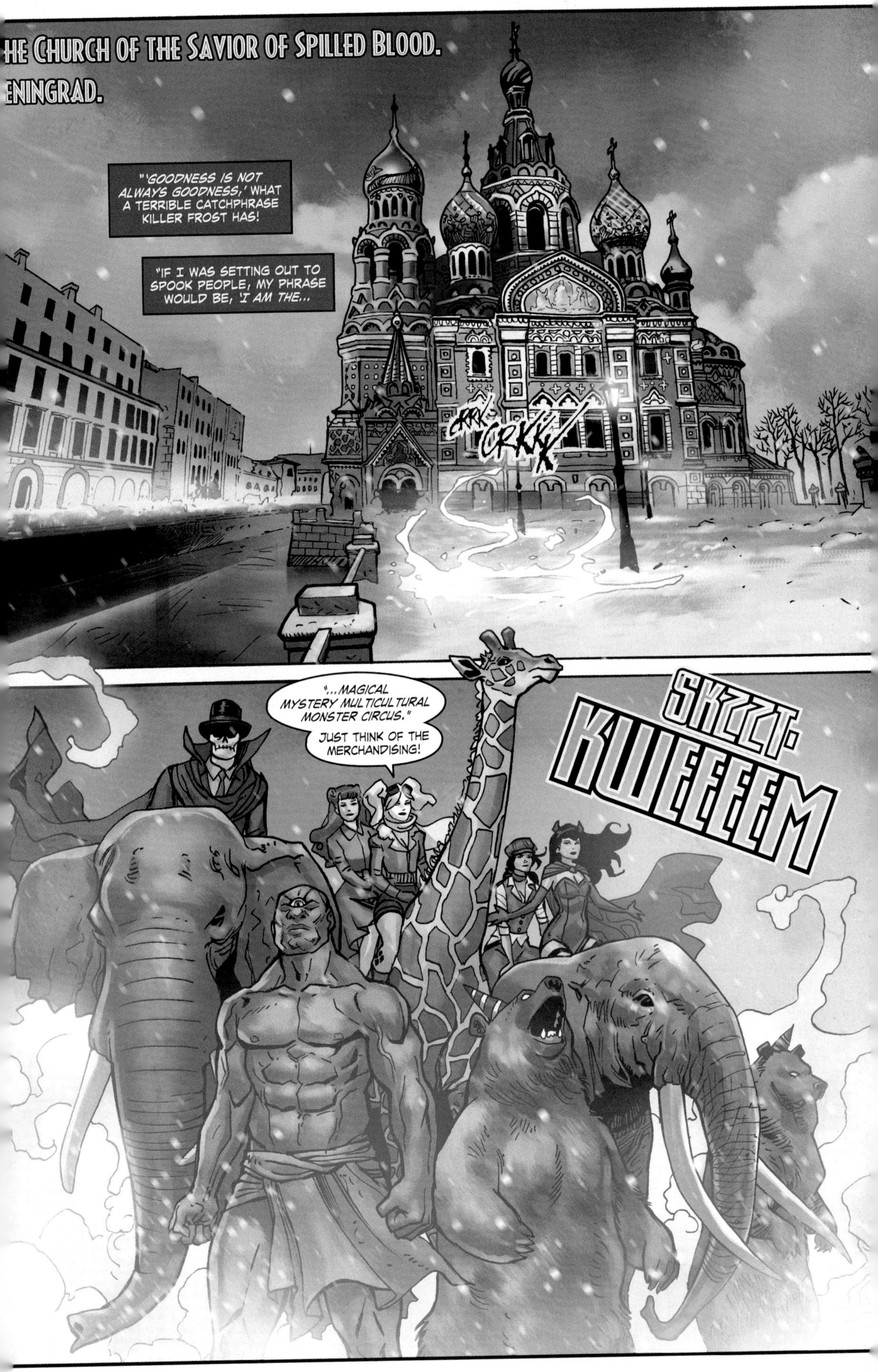
HE CHURCH OF THE SAVIOR OF SPILLED BLOOD.
ENINGRAD.
"'GOODNESS IS NOT ALWAYS GOODNESS,' WHAT A TERRIBLE CATCHPHRASE KILLER FROST HAS!
"IF I WAS SETTING OUT TO SPOOK PEOPLE, MY PHRASE WOULD BE, 'I AM THE...
CRRK CRKK
"...MAGICAL MYSTERY MULTICULTURAL MONSTER CIRCUS."
JUST THINK OF THE MERCHANDISING!
SKZZZT-KWEEEEM

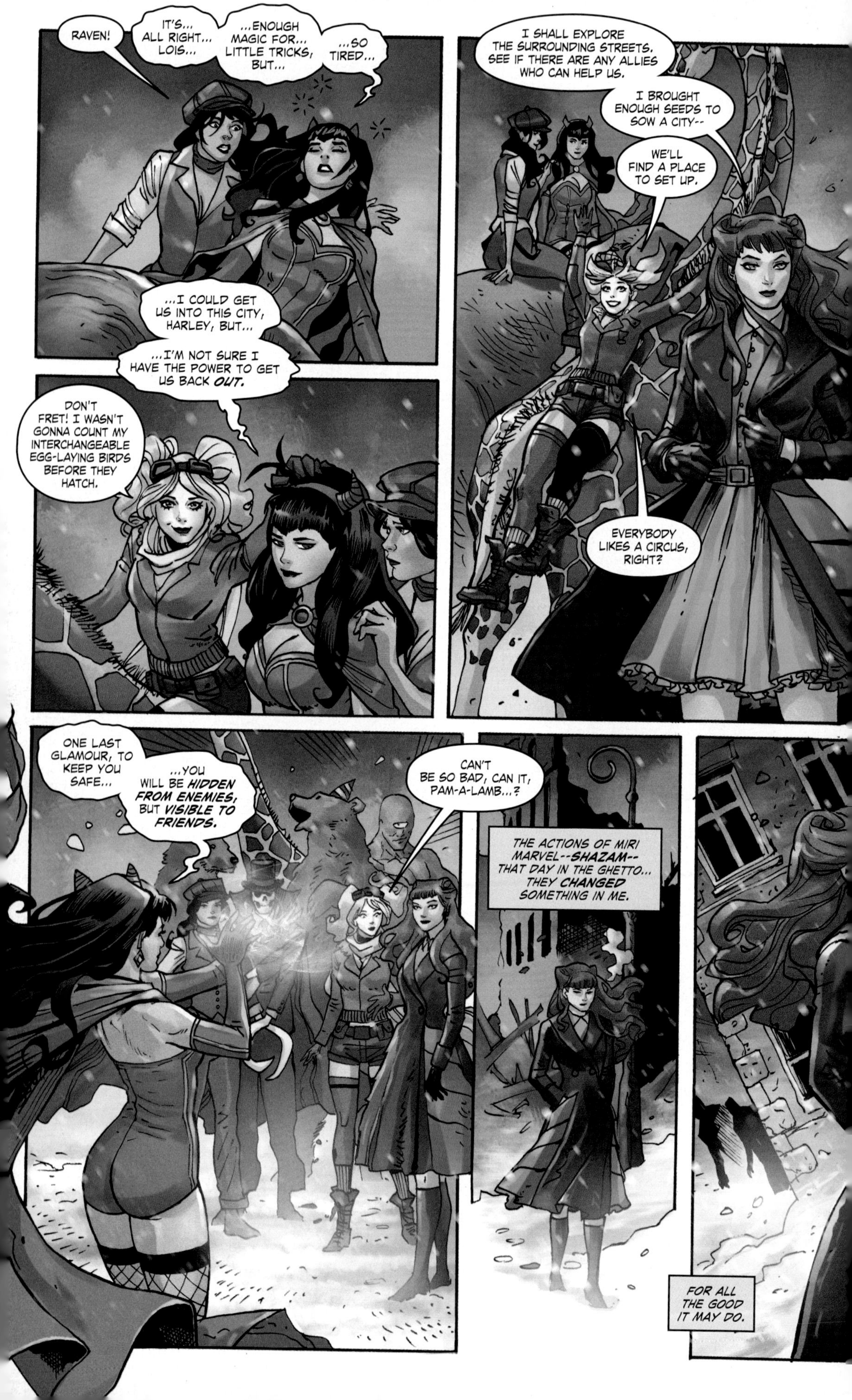
RAVEN!
IT'S... ALL RIGHT... LOIS...
...ENOUGH MAGIC FOR... LITTLE TRICKS, BUT...
...SO TIRED...
...I COULD GET US INTO THIS CITY, HARLEY, BUT...
...I'M NOT SURE I HAVE THE POWER TO GET US BACK OUT.
DON'T FRET! I WASN'T GONNA COUNT MY INTERCHANGEABLE EGG-LAYING BIRDS BEFORE THEY HATCH.
I SHALL EXPLORE THE SURROUNDING STREETS. SEE IF THERE ARE ANY ALLIES WHO CAN HELP US.
I BROUGHT ENOUGH SEEDS TO SOW A CITY--
WE'LL FIND A PLACE TO SET UP.
EVERYBODY LIKES A CIRCUS, RIGHT?
ONE LAST GLAMOUR, TO KEEP YOU SAFE...
...YOU WILL BE HIDDEN FROM ENEMIES, BUT VISIBLE TO FRIENDS.
CAN'T BE SO BAD, CAN IT, PAM-A-LAMB...?
THE ACTIONS OF MIRI MARVEL--SHAZAM--THAT DAY IN THE GHETTO... THEY CHANGED SOMETHING IN ME.
FOR ALL THE GOOD IT MAY DO.

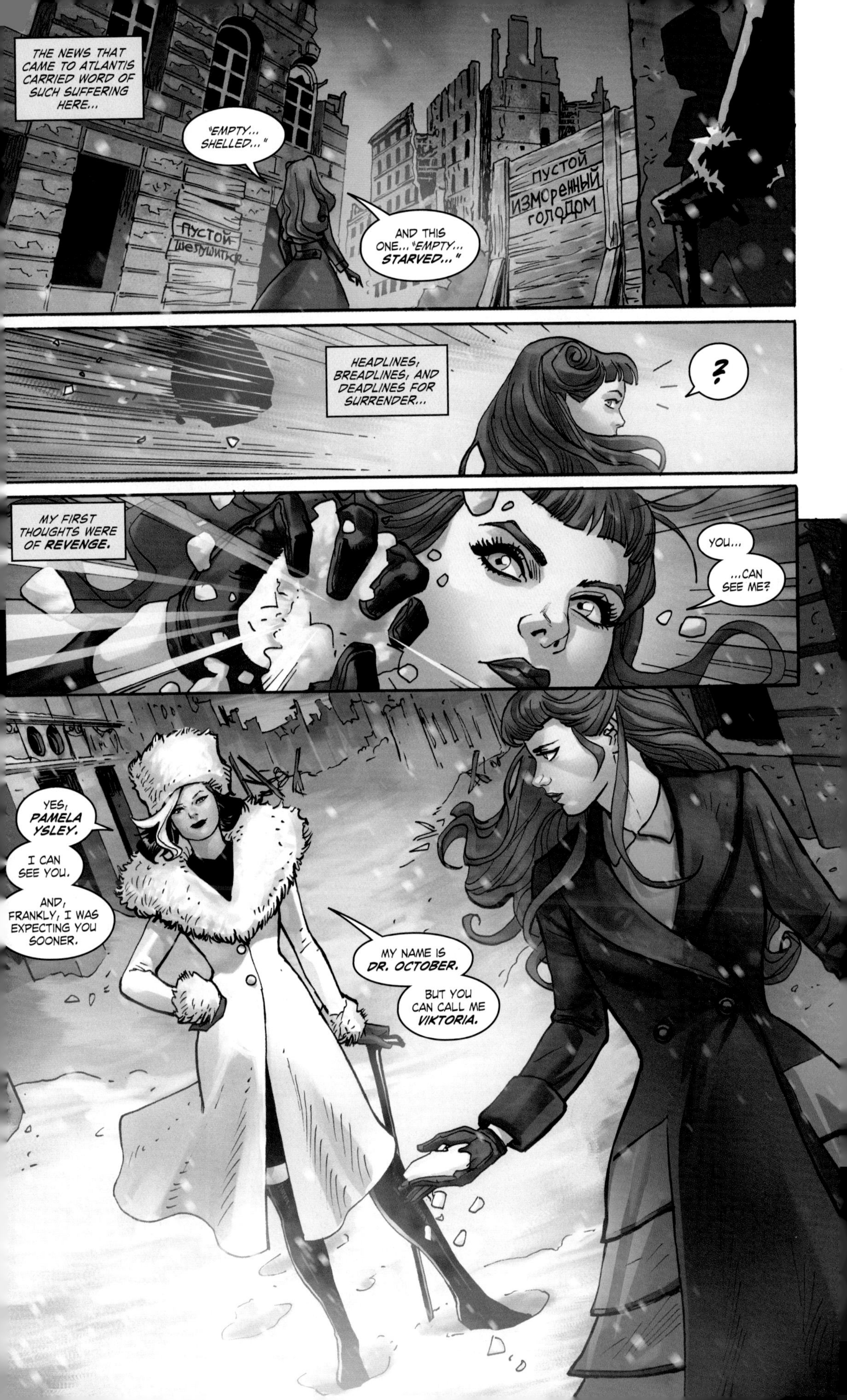

THE NEWS THAT CAME TO ATLANTIS CARRIED WORD OF SUCH SUFFERING HERE...
"EMPTY... SHELLED..."
ПУСТОЙ
AND THIS ONE... "EMPTY... STARVED..."
ПУСТОЙ ИЗМОРЕННЫЙ ГОЛОДОМ
HEADLINES, BREADLINES, AND DEADLINES FOR SURRENDER...
?
MY FIRST THOUGHTS WERE OF REVENGE.
YOU...
...CAN SEE ME?
YES, PAMELA YSLEY.
I CAN SEE YOU.
AND, FRANKLY, I WAS EXPECTING YOU SOONER.
MY NAME IS DR. OCTOBER.
BUT YOU CAN CALL ME VIKTORIA.

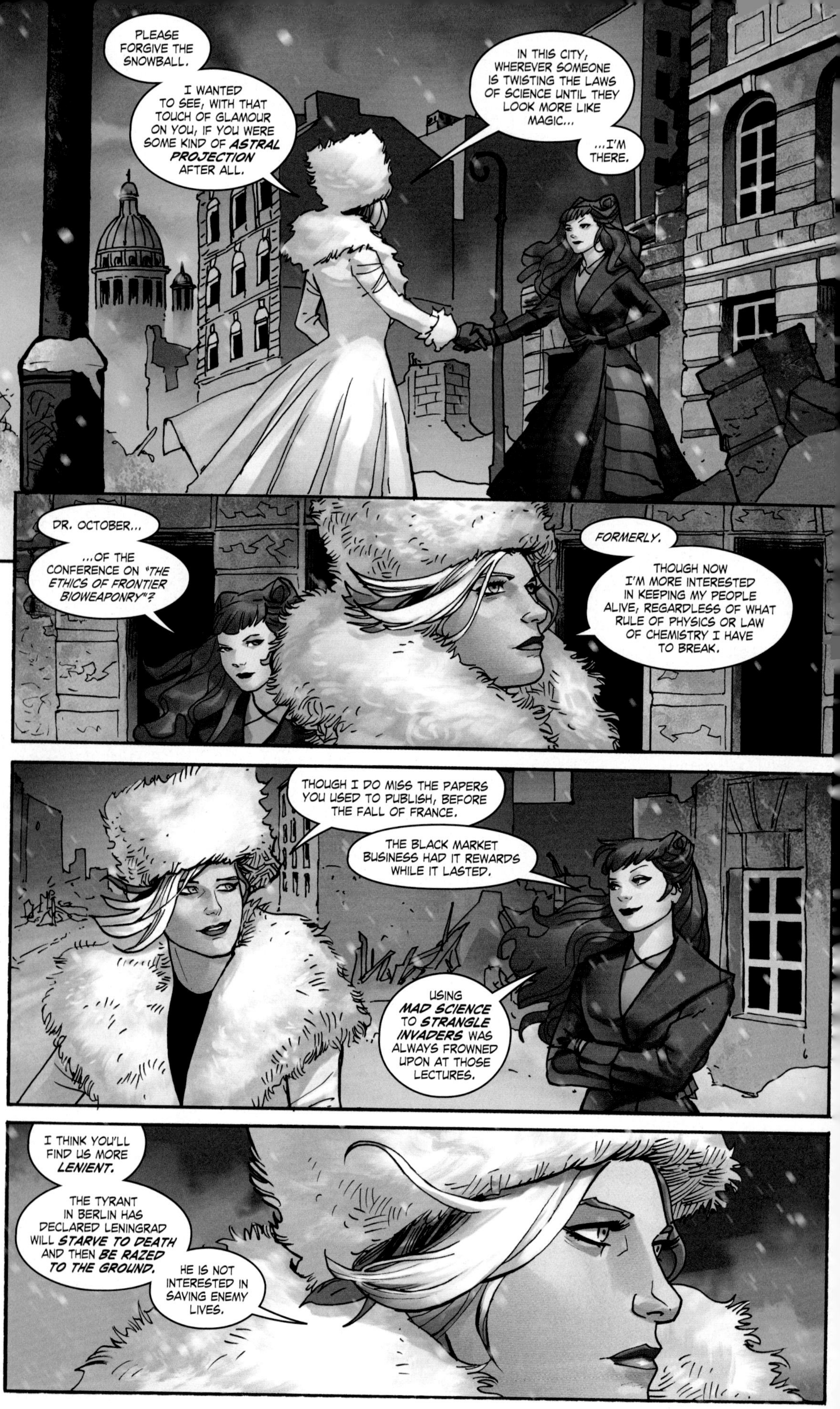
PLEASE FORGIVE THE SNOWBALL.
I WANTED TO SEE, WITH THAT TOUCH OF GLAMOUR ON YOU, IF YOU WERE SOME KIND OF ASTRAL PROJECTION AFTER ALL.
IN THIS CITY, WHEREVER SOMEONE IS TWISTING THE LAWS OF SCIENCE UNTIL THEY LOOK MORE LIKE MAGIC...
...I'M THERE.
DR. OCTOBER...
...OF THE CONFERENCE ON "THE ETHICS OF FRONTIER BIOWEAPONRY"?
FORMERLY.
THOUGH NOW I'M MORE INTERESTED IN KEEPING MY PEOPLE ALIVE, REGARDLESS OF WHAT RULE OF PHYSICS OR LAW OF CHEMISTRY I HAVE TO BREAK.
THOUGH I DO MISS THE PAPERS YOU USED TO PUBLISH, BEFORE THE FALL OF FRANCE.
THE BLACK MARKET BUSINESS HAD IT REWARDS WHILE IT LASTED.
USING MAD SCIENCE TO STRANGLE INVADERS WAS ALWAYS FROWNED UPON AT THOSE LECTURES.
I THINK YOU'LL FIND US MORE LENIENT.
THE TYRANT IN BERLIN HAS DECLARED LENINGRAD WILL STARVE TO DEATH AND THEN BE RAZED TO THE GROUND.
HE IS NOT INTERESTED IN SAVING ENEMY LIVES.

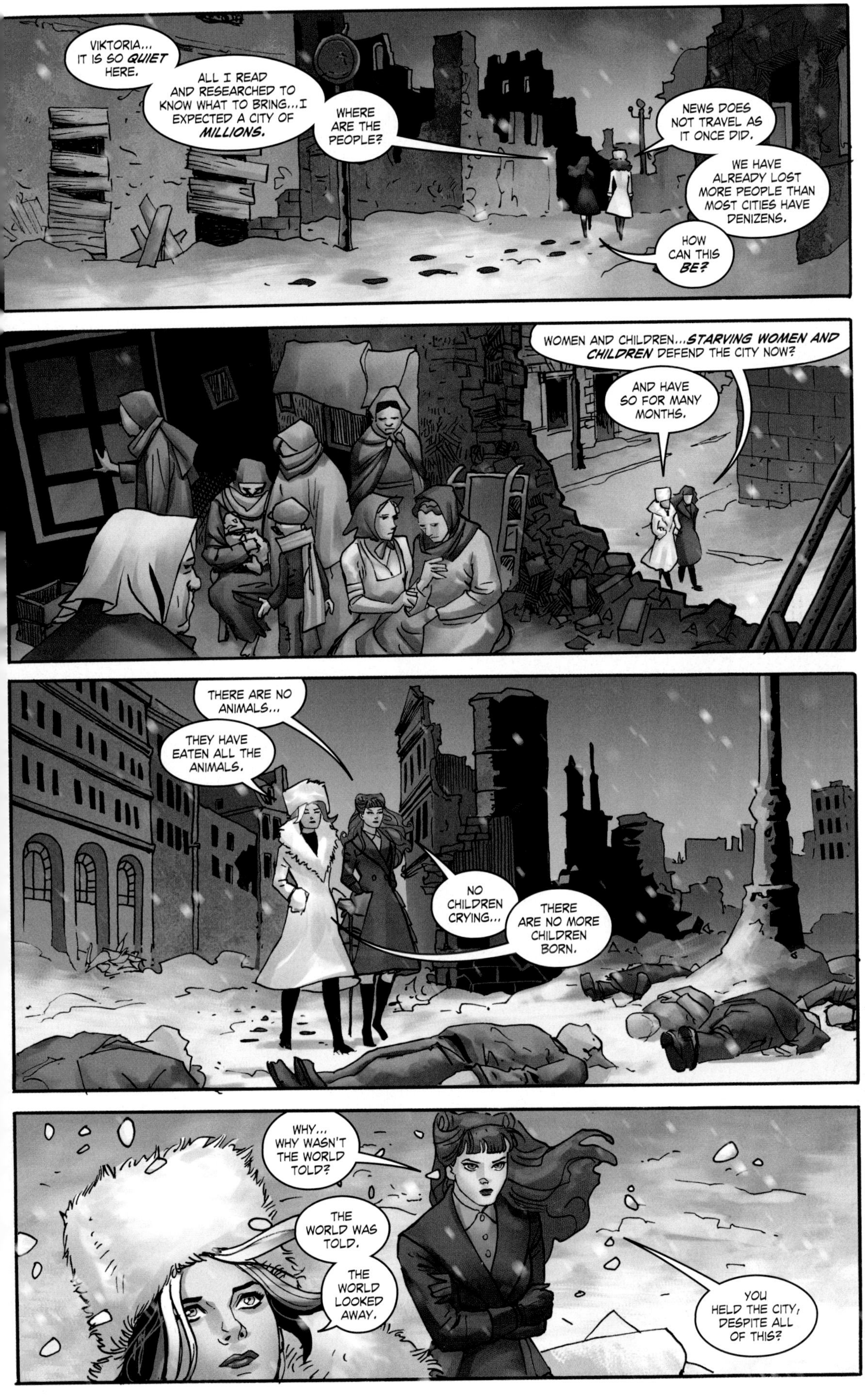
VIKTORIA... IT IS SO *QUIET* HERE.
ALL I READ AND RESEARCHED TO KNOW WHAT TO BRING...I EXPECTED A CITY OF *MILLIONS.*
WHERE ARE THE PEOPLE?
NEWS DOES NOT TRAVEL AS IT ONCE DID.
WE HAVE ALREADY LOST MORE PEOPLE THAN MOST CITIES HAVE DENIZENS.
HOW CAN THIS *BE?*
WOMEN AND CHILDREN...*STARVING WOMEN AND CHILDREN* DEFEND THE CITY NOW?
AND HAVE SO FOR MANY MONTHS.
THERE ARE NO ANIMALS...
THEY HAVE EATEN ALL THE ANIMALS.
NO CHILDREN CRYING...
THERE ARE NO MORE CHILDREN BORN.
WHY... WHY WASN'T THE WORLD TOLD?
THE WORLD WAS TOLD.
THE WORLD LOOKED AWAY.
YOU HELD THE CITY, DESPITE ALL OF THIS?

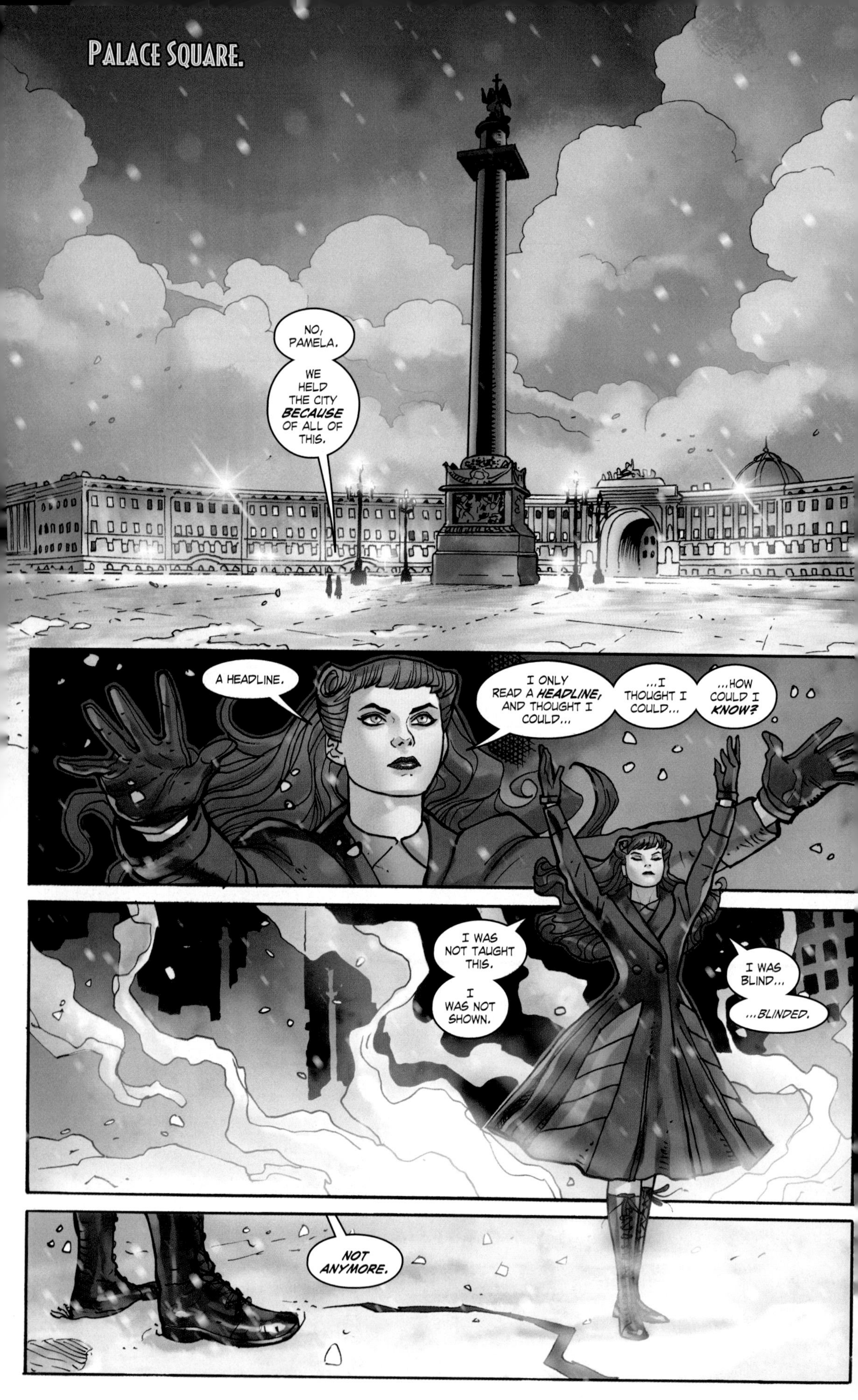
PALACE SQUARE.
NO, PAMELA.
WE HELD THE CITY *BECAUSE* OF ALL OF THIS.
A HEADLINE.
I ONLY READ A *HEADLINE,* AND THOUGHT I COULD...
...I THOUGHT I COULD...
...HOW COULD I *KNOW?*
I WAS NOT TAUGHT THIS.
I WAS NOT SHOWN.
I WAS BLIND...
...*BLINDED.*
NOT ANYMORE.

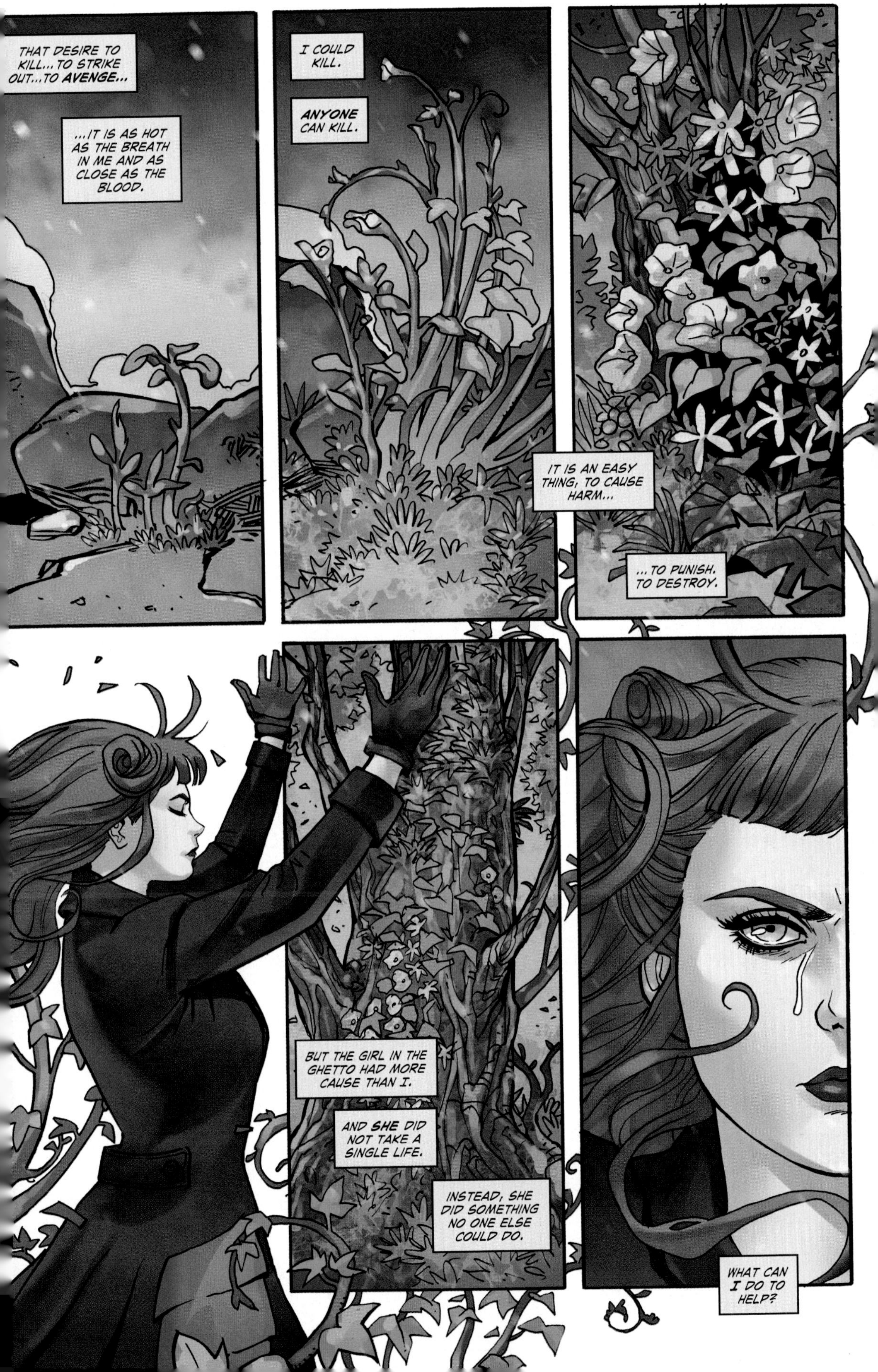
THAT DESIRE TO KILL...TO STRIKE OUT...TO AVENGE...
...IT IS AS HOT AS THE BREATH IN ME AND AS CLOSE AS THE BLOOD.
I COULD KILL.
ANYONE CAN KILL.
IT IS AN EASY THING, TO CAUSE HARM...
...TO PUNISH. TO DESTROY.
BUT THE GIRL IN THE GHETTO HAD MORE CAUSE THAN I.
AND SHE DID NOT TAKE A SINGLE LIFE.
INSTEAD, SHE DID SOMETHING NO ONE ELSE COULD DO.
WHAT CAN I DO TO HELP?

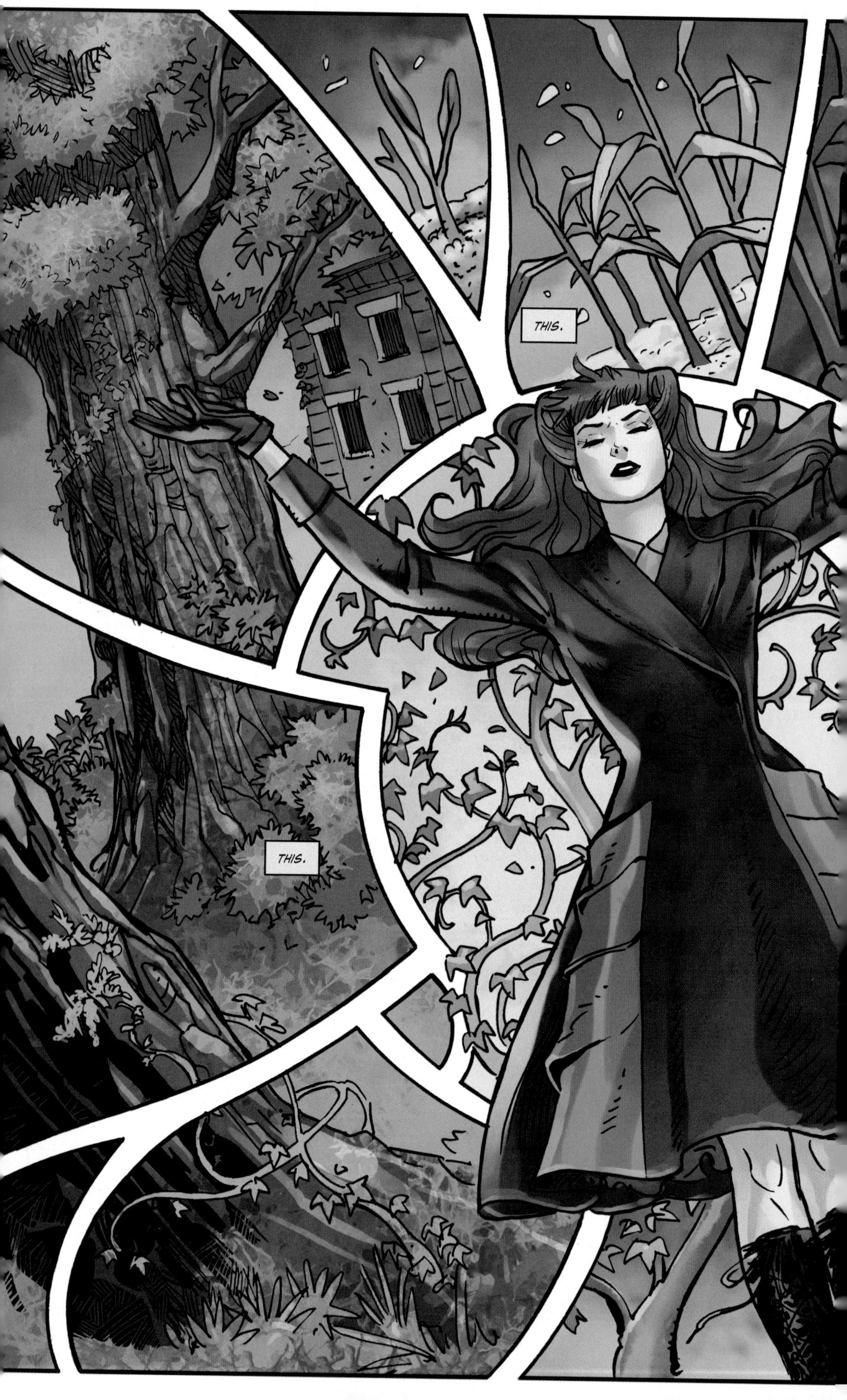
THIS.
THIS.

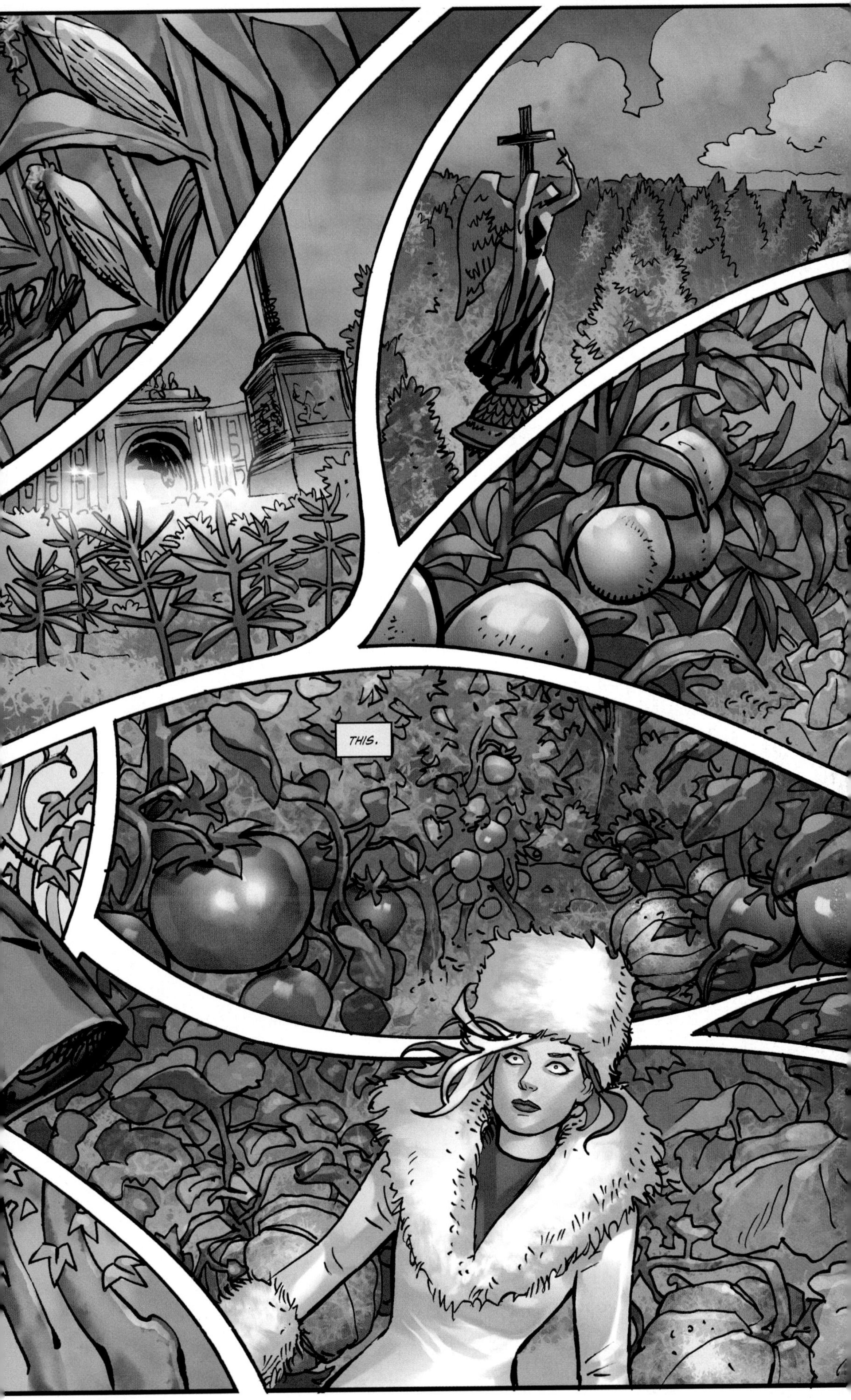
THIS.

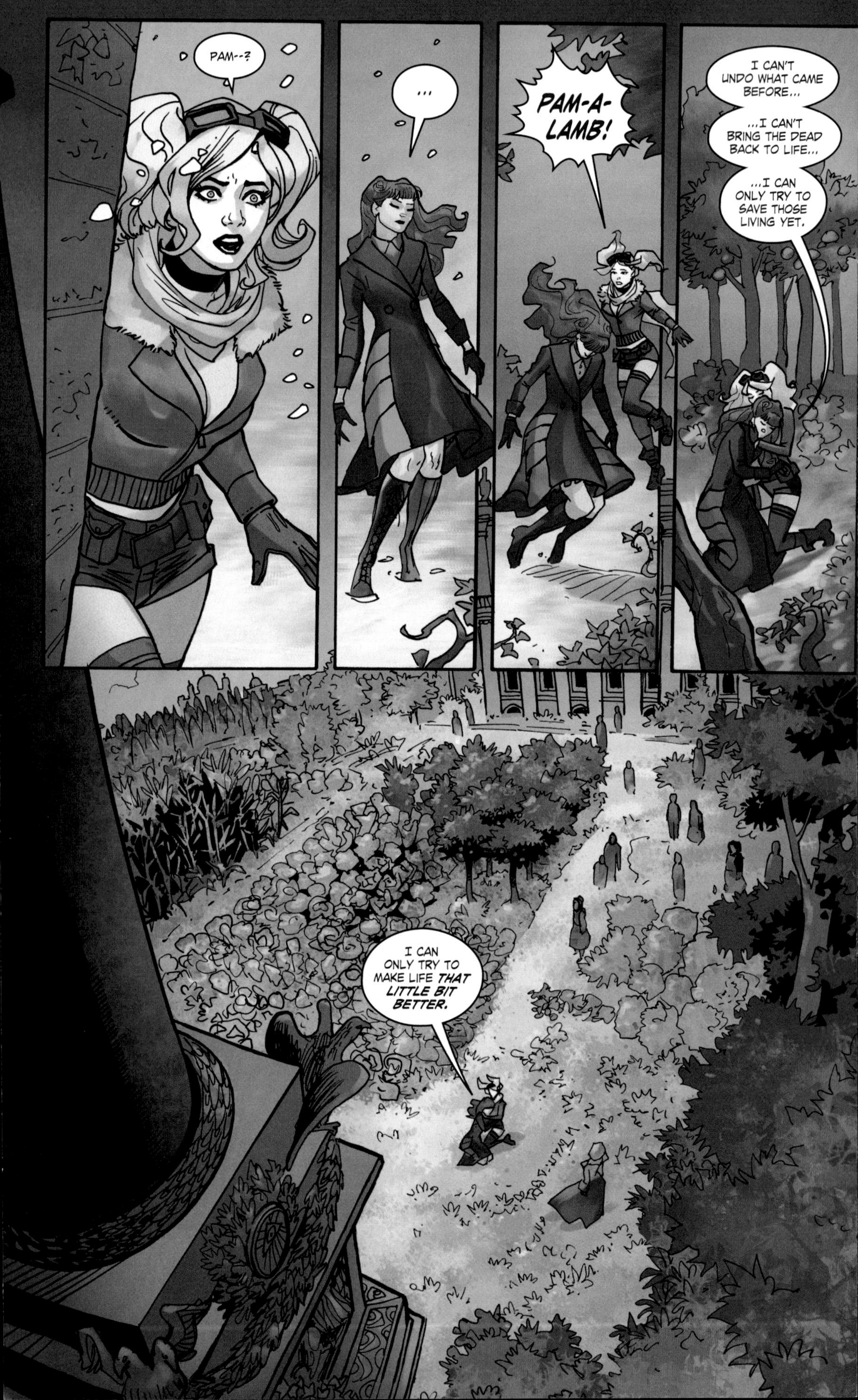
PAM--?
...
PAM-A-LAMB!
I CAN'T UNDO WHAT CAME BEFORE...
...I CAN'T BRING THE DEAD BACK TO LIFE...
...I CAN ONLY TRY TO SAVE THOSE LIVING YET.
I CAN ONLY TRY TO MAKE LIFE THAT LITTLE BIT BETTER.

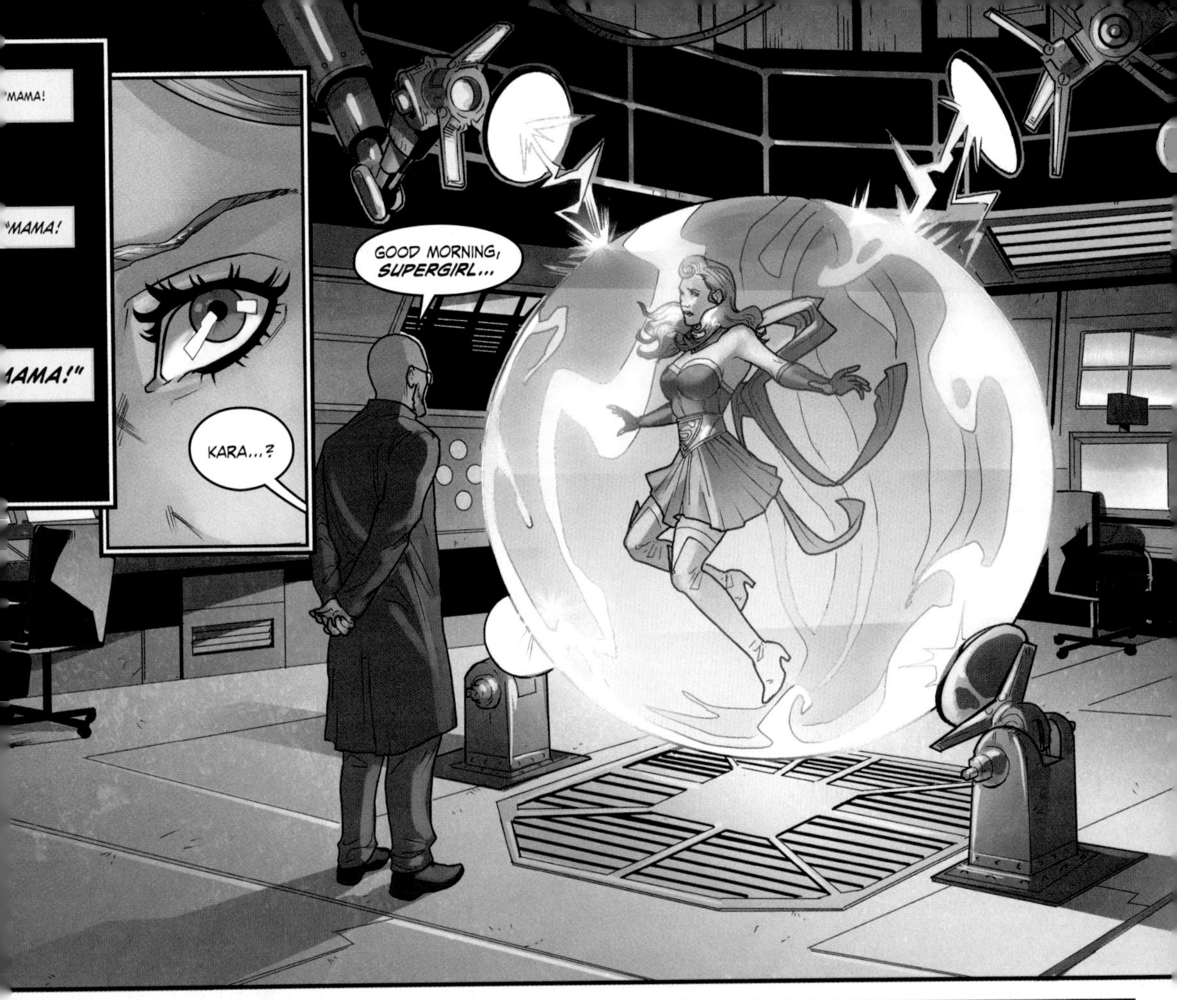
"MAMA!
"MAMA!
MAMA!"
KARA...?
GOOD MORNING, SUPERGIRL...

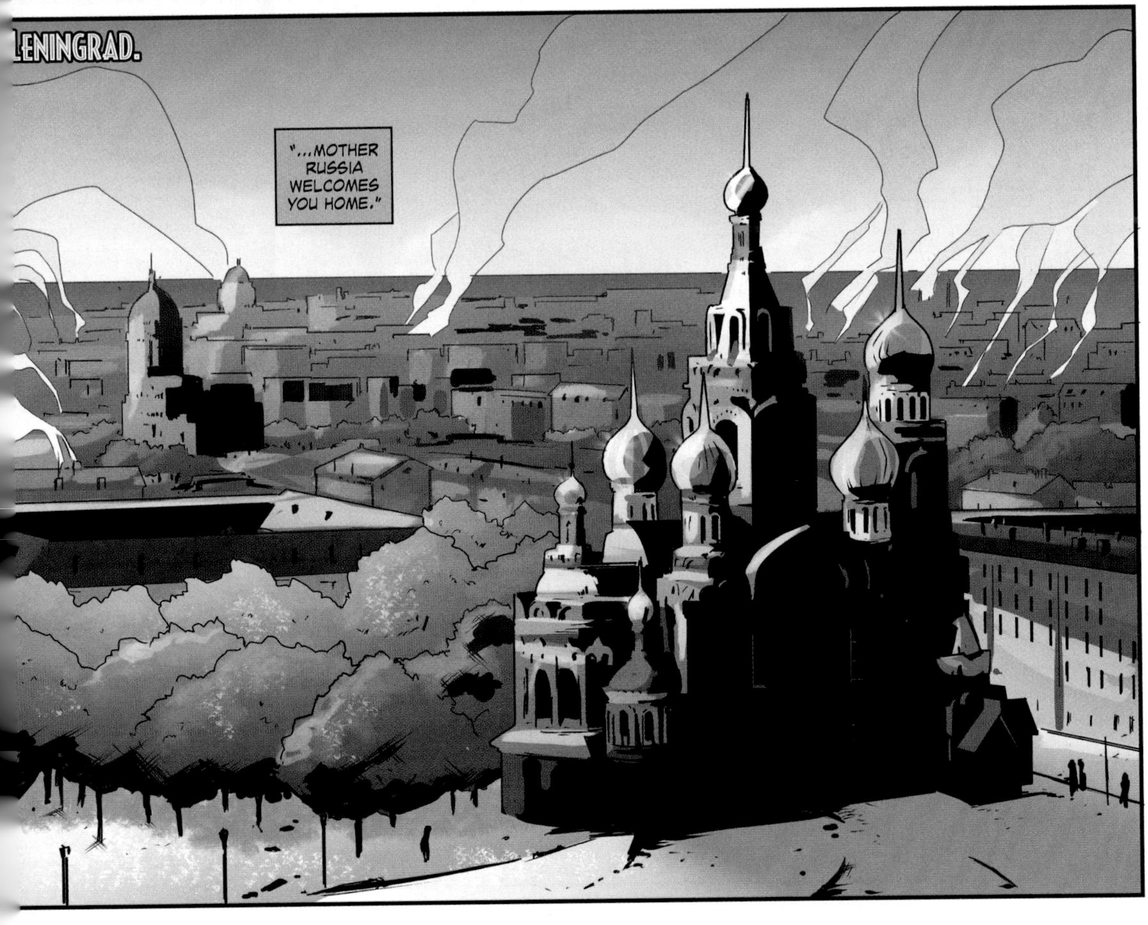
LENINGRAD.
"...MOTHER RUSSIA WELCOMES YOU HOME."

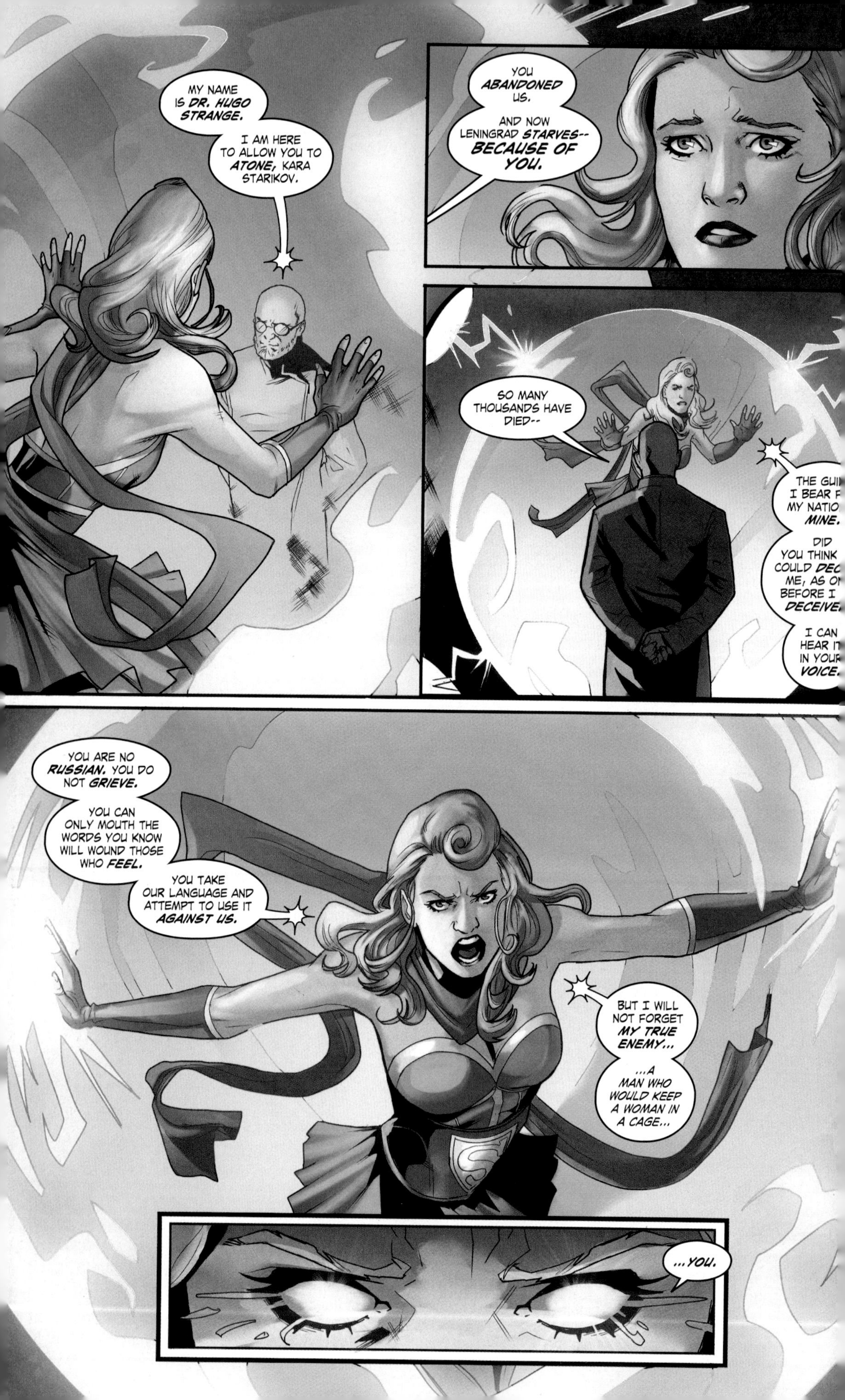
MY NAME IS DR. HUGO STRANGE.
I AM HERE TO ALLOW YOU TO ATONE, KARA STARIKOV.
YOU ABANDONED US.
AND NOW LENINGRAD STARVES-- BECAUSE OF YOU.
SO MANY THOUSANDS HAVE DIED--
THE GUI I BEAR F MY NATIO MINE.
DID YOU THINK COULD DEC ME, AS O BEFORE I DECEIVE
I CAN HEAR IT IN YOUR VOICE.
YOU ARE NO RUSSIAN. YOU DO NOT GRIEVE.
YOU CAN ONLY MOUTH THE WORDS YOU KNOW WILL WOUND THOSE WHO FEEL.
YOU TAKE OUR LANGUAGE AND ATTEMPT TO USE IT AGAINST US.
BUT I WILL NOT FORGET MY TRUE ENEMY...
...A MAN WHO WOULD KEEP A WOMAN IN A CAGE...
...YOU.

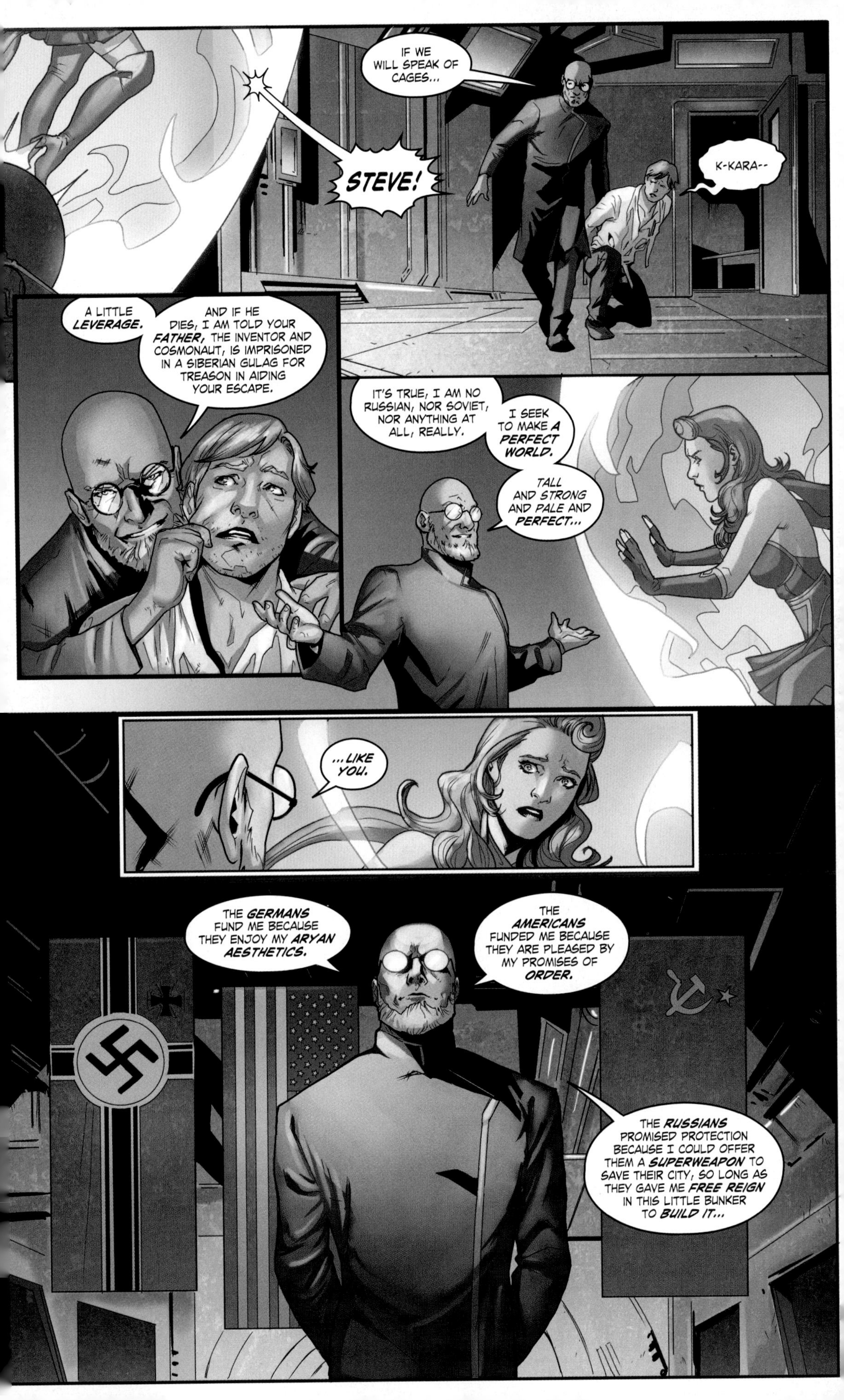
IF WE WILL SPEAK OF CAGES...
STEVE!
K-KARA--
A LITTLE LEVERAGE.
AND IF HE DIES, I AM TOLD YOUR FATHER, THE INVENTOR AND COSMONAUT, IS IMPRISONED IN A SIBERIAN GULAG FOR TREASON IN AIDING YOUR ESCAPE.
IT'S TRUE, I AM NO RUSSIAN, NOR SOVIET, NOR ANYTHING AT ALL, REALLY.
I SEEK TO MAKE A PERFECT WORLD.
TALL AND STRONG AND PALE AND PERFECT...
...LIKE YOU.
THE GERMANS FUND ME BECAUSE THEY ENJOY MY ARYAN AESTHETICS.
THE AMERICANS FUNDED ME BECAUSE THEY ARE PLEASED BY MY PROMISES OF ORDER.
THE RUSSIANS PROMISED PROTECTION BECAUSE I COULD OFFER THEM A SUPERWEAPON TO SAVE THEIR CITY, SO LONG AS THEY GAVE ME FREE REIGN IN THIS LITTLE BUNKER TO BUILD IT...

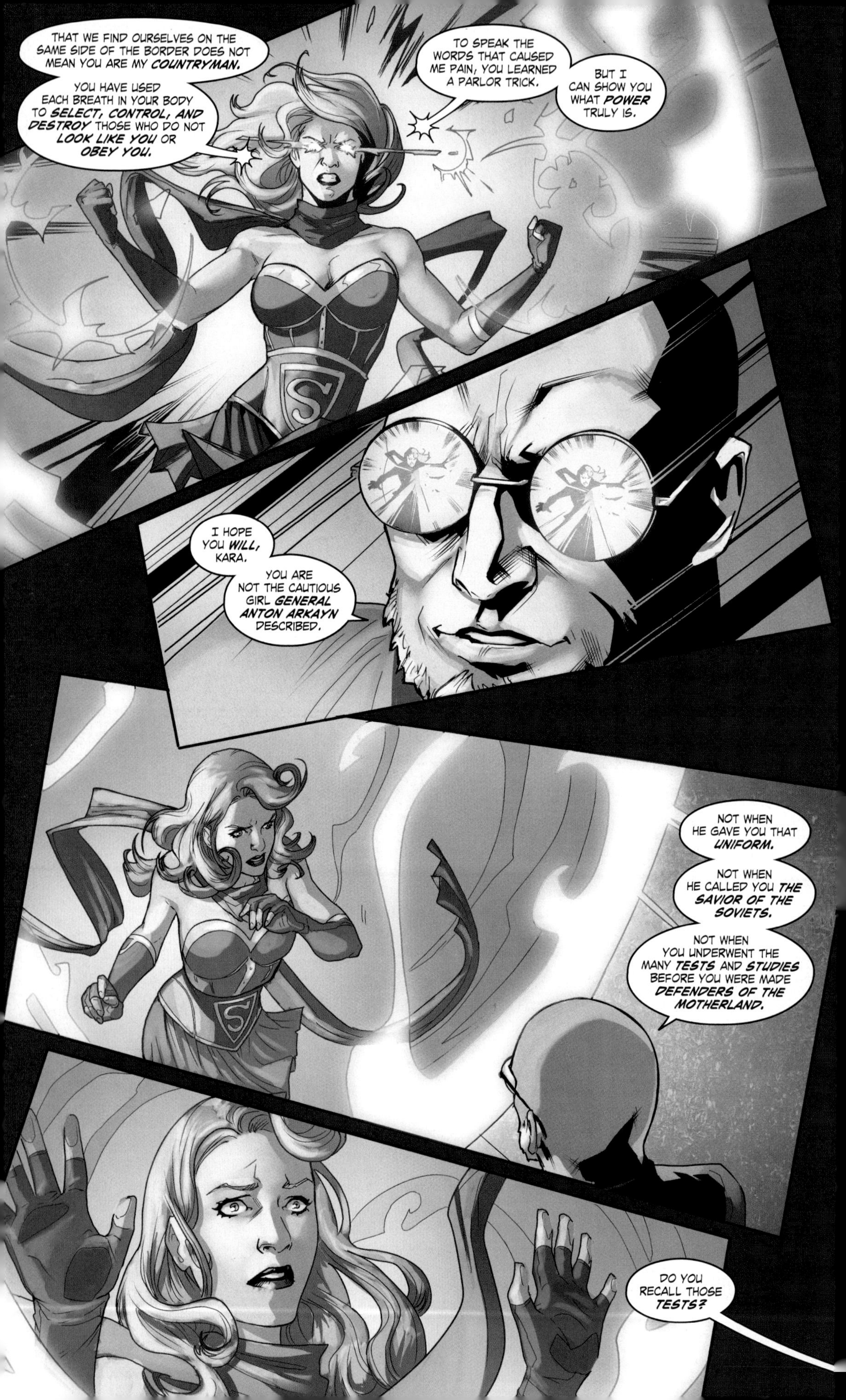
THAT WE FIND OURSELVES ON THE SAME SIDE OF THE BORDER DOES NOT MEAN YOU ARE MY COUNTRYMAN.
YOU HAVE USED EACH BREATH IN YOUR BODY TO SELECT, CONTROL, AND DESTROY THOSE WHO DO NOT LOOK LIKE YOU OR OBEY YOU.
TO SPEAK THE WORDS THAT CAUSED ME PAIN, YOU LEARNED A PARLOR TRICK.
BUT I CAN SHOW YOU WHAT POWER TRULY IS.
I HOPE YOU WILL, KARA.
YOU ARE NOT THE CAUTIOUS GIRL GENERAL ANTON ARKAYN DESCRIBED.
NOT WHEN HE GAVE YOU THAT UNIFORM.
NOT WHEN HE CALLED YOU THE SAVIOR OF THE SOVIETS.
NOT WHEN YOU UNDERWENT THE MANY TESTS AND STUDIES BEFORE YOU WERE MADE DEFENDERS OF THE MOTHERLAND.
DO YOU RECALL THOSE TESTS?

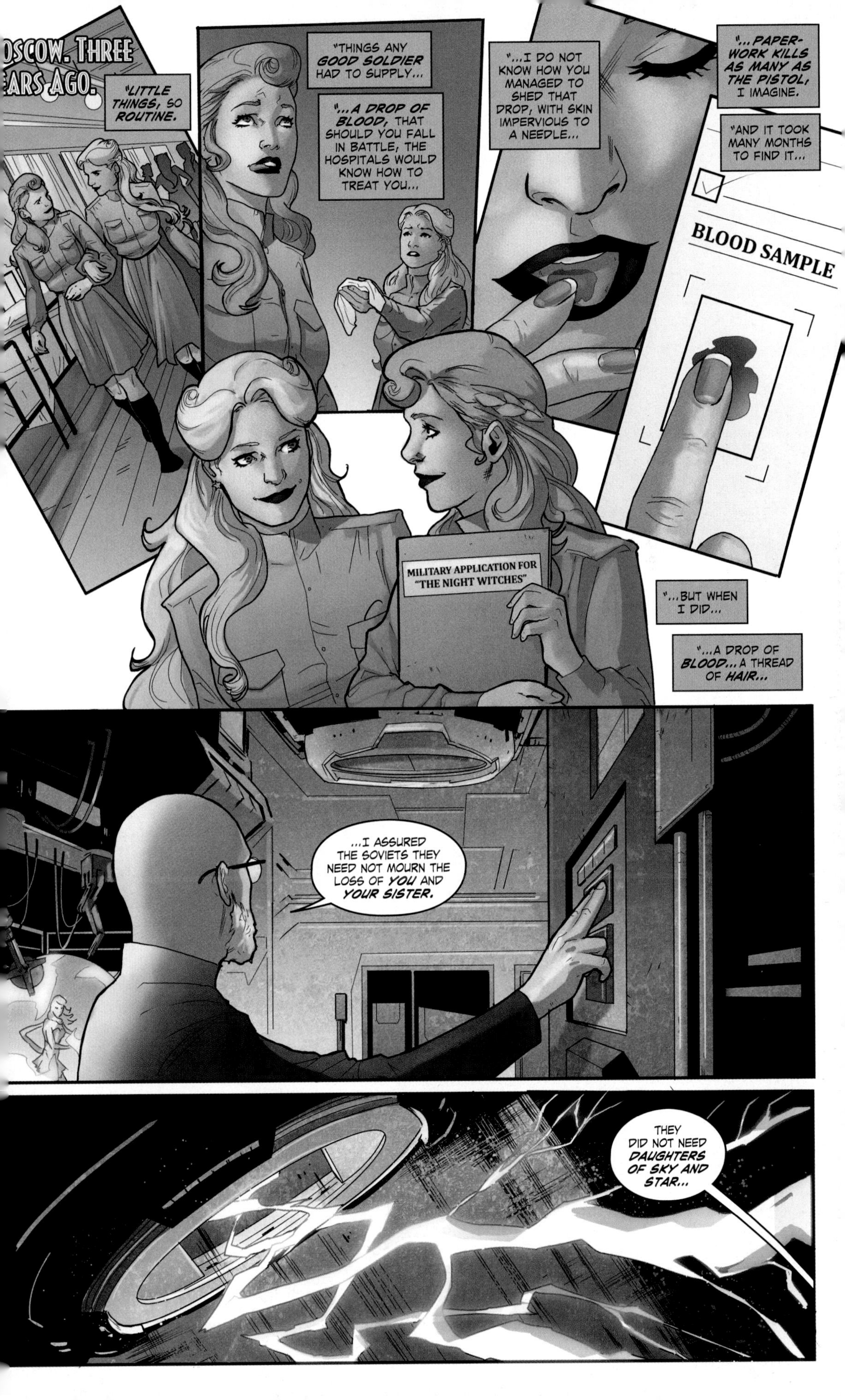
OSCOW. THREE
EARS AGO.
"LITTLE THINGS, SO ROUTINE.
"THINGS ANY GOOD SOLDIER HAD TO SUPPLY...
"...A DROP OF BLOOD, THAT SHOULD YOU FALL IN BATTLE, THE HOSPITALS WOULD KNOW HOW TO TREAT YOU...
"...I DO NOT KNOW HOW YOU MANAGED TO SHED THAT DROP, WITH SKIN IMPERVIOUS TO A NEEDLE...
"...PAPERWORK KILLS AS MANY AS THE PISTOL, I IMAGINE.
"AND IT TOOK MANY MONTHS TO FIND IT...
BLOOD SAMPLE
MILITARY APPLICATION FOR "THE NIGHT WITCHES"
"...BUT WHEN I DID...
"...A DROP OF BLOOD...A THREAD OF HAIR...
...I ASSURED THE SOVIETS THEY NEED NOT MOURN THE LOSS OF YOU AND YOUR SISTER.
THEY DID NOT NEED DAUGHTERS OF SKY AND STAR...

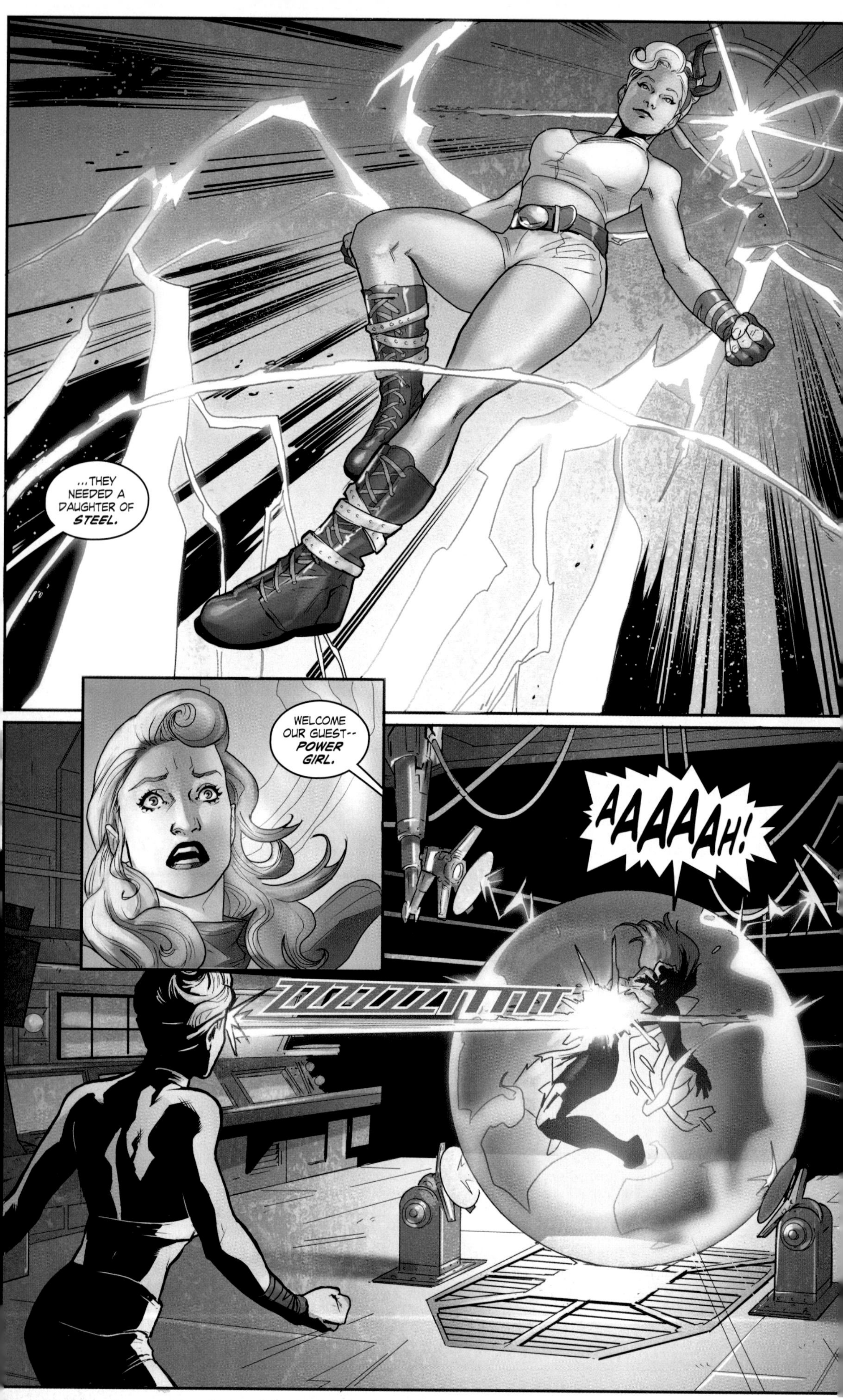
...THEY NEEDED A DAUGHTER OF STEEL.
WELCOME OUR GUEST-- POWER GIRL.
AAAAAH!
ZZZZZZTTTTT

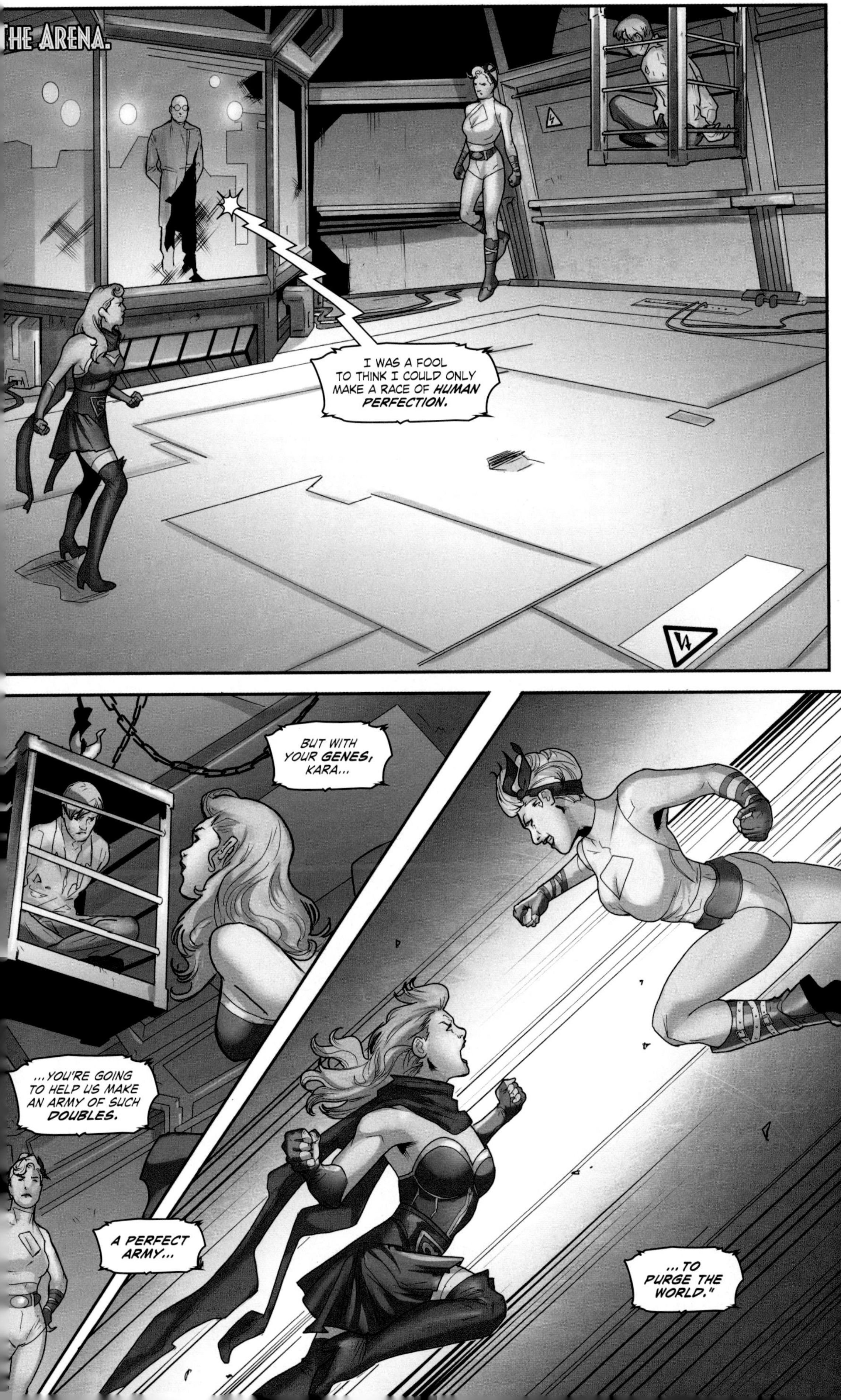
THE ARENA.
I WAS A FOOL TO THINK I COULD ONLY MAKE A RACE OF HUMAN PERFECTION.
BUT WITH YOUR GENES, KARA...
...YOU'RE GOING TO HELP US MAKE AN ARMY OF SUCH DOUBLES.
A PERFECT ARMY...
...TO PURGE THE WORLD."

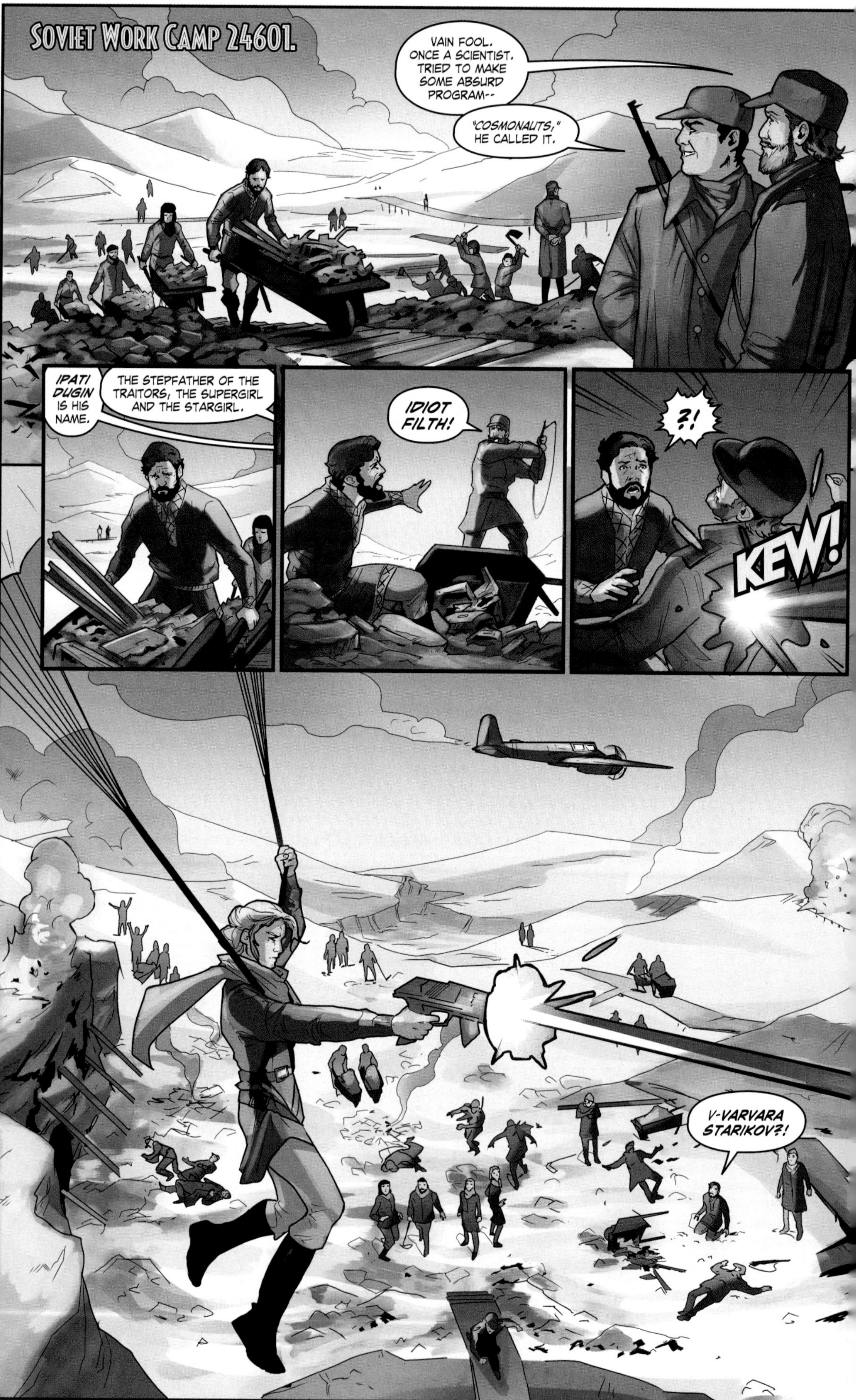
SOVIET WORK CAMP 24601.
VAIN FOOL. ONCE A SCIENTIST. TRIED TO MAKE SOME ABSURD PROGRAM--
"COSMONAUTS," HE CALLED IT.
IPATI DUGIN IS HIS NAME.
THE STEPFATHER OF THE TRAITORS, THE SUPERGIRL AND THE STARGIRL.
IDIOT FILTH!
?!
KEW!
V-VARVARA STARIKOV?!

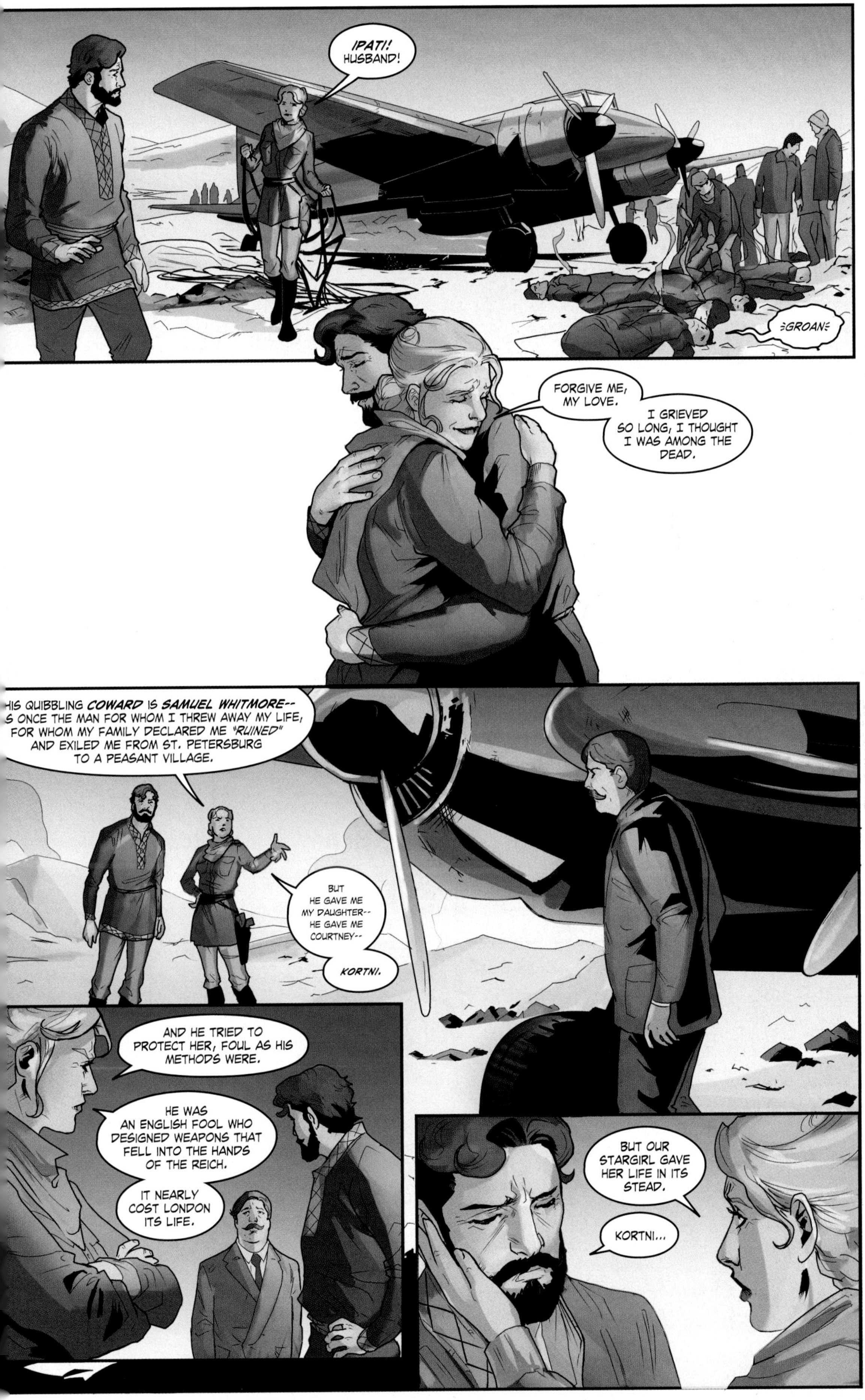

IPATI! HUSBAND!
GROAN
FORGIVE ME, MY LOVE.
I GRIEVED SO LONG, I THOUGHT I WAS AMONG THE DEAD.
HIS QUIBBLING COWARD IS SAMUEL WHITMORE-- S ONCE THE MAN FOR WHOM I THREW AWAY MY LIFE, FOR WHOM MY FAMILY DECLARED ME "RUINED" AND EXILED ME FROM ST. PETERSBURG TO A PEASANT VILLAGE.
BUT HE GAVE ME MY DAUGHTER-- HE GAVE ME COURTNEY--
KORTNI.
AND HE TRIED TO PROTECT HER, FOUL AS HIS METHODS WERE.
HE WAS AN ENGLISH FOOL WHO DESIGNED WEAPONS THAT FELL INTO THE HANDS OF THE REICH.
IT NEARLY COST LONDON ITS LIFE.
BUT OUR STARGIRL GAVE HER LIFE IN ITS STEAD.
KORTNI...

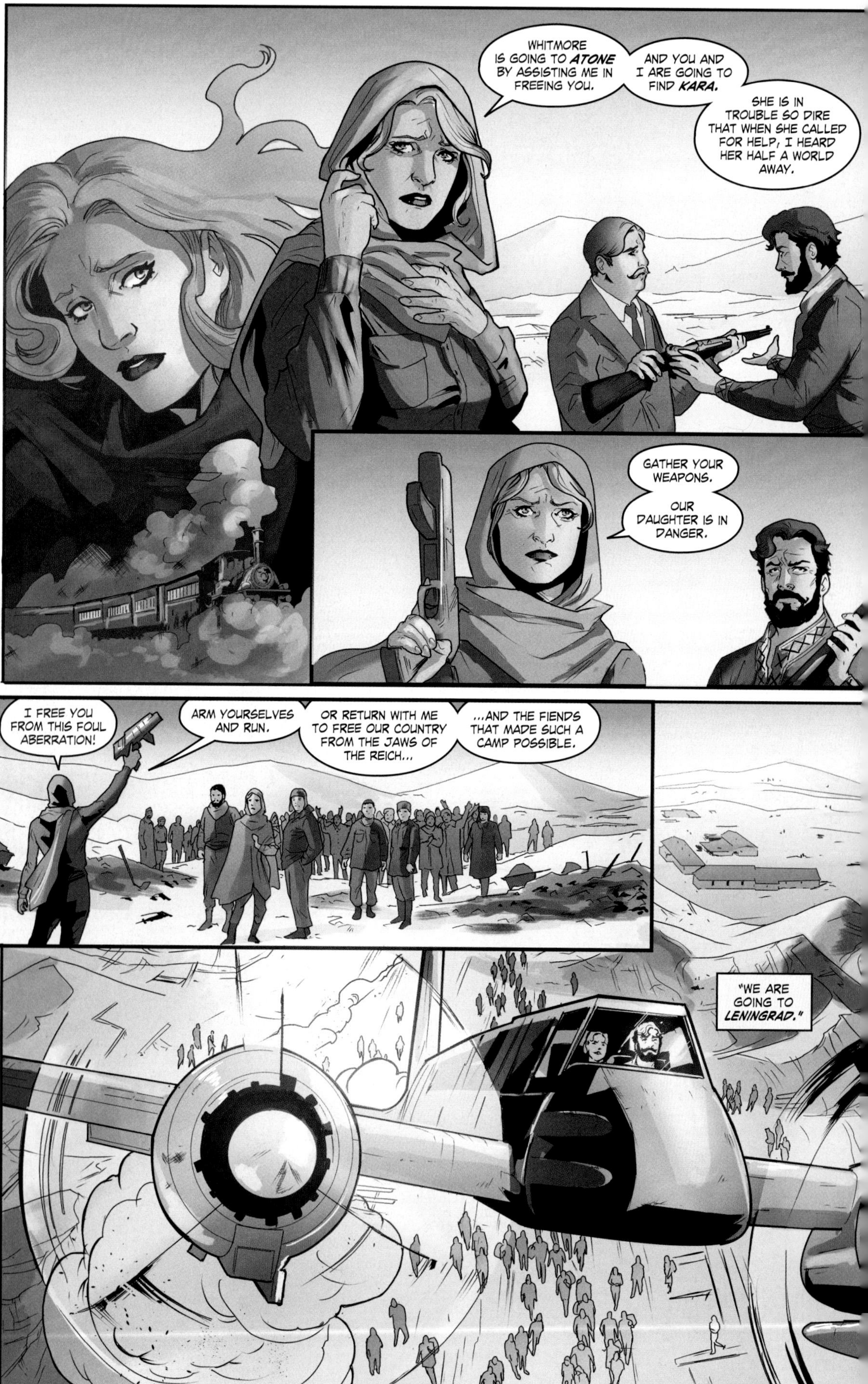
WHITMORE IS GOING TO ATONE BY ASSISTING ME IN FREEING YOU.
AND YOU AND I ARE GOING TO FIND KARA.
SHE IS IN TROUBLE SO DIRE THAT WHEN SHE CALLED FOR HELP, I HEARD HER HALF A WORLD AWAY.
GATHER YOUR WEAPONS.
OUR DAUGHTER IS IN DANGER.
I FREE YOU FROM THIS FOUL ABERRATION!
ARM YOURSELVES AND RUN.
OR RETURN WITH ME TO FREE OUR COUNTRY FROM THE JAWS OF THE REICH...
...AND THE FIENDS THAT MADE SUCH A CAMP POSSIBLE.
"WE ARE GOING TO LENINGRAD."

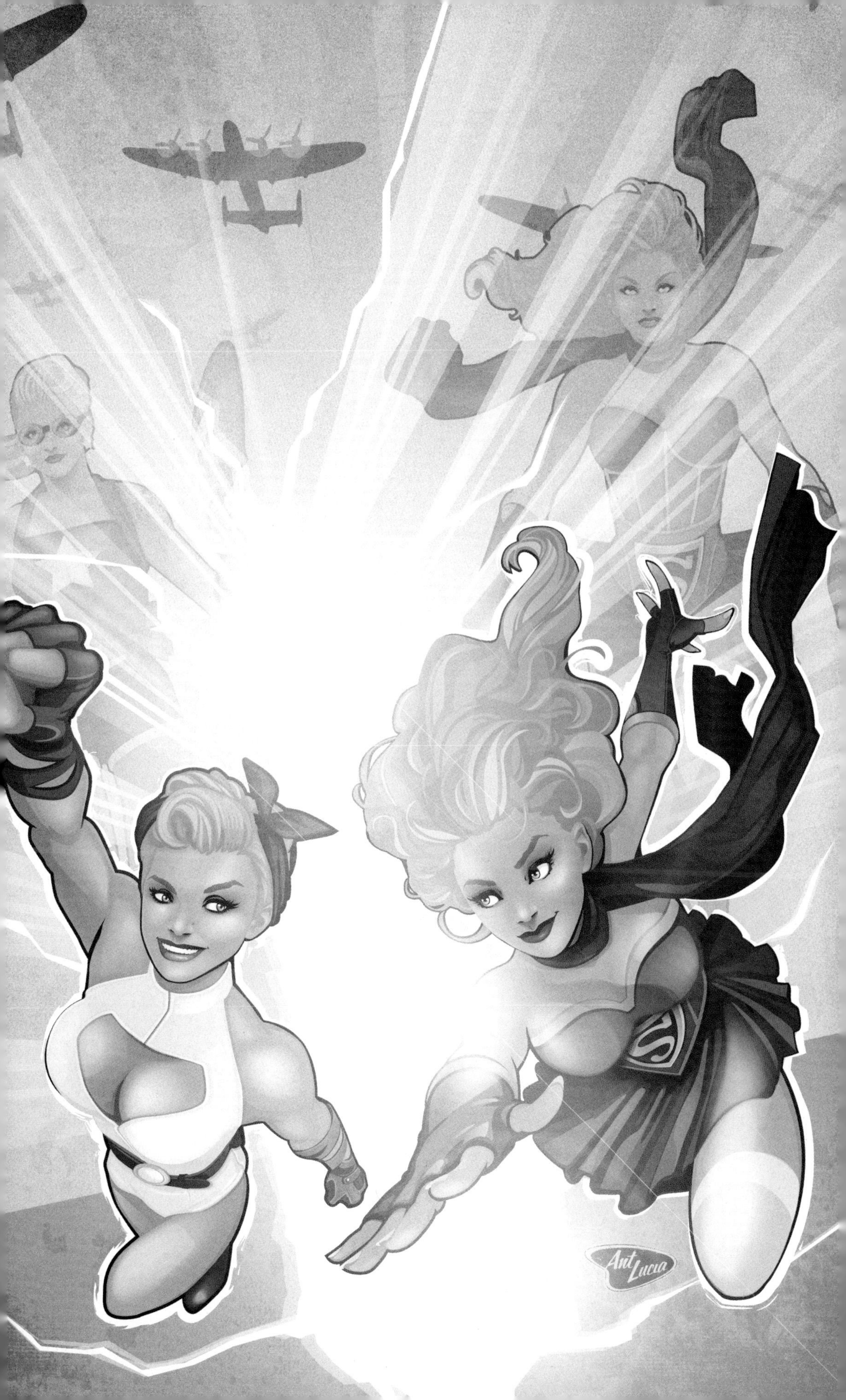
Ant Lucia

SUPER WEAPON

MARGUERITE BENNETT
Writer

LAURA BRAGA
ANEKE
Artists

J. NANJAN
WENDY BROOME
Colorists

Cover by
ANT LUCIA

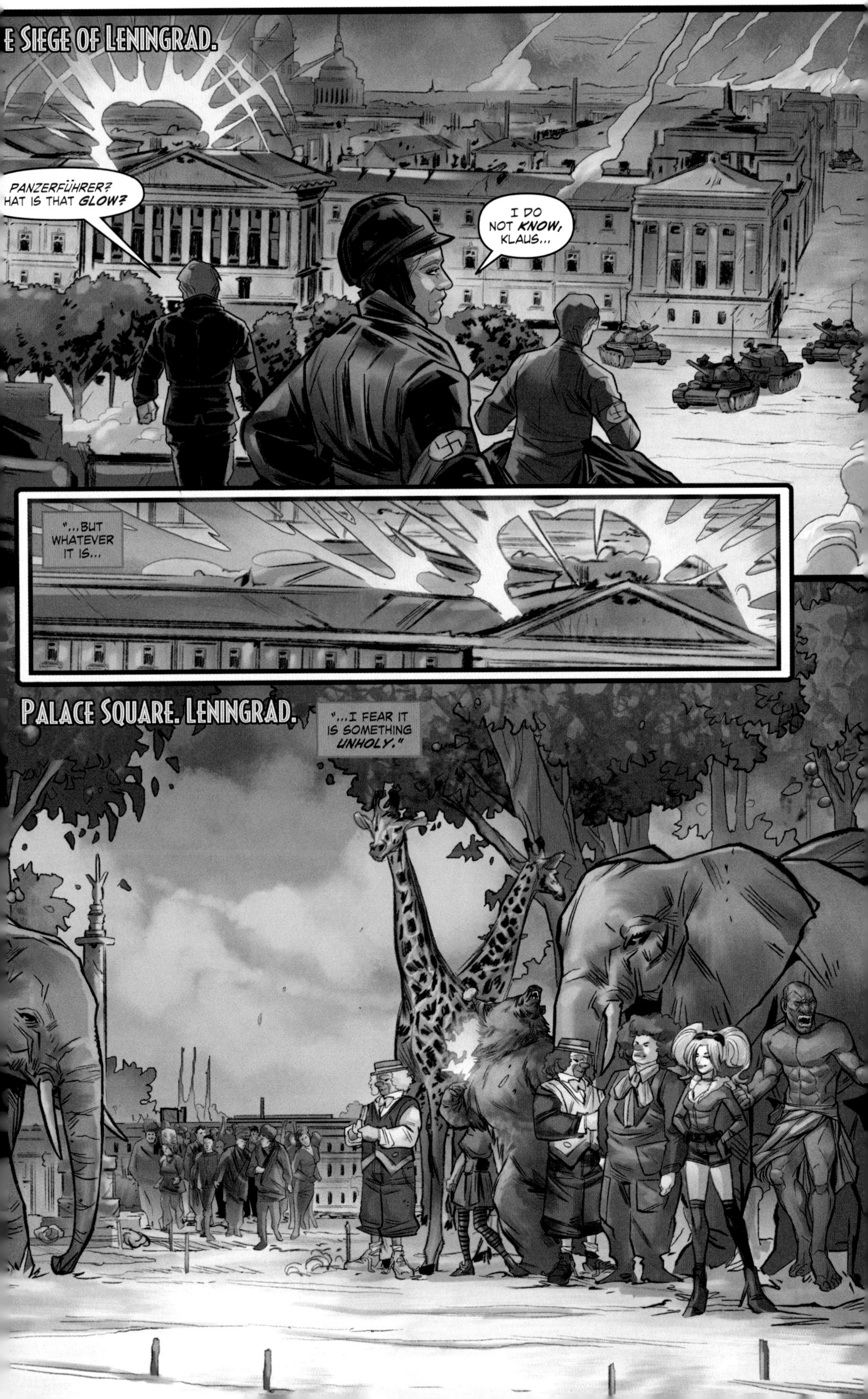
E SIEGE OF LENINGRAD.
PANZERFÜHRER? HAT IS THAT GLOW?
I DO NOT KNOW, KLAUS...
"...BUT WHATEVER IT IS...
PALACE SQUARE. LENINGRAD.
"...I FEAR IT IS SOMETHING UNHOLY."

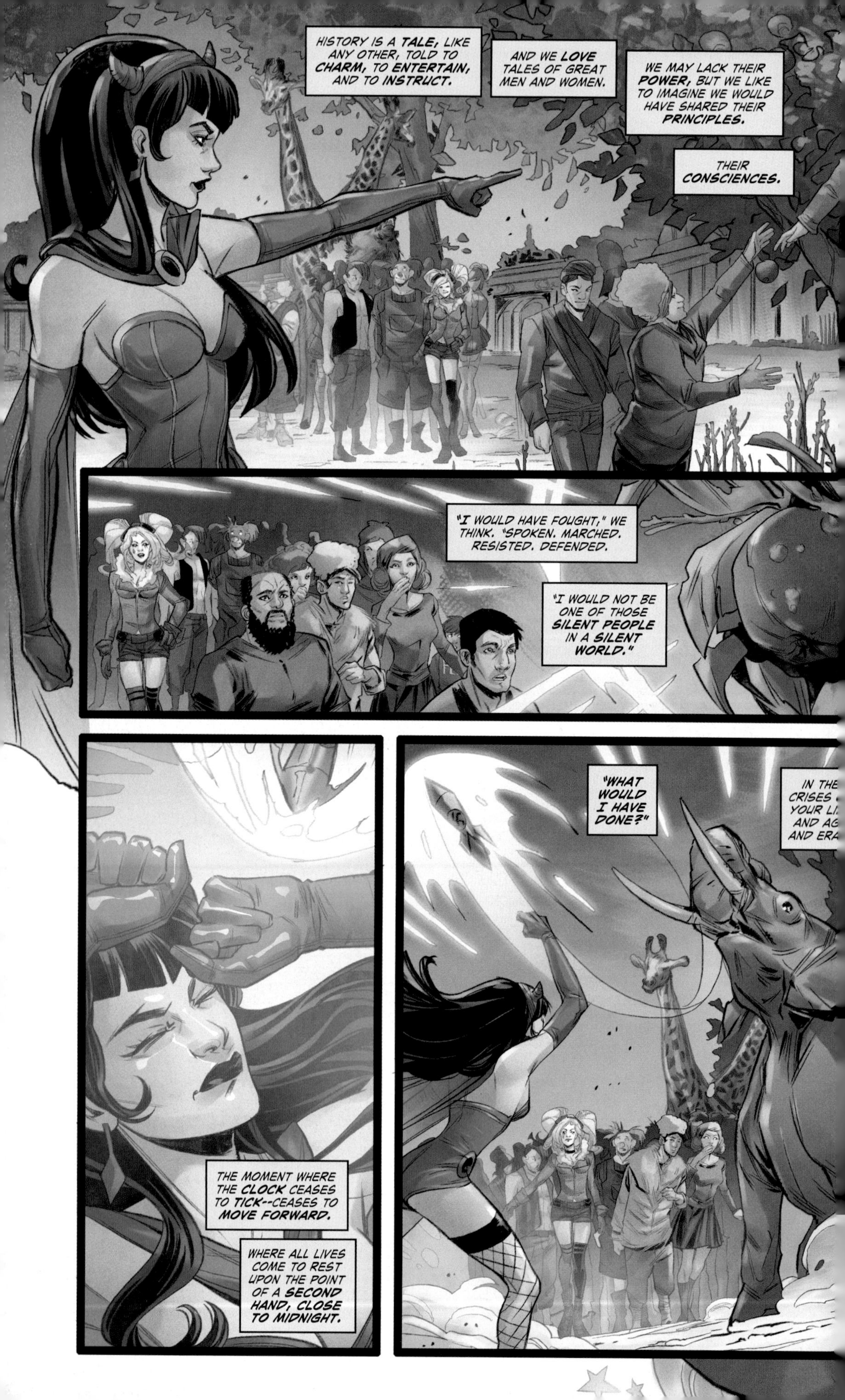
HISTORY IS A TALE, LIKE ANY OTHER, TOLD TO CHARM, TO ENTERTAIN, AND TO INSTRUCT.
AND WE LOVE TALES OF GREAT MEN AND WOMEN.
WE MAY LACK THEIR POWER, BUT WE LIKE TO IMAGINE WE WOULD HAVE SHARED THEIR PRINCIPLES.
THEIR CONSCIENCES.
"I WOULD HAVE FOUGHT," WE THINK. "SPOKEN. MARCHED. RESISTED. DEFENDED.
"I WOULD NOT BE ONE OF THOSE SILENT PEOPLE IN A SILENT WORLD."
THE MOMENT WHERE THE CLOCK CEASES TO TICK--CEASES TO MOVE FORWARD.
WHERE ALL LIVES COME TO REST UPON THE POINT OF A SECOND HAND, CLOSE TO MIDNIGHT.
"WHAT WOULD I HAVE DONE?"

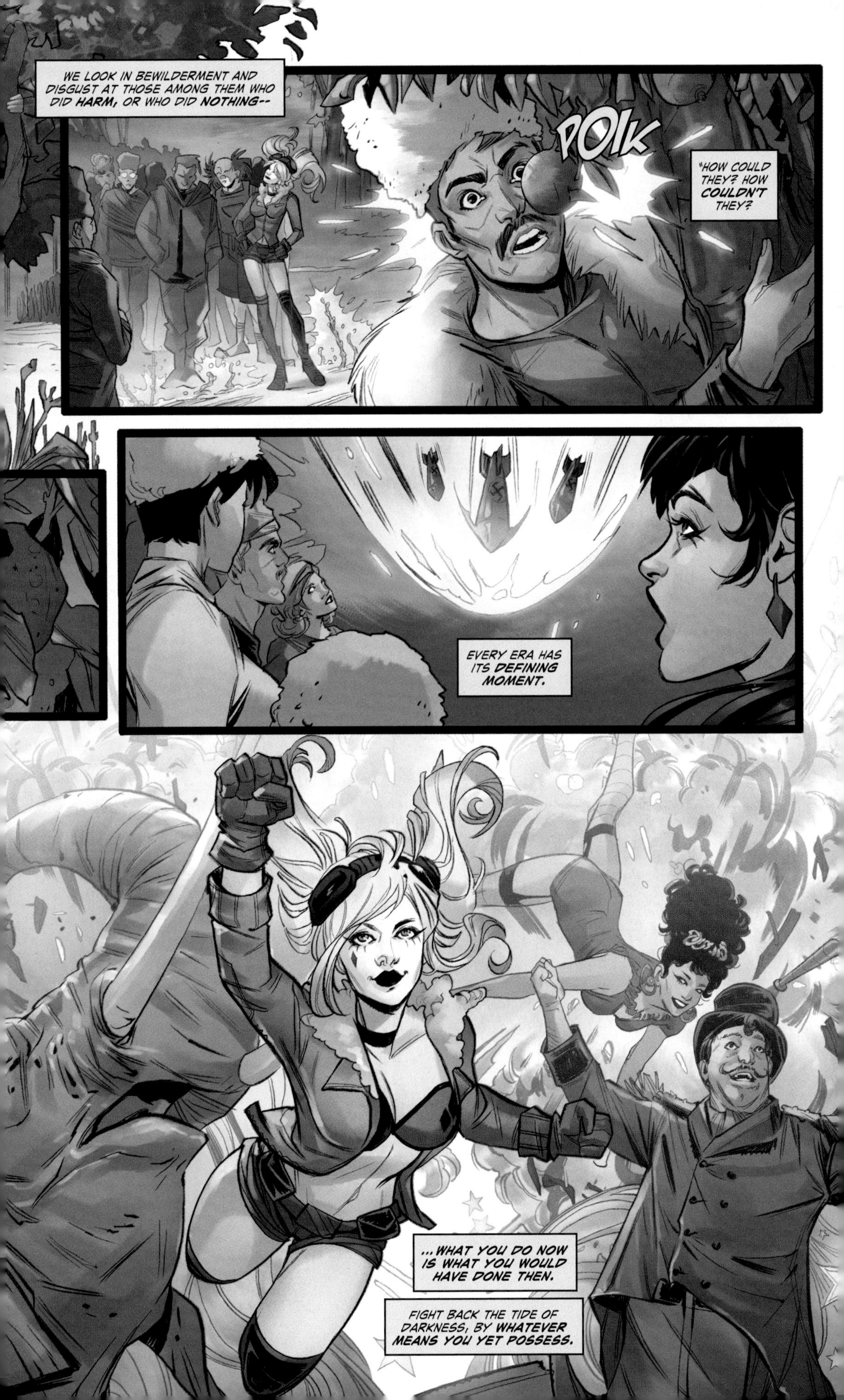
WE LOOK IN BEWILDERMENT AND DISGUST AT THOSE AMONG THEM WHO DID HARM, OR WHO DID NOTHING--
POIK
"HOW COULD THEY? HOW COULDN'T THEY?
EVERY ERA HAS ITS DEFINING MOMENT.
...WHAT YOU DO NOW IS WHAT YOU WOULD HAVE DONE THEN.
FIGHT BACK THE TIDE OF DARKNESS, BY WHATEVER MEANS YOU YET POSSESS.

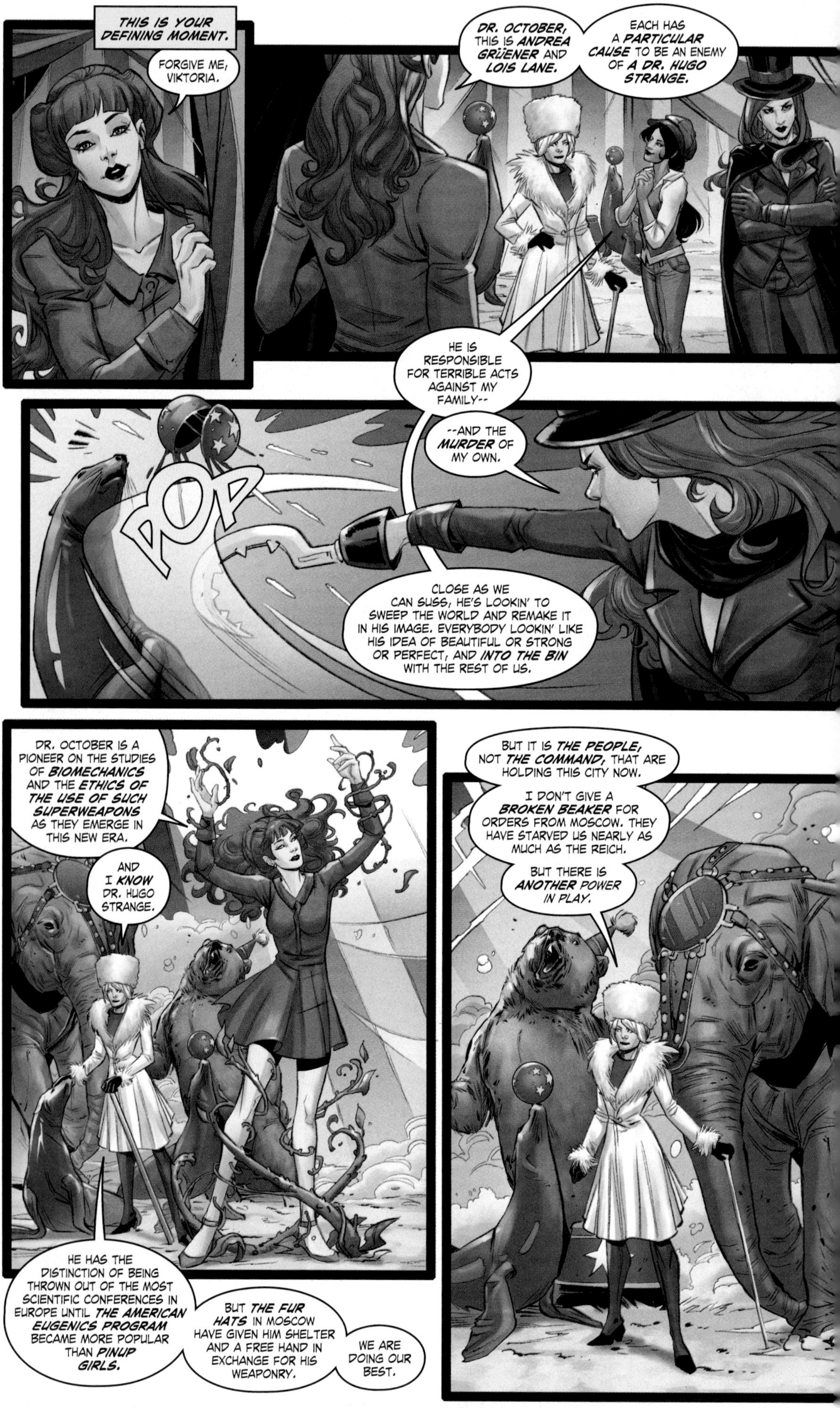
THIS IS YOUR DEFINING MOMENT.
FORGIVE ME, VIKTORIA.
DR. OCTOBER, THIS IS ANDREA GRÜENER AND LOIS LANE.
EACH HAS A PARTICULAR CAUSE TO BE AN ENEMY OF A DR. HUGO STRANGE.
HE IS RESPONSIBLE FOR TERRIBLE ACTS AGAINST MY FAMILY--
--AND THE MURDER OF MY OWN.
POP
CLOSE AS WE CAN SUSS, HE'S LOOKIN' TO SWEEP THE WORLD AND REMAKE IT IN HIS IMAGE. EVERYBODY LOOKIN' LIKE HIS IDEA OF BEAUTIFUL OR STRONG OR PERFECT, AND INTO THE BIN WITH THE REST OF US.
DR. OCTOBER IS A PIONEER ON THE STUDIES OF BIOMECHANICS AND THE ETHICS OF THE USE OF SUCH SUPERWEAPONS AS THEY EMERGE IN THIS NEW ERA.
AND I KNOW DR. HUGO STRANGE.
HE HAS THE DISTINCTION OF BEING THROWN OUT OF THE MOST SCIENTIFIC CONFERENCES IN EUROPE UNTIL THE AMERICAN EUGENICS PROGRAM BECAME MORE POPULAR THAN PINUP GIRLS.
BUT THE FUR HATS IN MOSCOW HAVE GIVEN HIM SHELTER AND A FREE HAND IN EXCHANGE FOR HIS WEAPONRY.
WE ARE DOING OUR BEST.
BUT IT IS THE PEOPLE, NOT THE COMMAND, THAT ARE HOLDING THIS CITY NOW.
I DON'T GIVE A BROKEN BEAKER FOR ORDERS FROM MOSCOW. THEY HAVE STARVED US NEARLY AS MUCH AS THE REICH.
BUT THERE IS ANOTHER POWER IN PLAY.

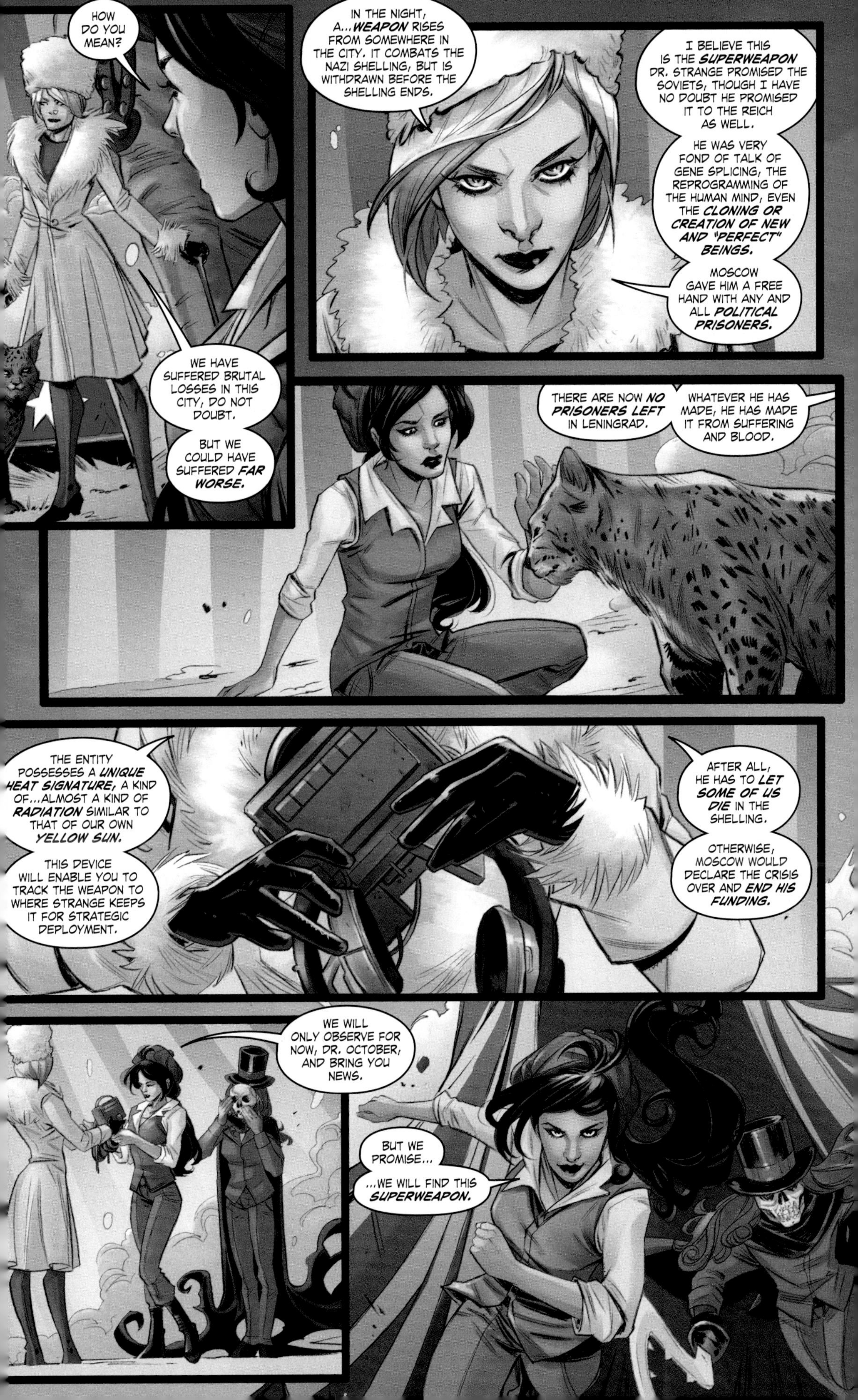

HOW DO YOU MEAN?
IN THE NIGHT, A... WEAPON RISES FROM SOMEWHERE IN THE CITY. IT COMBATS THE NAZI SHELLING, BUT IS WITHDRAWN BEFORE THE SHELLING ENDS.
I BELIEVE THIS IS THE SUPERWEAPON DR. STRANGE PROMISED THE SOVIETS, THOUGH I HAVE NO DOUBT HE PROMISED IT TO THE REICH AS WELL.
HE WAS VERY FOND OF TALK OF GENE SPLICING, THE REPROGRAMMING OF THE HUMAN MIND, EVEN THE CLONING OR CREATION OF NEW AND "PERFECT" BEINGS.
MOSCOW GAVE HIM A FREE HAND WITH ANY AND ALL POLITICAL PRISONERS.
WE HAVE SUFFERED BRUTAL LOSSES IN THIS CITY, DO NOT DOUBT.
BUT WE COULD HAVE SUFFERED FAR WORSE.
THERE ARE NOW NO PRISONERS LEFT IN LENINGRAD.
WHATEVER HE HAS MADE, HE HAS MADE IT FROM SUFFERING AND BLOOD.
THE ENTITY POSSESSES A UNIQUE HEAT SIGNATURE, A KIND OF...ALMOST A KIND OF RADIATION SIMILAR TO THAT OF OUR OWN YELLOW SUN.
THIS DEVICE WILL ENABLE YOU TO TRACK THE WEAPON TO WHERE STRANGE KEEPS IT FOR STRATEGIC DEPLOYMENT.
AFTER ALL, HE HAS TO LET SOME OF US DIE IN THE SHELLING.
OTHERWISE, MOSCOW WOULD DECLARE THE CRISIS OVER AND END HIS FUNDING.
WE WILL ONLY OBSERVE FOR NOW, DR. OCTOBER, AND BRING YOU NEWS.
BUT WE PROMISE...
...WE WILL FIND THIS SUPERWEAPON.

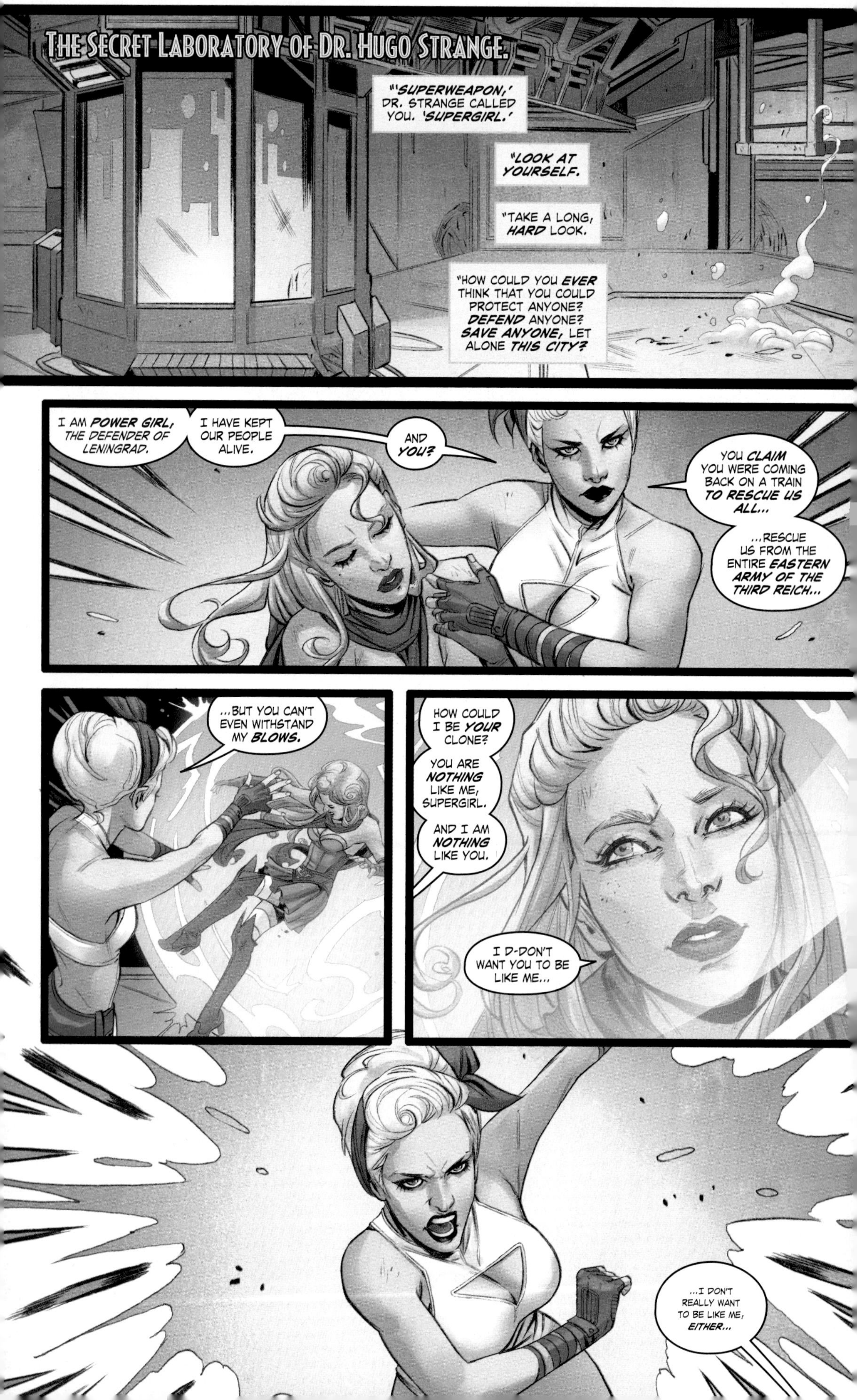

THE SECRET LABORATORY OF DR. HUGO STRANGE.
"'SUPERWEAPON,' DR. STRANGE CALLED YOU. 'SUPERGIRL.'
"LOOK AT YOURSELF.
"TAKE A LONG, HARD LOOK.
"HOW COULD YOU EVER THINK THAT YOU COULD PROTECT ANYONE? DEFEND ANYONE? SAVE ANYONE, LET ALONE THIS CITY?
I AM POWER GIRL, THE DEFENDER OF LENINGRAD.
I HAVE KEPT OUR PEOPLE ALIVE.
AND YOU?
YOU CLAIM YOU WERE COMING BACK ON A TRAIN TO RESCUE US ALL...
...RESCUE US FROM THE ENTIRE EASTERN ARMY OF THE THIRD REICH...
...BUT YOU CAN'T EVEN WITHSTAND MY BLOWS.
HOW COULD I BE YOUR CLONE?
YOU ARE NOTHING LIKE ME, SUPERGIRL.
AND I AM NOTHING LIKE YOU.
I D-DON'T WANT YOU TO BE LIKE ME...
...I DON'T REALLY WANT TO BE LIKE ME, EITHER...

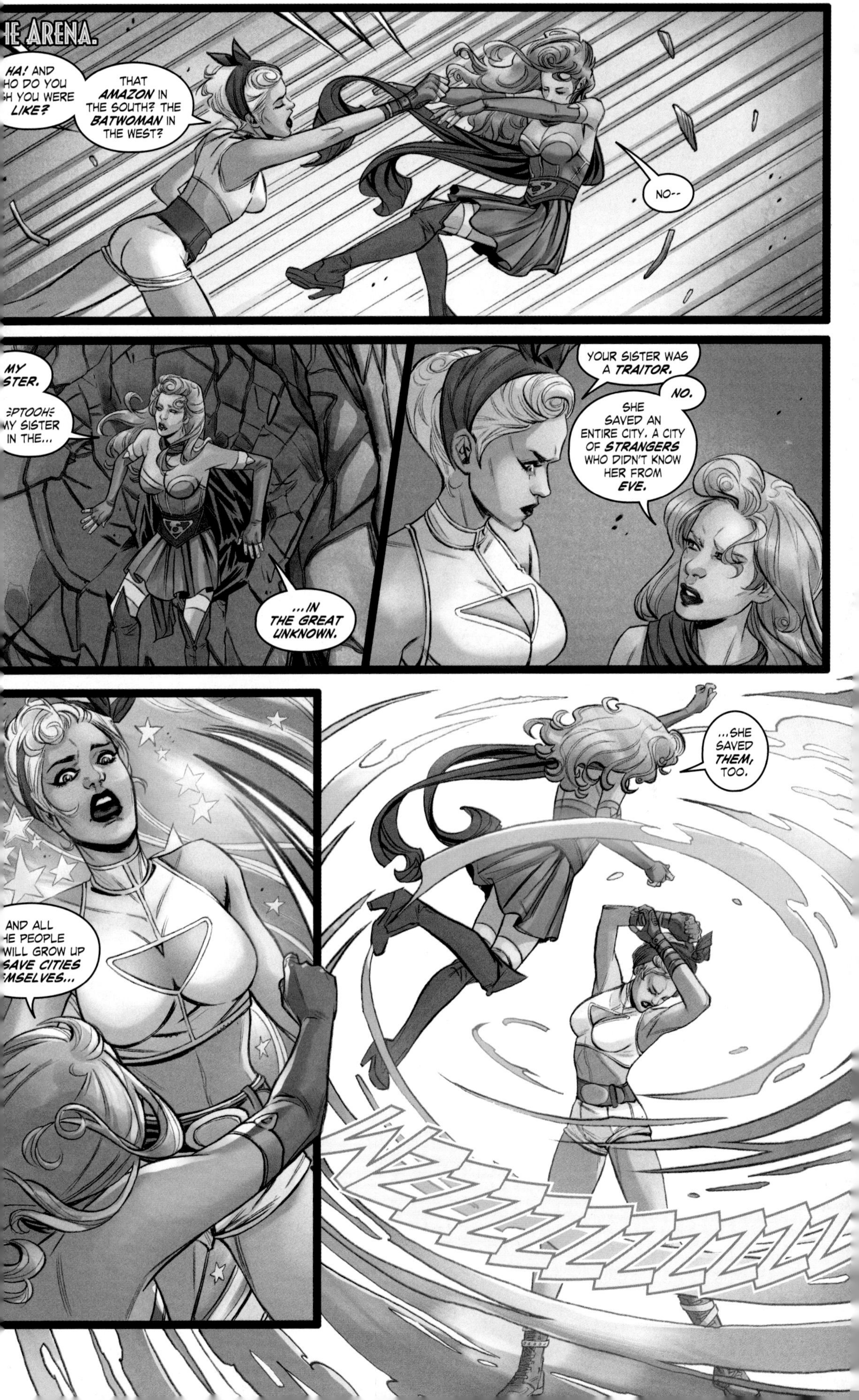
HE ARENA.
HA! AND HO DO YOU GH YOU WERE LIKE?
THAT AMAZON IN THE SOUTH? THE BATWOMAN IN THE WEST?
NO--
MY STER.
PTOOH! MY SISTER IN THE...
...IN THE GREAT UNKNOWN.
YOUR SISTER WAS A TRAITOR.
NO.
SHE SAVED AN ENTIRE CITY. A CITY OF STRANGERS WHO DIDN'T KNOW HER FROM EVE.
AND ALL HE PEOPLE WILL GROW UP SAVE CITIES MSELVES...
...SHE SAVED THEM, TOO.
WZZZZZZZZZZZZ

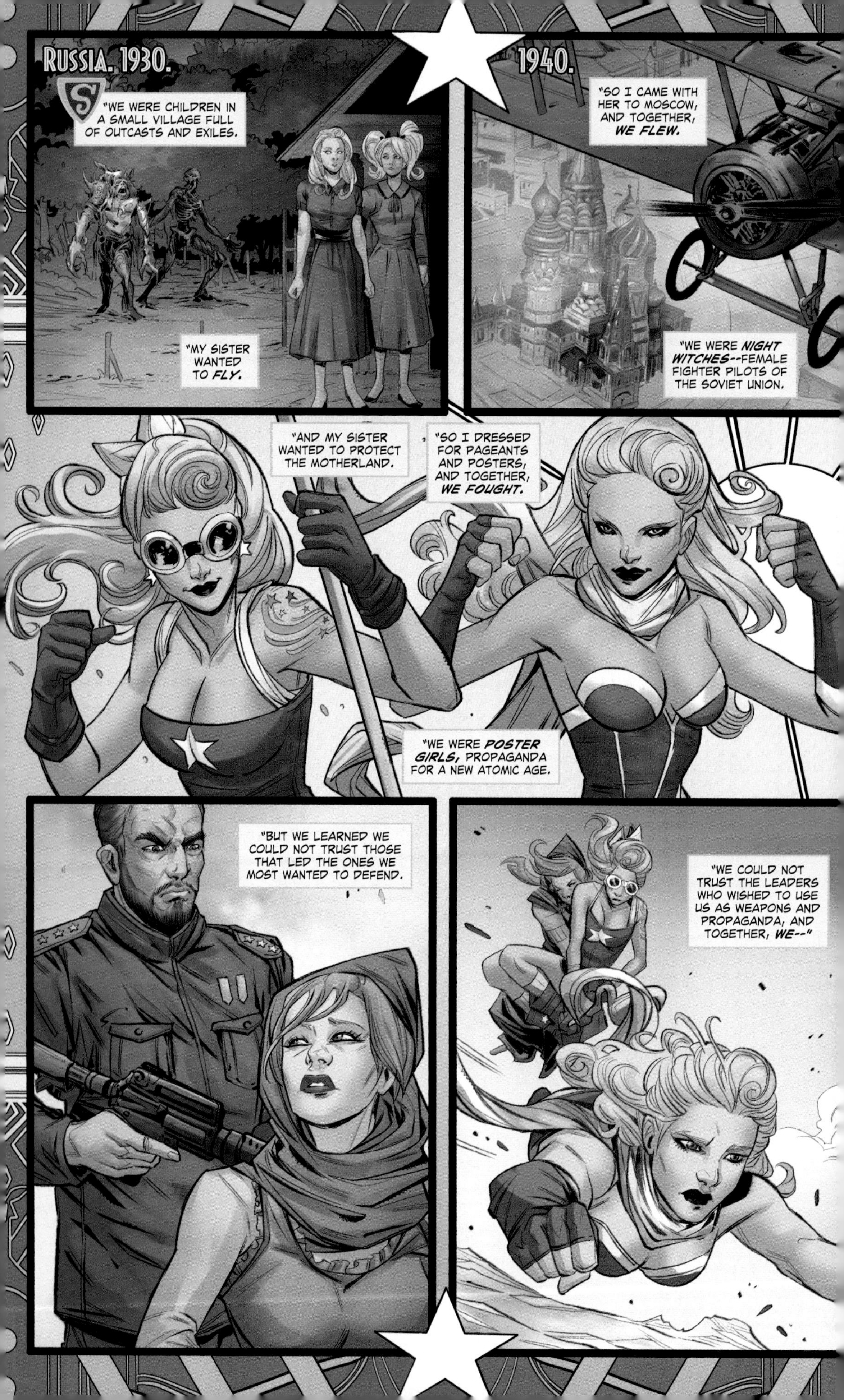
RUSSIA. 1930.
"WE WERE CHILDREN IN A SMALL VILLAGE FULL OF OUTCASTS AND EXILES.
"MY SISTER WANTED TO FLY.
1940.
"SO I CAME WITH HER TO MOSCOW, AND TOGETHER, WE FLEW.
"WE WERE NIGHT WITCHES--FEMALE FIGHTER PILOTS OF THE SOVIET UNION.
"AND MY SISTER WANTED TO PROTECT THE MOTHERLAND.
"SO I DRESSED FOR PAGEANTS AND POSTERS, AND TOGETHER, WE FOUGHT.
"WE WERE POSTER GIRLS, PROPAGANDA FOR A NEW ATOMIC AGE.
"BUT WE LEARNED WE COULD NOT TRUST THOSE THAT LED THE ONES WE MOST WANTED TO DEFEND.
"WE COULD NOT TRUST THE LEADERS WHO WISHED TO USE US AS WEAPONS AND PROPAGANDA, AND TOGETHER, WE--"

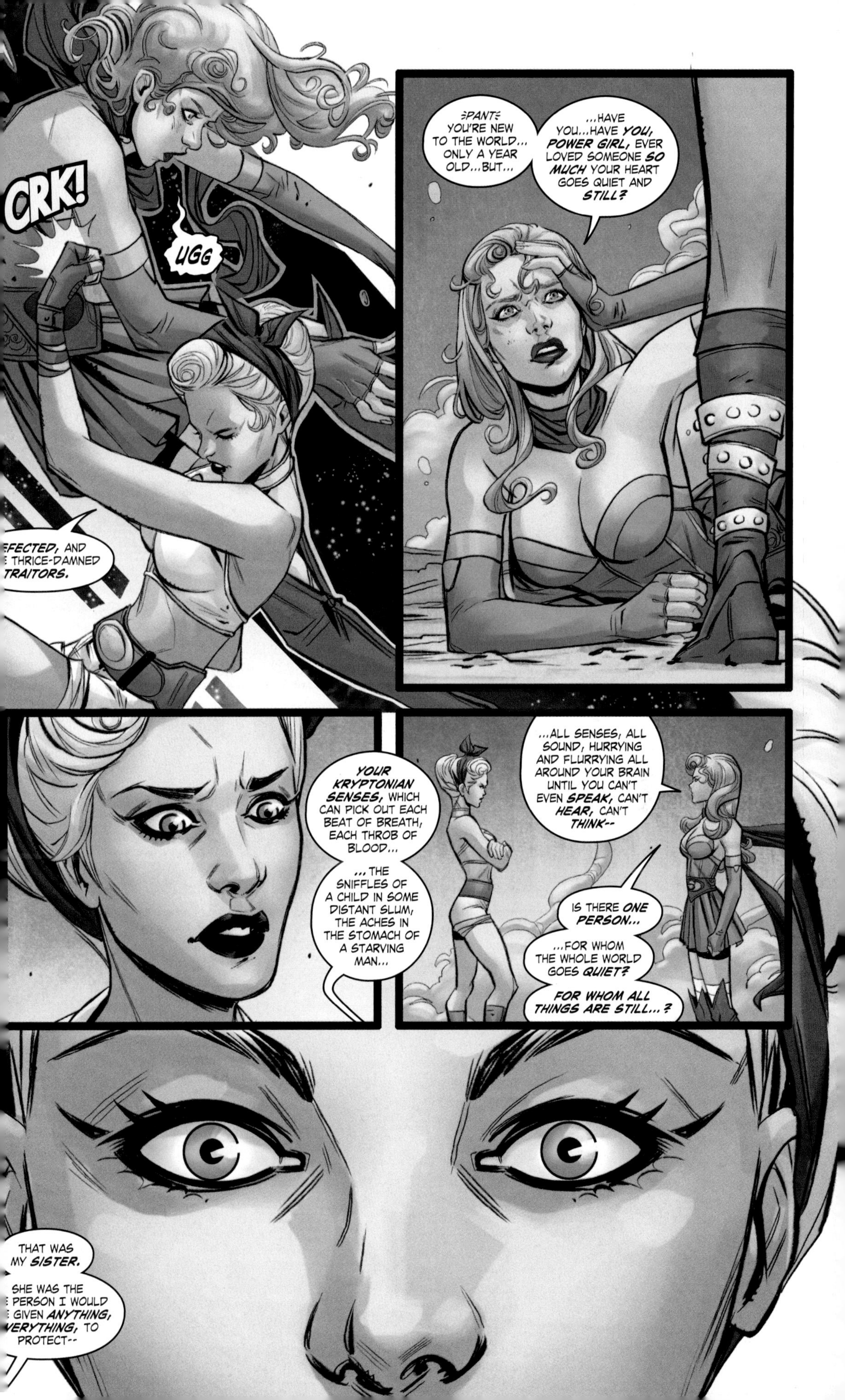
CRK!
UGG
...FECTED, AND ...E THRICE-DAMNED TRAITORS.
=PANT= YOU'RE NEW TO THE WORLD... ONLY A YEAR OLD...BUT...
...HAVE YOU...HAVE YOU, POWER GIRL, EVER LOVED SOMEONE SO MUCH YOUR HEART GOES QUIET AND STILL?
YOUR KRYPTONIAN SENSES, WHICH CAN PICK OUT EACH BEAT OF BREATH, EACH THROB OF BLOOD...
...THE SNIFFLES OF A CHILD IN SOME DISTANT SLUM, THE ACHES IN THE STOMACH OF A STARVING MAN...
...ALL SENSES, ALL SOUND, HURRYING AND FLURRYING ALL AROUND YOUR BRAIN UNTIL YOU CAN'T EVEN SPEAK, CAN'T HEAR, CAN'T THINK--
IS THERE ONE PERSON...
...FOR WHOM THE WHOLE WORLD GOES QUIET?
FOR WHOM ALL THINGS ARE STILL...?
THAT WAS MY SISTER.
SHE WAS THE ...E PERSON I WOULD ...E GIVEN ANYTHING, ...VERYTHING, TO PROTECT--

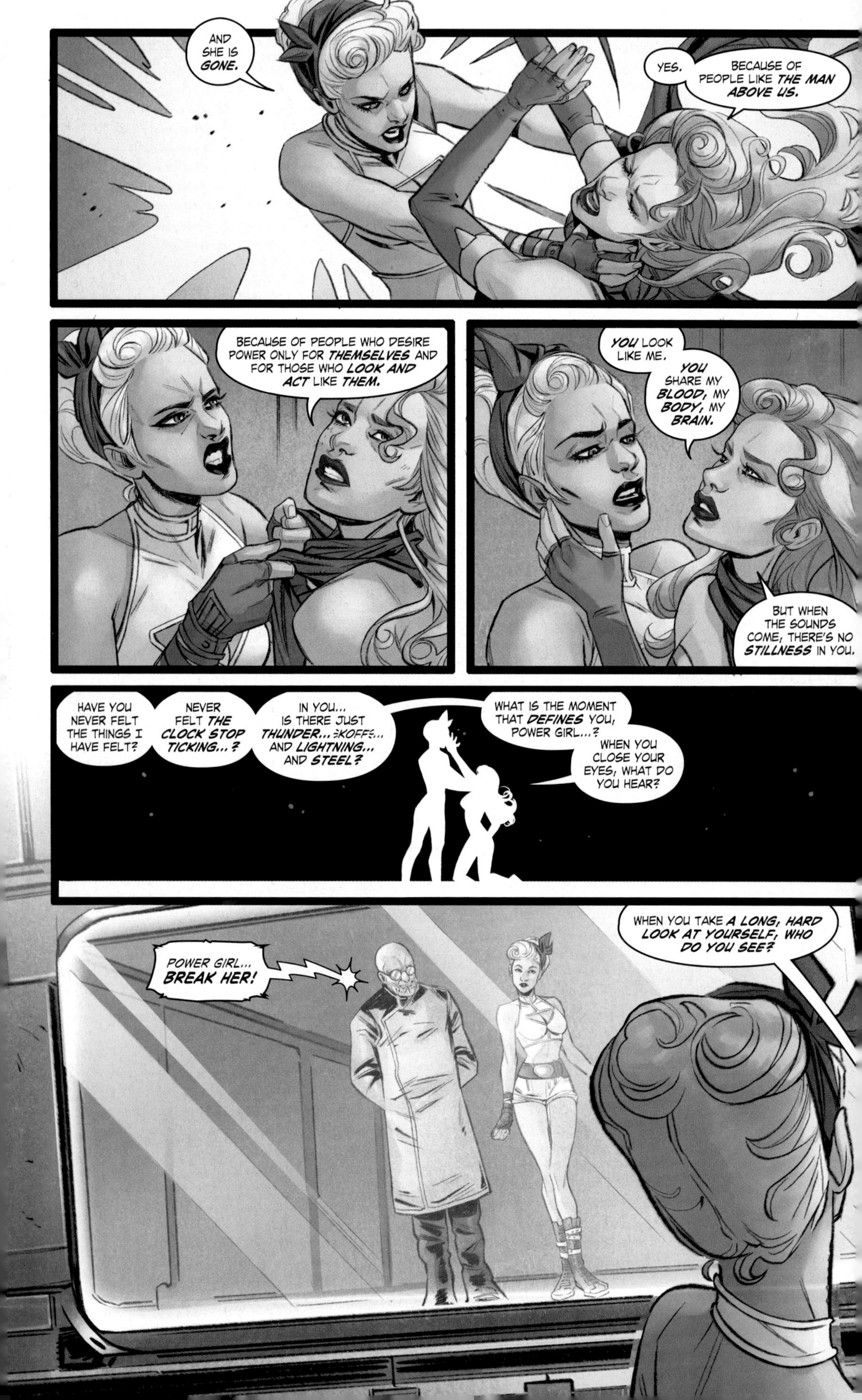
AND SHE IS GONE.
YES.
BECAUSE OF PEOPLE LIKE THE MAN ABOVE US.
BECAUSE OF PEOPLE WHO DESIRE POWER ONLY FOR THEMSELVES AND FOR THOSE WHO LOOK AND ACT LIKE THEM.
YOU LOOK LIKE ME.
YOU SHARE MY BLOOD, MY BODY, MY BRAIN.
BUT WHEN THE SOUNDS COME, THERE'S NO STILLNESS IN YOU.
HAVE YOU NEVER FELT THE THINGS I HAVE FELT?
NEVER FELT THE CLOCK STOP TICKING...?
IN YOU... IS THERE JUST THUNDER... SKOFFS... AND LIGHTNING... AND STEEL?
WHAT IS THE MOMENT THAT DEFINES YOU, POWER GIRL...?
WHEN YOU CLOSE YOUR EYES, WHAT DO YOU HEAR?
POWER GIRL... BREAK HER!
WHEN YOU TAKE A LONG, HARD LOOK AT YOURSELF, WHO DO YOU SEE?

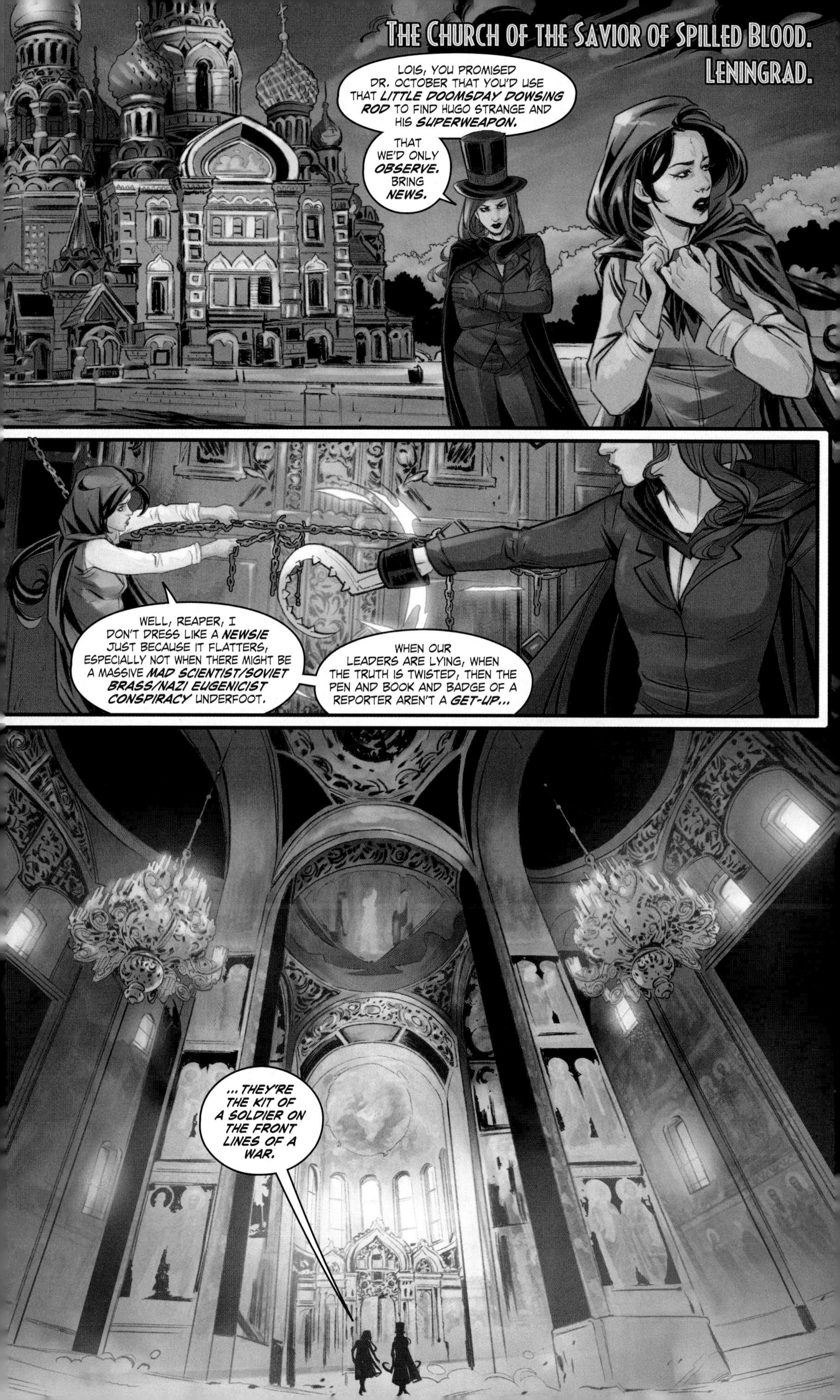
THE CHURCH OF THE SAVIOR OF SPILLED BLOOD. LENINGRAD.
LOIS, YOU PROMISED DR. OCTOBER THAT YOU'D USE THAT LITTLE DOOMSDAY DOWSING ROD TO FIND HUGO STRANGE AND HIS SUPERWEAPON.
THAT WE'D ONLY OBSERVE. BRING NEWS.
WELL, REAPER, I DON'T DRESS LIKE A NEWSIE JUST BECAUSE IT FLATTERS, ESPECIALLY NOT WHEN THERE MIGHT BE A MASSIVE MAD SCIENTIST/SOVIET BRASS/NAZI EUGENICIST CONSPIRACY UNDERFOOT.
WHEN OUR LEADERS ARE LYING, WHEN THE TRUTH IS TWISTED, THEN THE PEN AND BOOK AND BADGE OF A REPORTER AREN'T A GET-UP...
...THEY'RE THE KIT OF A SOLDIER ON THE FRONT LINES OF A WAR.

LOIS, IF YOU WERE ALWAYS PLANNING ON DOING A LITTLE MORE THAN *RECONNAISSANCE*, I WON'T GET IN TROUBLE FOR *CROSSING MY HOOKS* BEHIND MY BACK?

I'M NOT SAYING LET'S GET INTO A *SCRAPE*.

SPEAKING OF-- GOLLY, EVERY SCRAP OF GOLD IN HERE HAS BEEN SCRATCHED OR PLUCKED AND BOILED DOWN, HASN'T IT...?

"OPIATE OF THE MASSES," "HOARDING OF WEALTH," AND SO ON.

THE GOLD WAS USED TO FUND THE *STATE* INSTEAD. SCHOOLS AND SOLDIERS, IDEALLY.

HM.

LOOK, YOU WANT TO TALK MORAL RELATIVISM WITH A REVENGE KILLER IN A FORBIDDEN CHURCH, OR YOU WANT TO GO PUNCH OUR MORTAL FOE?

OH, *PUNCH*, DEFINITELY.

HM. *THIS* PIECE OF GOLD HASN'T BEEN TAKEN. HOW COULD IT HAVE BEEN MISSED?

I DON'T THINK IT WAS...IT'S ST. ANTHONY...HE'S THE FINDER OF MISSING PERSONS AND LOST THINGS.

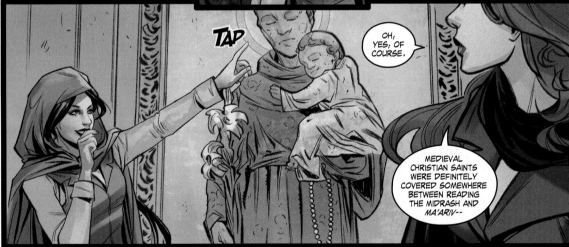

TAP

OH, YES, OF COURSE.

MEDIEVAL CHRISTIAN SAINTS WERE DEFINITELY COVERED SOMEWHERE BETWEEN READING THE MIDRASH AND MA'ARIV--

WHIRRRRRRR

LOIS!

!!

THE FLOOR IS LOWERING!

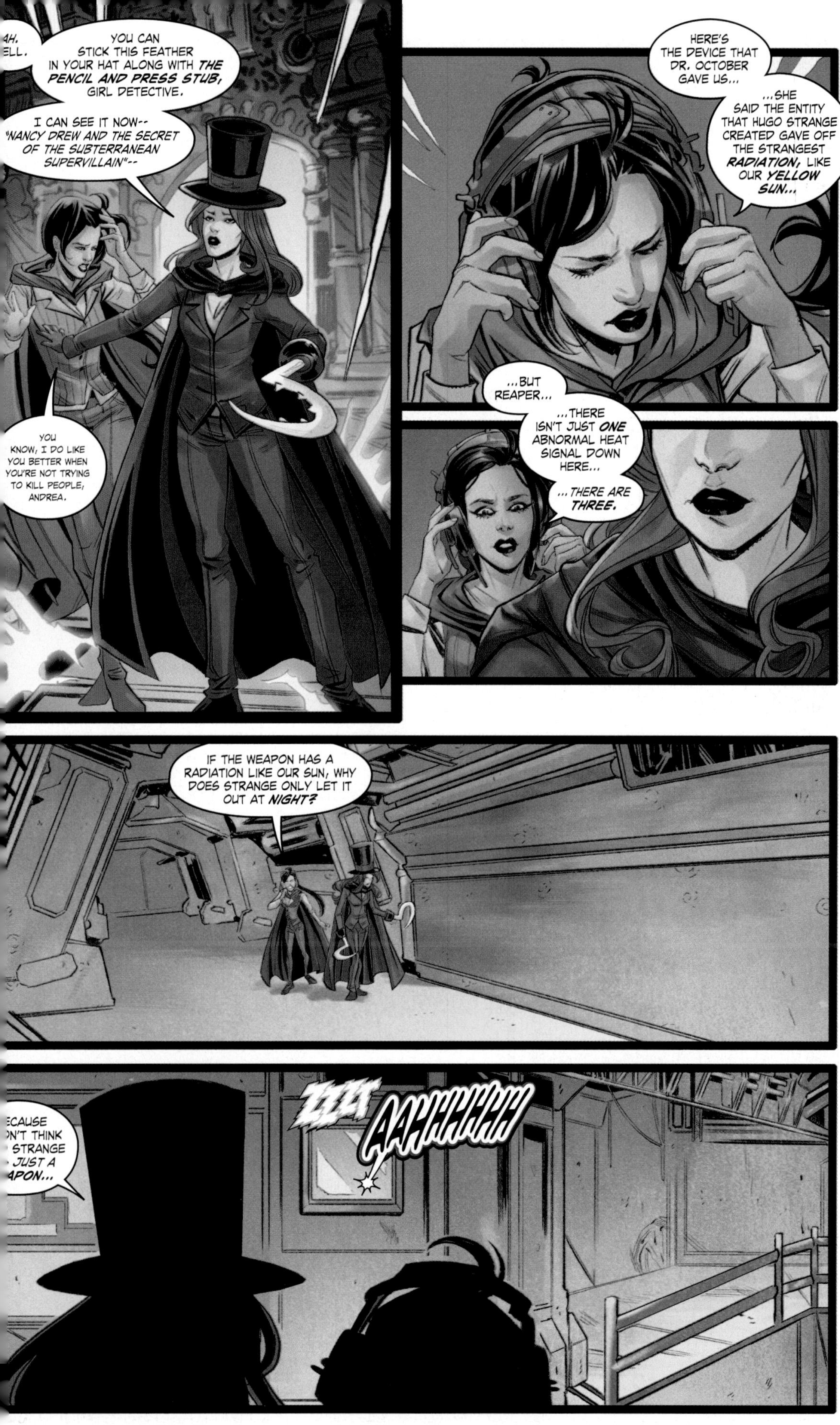

AH.
ELL.
YOU CAN STICK THIS FEATHER IN YOUR HAT ALONG WITH THE PENCIL AND PRESS STUB, GIRL DETECTIVE.
I CAN SEE IT NOW-- "NANCY DREW AND THE SECRET OF THE SUBTERRANEAN SUPERVILLAIN"--
YOU KNOW, I DO LIKE YOU BETTER WHEN YOU'RE NOT TRYING TO KILL PEOPLE, ANDREA.
HERE'S THE DEVICE THAT DR. OCTOBER GAVE US...
...SHE SAID THE ENTITY THAT HUGO STRANGE CREATED GAVE OFF THE STRANGEST RADIATION, LIKE OUR YELLOW SUN...
...BUT REAPER...
...THERE ISN'T JUST ONE ABNORMAL HEAT SIGNAL DOWN HERE...
...THERE ARE THREE.
IF THE WEAPON HAS A RADIATION LIKE OUR SUN, WHY DOES STRANGE ONLY LET IT OUT AT NIGHT?
ECAUSE
ON'T THINK
STRANGE
JUST A
APON...
ZZZT
AAHHHHHHH

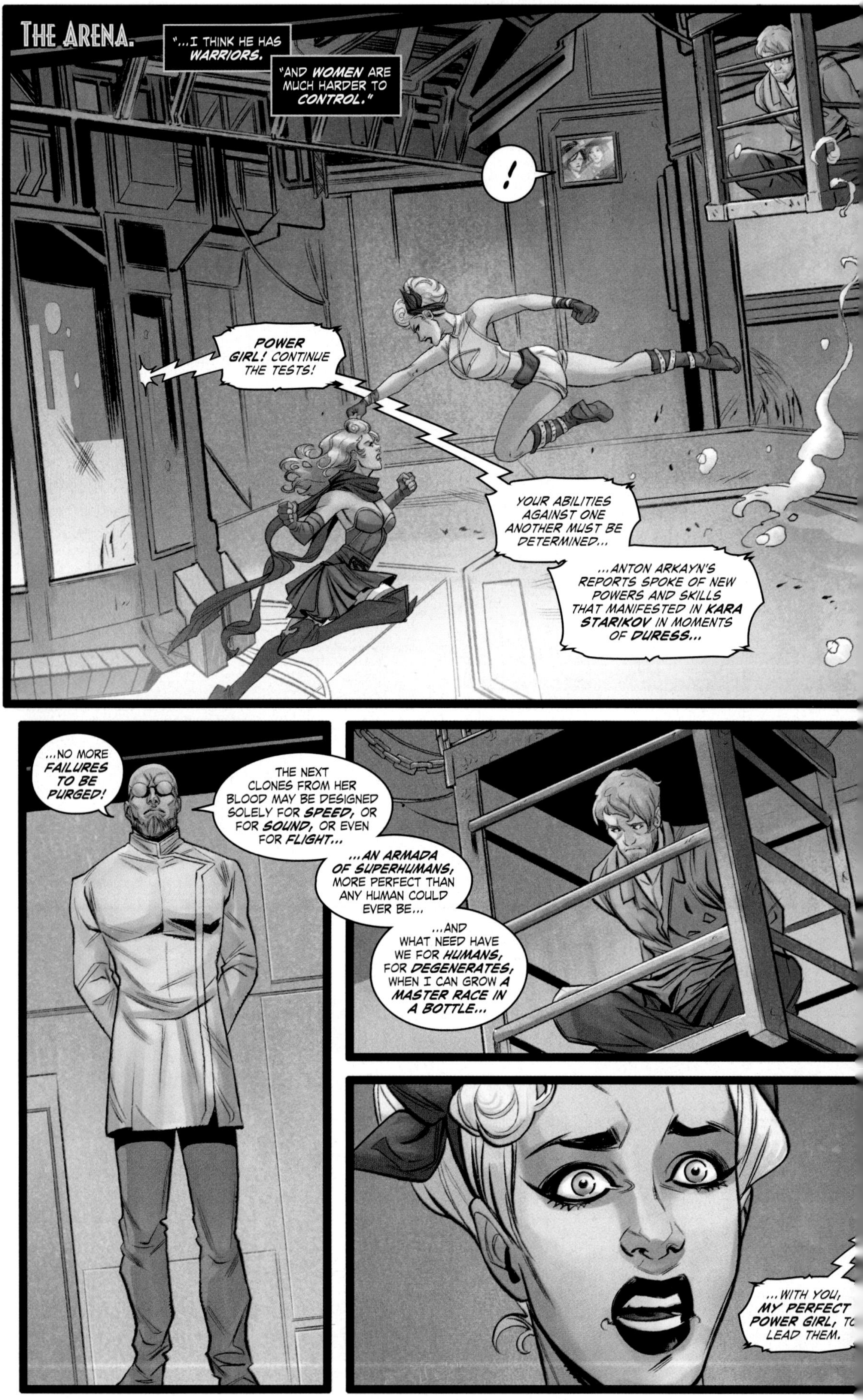
The Arena.
"...I think he has warriors.
"And women are much harder to control."
!
Power Girl! Continue the tests!
Your abilities against one another must be determined...
...Anton Arkayn's reports spoke of new powers and skills that manifested in Kara Starikov in moments of duress...
...No more failures to be purged!
The next clones from her blood may be designed solely for speed, or for sound, or even for flight...
...An armada of superhumans, more perfect than any human could ever be...
...And what need have we for humans, for degenerates, when I can grow a master race in a bottle...
...With you, my perfect Power Girl, to lead them.

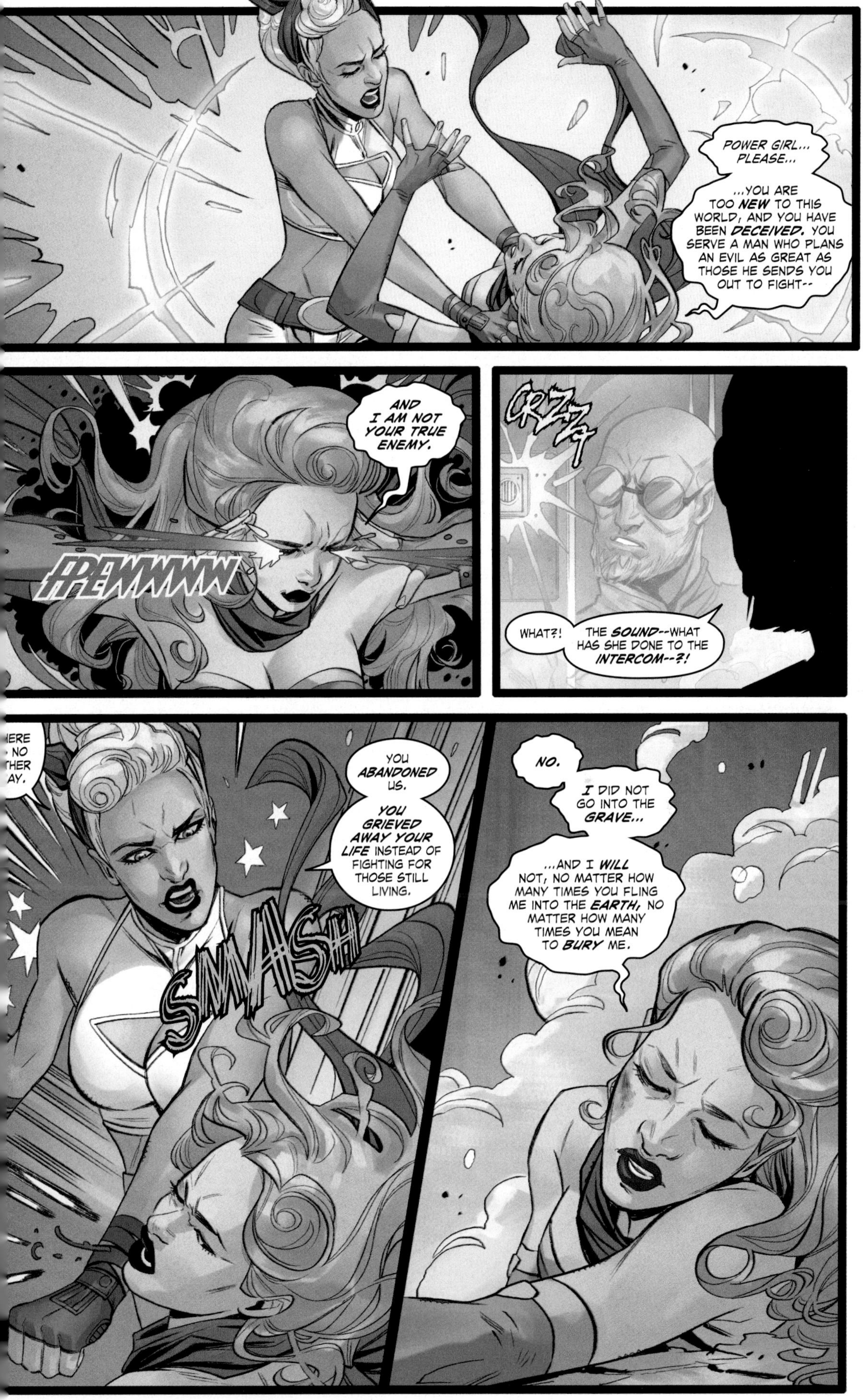
POWER GIRL... PLEASE...
...YOU ARE TOO NEW TO THIS WORLD, AND YOU HAVE BEEN DECEIVED. YOU SERVE A MAN WHO PLANS AN EVIL AS GREAT AS THOSE HE SENDS YOU OUT TO FIGHT--
AND I AM NOT YOUR TRUE ENEMY.
FFEWWWWW
CRZZZT
WHAT?!
THE SOUND--WHAT HAS SHE DONE TO THE INTERCOM--?!
YOU ABANDONED US.
YOU GRIEVED AWAY YOUR LIFE INSTEAD OF FIGHTING FOR THOSE STILL LIVING.
SMASH
NO.
I DID NOT GO INTO THE GRAVE...
...AND I WILL NOT, NO MATTER HOW MANY TIMES YOU FLING ME INTO THE EARTH, NO MATTER HOW MANY TIMES YOU MEAN TO BURY ME.

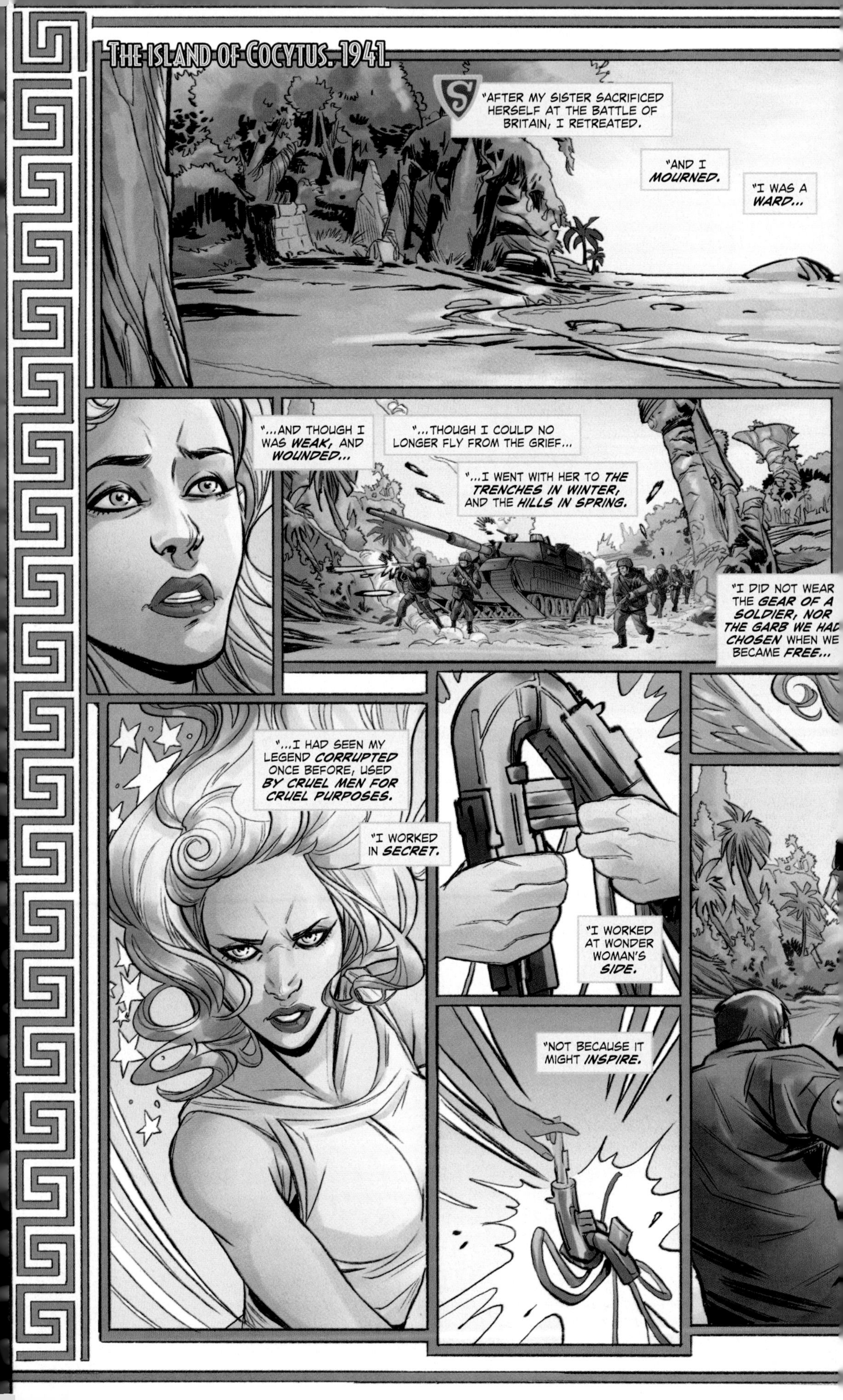

THE ISLAND OF COCYTUS. 1941.
"AFTER MY SISTER SACRIFICED HERSELF AT THE BATTLE OF BRITAIN, I RETREATED.
"AND I MOURNED.
"I WAS A WARD...
"...AND THOUGH I WAS WEAK, AND WOUNDED...
"...THOUGH I COULD NO LONGER FLY FROM THE GRIEF...
"...I WENT WITH HER TO THE TRENCHES IN WINTER, AND THE HILLS IN SPRING.
"I DID NOT WEAR THE GEAR OF A SOLDIER, NOR THE GARB WE HAD CHOSEN WHEN WE BECAME FREE...
"...I HAD SEEN MY LEGEND CORRUPTED ONCE BEFORE, USED BY CRUEL MEN FOR CRUEL PURPOSES.
"I WORKED IN SECRET.
"I WORKED AT WONDER WOMAN'S SIDE.
"NOT BECAUSE IT MIGHT INSPIRE.

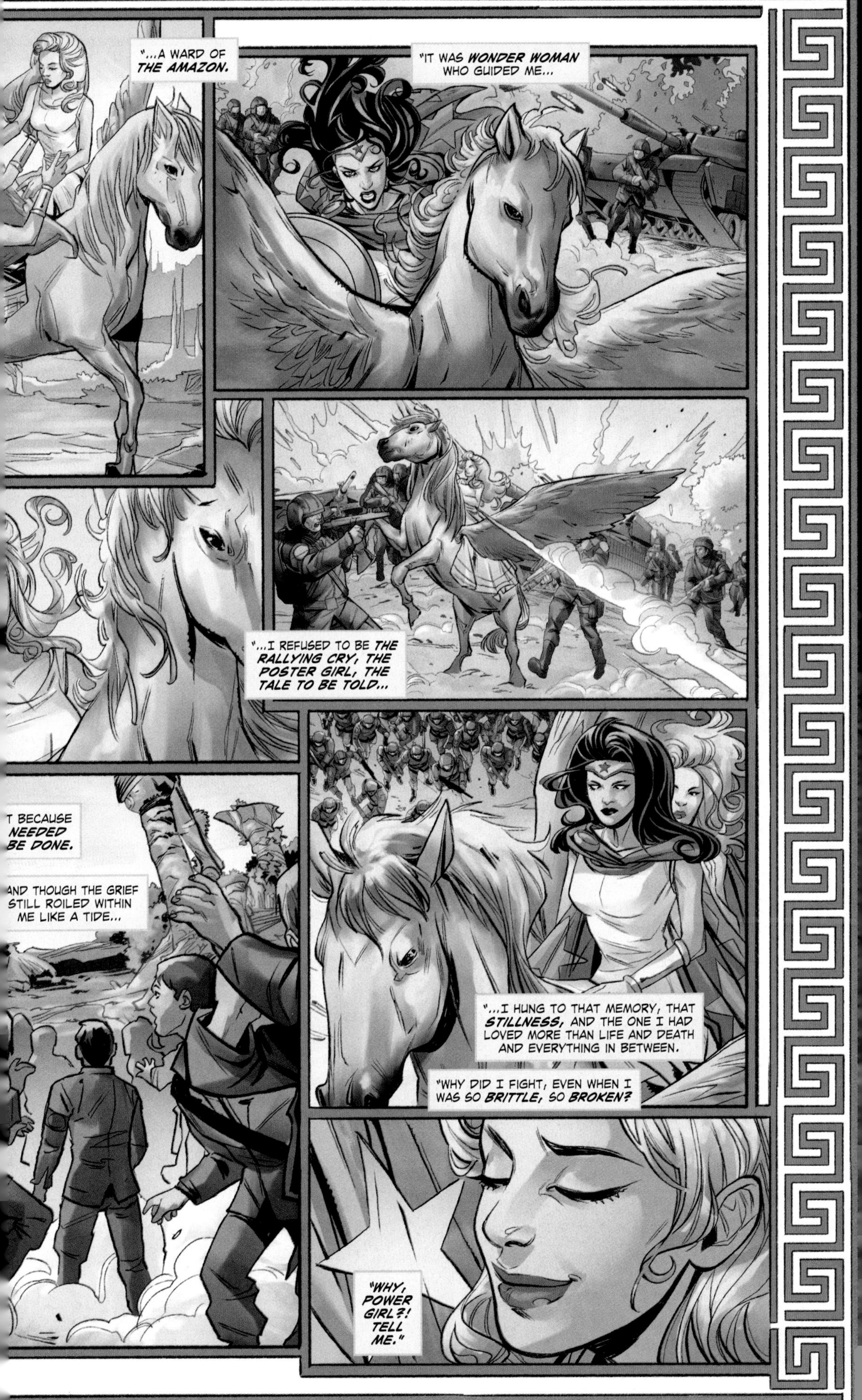
"...A WARD OF THE AMAZON.
"IT WAS WONDER WOMAN WHO GUIDED ME...
"...I REFUSED TO BE THE RALLYING CRY, THE POSTER GIRL, THE TALE TO BE TOLD...
T BECAUSE NEEDED BE DONE.
AND THOUGH THE GRIEF STILL ROILED WITHIN ME LIKE A TIDE...
"...I HUNG TO THAT MEMORY, THAT STILLNESS, AND THE ONE I HAD LOVED MORE THAN LIFE AND DEATH AND EVERYTHING IN BETWEEN.
"WHY DID I FIGHT, EVEN WHEN I WAS SO BRITTLE, SO BROKEN?
"WHY, POWER GIRL?! TELL ME."

BECAUSE... ...BECAUSE OF *YOUR SISTER.*

BECAUSE SHE HAD SAVED *YOU,* TOO...

...AND FOR HER *MEMORY,* YOU HAD TO GO ON FIGHTING.

YOU DIDN'T... *TRULY* BETRAY US, IF YOU KEPT FIGHTING, EVEN AFTER YOU FLED...

"...YOU WOULDN'T LET THE LEGACY...SHE HAD LEFT YOU BECOME... CORRUPTED BY GREEDY, GRASPING *TYRANTS.*

"YOU HAD TO RESIST OUT OF... OUT OF *LOVE.*"

REAPER...

...HOW ABO... A LITTLE LE... RECONNAISSAN... AND A LITTLE M... *RESISTANCE*...

YOU KNOW, LOIS, WHEN YOU'RE NOT TRYING TO SABOTAGE MY REVENGE SCHEMES...

...I LIKE *YOU* BETTER, TOO.

KRRON-ZZZZ

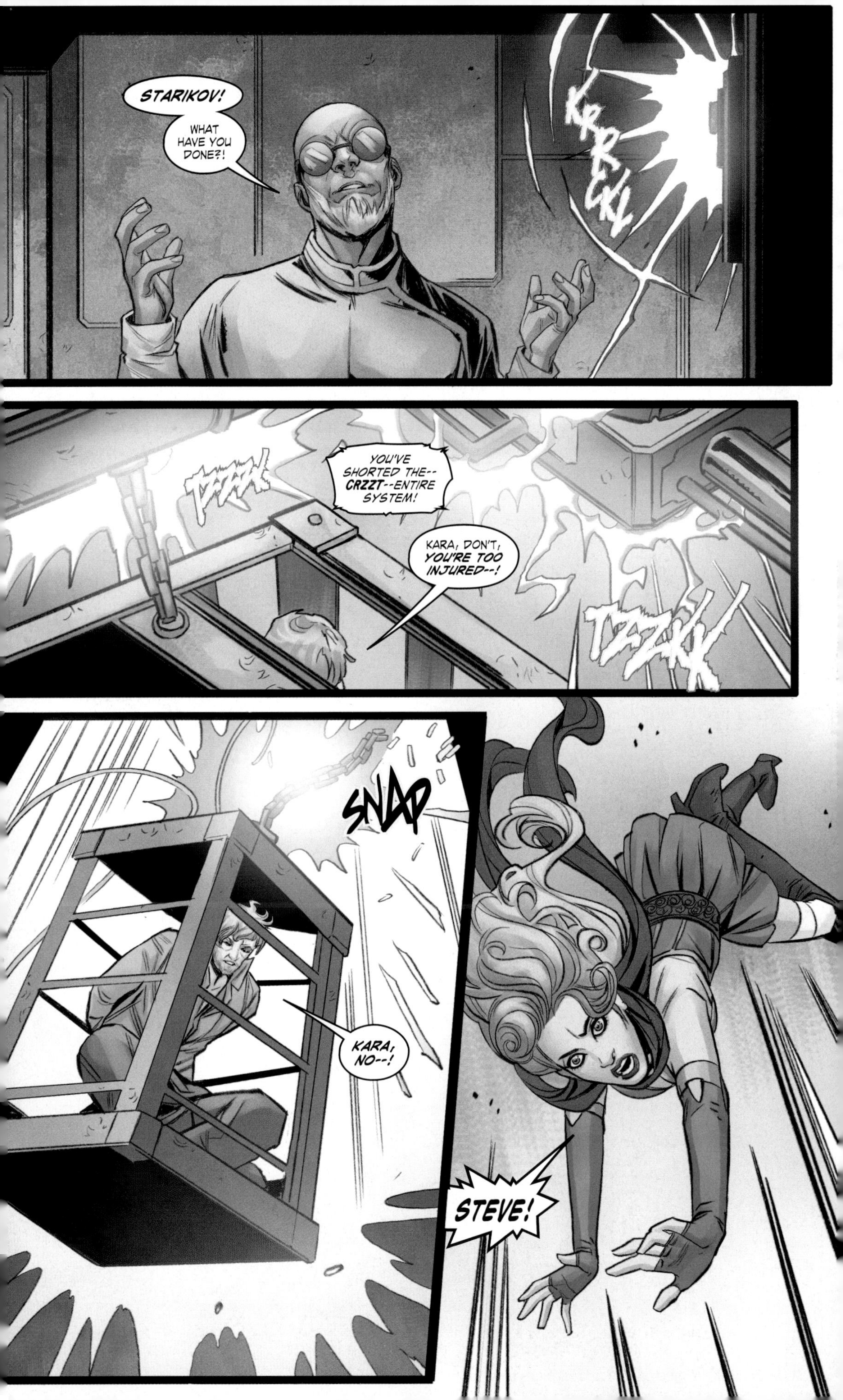

STARIKOV!
WHAT HAVE YOU DONE?!
KRRRCKK
TZZKK
YOU'VE SHORTED THE--CRZZT--ENTIRE SYSTEM!
KARA, DON'T, YOU'RE TOO INJURED--!
TZZKK
SNAP
KARA, NO--!
STEVE!

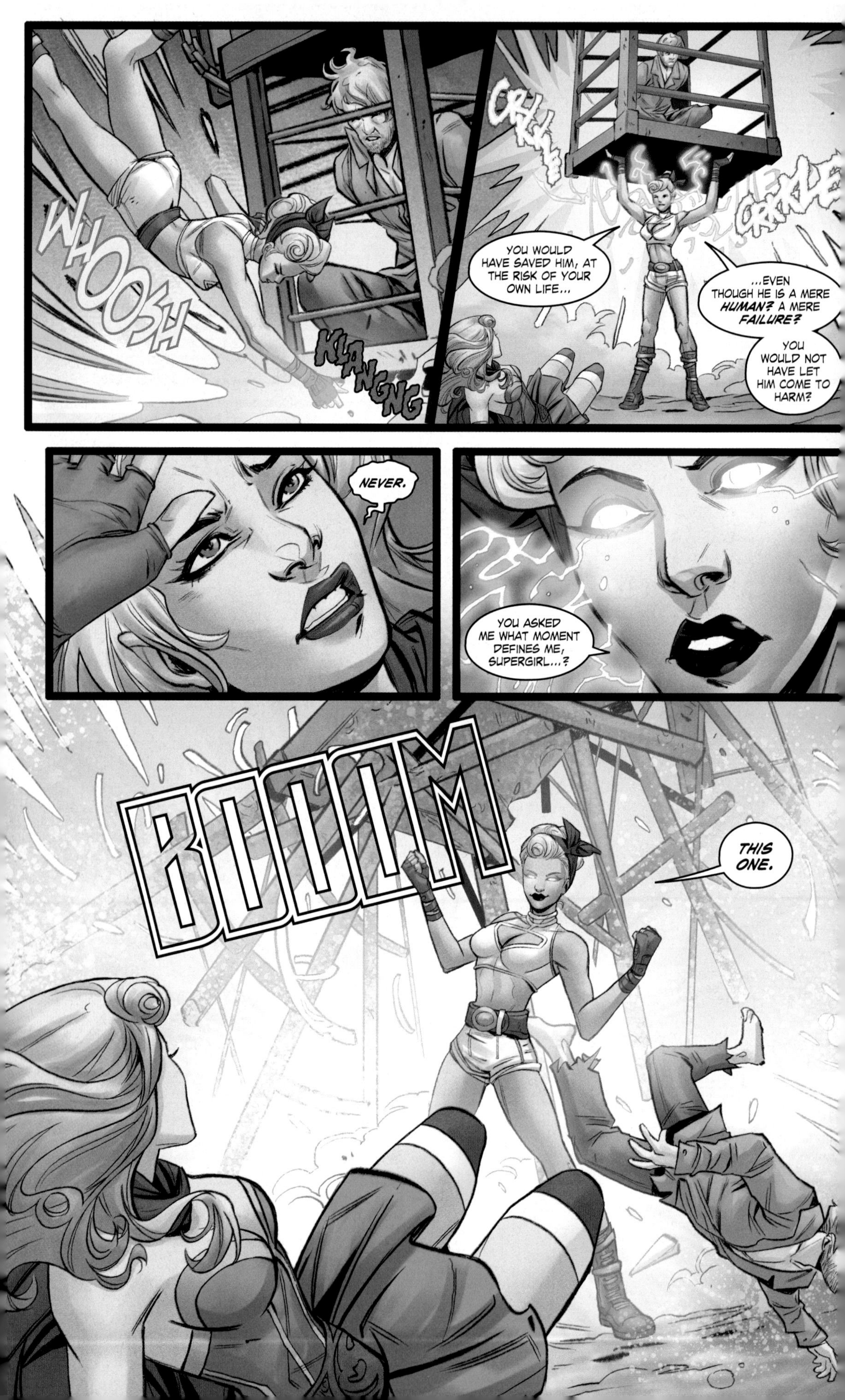
WHOOSH
KLANGNG
CRKLE
CRKKLE
YOU WOULD HAVE SAVED HIM, AT THE RISK OF YOUR OWN LIFE...
...EVEN THOUGH HE IS A MERE HUMAN? A MERE FAILURE?
YOU WOULD NOT HAVE LET HIM COME TO HARM?
NEVER.
YOU ASKED ME WHAT MOMENT DEFINES ME, SUPERGIRL...?
BOOOM
THIS ONE.

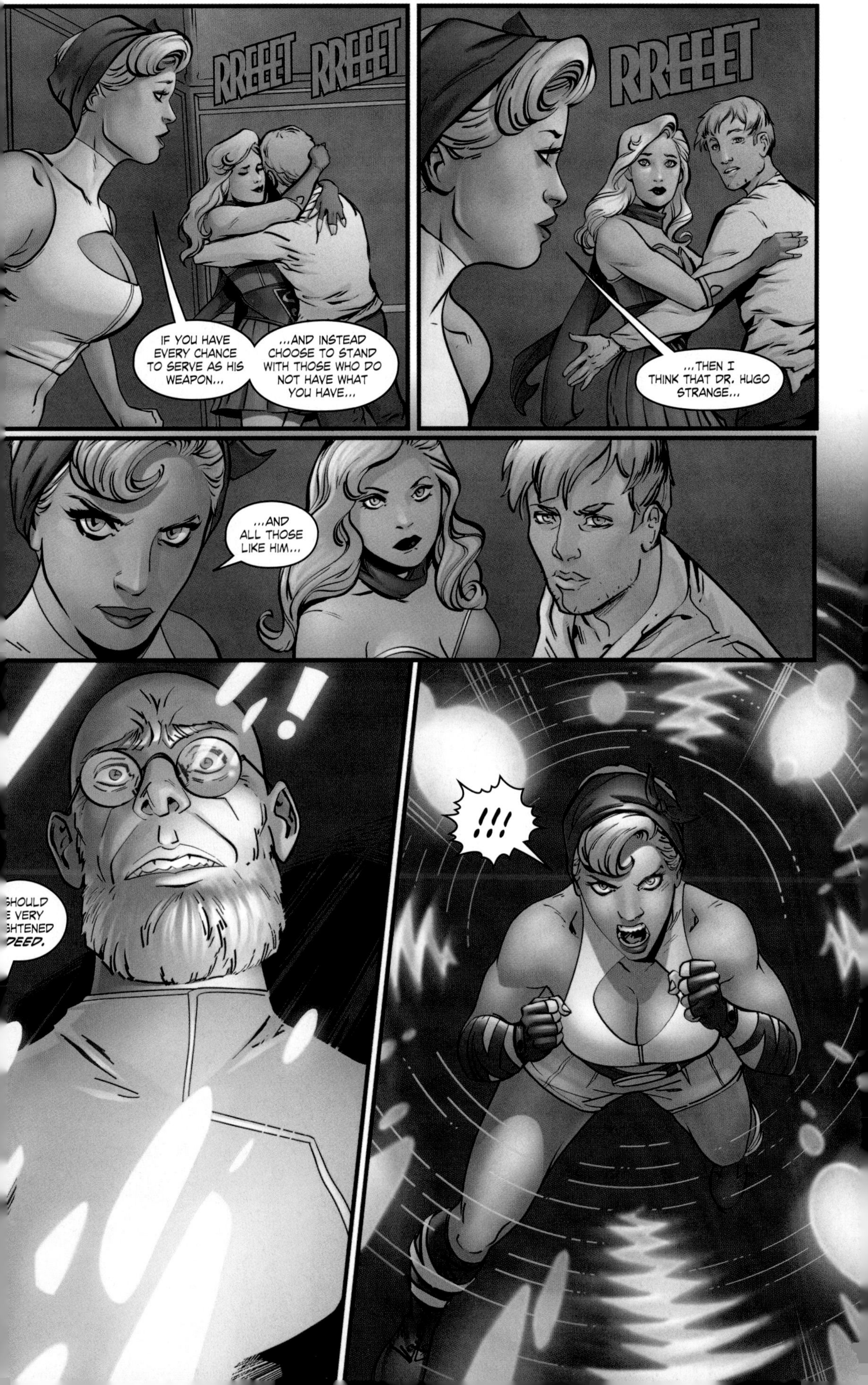
RREEET RREEET
IF YOU HAVE EVERY CHANCE TO SERVE AS HIS WEAPON...
...AND INSTEAD CHOOSE TO STAND WITH THOSE WHO DO NOT HAVE WHAT YOU HAVE...
RREEET
...THEN I THINK THAT DR. HUGO STRANGE...
...AND ALL THOSE LIKE HIM...
SHOULD
E VERY
GHTENED
DEED.
!!!

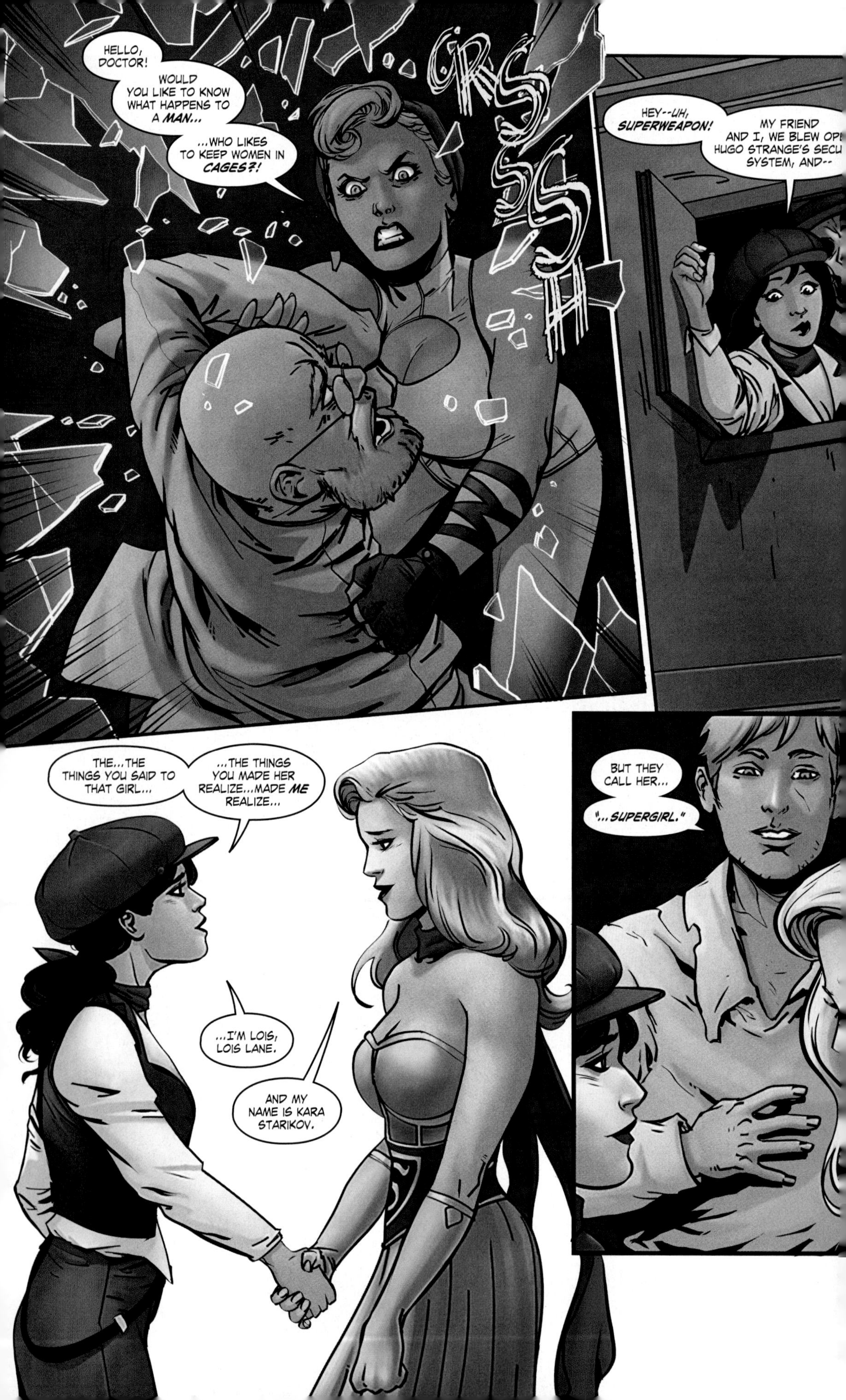
HELLO, DOCTOR!
WOULD YOU LIKE TO KNOW WHAT HAPPENS TO A MAN...
...WHO LIKES TO KEEP WOMEN IN CAGES?!
CRSSSH
HEY--UH, SUPERWEAPON!
MY FRIEND AND I, WE BLEW OPE HUGO STRANGE'S SECU SYSTEM, AND--
THE...THE THINGS YOU SAID TO THAT GIRL...
...THE THINGS YOU MADE HER REALIZE...MADE ME REALIZE...
...I'M LOIS, LOIS LANE.
AND MY NAME IS KARA STARIKOV.
BUT THEY CALL HER...
"...SUPERGIRL."

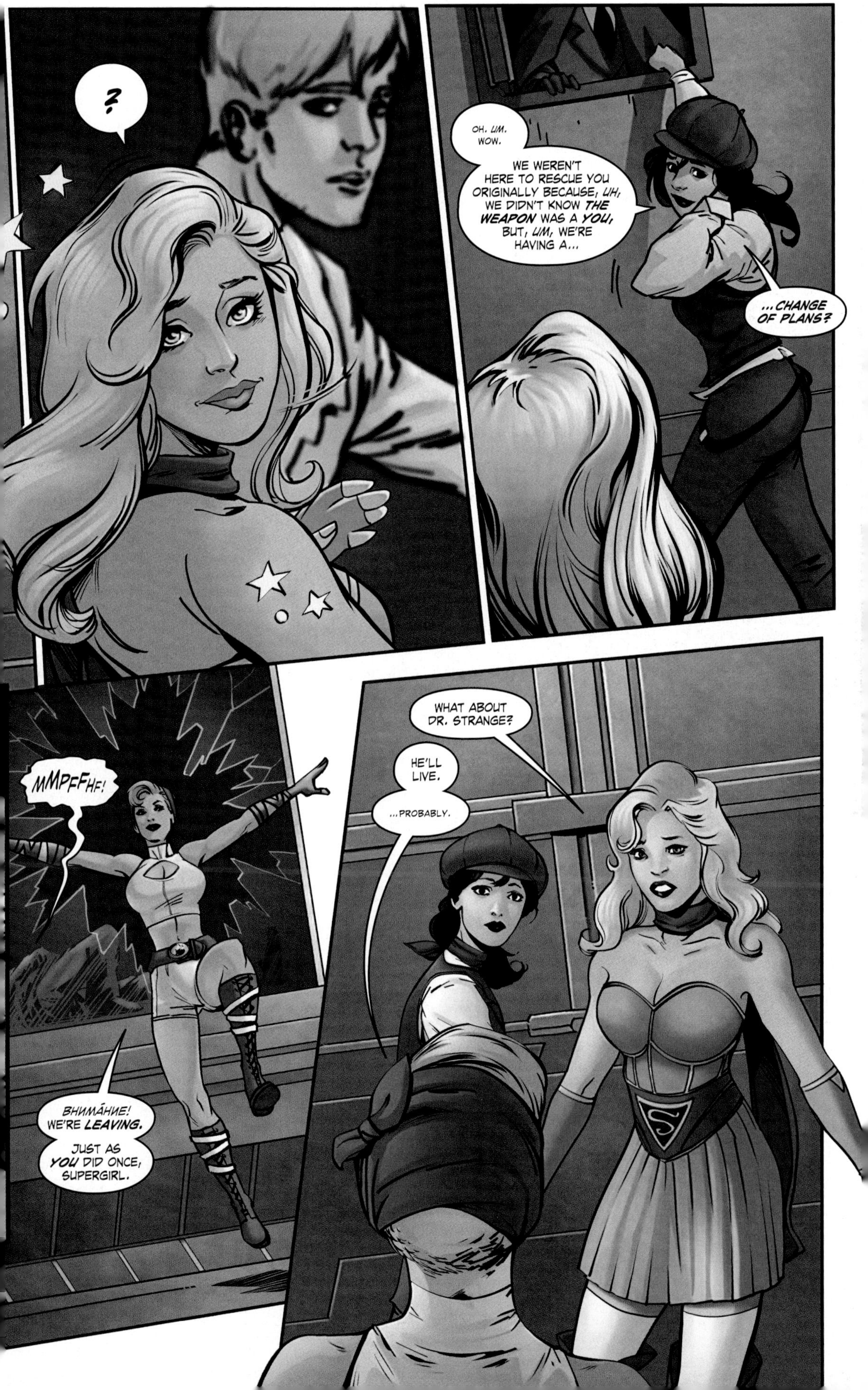
?
OH. UM. WOW.
WE WEREN'T HERE TO RESCUE YOU ORIGINALLY BECAUSE, UH, WE DIDN'T KNOW THE WEAPON WAS A YOU, BUT, UM, WE'RE HAVING A...
...CHANGE OF PLANS?
MMPFFHF!
ВНИМÁНИЕ! WE'RE LEAVING.
JUST AS YOU DID ONCE, SUPERGIRL.
WHAT ABOUT DR. STRANGE?
HE'LL LIVE.
...PROBABLY.

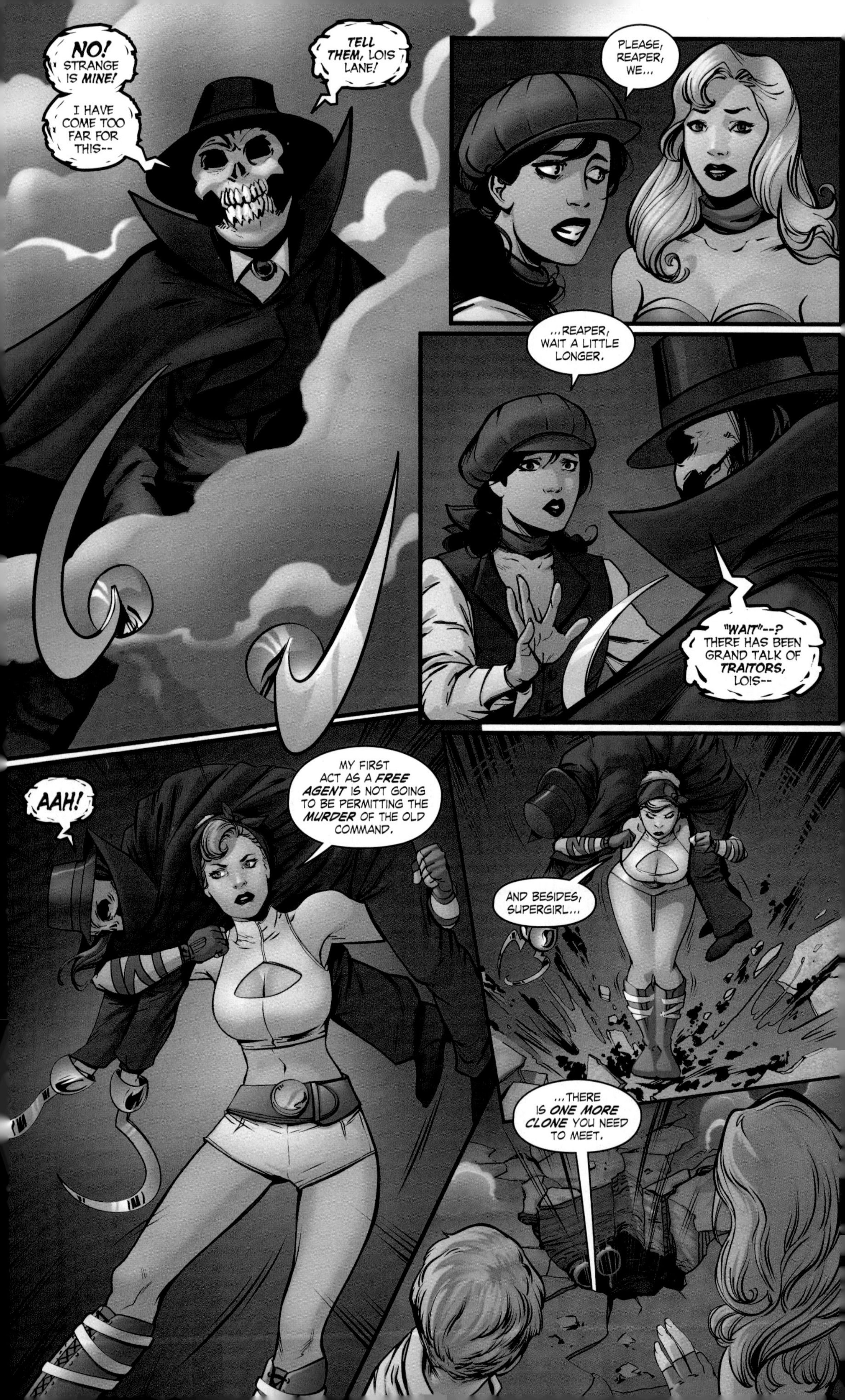
NO! STRANGE IS MINE!
I HAVE COME TOO FAR FOR THIS--
TELL THEM, LOIS LANE!
PLEASE, REAPER, WE...
...REAPER, WAIT A LITTLE LONGER.
"WAIT"--? THERE HAS BEEN GRAND TALK OF TRAITORS, LOIS--
AAH!
MY FIRST ACT AS A FREE AGENT IS NOT GOING TO BE PERMITTING THE MURDER OF THE OLD COMMAND.
AND BESIDES, SUPERGIRL...
...THERE IS ONE MORE CLONE YOU NEED TO MEET.

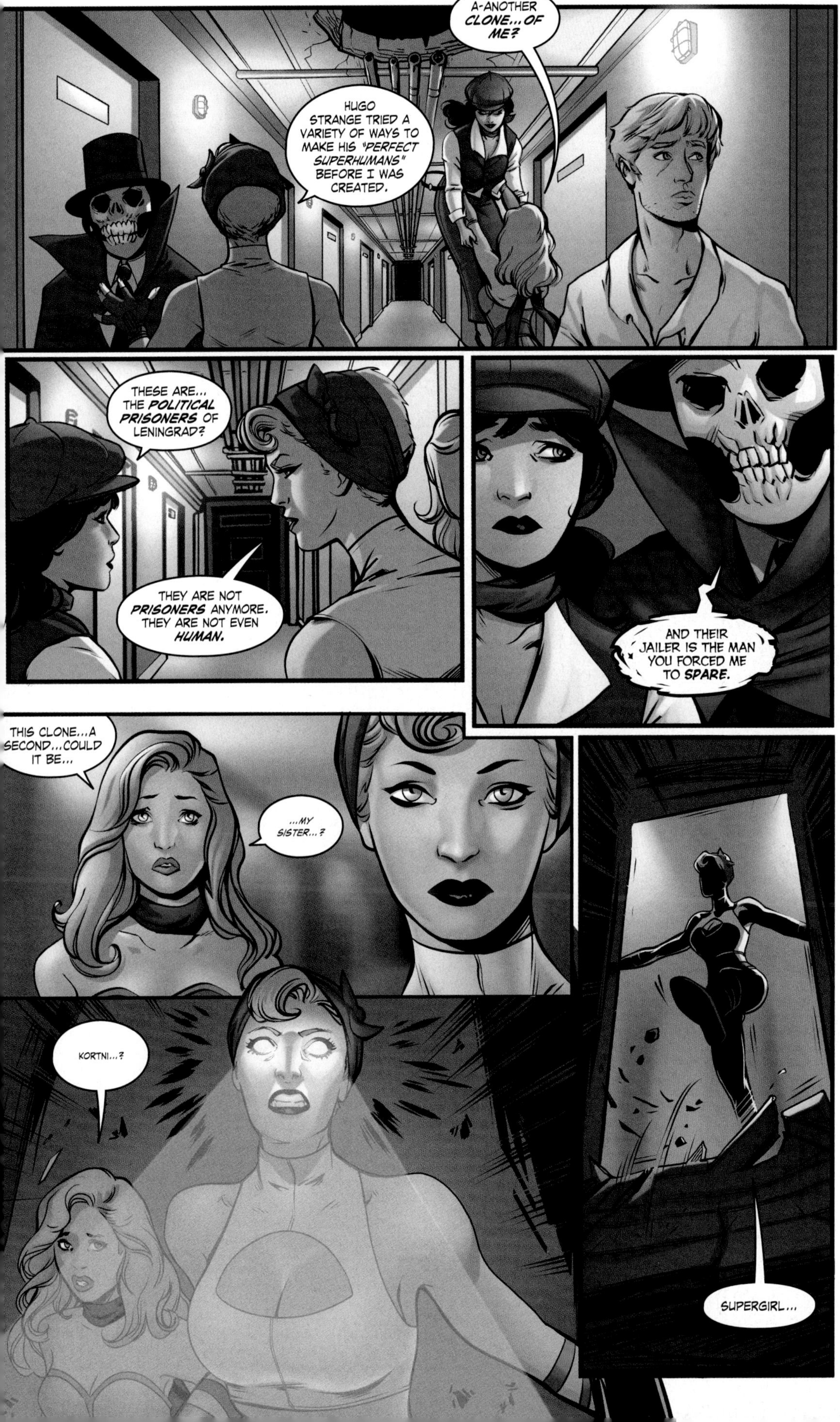
HUGO STRANGE TRIED A VARIETY OF WAYS TO MAKE HIS "PERFECT SUPERHUMANS" BEFORE I WAS CREATED.
A-ANOTHER CLONE... OF ME?
THESE ARE... THE POLITICAL PRISONERS OF LENINGRAD?
THEY ARE NOT PRISONERS ANYMORE. THEY ARE NOT EVEN HUMAN.
AND THEIR JAILER IS THE MAN YOU FORCED ME TO SPARE.
THIS CLONE...A SECOND...COULD IT BE...
...MY SISTER...?
KORTNI...?
SUPERGIRL...

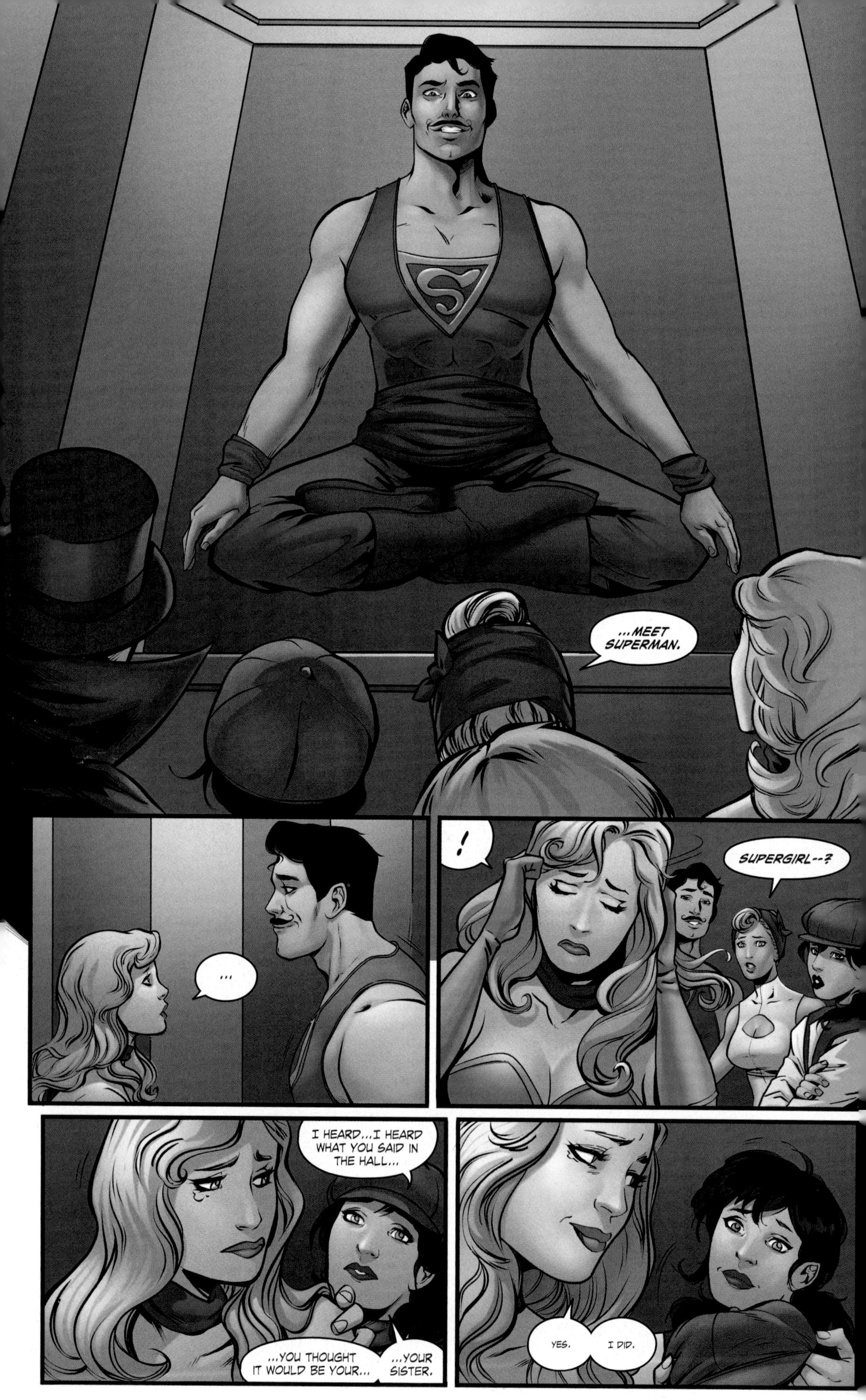
...MEET SUPERMAN.
...
!
SUPERGIRL--?
I HEARD...I HEARD WHAT YOU SAID IN THE HALL...
...YOU THOUGHT IT WOULD BE YOUR...
...YOUR SISTER.
YES.
I DID.

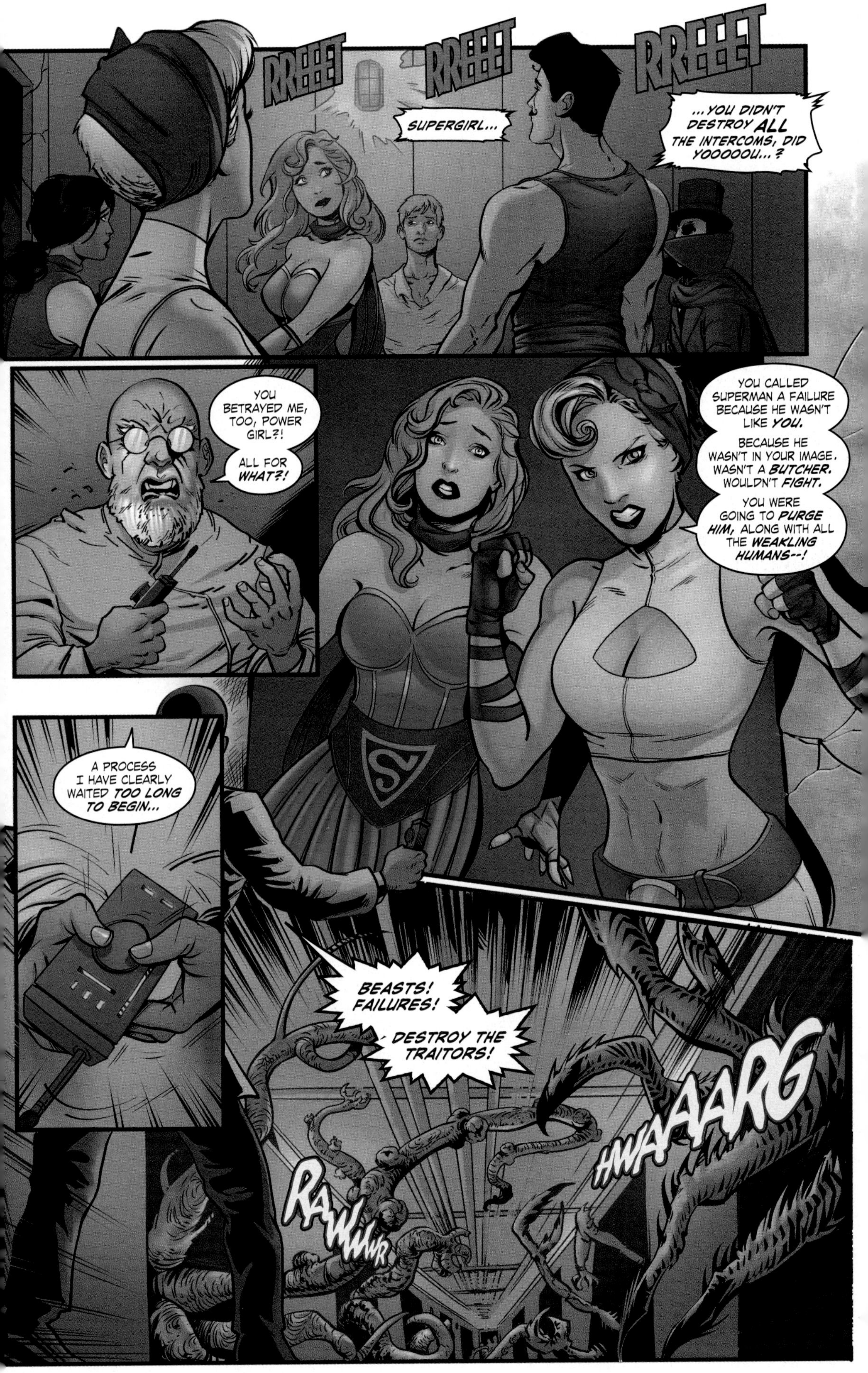
RREEET
RREEET
RREEET
SUPERGIRL...
...YOU DIDN'T DESTROY ALL THE INTERCOMS, DID YOOOOOU...?
YOU BETRAYED ME, TOO, POWER GIRL?!
ALL FOR WHAT?!
YOU CALLED SUPERMAN A FAILURE BECAUSE HE WASN'T LIKE YOU.
BECAUSE HE WASN'T IN YOUR IMAGE. WASN'T A BUTCHER. WOULDN'T FIGHT.
YOU WERE GOING TO PURGE HIM, ALONG WITH ALL THE WEAKLING HUMANS--!
A PROCESS I HAVE CLEARLY WAITED TOO LONG TO BEGIN...
BEASTS! FAILURES!
DESTROY THE TRAITORS!
HWAAARG
RAWWWR

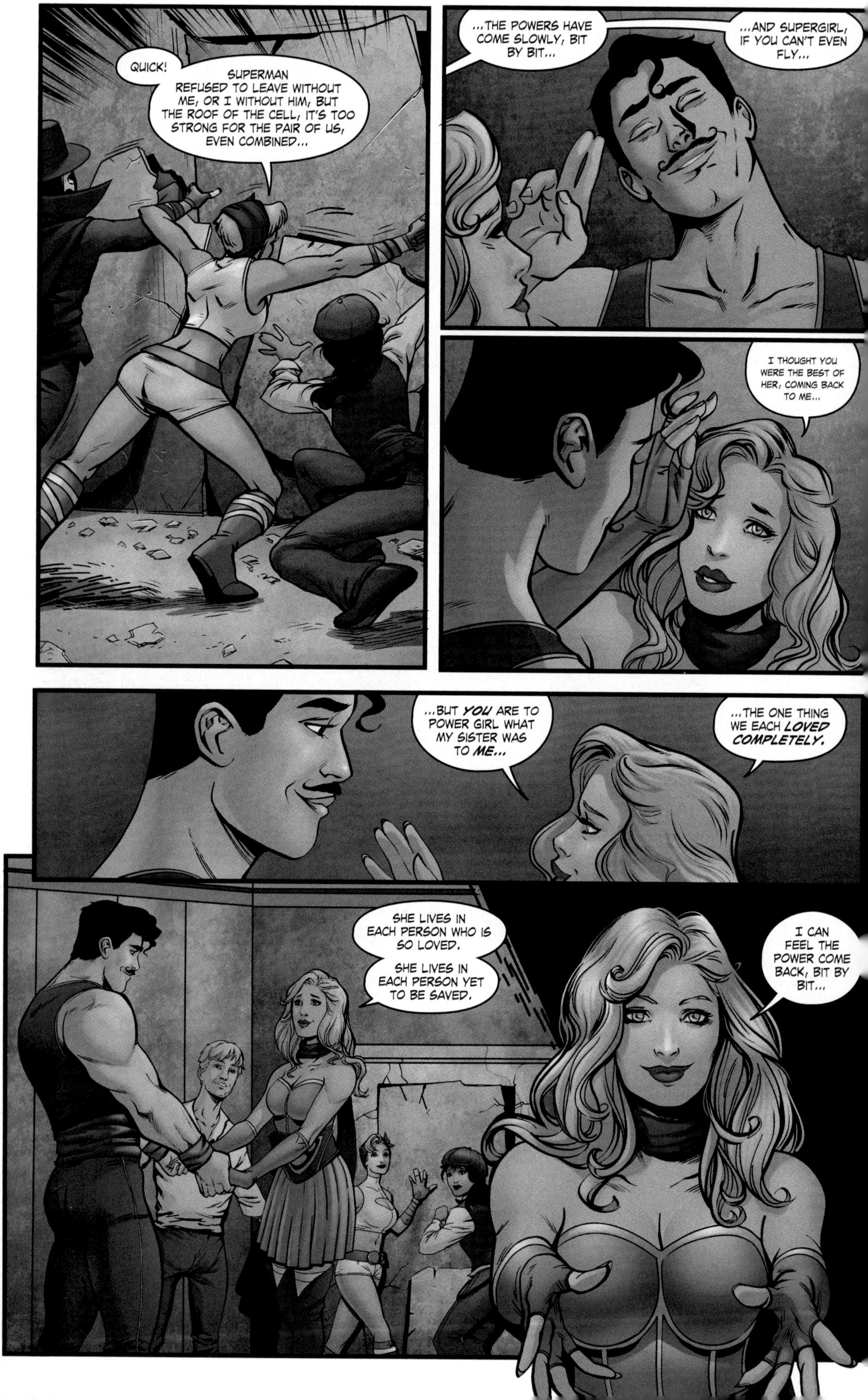
QUICK!
SUPERMAN REFUSED TO LEAVE WITHOUT ME, OR I WITHOUT HIM, BUT THE ROOF OF THE CELL, IT'S TOO STRONG FOR THE PAIR OF US, EVEN COMBINED...
...THE POWERS HAVE COME SLOWLY, BIT BY BIT...
...AND SUPERGIRL, IF YOU CAN'T EVEN FLY...
I THOUGHT YOU WERE THE BEST OF HER, COMING BACK TO ME...
...BUT YOU ARE TO POWER GIRL WHAT MY SISTER WAS TO ME...
...THE ONE THING WE EACH LOVED COMPLETELY.
SHE LIVES IN EACH PERSON WHO IS SO LOVED.
SHE LIVES IN EACH PERSON YET TO BE SAVED.
I CAN FEEL THE POWER COME BACK, BIT BY BIT...

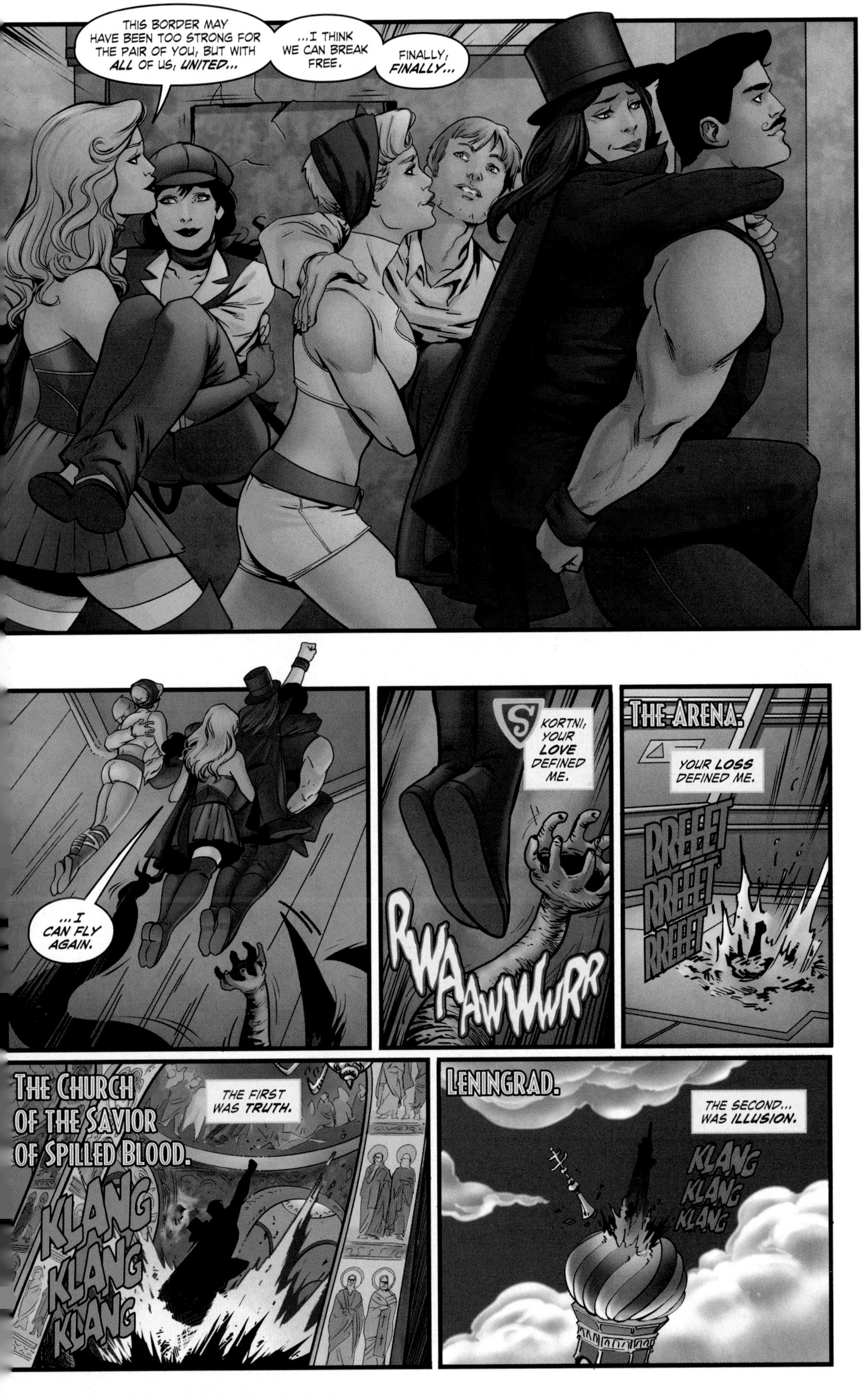
THIS BORDER MAY HAVE BEEN TOO STRONG FOR THE PAIR OF YOU, BUT WITH ALL OF US, UNITED...
...I THINK WE CAN BREAK FREE.
FINALLY, FINALLY...
...I CAN FLY AGAIN.
KORTNI, YOUR LOVE DEFINED ME.
RWAAAWWWURR
THE ARENA.
YOUR LOSS DEFINED ME.
RREEEET RREEEET RREEEET
THE CHURCH OF THE SAVIOR OF SPILLED BLOOD.
THE FIRST WAS TRUTH.
KLANG KLANG KLANG
LENINGRAD.
THE SECOND... WAS ILLUSION.
KLANG KLANG KLANG

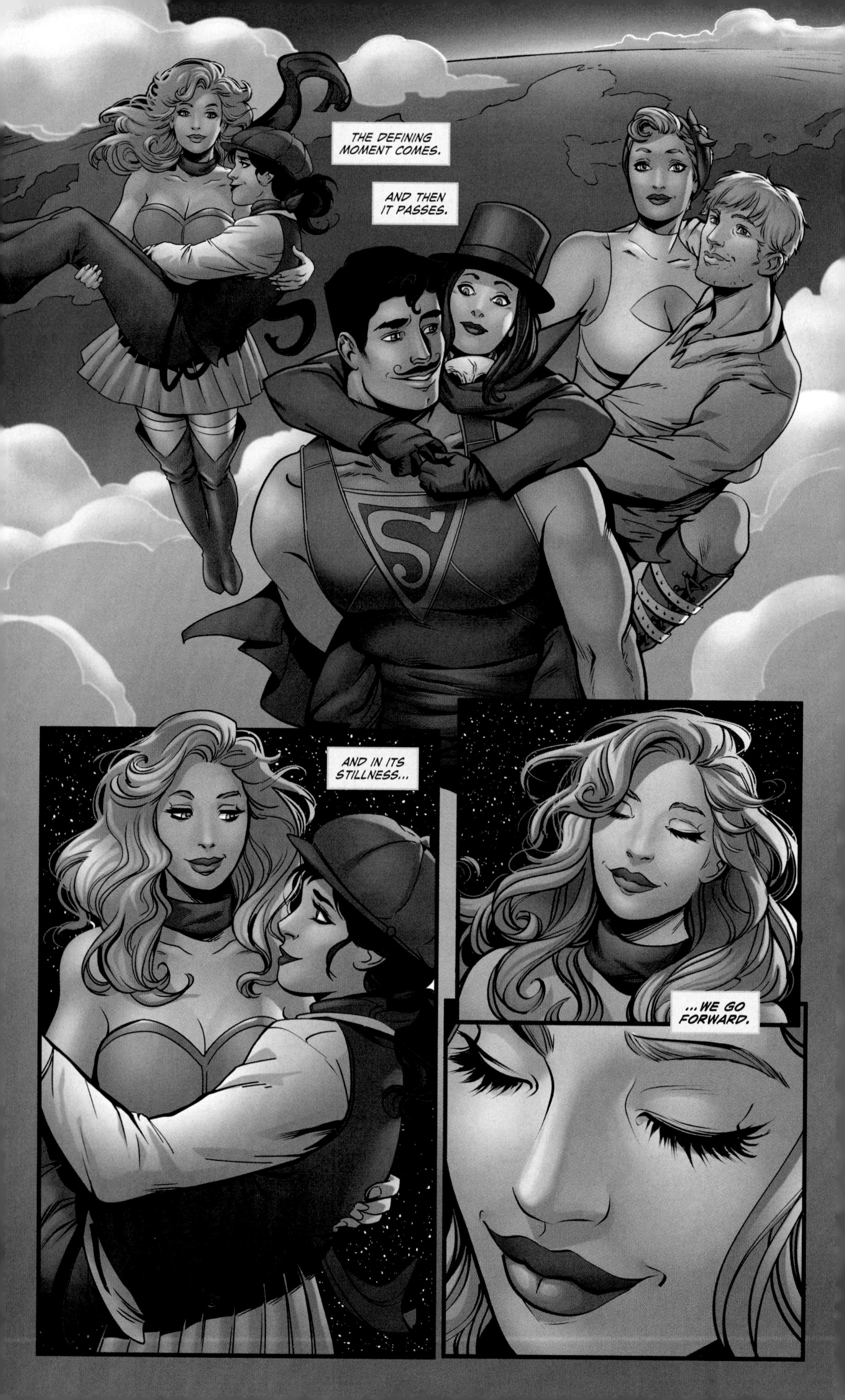
THE DEFINING MOMENT COMES.
AND THEN IT PASSES.
AND IN ITS STILLNESS...
...WE GO FORWARD.

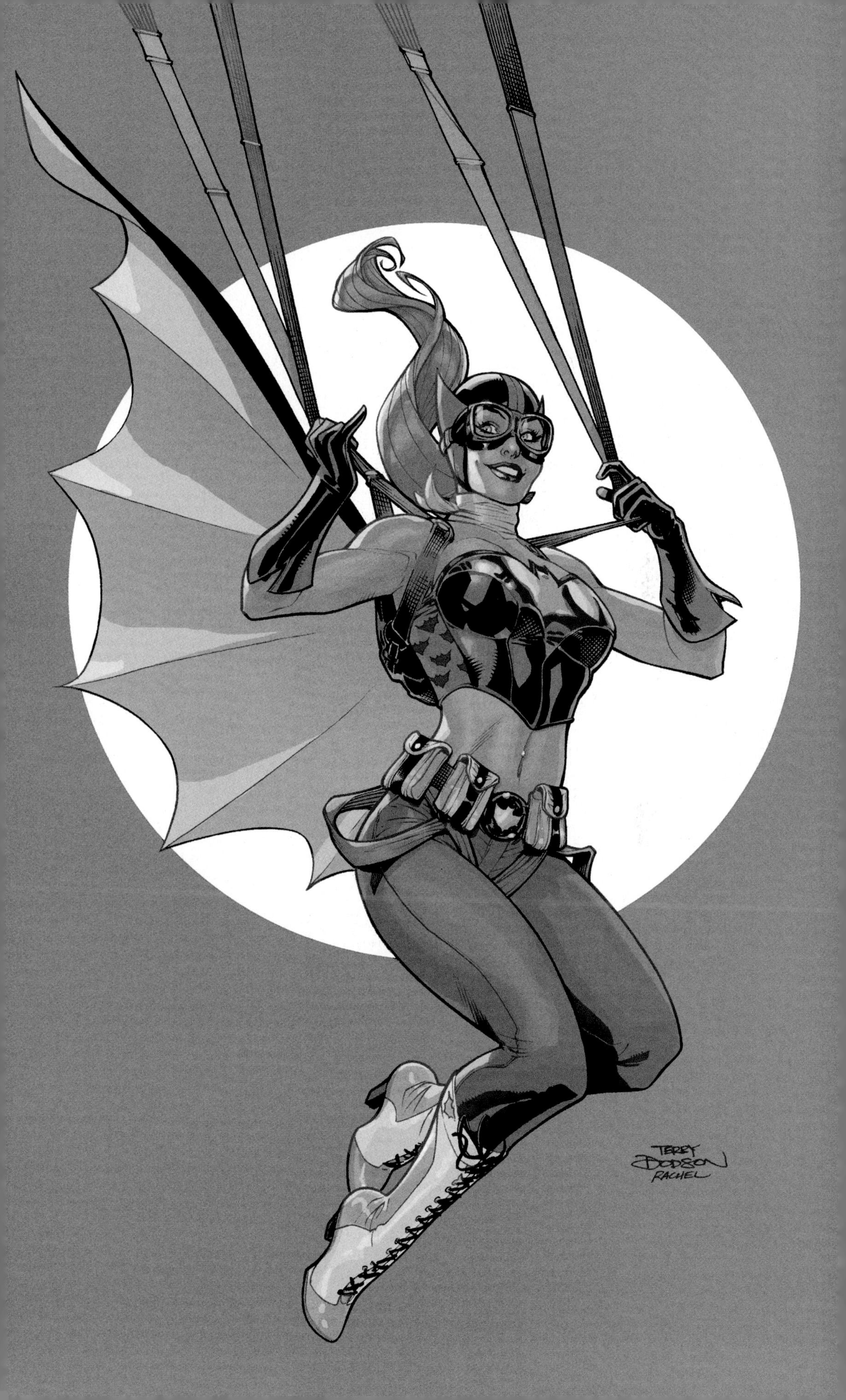
TERRY
DODSON
RACHEL

DOUBLE FEATURE

MARGUERITE BENNETT
Writer

ELSA CHARRETIER
Artist

HI-FI
Colorist

Cover by
TERRY AND RACHEL DODSON

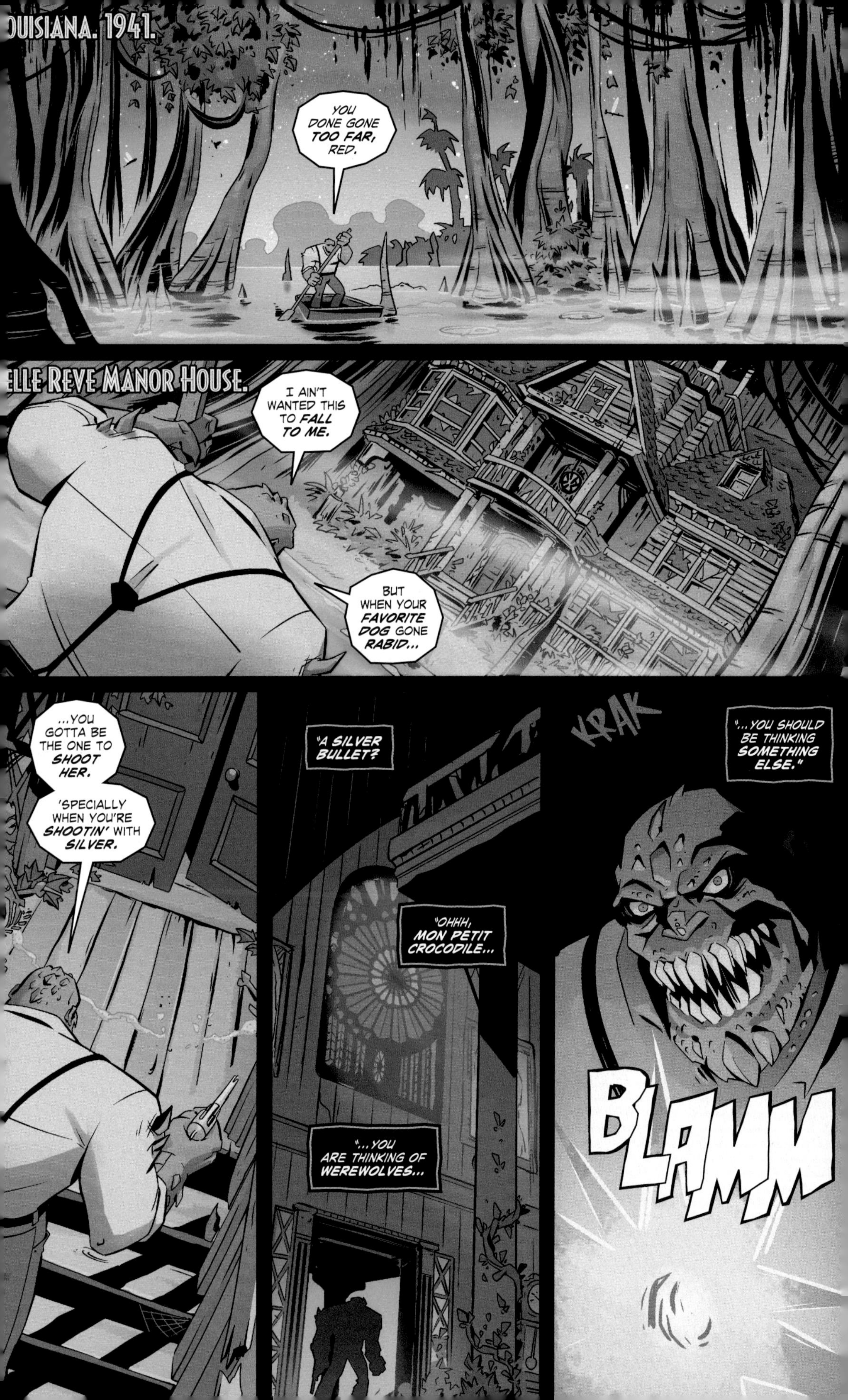
OUISIANA. 1941.
YOU DONE GONE TOO FAR, RED.
ELLE REVE MANOR HOUSE.
I AIN'T WANTED THIS TO FALL TO ME.
BUT WHEN YOUR FAVORITE DOG GONE RABID...
...YOU GOTTA BE THE ONE TO SHOOT HER.
'SPECIALLY WHEN YOU'RE SHOOTIN' WITH SILVER.
"A SILVER BULLET?
"OHHH, MON PETIT CROCODILE...
"...YOU ARE THINKING OF WEREWOLVES...
KRAK
"...YOU SHOULD BE THINKING SOMETHING ELSE."
BLAMM

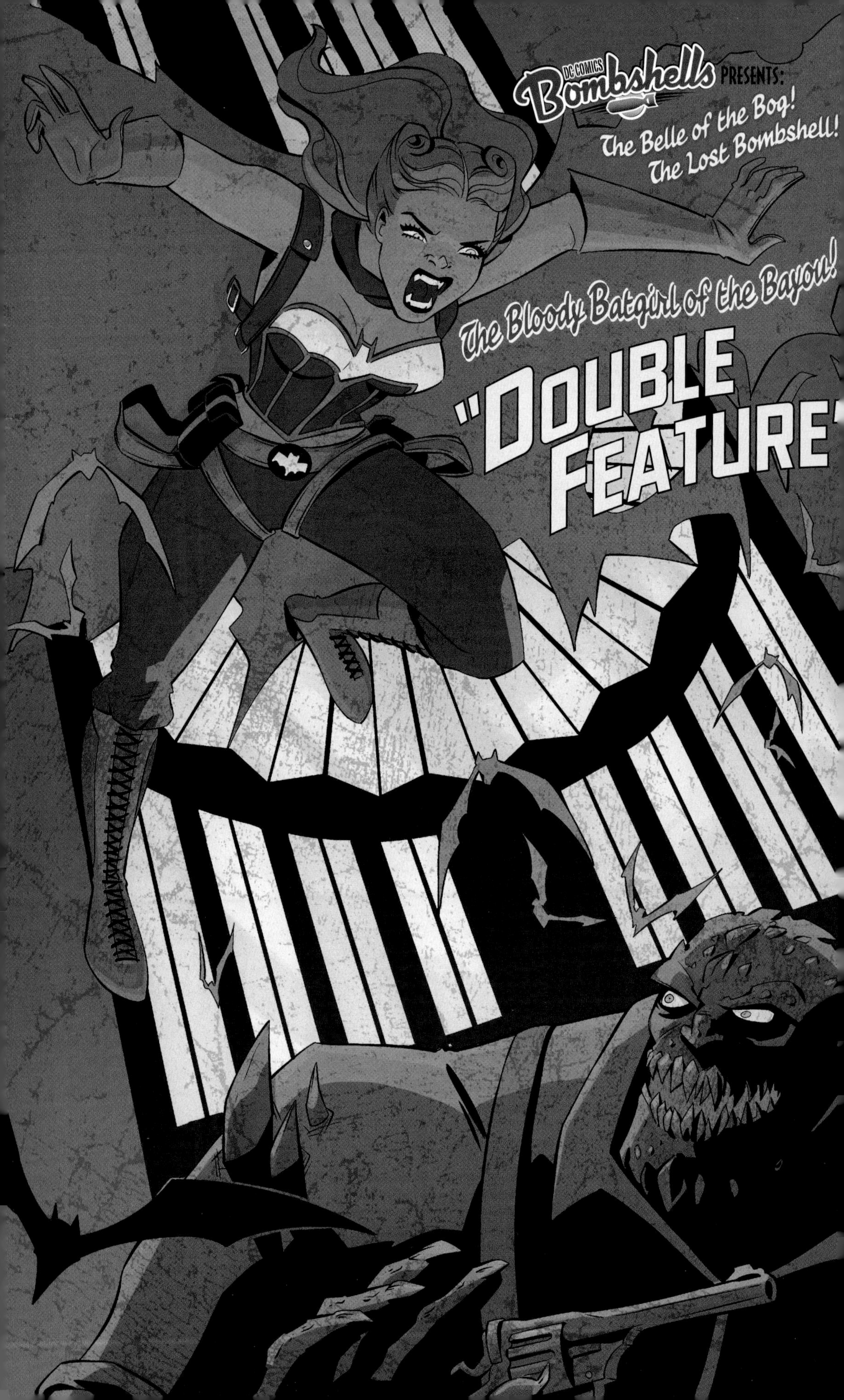
DC COMICS Bombshells PRESENTS:
The Belle of the Bog!
The Lost Bombshell!
The Bloody Batgirl of the Bayou!
"DOUBLE FEATURE"

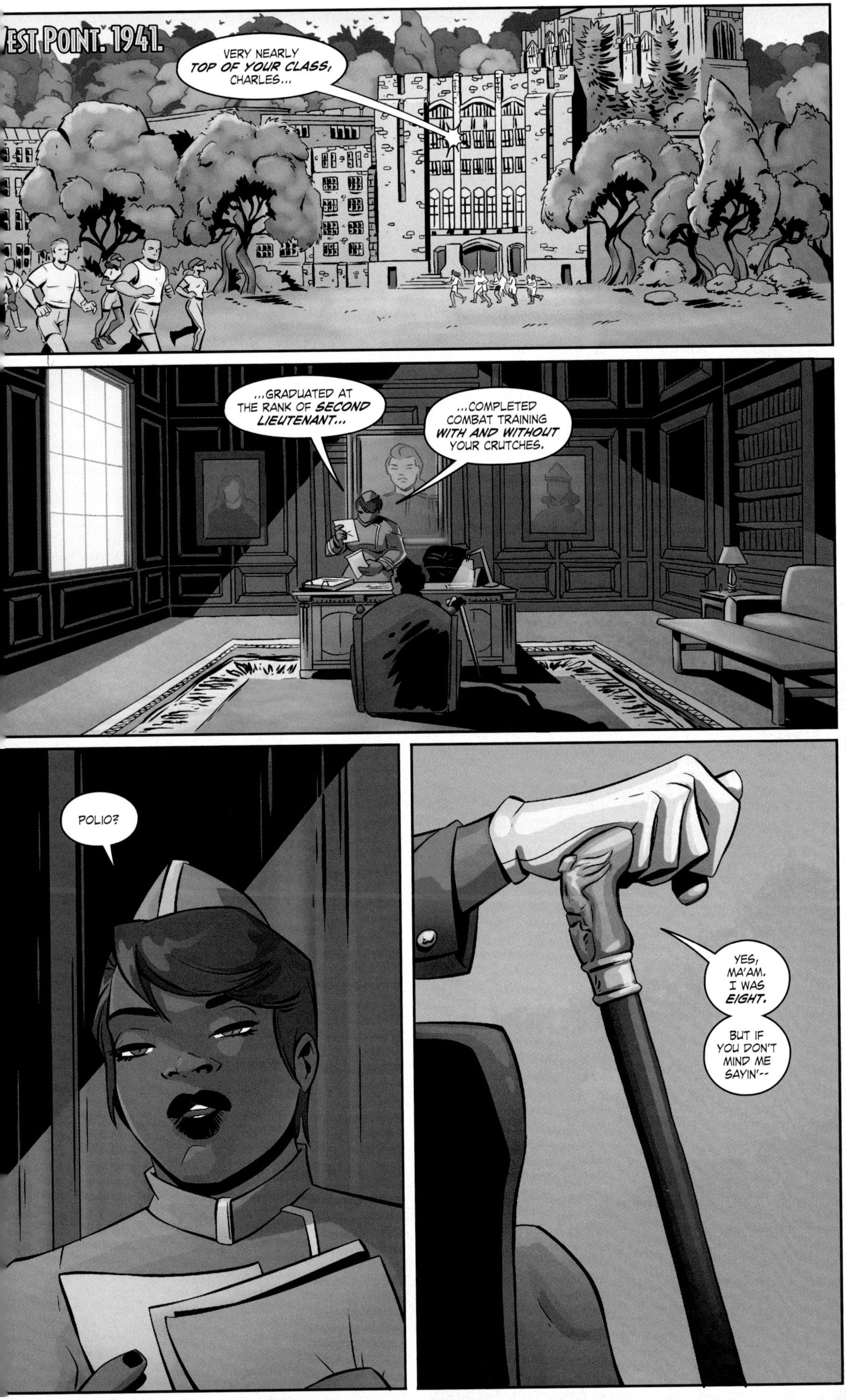
EST POINT. 1941.
VERY NEARLY TOP OF YOUR CLASS, CHARLES...
...GRADUATED AT THE RANK OF SECOND LIEUTENANT...
...COMPLETED COMBAT TRAINING WITH AND WITHOUT YOUR CRUTCHES.
POLIO?
YES, MA'AM. I WAS EIGHT.
BUT IF YOU DON'T MIND ME SAYIN'--

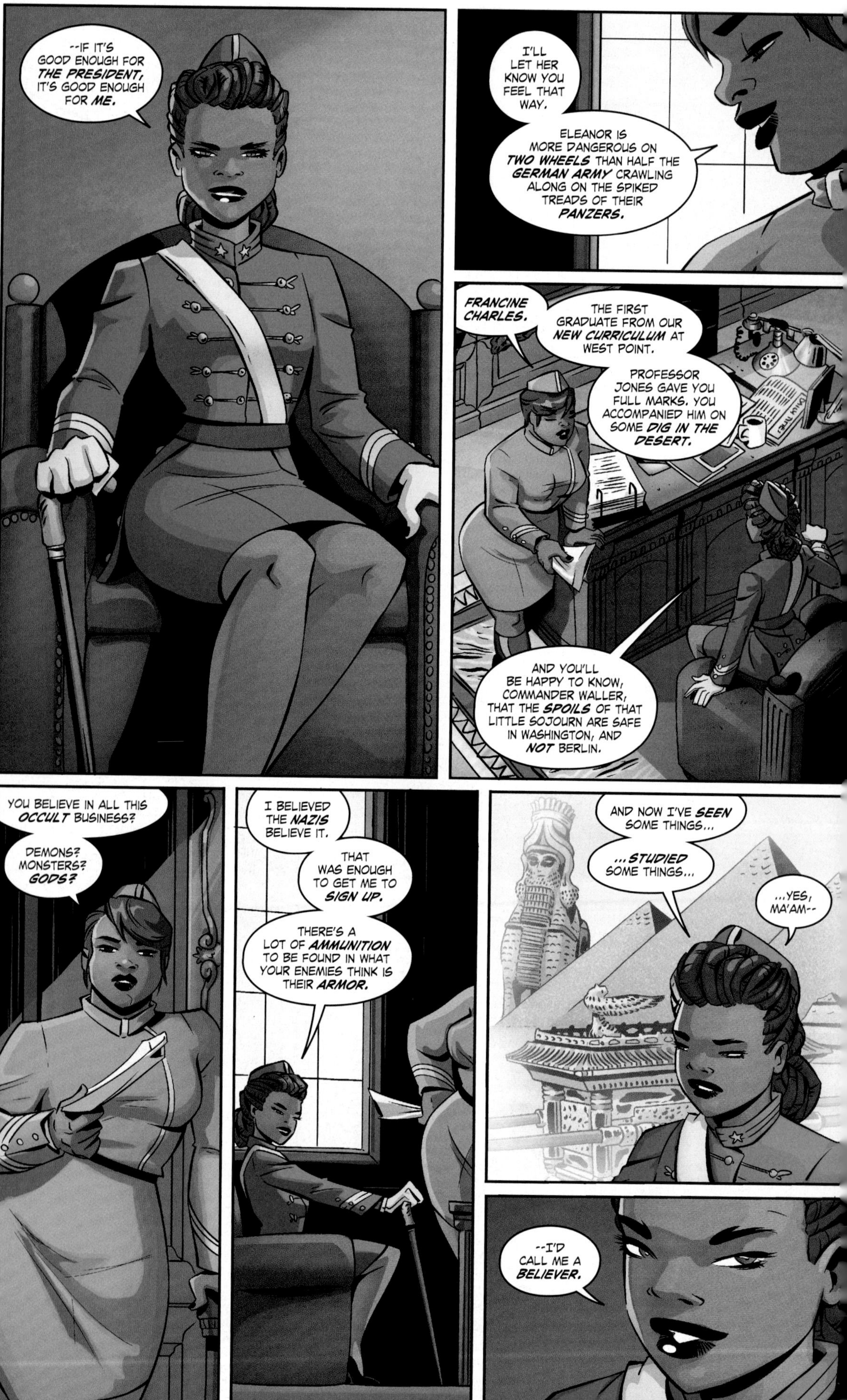
--IF IT'S GOOD ENOUGH FOR *THE PRESIDENT,* IT'S GOOD ENOUGH FOR *ME.*
I'LL LET HER KNOW YOU FEEL THAT WAY.
ELEANOR IS MORE DANGEROUS ON *TWO WHEELS* THAN HALF THE *GERMAN ARMY* CRAWLING ALONG ON THE SPIKED TREADS OF THEIR *PANZERS.*
FRANCINE CHARLES.
THE FIRST GRADUATE FROM OUR *NEW CURRICULUM* AT WEST POINT.
PROFESSOR JONES GAVE YOU FULL MARKS. YOU ACCOMPANIED HIM ON SOME *DIG IN THE DESERT.*
AND YOU'LL BE HAPPY TO KNOW, COMMANDER WALLER, THAT THE *SPOILS* OF THAT LITTLE SOJOURN ARE SAFE IN WASHINGTON, AND *NOT* BERLIN.
YOU BELIEVE IN ALL THIS *OCCULT* BUSINESS?
DEMONS? MONSTERS? *GODS?*
I BELIEVED THE *NAZIS* BELIEVE IT.
THAT WAS ENOUGH TO GET ME TO *SIGN UP.*
THERE'S A LOT OF *AMMUNITION* TO BE FOUND IN WHAT YOUR ENEMIES THINK IS THEIR *ARMOR.*
AND NOW I'VE *SEEN* SOME THINGS...
...STUDIED SOME THINGS...
...YES, MA'AM--
--I'D CALL ME A *BELIEVER.*

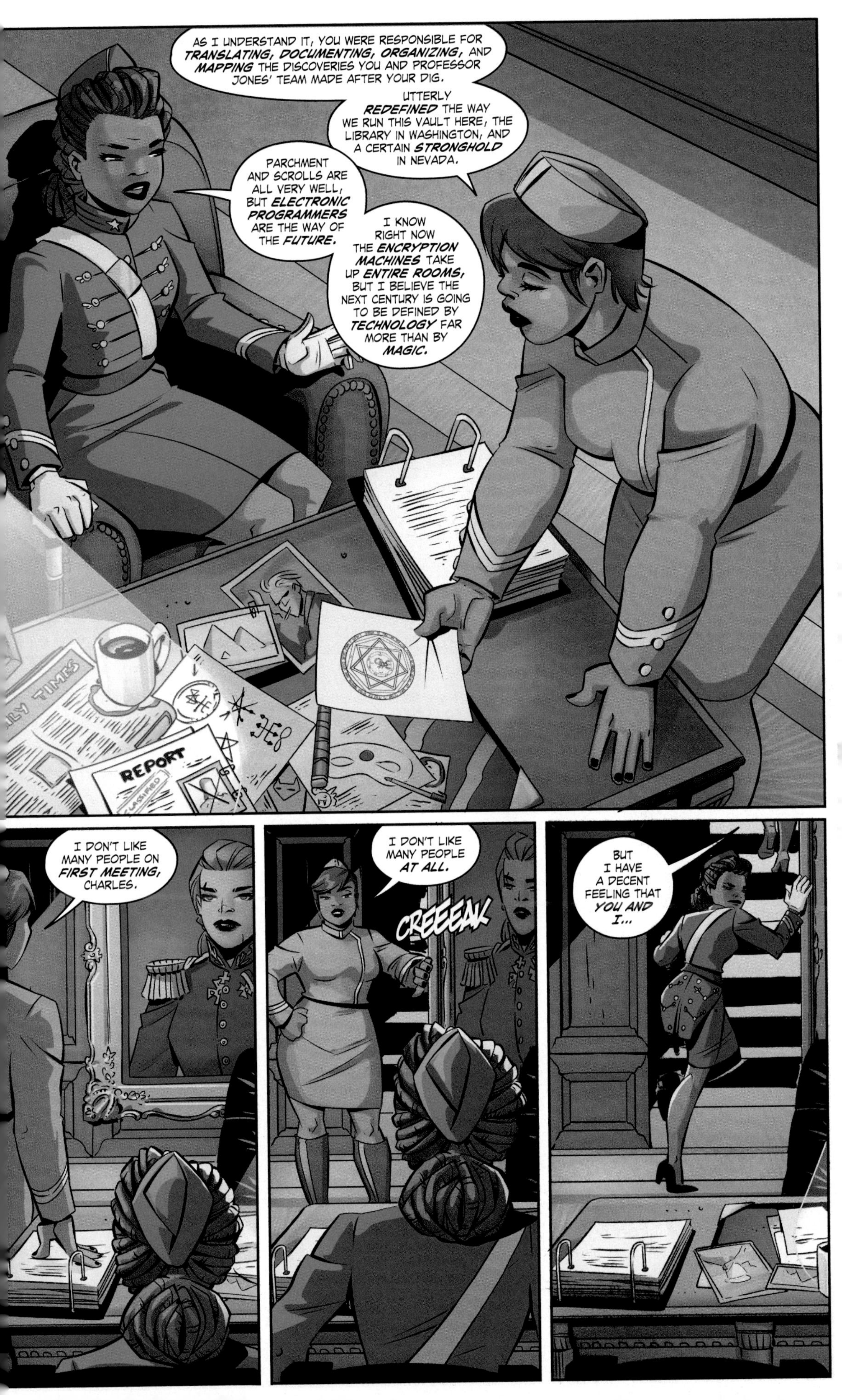
AS I UNDERSTAND IT, YOU WERE RESPONSIBLE FOR TRANSLATING, DOCUMENTING, ORGANIZING, AND MAPPING THE DISCOVERIES YOU AND PROFESSOR JONES' TEAM MADE AFTER YOUR DIG.
UTTERLY REDEFINED THE WAY WE RUN THIS VAULT HERE, THE LIBRARY IN WASHINGTON, AND A CERTAIN STRONGHOLD IN NEVADA.
PARCHMENT AND SCROLLS ARE ALL VERY WELL, BUT ELECTRONIC PROGRAMMERS ARE THE WAY OF THE FUTURE.
I KNOW RIGHT NOW THE ENCRYPTION MACHINES TAKE UP ENTIRE ROOMS, BUT I BELIEVE THE NEXT CENTURY IS GOING TO BE DEFINED BY TECHNOLOGY FAR MORE THAN BY MAGIC.
REPORT
I DON'T LIKE MANY PEOPLE ON FIRST MEETING, CHARLES.
I DON'T LIKE MANY PEOPLE AT ALL.
CREEEAK
BUT I HAVE A DECENT FEELING THAT YOU AND I...

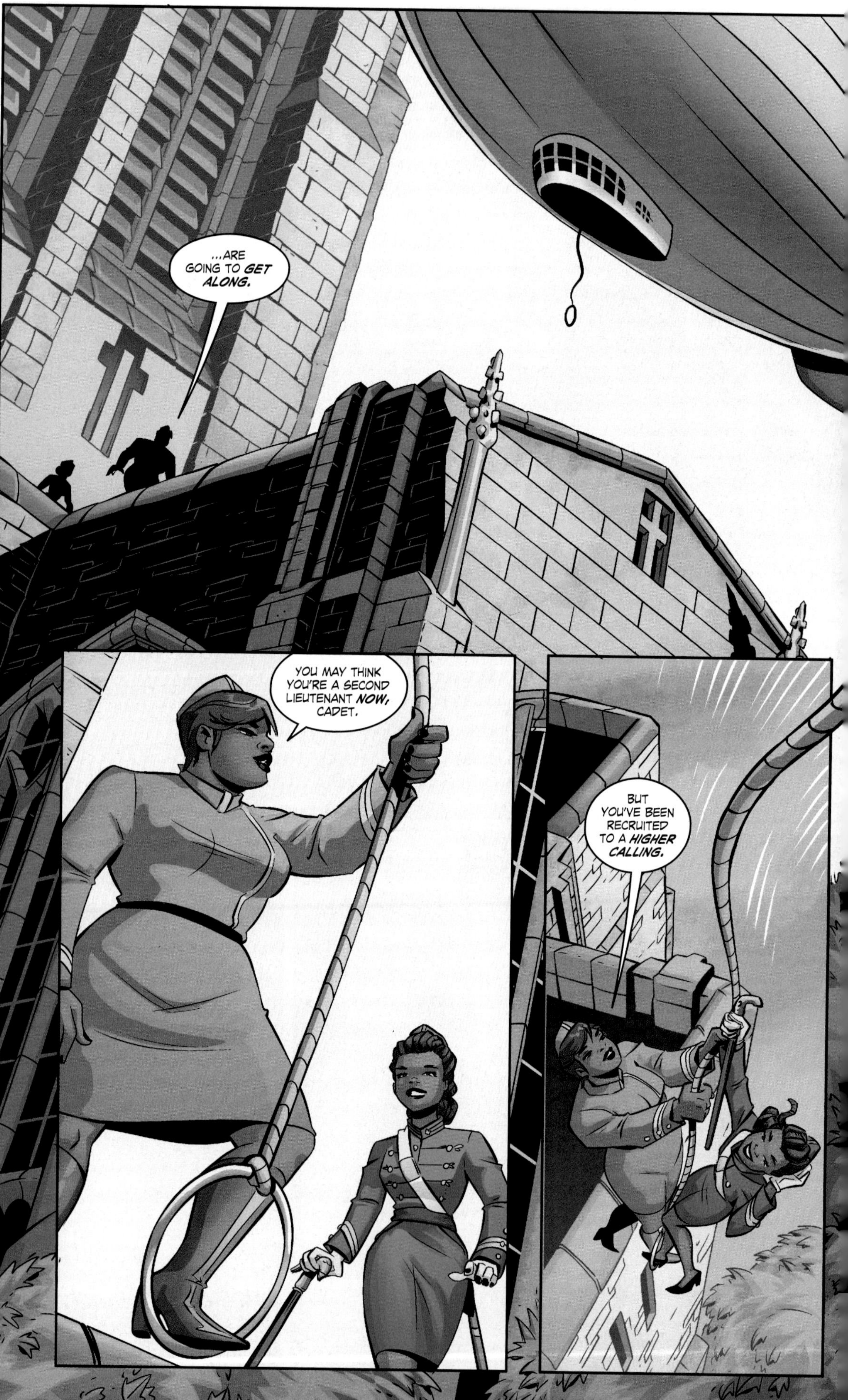
...ARE GOING TO GET ALONG.
YOU MAY THINK YOU'RE A SECOND LIEUTENANT NOW, CADET.
BUT YOU'VE BEEN RECRUITED TO A HIGHER CALLING.

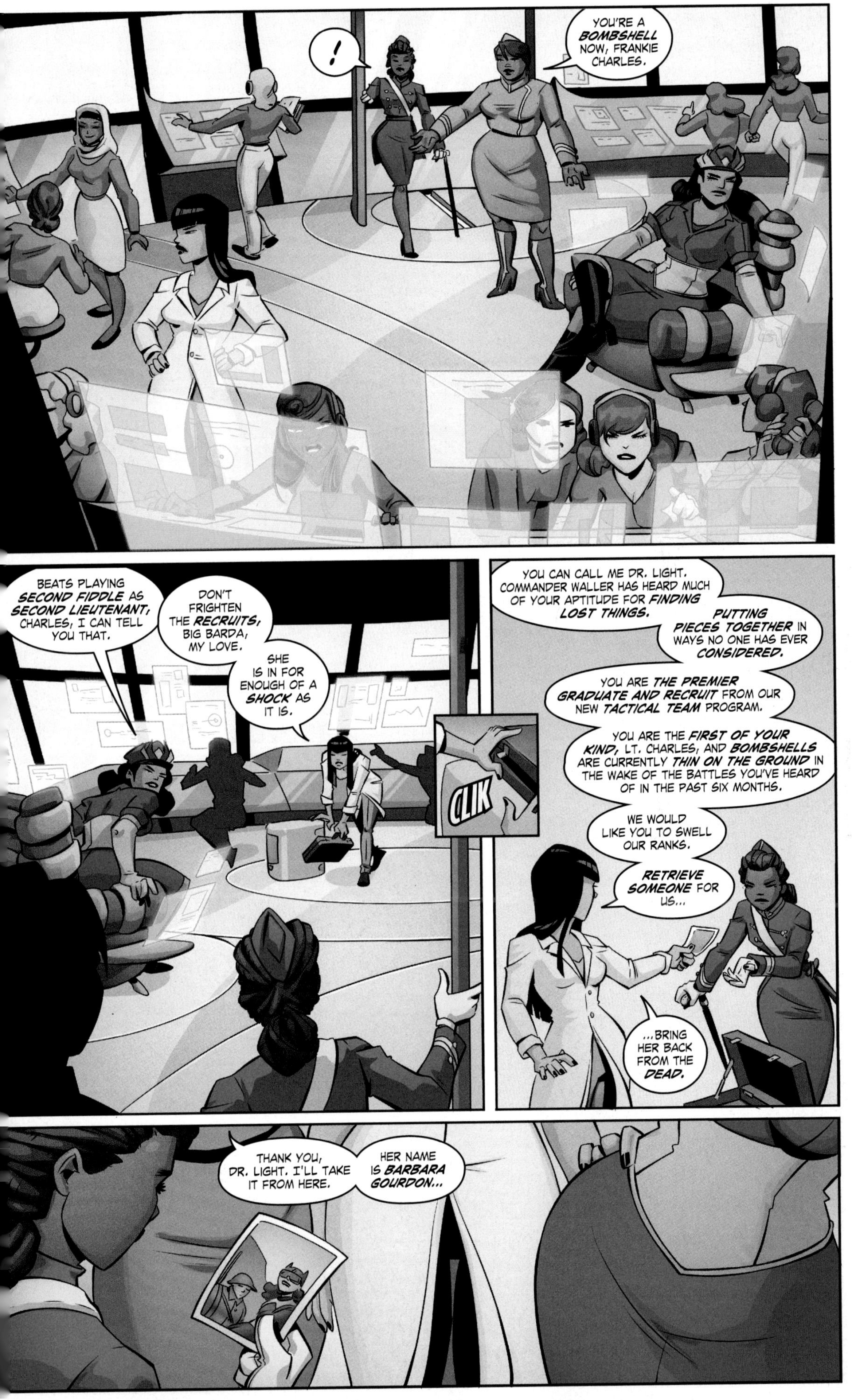
!
YOU'RE A BOMBSHELL NOW, FRANKIE CHARLES.
BEATS PLAYING SECOND FIDDLE AS SECOND LIEUTENANT, CHARLES, I CAN TELL YOU THAT.
DON'T FRIGHTEN THE RECRUITS, BIG BARDA, MY LOVE.
SHE IS IN FOR ENOUGH OF A SHOCK AS IT IS.
CLIK
YOU CAN CALL ME DR. LIGHT. COMMANDER WALLER HAS HEARD MUCH OF YOUR APTITUDE FOR FINDING LOST THINGS.
PUTTING PIECES TOGETHER IN WAYS NO ONE HAS EVER CONSIDERED.
YOU ARE THE PREMIER GRADUATE AND RECRUIT FROM OUR NEW TACTICAL TEAM PROGRAM.
YOU ARE THE FIRST OF YOUR KIND, LT. CHARLES, AND BOMBSHELLS ARE CURRENTLY THIN ON THE GROUND IN THE WAKE OF THE BATTLES YOU'VE HEARD OF IN THE PAST SIX MONTHS.
WE WOULD LIKE YOU TO SWELL OUR RANKS.
RETRIEVE SOMEONE FOR US...
...BRING HER BACK FROM THE DEAD.
THANK YOU, DR. LIGHT. I'LL TAKE IT FROM HERE.
HER NAME IS BARBARA GOURDON...

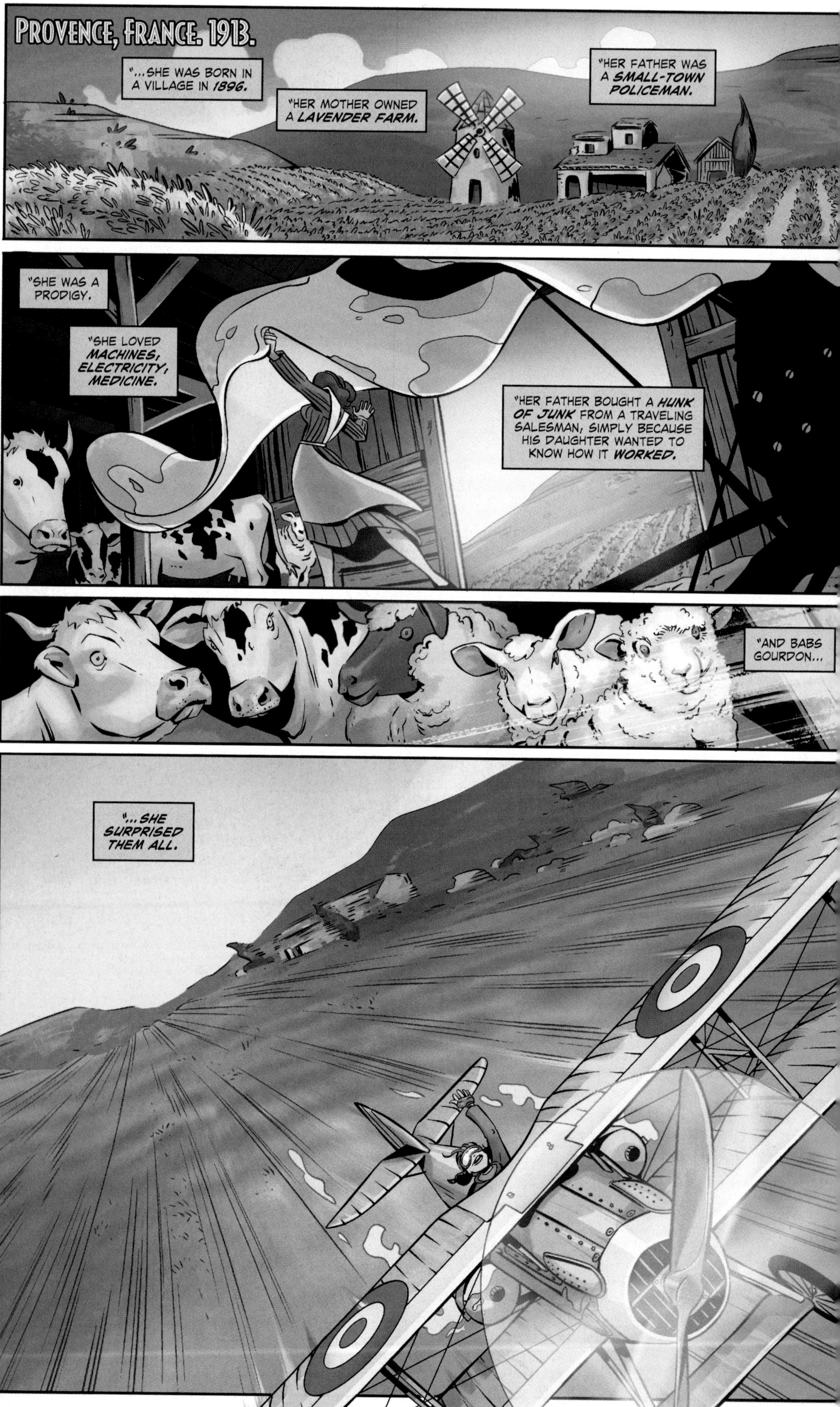
PROVENCE, FRANCE. 1913.
"...SHE WAS BORN IN A VILLAGE IN 1896.
"HER MOTHER OWNED A LAVENDER FARM.
"HER FATHER WAS A SMALL-TOWN POLICEMAN.
"SHE WAS A PRODIGY.
"SHE LOVED MACHINES, ELECTRICITY, MEDICINE.
"HER FATHER BOUGHT A HUNK OF JUNK FROM A TRAVELING SALESMAN, SIMPLY BECAUSE HIS DAUGHTER WANTED TO KNOW HOW IT WORKED.
"AND BABS GOURDON...
"...SHE SURPRISED THEM ALL.

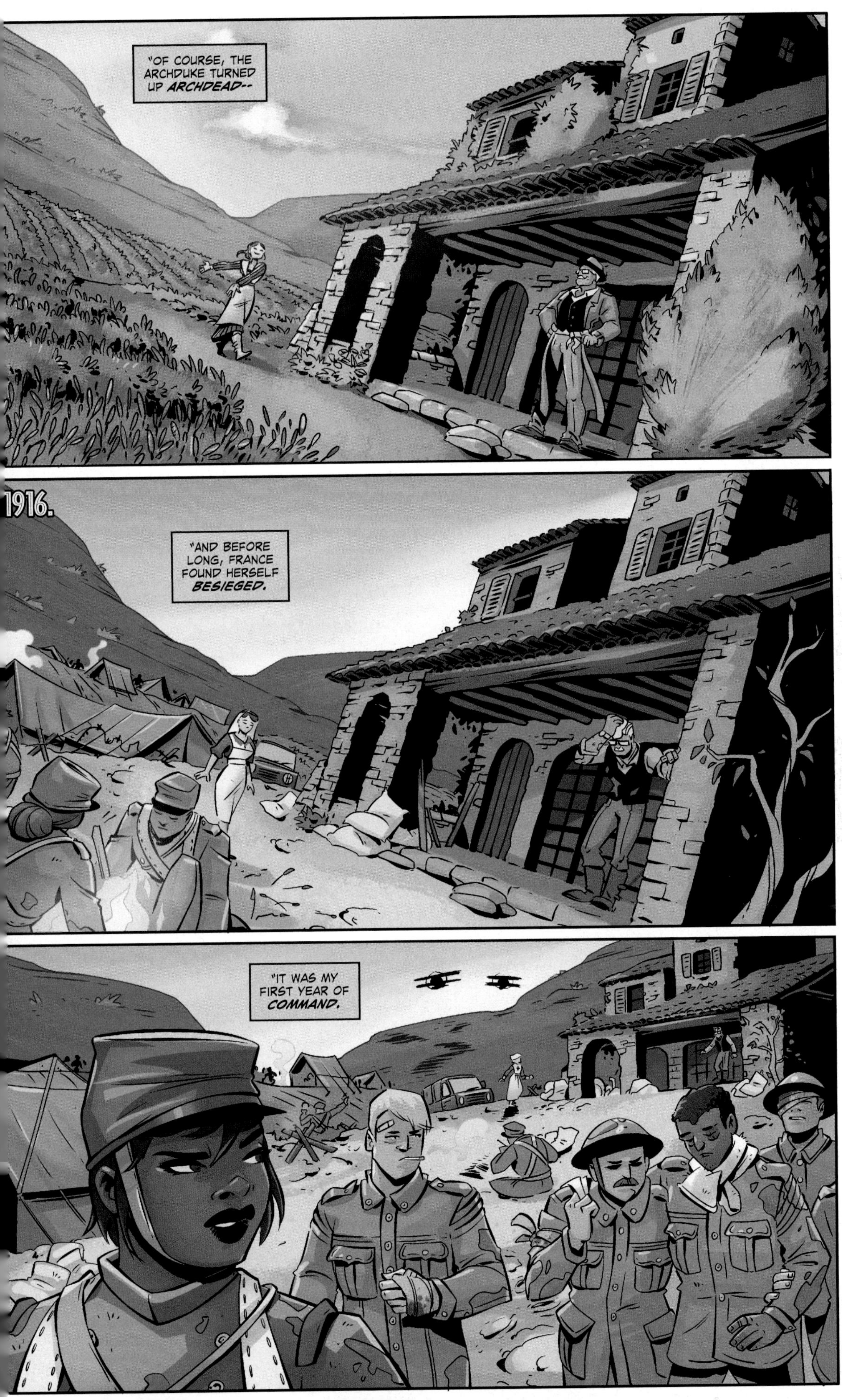
"OF COURSE, THE ARCHDUKE TURNED UP ARCHDEAD--
1916.
"AND BEFORE LONG, FRANCE FOUND HERSELF BESIEGED.
"IT WAS MY FIRST YEAR OF COMMAND.

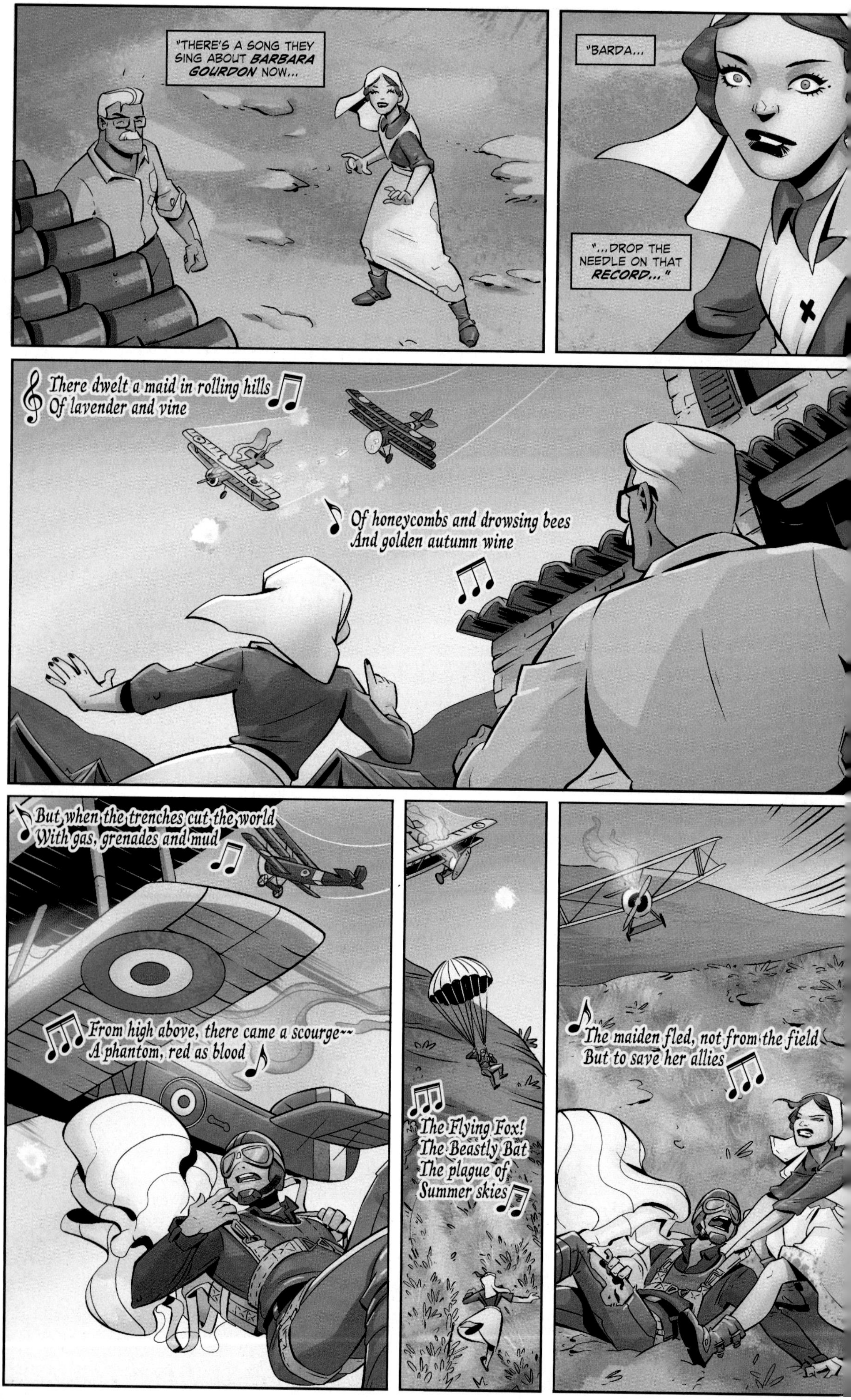
"THERE'S A SONG THEY SING ABOUT BARBARA GOURDON NOW...
"BARDA...
"...DROP THE NEEDLE ON THAT RECORD..."
There dwelt a maid in rolling hills
Of lavender and vine
Of honeycombs and drowsing bees
And golden autumn wine
But when the trenches cut the world
With gas, grenades and mud
From high above, there came a scourge--
A phantom, red as blood
The Flying Fox!
The Beastly Bat
The plague of
Summer skies
The maiden fled, not from the field
But to save her allies

♫♫ The scent of fire, the scent of oil
The scent of blooming fields
The lavender all burning bright
And crushed by hobnailed heels ♫

She would not let her world burn
And take all that was dear ♫♫

♫♫ The home she loved,
The land, the kin ♫

♫ The maiden showed no fear! ♫♫

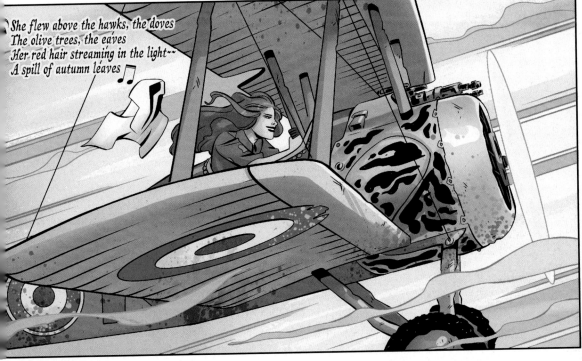

♫ She flew above the hawks, the doves
The olive trees, the eaves
Her red hair streaming in the light~~
A spill of autumn leaves ♫♫

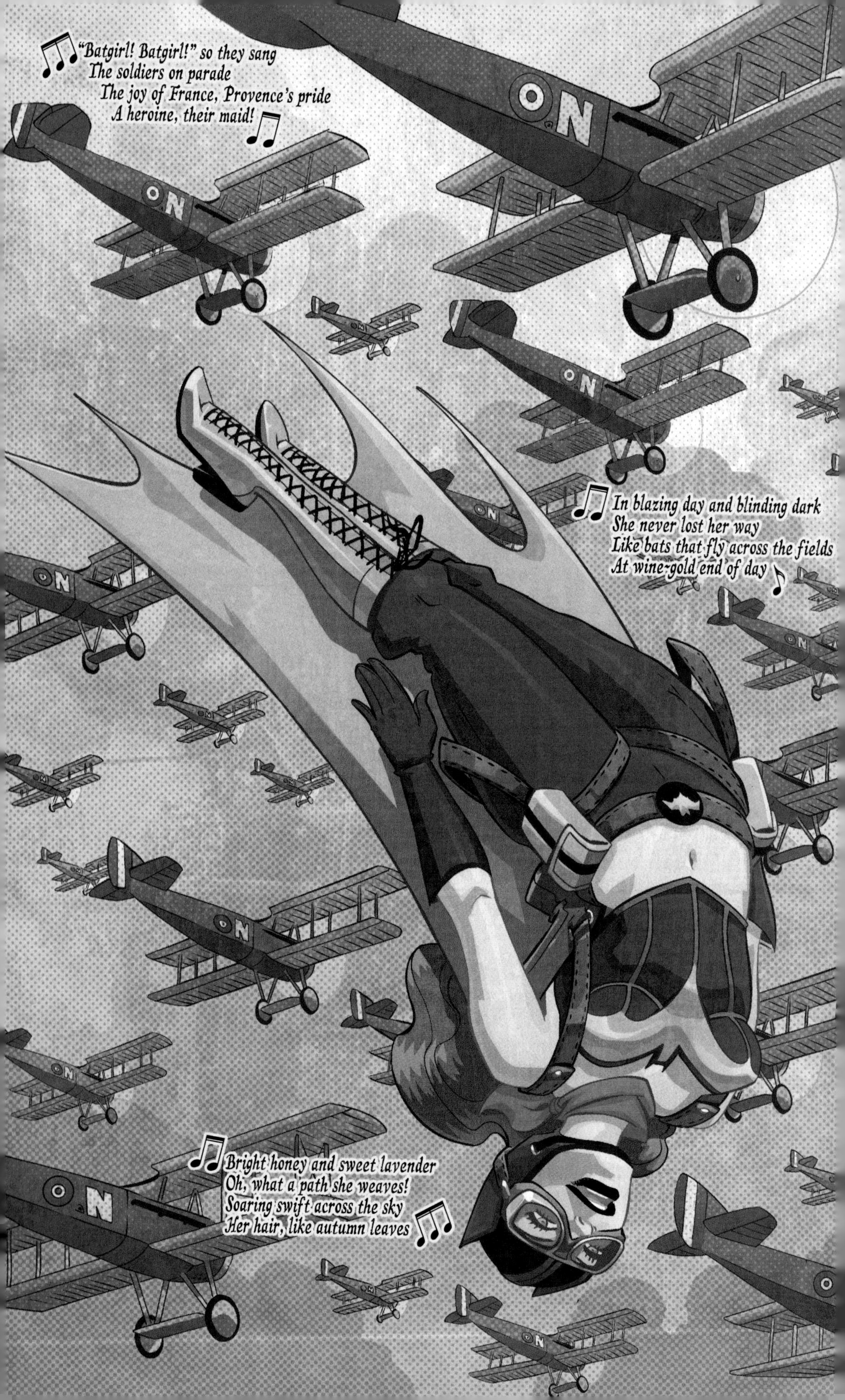
"Batgirl! Batgirl!" so they sang
The soldiers on parade
The joy of France, Provence's pride
A heroine, their maid!
In blazing day and blinding dark
She never lost her way
Like bats that fly across the fields
At wine-gold end of day
Bright honey and sweet lavender
Oh, what a path she weaves!
Soaring swift across the sky
Her hair, like autumn leaves

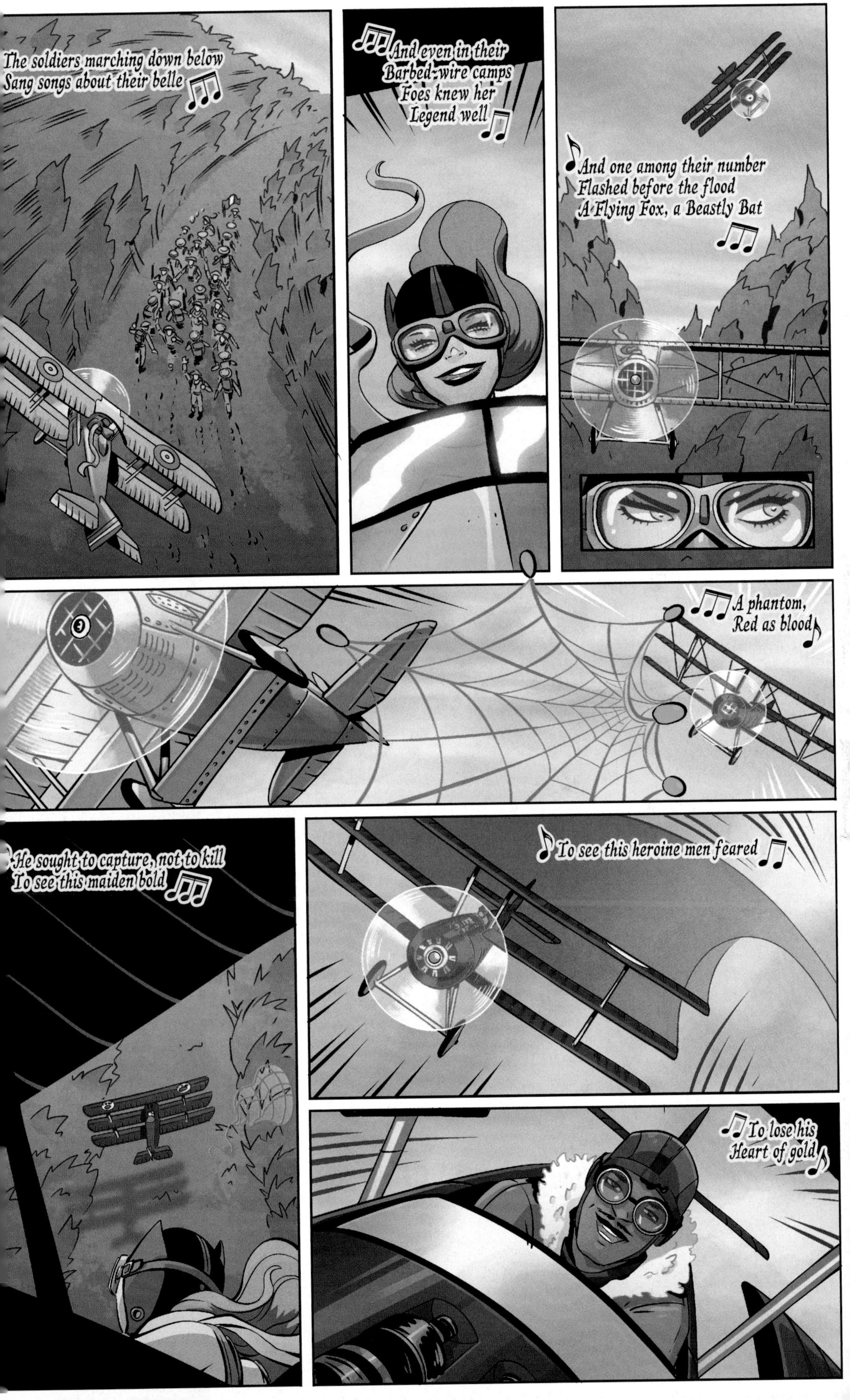

The soldiers marching down below
Sang songs about their belle
And even in their
Barbed-wire camps
Foes knew her
Legend well
And one among their number
Flashed before the flood
A Flying Fox, a Beastly Bat
A phantom,
Red as blood
He sought to capture, not to kill
To see this maiden bold
To see this heroine men feared
To lose his
Heart of gold

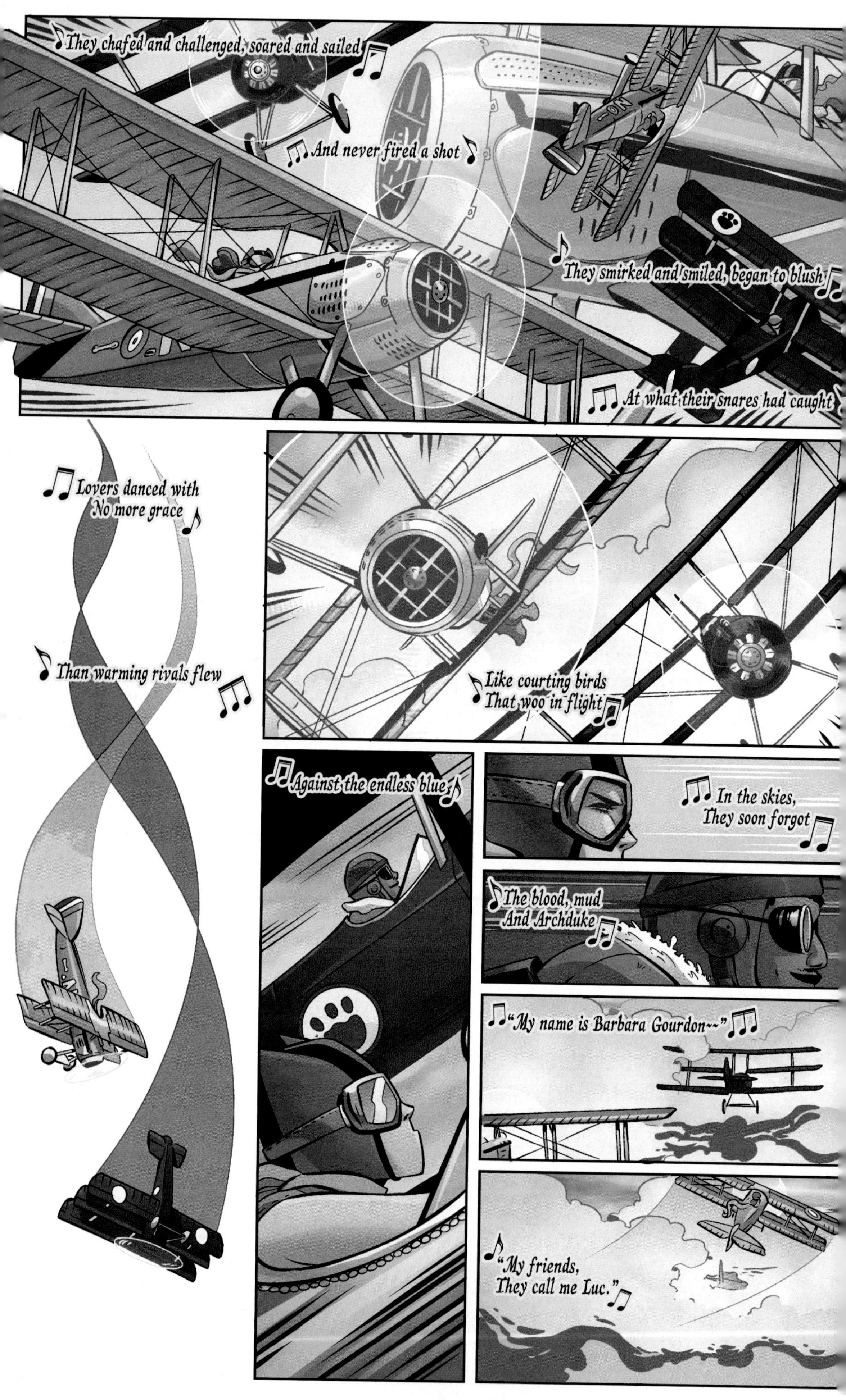
They chafed and challenged, soared and sailed
And never fired a shot
They smirked and smiled, began to blush
At what their snares had caught
Lovers danced with
No more grace
Than warming rivals flew
Like courting birds
That woo in flight
Against the endless blue
In the skies,
They soon forgot
The blood, mud
And Archduke
"My name is Barbara Gourdon~~"
"My friends,
They call me Luc."

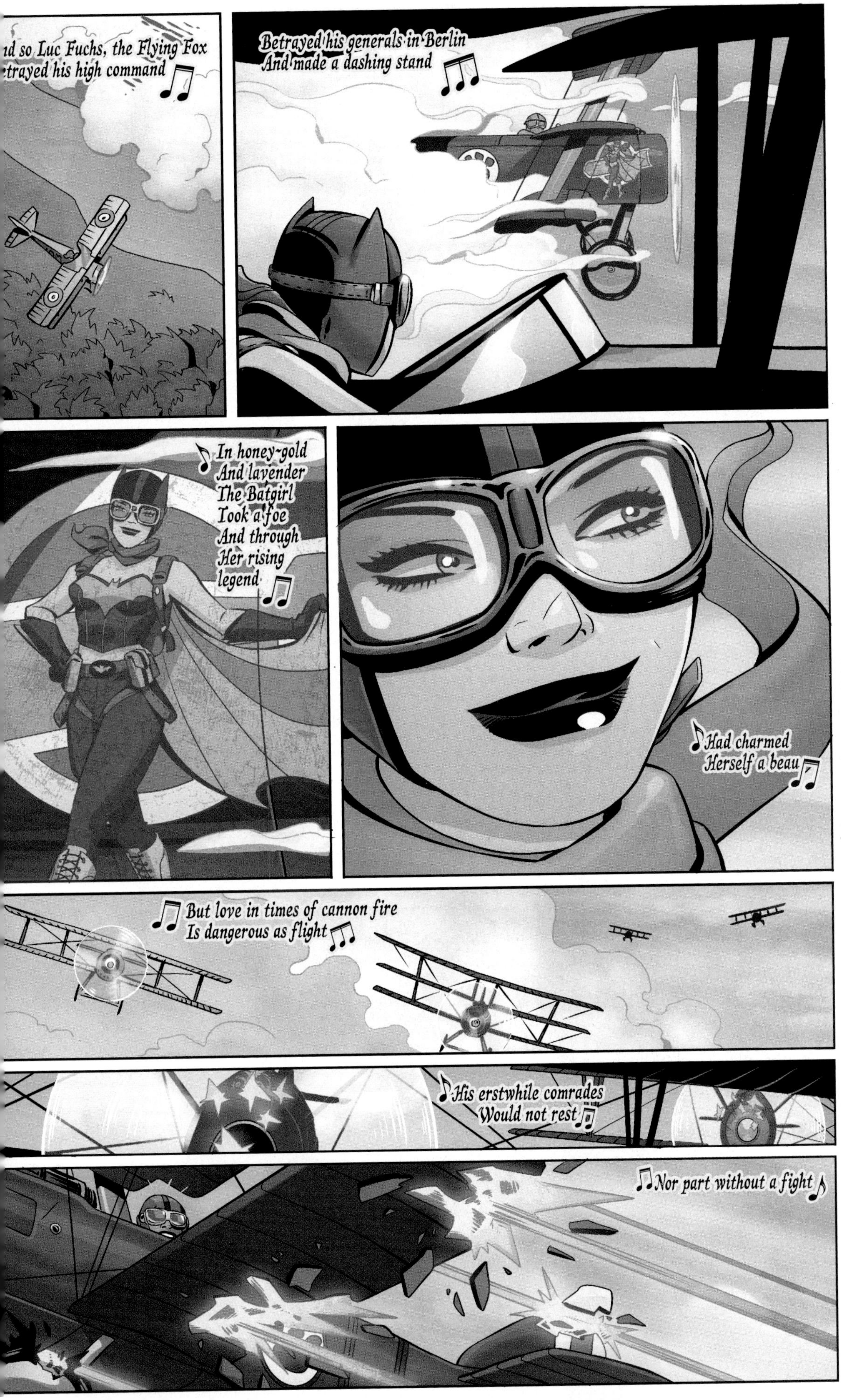

nd so Luc Fuchs, the Flying Fox
etrayed his high command
Betrayed his generals in Berlin
And made a dashing stand
In honey-gold
And lavender
The Batgirl
Took a foe
And through
Her rising
legend
Had charmed
Herself a beau
But love in times of cannon fire
Is dangerous as flight
His erstwhile comrades
Would not rest
Nor part without a fight

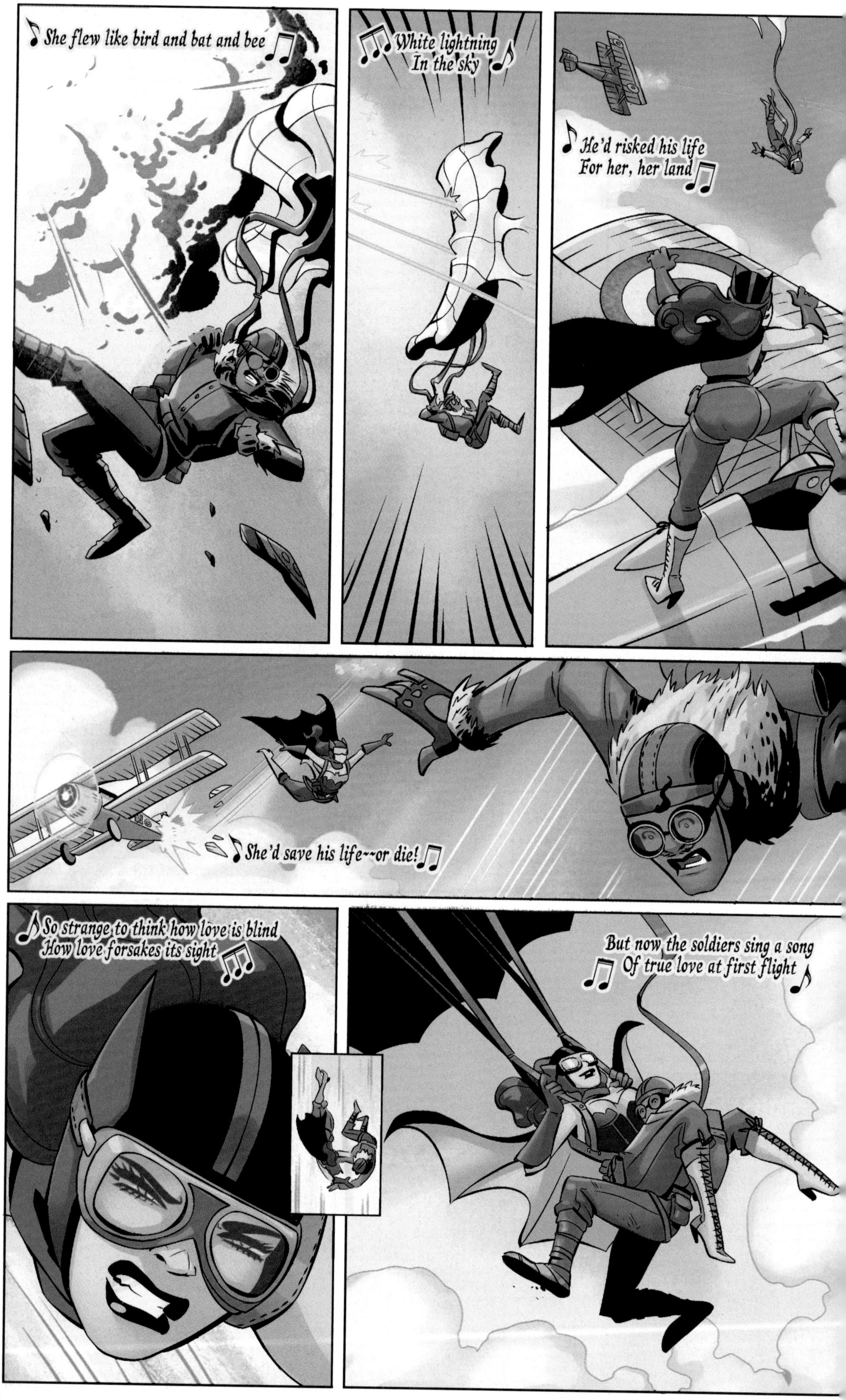
She flew like bird and bat and bee
White lightning In the sky
He'd risked his life For her, her land
She'd save his life--or die!
So strange to think how love is blind How love forsakes its sight
But now the soldiers sing a song Of true love at first flight

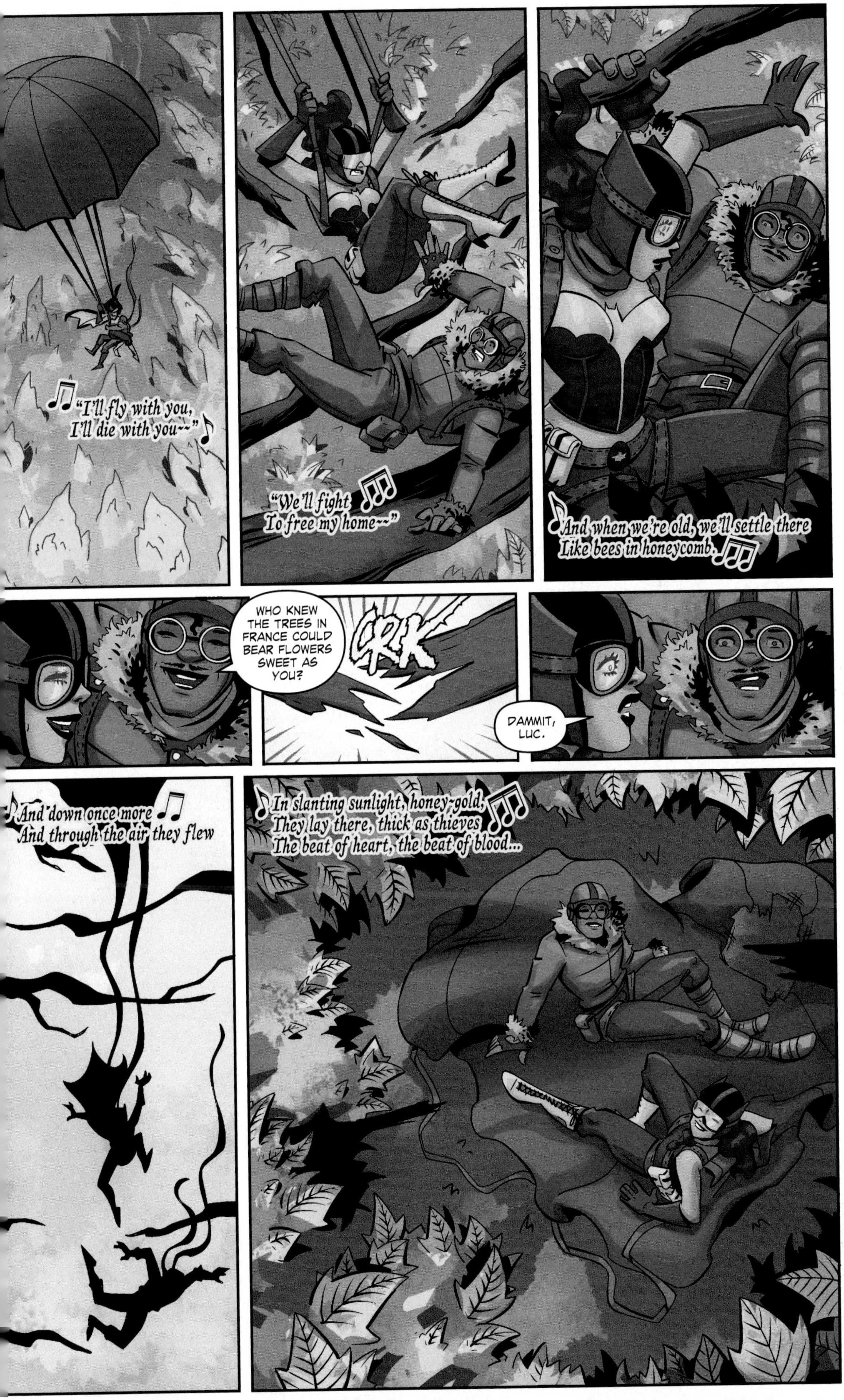
"I'll fly with you,
I'll die with you~~"
"We'll fight
To free my home~~"
And when we're old, we'll settle there
Like bees in honeycomb.
WHO KNEW THE TREES IN FRANCE COULD BEAR FLOWERS SWEET AS YOU?
CRK
DAMMIT, LUC.
And down once more
And through the air they flew
In slanting sunlight, honey-gold,
They lay there, thick as thieves
The beat of heart, the beat of blood...

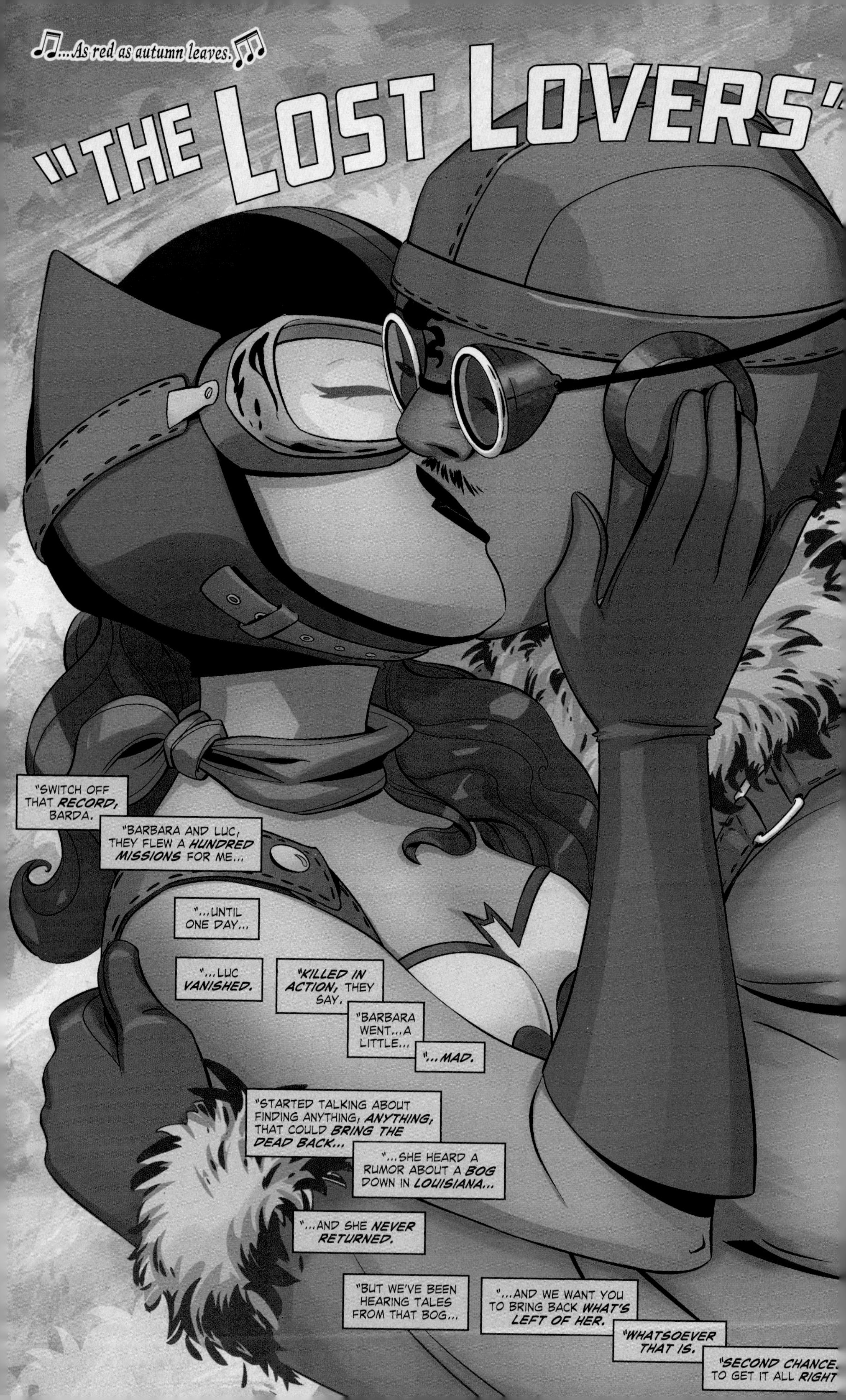

♫...As red as autumn leaves.♫
"THE LOST LOVERS"
"SWITCH OFF THAT RECORD, BARDA.
"BARBARA AND LUC, THEY FLEW A HUNDRED MISSIONS FOR ME...
"...UNTIL ONE DAY...
"...LUC VANISHED.
"KILLED IN ACTION, THEY SAY.
"BARBARA WENT...A LITTLE...
"...MAD.
"STARTED TALKING ABOUT FINDING ANYTHING, ANYTHING, THAT COULD BRING THE DEAD BACK...
"...SHE HEARD A RUMOR ABOUT A BOG DOWN IN LOUISIANA...
"...AND SHE NEVER RETURNED.
"BUT WE'VE BEEN HEARING TALES FROM THAT BOG...
"...AND WE WANT YOU TO BRING BACK WHAT'S LEFT OF HER.
"WHATSOEVER THAT IS.
"SECOND CHANCE TO GET IT ALL RIGHT

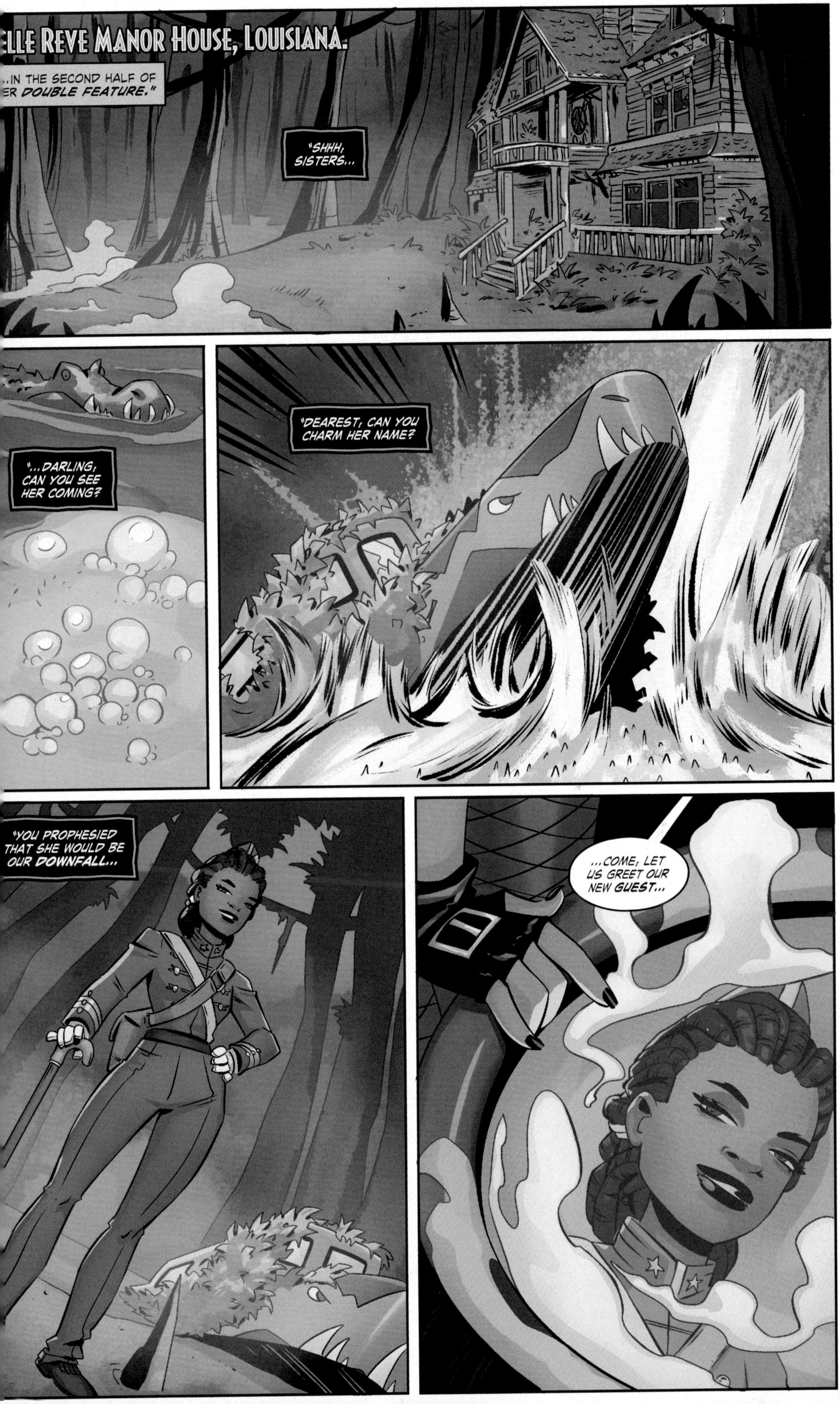

ELLE REVE MANOR HOUSE, LOUISIANA.
...IN THE SECOND HALF OF
ER DOUBLE FEATURE."
"SHHH, SISTERS...
"...DARLING, CAN YOU SEE HER COMING?
"DEAREST, CAN YOU CHARM HER NAME?
"YOU PROPHESIED THAT SHE WOULD BE OUR DOWNFALL...
...COME, LET US GREET OUR NEW GUEST...

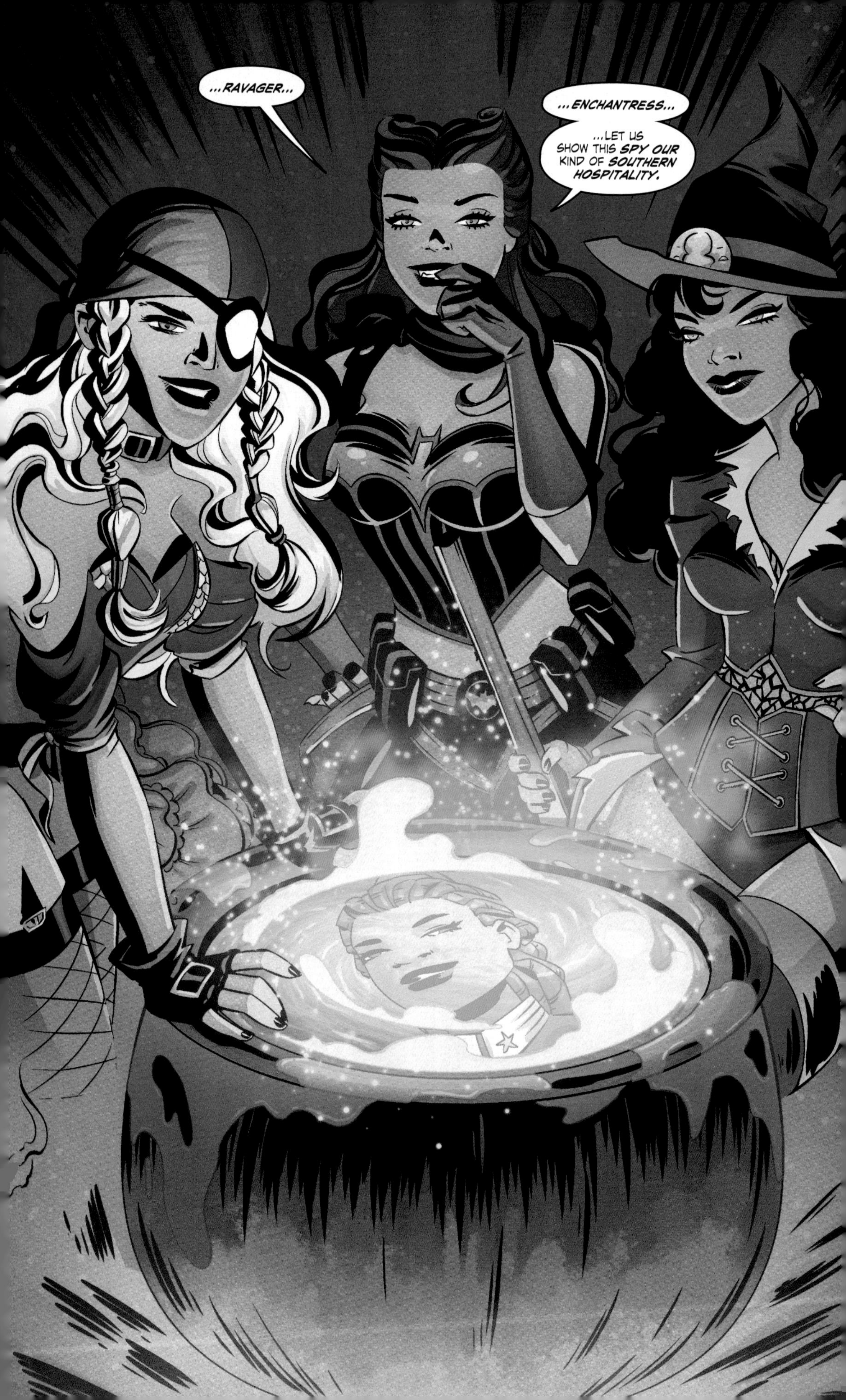
...RAVAGER...
...ENCHANTRESS...
...LET US SHOW THIS SPY OUR KIND OF SOUTHERN HOSPITALITY.

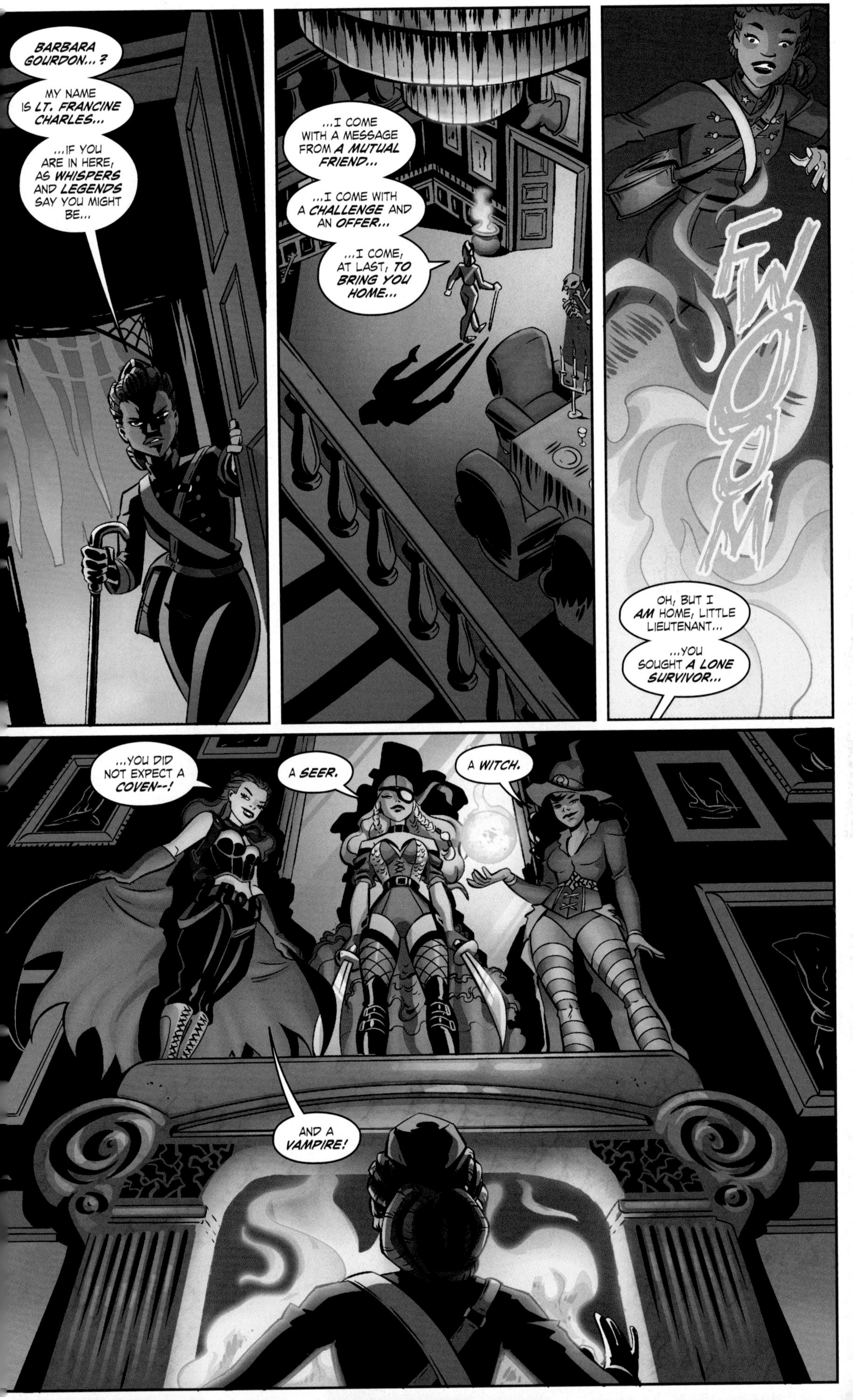
BARBARA GOURDON...?
MY NAME IS LT. FRANCINE CHARLES...
...IF YOU ARE IN HERE, AS WHISPERS AND LEGENDS SAY YOU MIGHT BE...
...I COME WITH A MESSAGE FROM A MUTUAL FRIEND...
...I COME WITH A CHALLENGE AND AN OFFER...
...I COME, AT LAST, TO BRING YOU HOME...
FWOOM
OH, BUT I AM HOME, LITTLE LIEUTENANT...
...YOU SOUGHT A LONE SURVIVOR...
...YOU DID NOT EXPECT A COVEN--!
A SEER.
A WITCH.
AND A VAMPIRE!

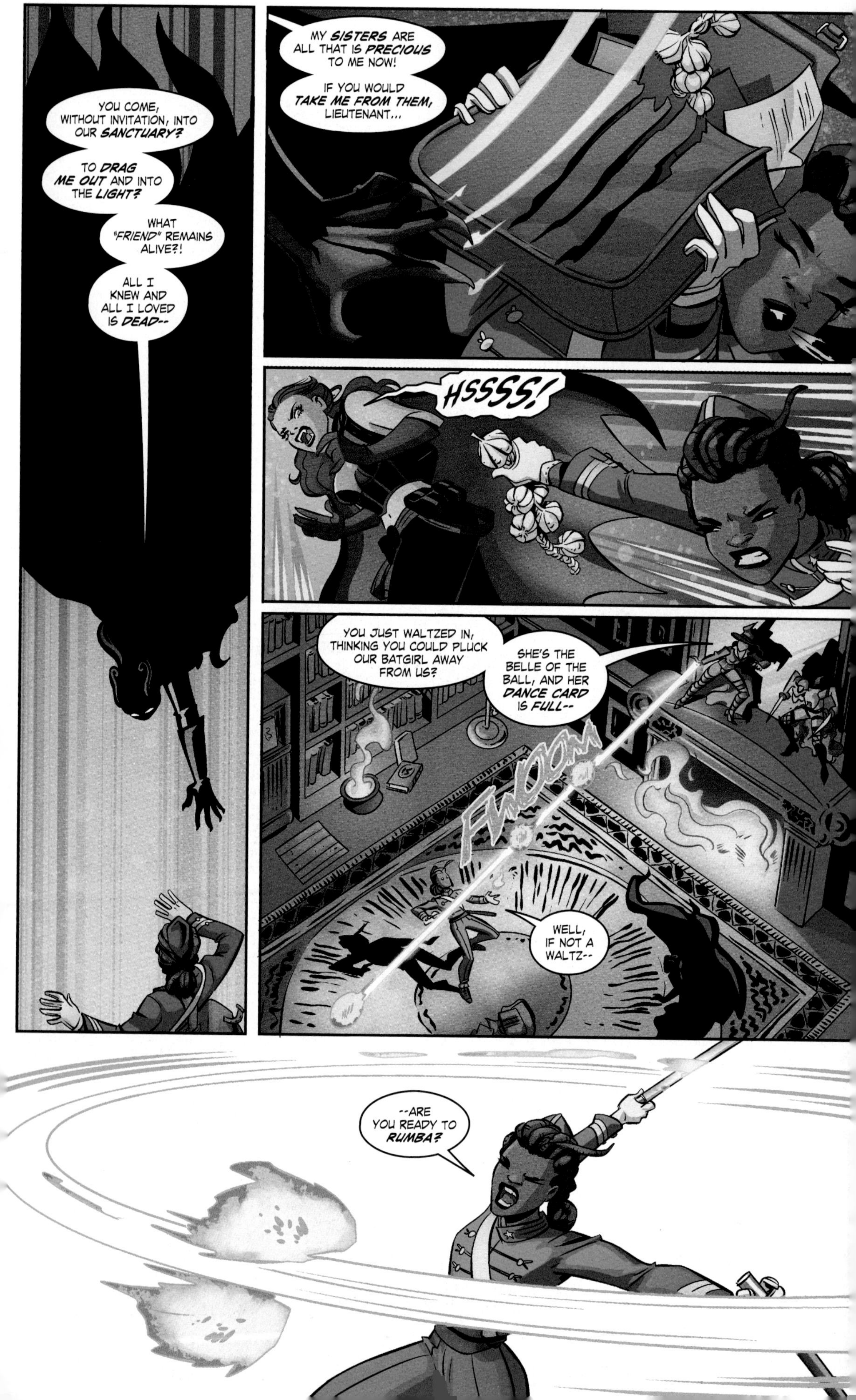
YOU COME, WITHOUT INVITATION, INTO OUR SANCTUARY?
TO DRAG ME OUT AND INTO THE LIGHT?
WHAT "FRIEND" REMAINS ALIVE?!
ALL I KNEW AND ALL I LOVED IS DEAD--
MY SISTERS ARE ALL THAT IS PRECIOUS TO ME NOW!
IF YOU WOULD TAKE ME FROM THEM, LIEUTENANT...
HSSSS!
YOU JUST WALTZED IN, THINKING YOU COULD PLUCK OUR BATGIRL AWAY FROM US?
SHE'S THE BELLE OF THE BALL, AND HER DANCE CARD IS FULL--
FWOOM
WELL, IF NOT A WALTZ--
--ARE YOU READY TO RUMBA?

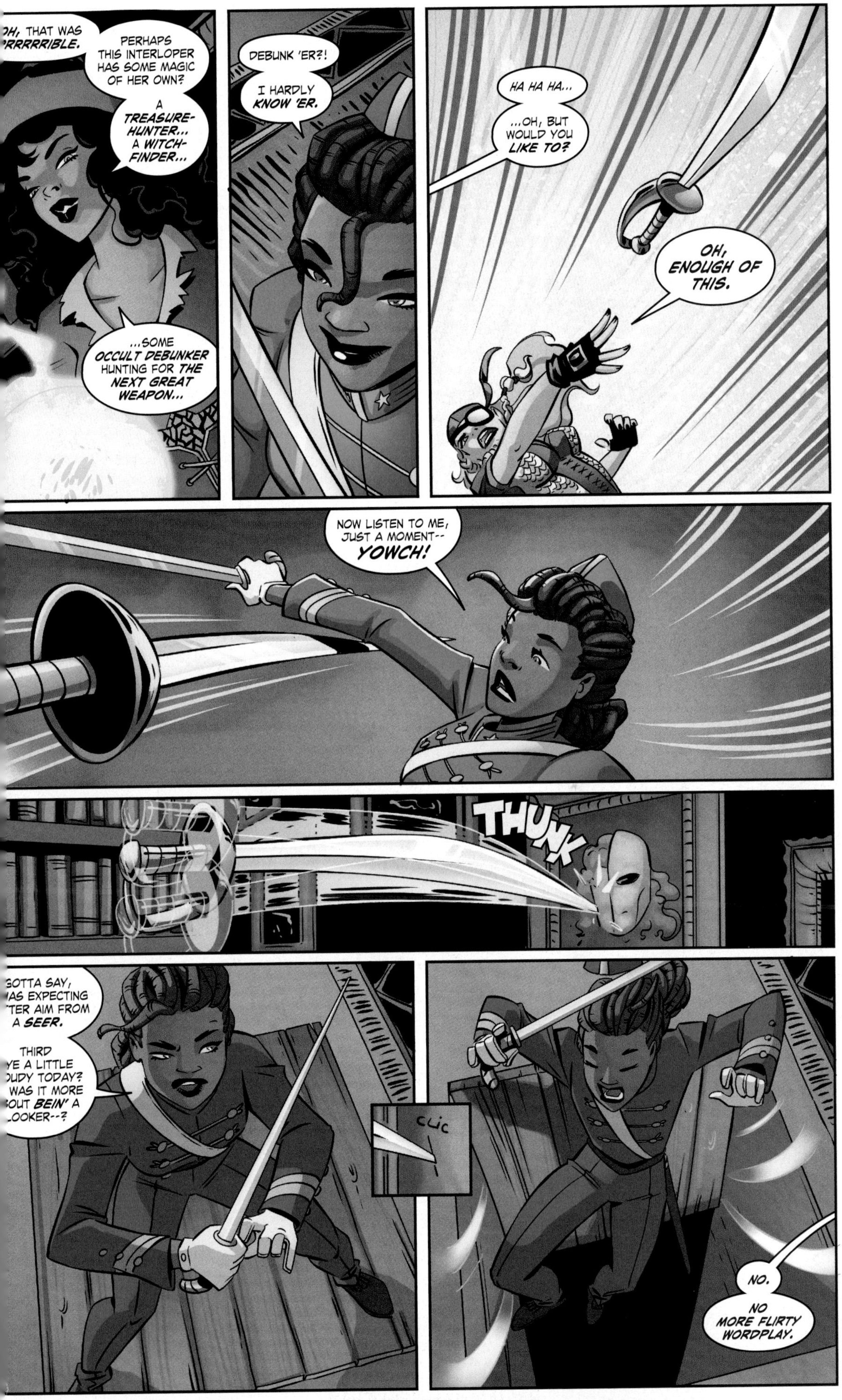

OH, THAT WAS
RRRRRIBLE.
PERHAPS THIS INTERLOPER HAS SOME MAGIC OF HER OWN?
A TREASURE-HUNTER... A WITCH-FINDER...
...SOME OCCULT DEBUNKER HUNTING FOR THE NEXT GREAT WEAPON...
DEBUNK 'ER?!
I HARDLY KNOW 'ER.
HA HA HA...
...OH, BUT WOULD YOU LIKE TO?
OH, ENOUGH OF THIS.
NOW LISTEN TO ME, JUST A MOMENT-- YOWCH!
THUNK
GOTTA SAY, WAS EXPECTING TTER AIM FROM A SEER.
THIRD YE A LITTLE OUDY TODAY? WAS IT MORE OUT BEIN' A LOOKER--?
CLIC
NO.
NO MORE FLIRTY WORDPLAY.

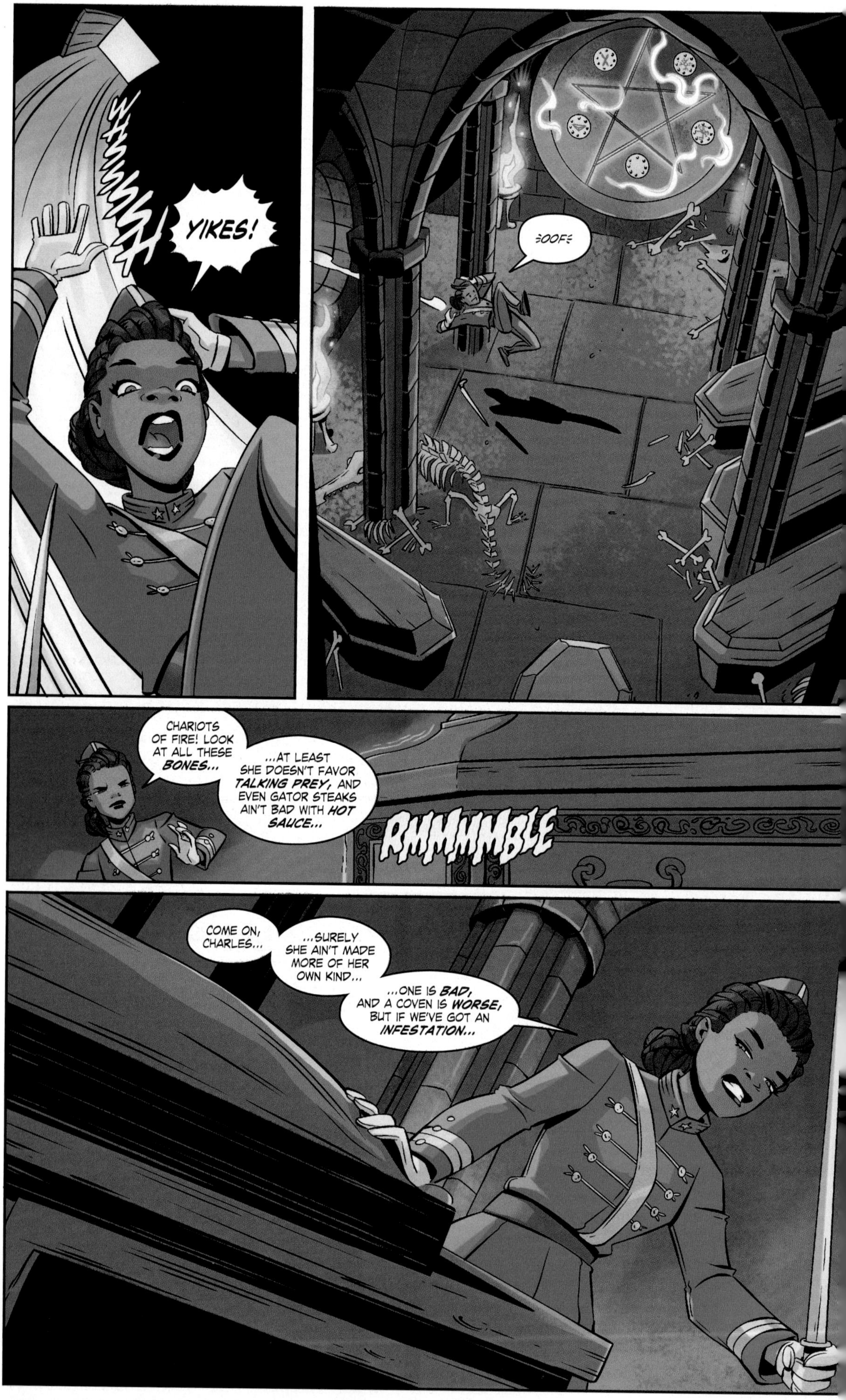

WHHWWWH
YIKES!
=OOF=
CHARIOTS OF FIRE! LOOK AT ALL THESE BONES...
...AT LEAST SHE DOESN'T FAVOR TALKING PREY, AND EVEN GATOR STEAKS AIN'T BAD WITH HOT SAUCE...
RMMMMBLE
COME ON, CHARLES...
...SURELY SHE AIN'T MADE MORE OF HER OWN KIND...
...ONE IS BAD, AND A COVEN IS WORSE, BUT IF WE'VE GOT AN INFESTATION...

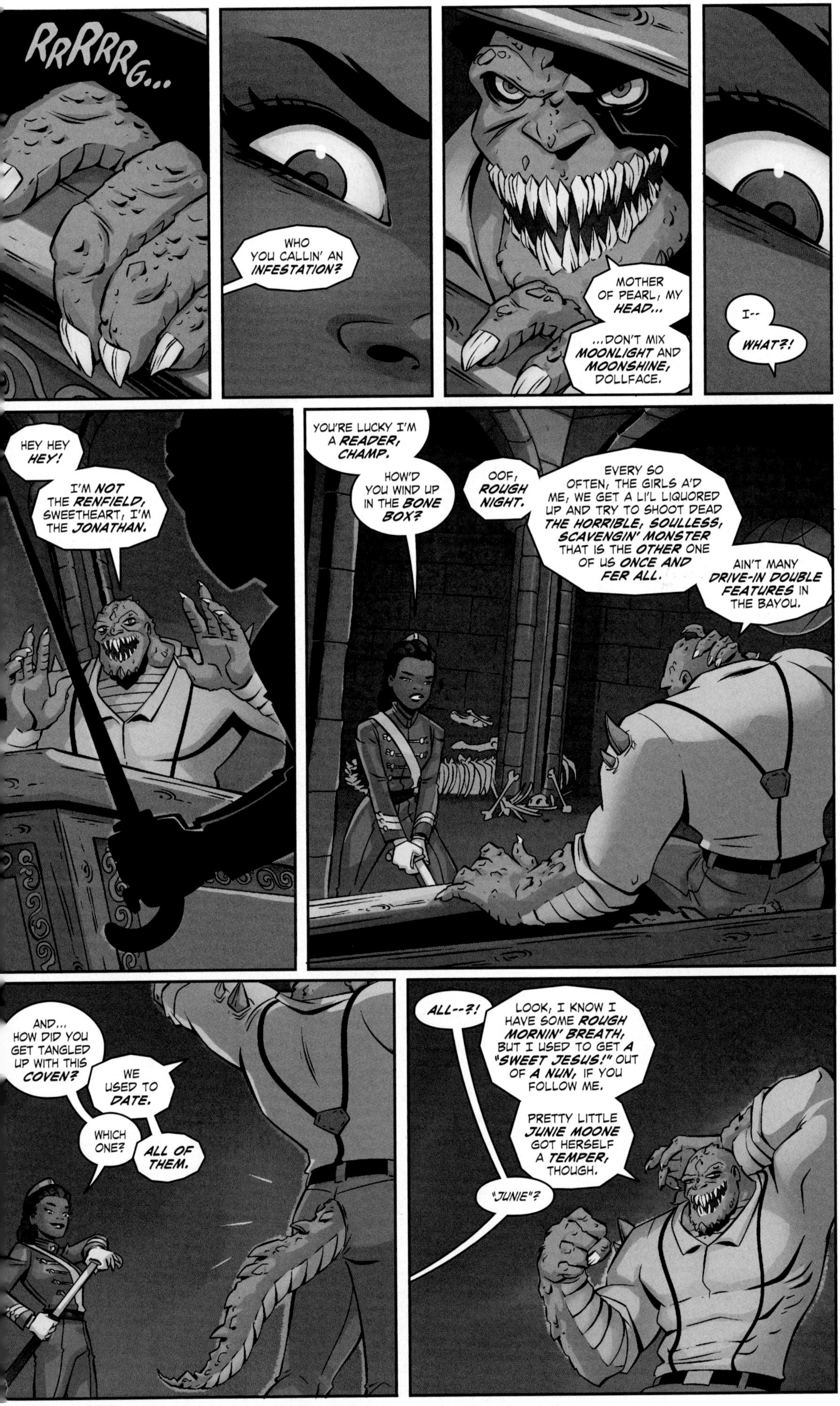
RRRRRG...
WHO YOU CALLIN' AN INFESTATION?
MOTHER OF PEARL, MY HEAD...
...DON'T MIX MOONLIGHT AND MOONSHINE, DOLLFACE.
I--
WHAT?!
HEY HEY HEY!
I'M NOT THE RENFIELD, SWEETHEART, I'M THE JONATHAN.
YOU'RE LUCKY I'M A READER, CHAMP.
HOW'D YOU WIND UP IN THE BONE BOX?
OOF, ROUGH NIGHT.
EVERY SO OFTEN, THE GIRLS A'D ME, WE GET A LI'L LIQUORED UP AND TRY TO SHOOT DEAD THE HORRIBLE, SOULLESS, SCAVENGIN' MONSTER THAT IS THE OTHER ONE OF US ONCE AND FER ALL.
AIN'T MANY DRIVE-IN DOUBLE FEATURES IN THE BAYOU.
AND... HOW DID YOU GET TANGLED UP WITH THIS COVEN?
WE USED TO DATE.
WHICH ONE?
ALL OF THEM.
ALL--?!
LOOK, I KNOW I HAVE SOME ROUGH MORNIN' BREATH, BUT I USED TO GET A "SWEET JESUS!" OUT OF A NUN, IF YOU FOLLOW ME.
PRETTY LITTLE JUNIE MOONE GOT HERSELF A TEMPER, THOUGH.
"JUNIE"?

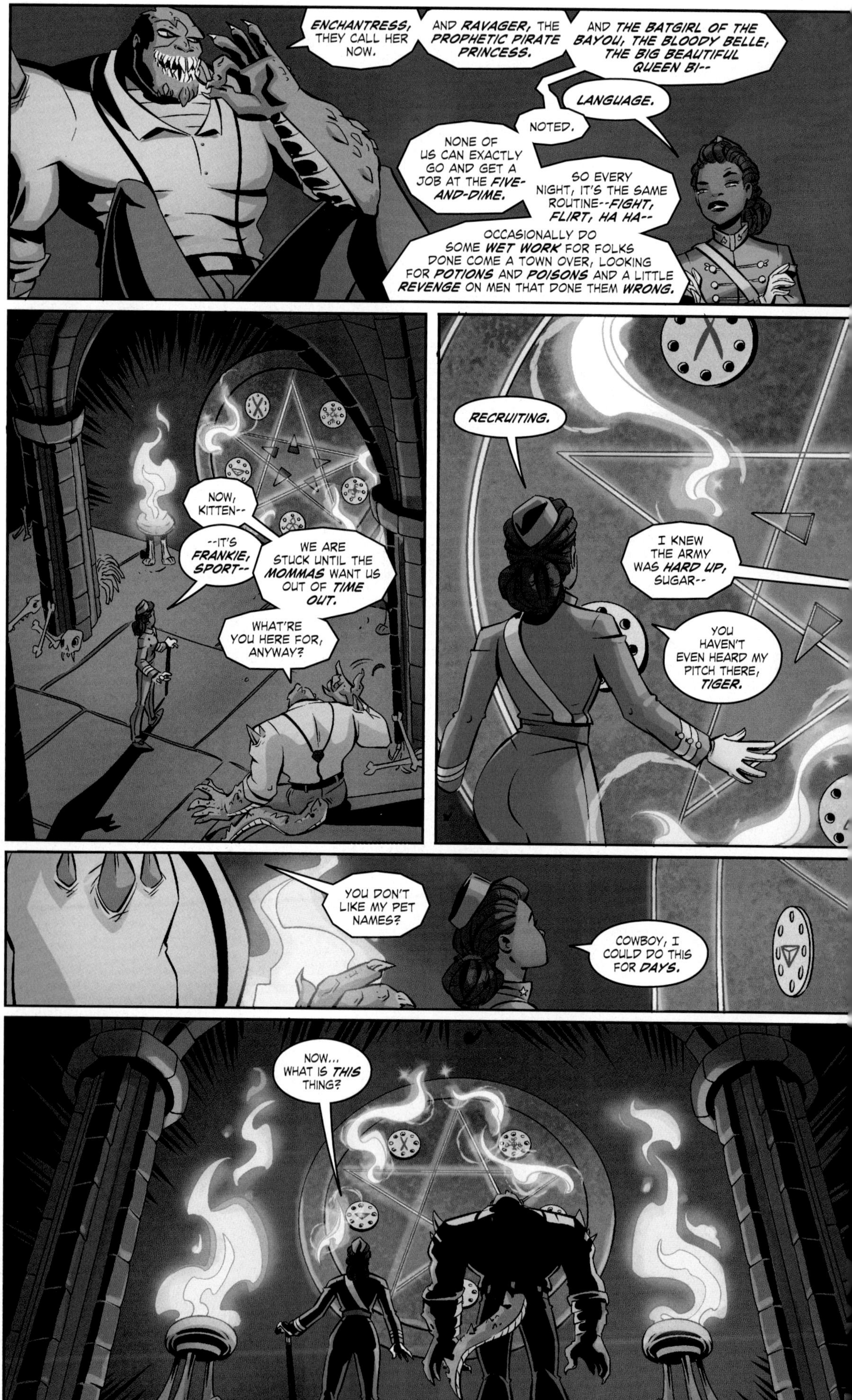
ENCHANTRESS, THEY CALL HER NOW.
AND RAVAGER, THE PROPHETIC PIRATE PRINCESS.
AND THE BATGIRL OF THE BAYOU, THE BLOODY BELLE, THE BIG BEAUTIFUL QUEEN BI--
LANGUAGE.
NOTED.
NONE OF US CAN EXACTLY GO AND GET A JOB AT THE FIVE-AND-DIME.
SO EVERY NIGHT, IT'S THE SAME ROUTINE--FIGHT, FLIRT, HA HA--
OCCASIONALLY DO SOME WET WORK FOR FOLKS DONE COME A TOWN OVER, LOOKING FOR POTIONS AND POISONS AND A LITTLE REVENGE ON MEN THAT DONE THEM WRONG.
NOW, KITTEN--
--IT'S FRANKIE, SPORT--
WE ARE STUCK UNTIL THE MOMMAS WANT US OUT OF TIME OUT.
WHAT'RE YOU HERE FOR, ANYWAY?
RECRUITING.
I KNEW THE ARMY WAS HARD UP, SUGAR--
YOU HAVEN'T EVEN HEARD MY PITCH THERE, TIGER.
YOU DON'T LIKE MY PET NAMES?
COWBOY, I COULD DO THIS FOR DAYS.
NOW... WHAT IS THIS THING?

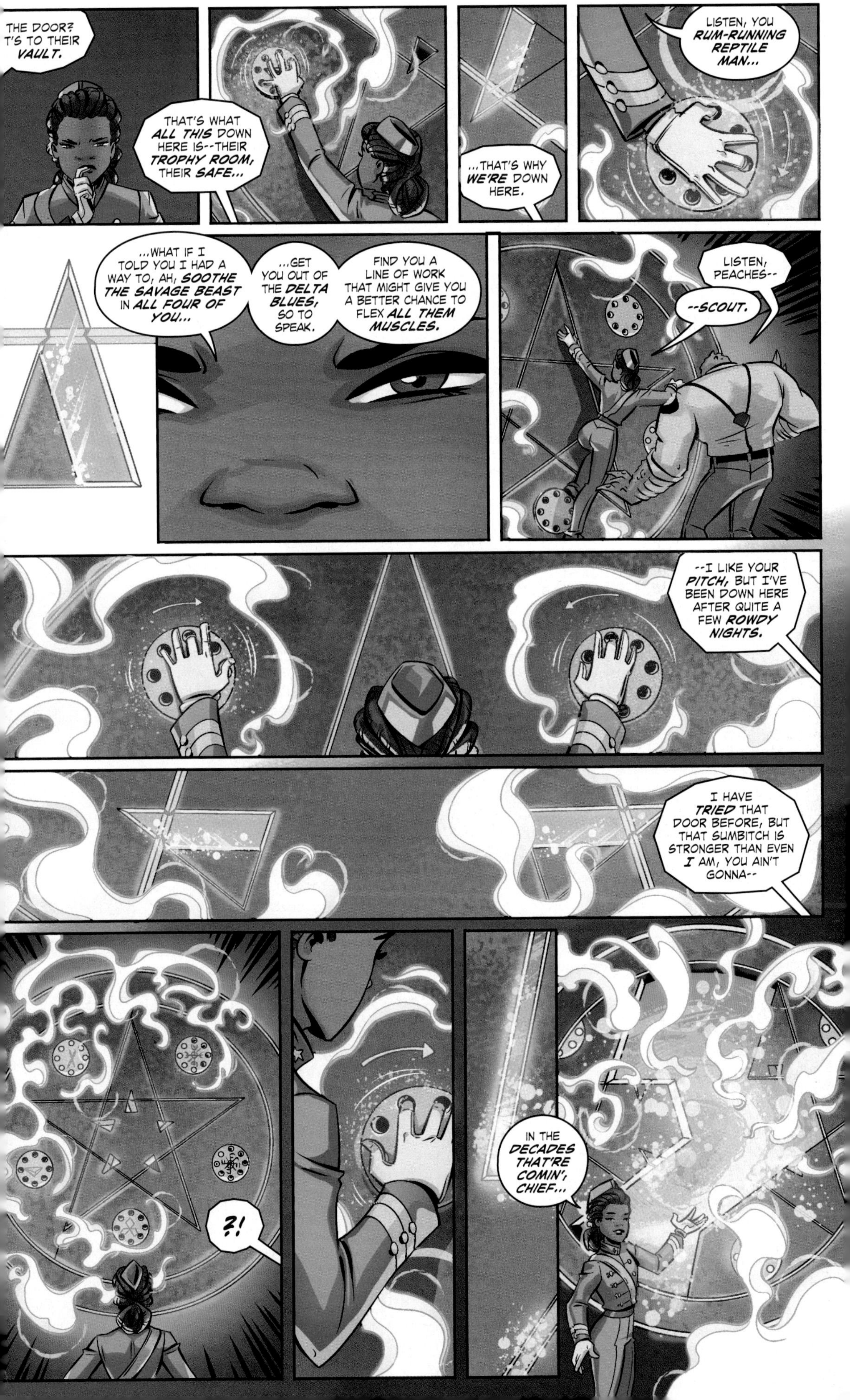
THE DOOR? T'S TO THEIR VAULT.
THAT'S WHAT ALL THIS DOWN HERE IS--THEIR TROPHY ROOM, THEIR SAFE...
...THAT'S WHY WE'RE DOWN HERE.
LISTEN, YOU RUM-RUNNING REPTILE MAN...
...WHAT IF I TOLD YOU I HAD A WAY TO, AH, SOOTHE THE SAVAGE BEAST IN ALL FOUR OF YOU...
...GET YOU OUT OF THE DELTA BLUES, SO TO SPEAK.
FIND YOU A LINE OF WORK THAT MIGHT GIVE YOU A BETTER CHANCE TO FLEX ALL THEM MUSCLES.
LISTEN, PEACHES--
--SCOUT.
--I LIKE YOUR PITCH, BUT I'VE BEEN DOWN HERE AFTER QUITE A FEW ROWDY NIGHTS.
I HAVE TRIED THAT DOOR BEFORE, BUT THAT SUMBITCH IS STRONGER THAN EVEN I AM, YOU AIN'T GONNA--
?!
IN THE DECADES THAT'RE COMIN', CHIEF...

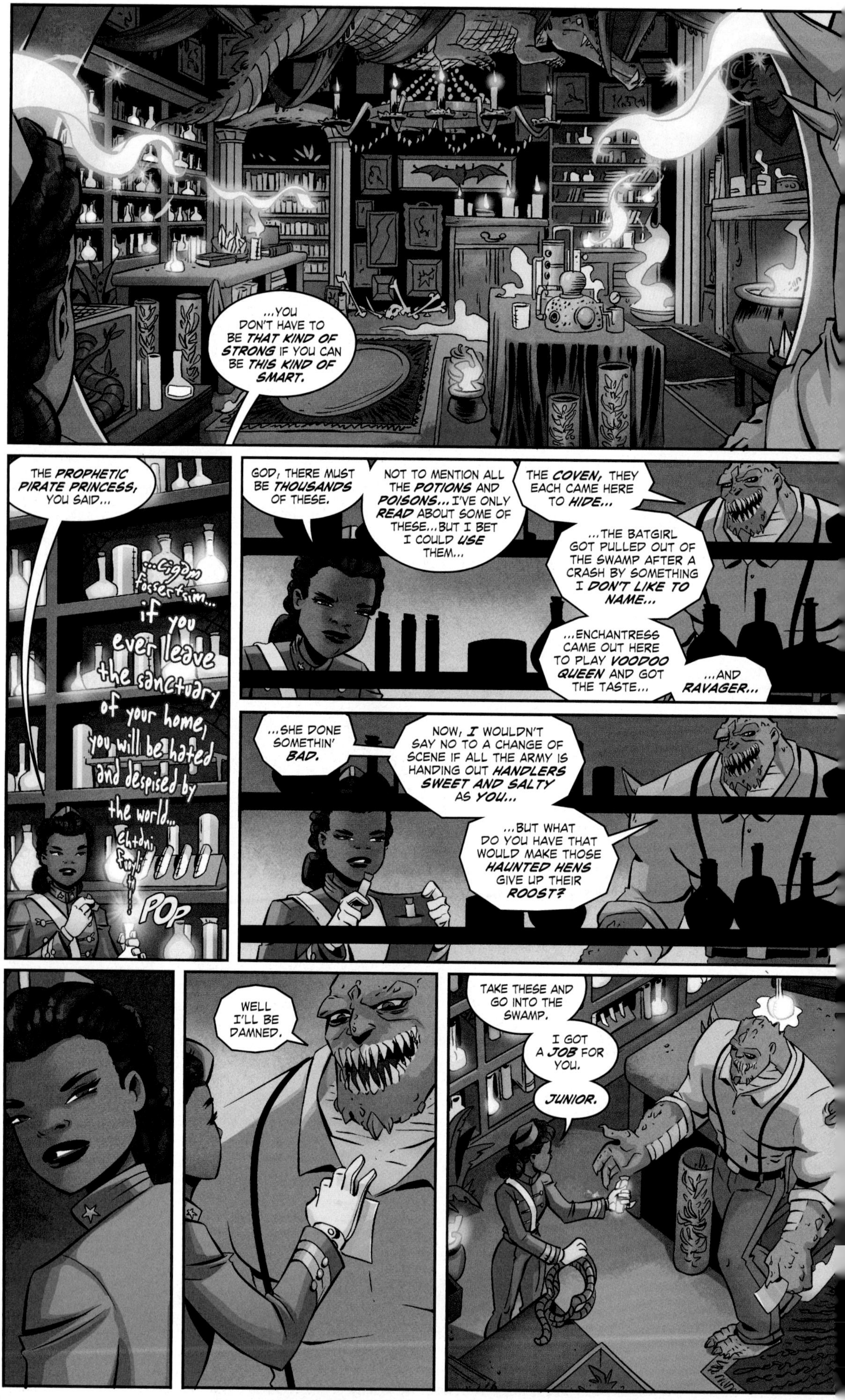
...YOU DON'T HAVE TO BE THAT KIND OF STRONG IF YOU CAN BE THIS KIND OF SMART.
THE PROPHETIC PIRATE PRINCESS, YOU SAID...
...cigam fossertsim... if you ever leave the sanctuary of your home, you will be hated and despised by the world... ehtdni fuoyli
POP
GOD, THERE MUST BE THOUSANDS OF THESE.
NOT TO MENTION ALL THE POTIONS AND POISONS... I'VE ONLY READ ABOUT SOME OF THESE... BUT I BET I COULD USE THEM...
THE COVEN, THEY EACH CAME HERE TO HIDE...
...THE BATGIRL GOT PULLED OUT OF THE SWAMP AFTER A CRASH BY SOMETHING I DON'T LIKE TO NAME...
...ENCHANTRESS CAME OUT HERE TO PLAY VOODOO QUEEN AND GOT THE TASTE...
...AND RAVAGER...
...SHE DONE SOMETHIN' BAD.
NOW, I WOULDN'T SAY NO TO A CHANGE OF SCENE IF ALL THE ARMY IS HANDING OUT HANDLERS SWEET AND SALTY AS YOU...
...BUT WHAT DO YOU HAVE THAT WOULD MAKE THOSE HAUNTED HENS GIVE UP THEIR ROOST?
WELL I'LL BE DAMNED.
TAKE THESE AND GO INTO THE SWAMP.
I GOT A JOB FOR YOU.
JUNIOR.

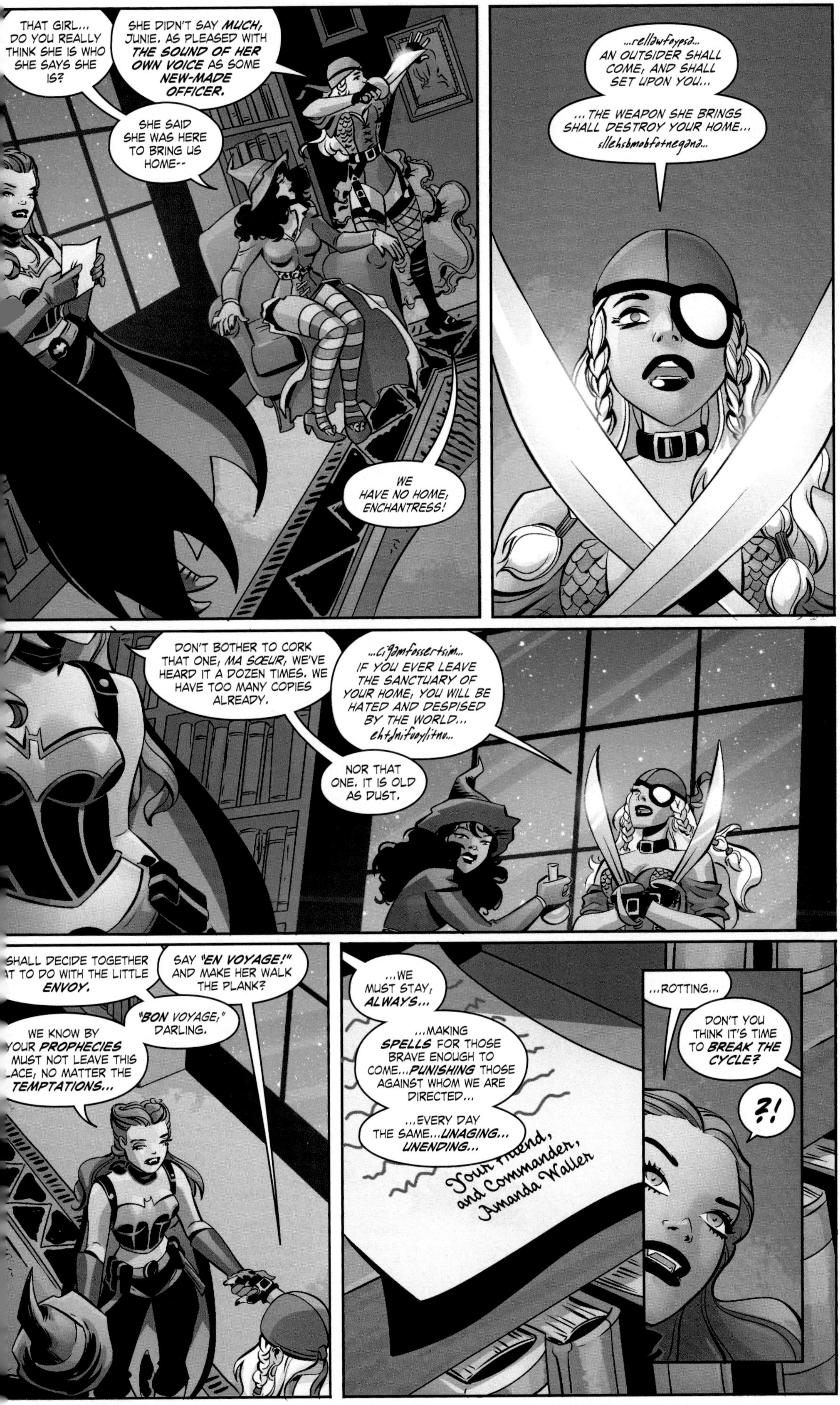

THAT GIRL... DO YOU REALLY THINK SHE IS WHO SHE SAYS SHE IS?
SHE DIDN'T SAY MUCH, JUNIE. AS PLEASED WITH THE SOUND OF HER OWN VOICE AS SOME NEW-MADE OFFICER.
SHE SAID SHE WAS HERE TO BRING US HOME--
WE HAVE NO HOME, ENCHANTRESS!
...rellawfoypsd... AN OUTSIDER SHALL COME, AND SHALL SET UPON YOU...
...THE WEAPON SHE BRINGS SHALL DESTROY YOUR HOME... sllehsbmobfotnegand...
DON'T BOTHER TO CORK THAT ONE, MA SŒUR, WE'VE HEARD IT A DOZEN TIMES. WE HAVE TOO MANY COPIES ALREADY.
...cigamfossertsim... IF YOU EVER LEAVE THE SANCTUARY OF YOUR HOME, YOU WILL BE HATED AND DESPISED BY THE WORLD... ehtdnifuoylitnu...
NOR THAT ONE. IT IS OLD AS DUST.
SHALL DECIDE TOGETHER AT TO DO WITH THE LITTLE ENVOY.
SAY "EN VOYAGE!" AND MAKE HER WALK THE PLANK?
"BON VOYAGE," DARLING.
WE KNOW BY YOUR PROPHECIES MUST NOT LEAVE THIS LACE, NO MATTER THE TEMPTATIONS...
...WE MUST STAY, ALWAYS...
...MAKING SPELLS FOR THOSE BRAVE ENOUGH TO COME...PUNISHING THOSE AGAINST WHOM WE ARE DIRECTED...
...EVERY DAY THE SAME...UNAGING... UNENDING...
Your Friend, and Commander, Amanda Waller
...ROTTING...
DON'T YOU THINK IT'S TIME TO BREAK THE CYCLE?
?!

HEY, GIRL, HEY.

THAT IS *OUR* ENTRANCE!

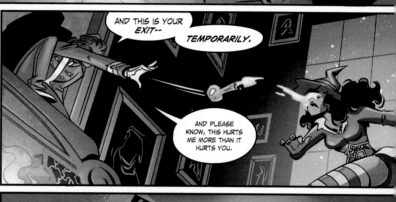

AND THIS IS YOUR *EXIT*--

TEMPORARILY.

AND PLEASE KNOW, THIS HURTS ME MORE THAN IT HURTS YOU.

DON'T *HOLLER.* IT'LL ONLY LAST A FEW MINUTES. A LITTLE TRIP DOWN MEMORY LANE.

BUT I THINK YOU MIGHT WANT TO *COOL* THAT *TEMPER* OF YOURS...

...THEN WE'LL TALK *DANCING.*

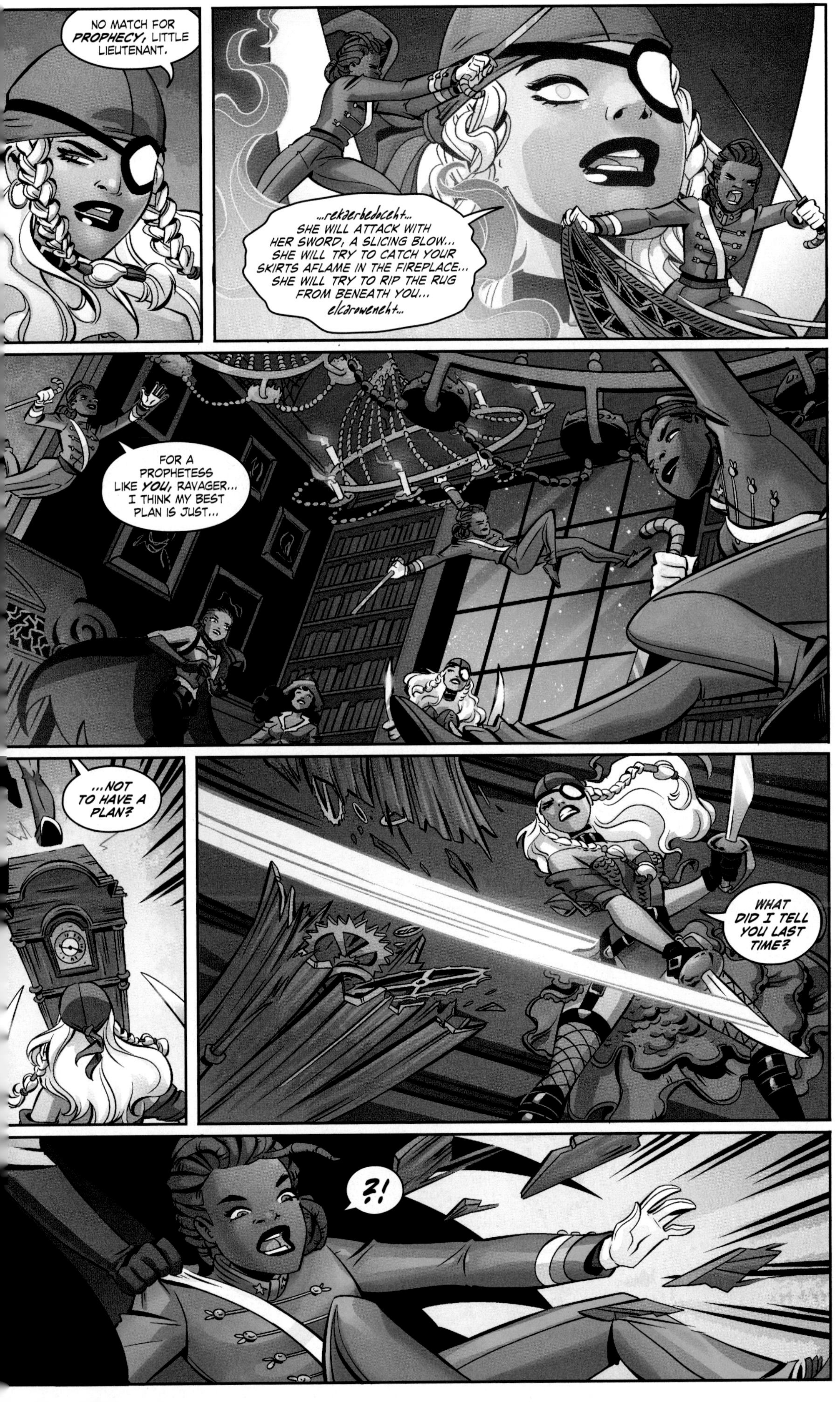
NO MATCH FOR PROPHECY, LITTLE LIEUTENANT.
...rekaerbedoceht... SHE WILL ATTACK WITH HER SWORD, A SLICING BLOW... SHE WILL TRY TO CATCH YOUR SKIRTS AFLAME IN THE FIREPLACE... SHE WILL TRY TO RIP THE RUG FROM BENEATH YOU... elcaroweneht...
FOR A PROPHETESS LIKE YOU, RAVAGER... I THINK MY BEST PLAN IS JUST...
...NOT TO HAVE A PLAN?
WHAT DID I TELL YOU LAST TIME?
?!

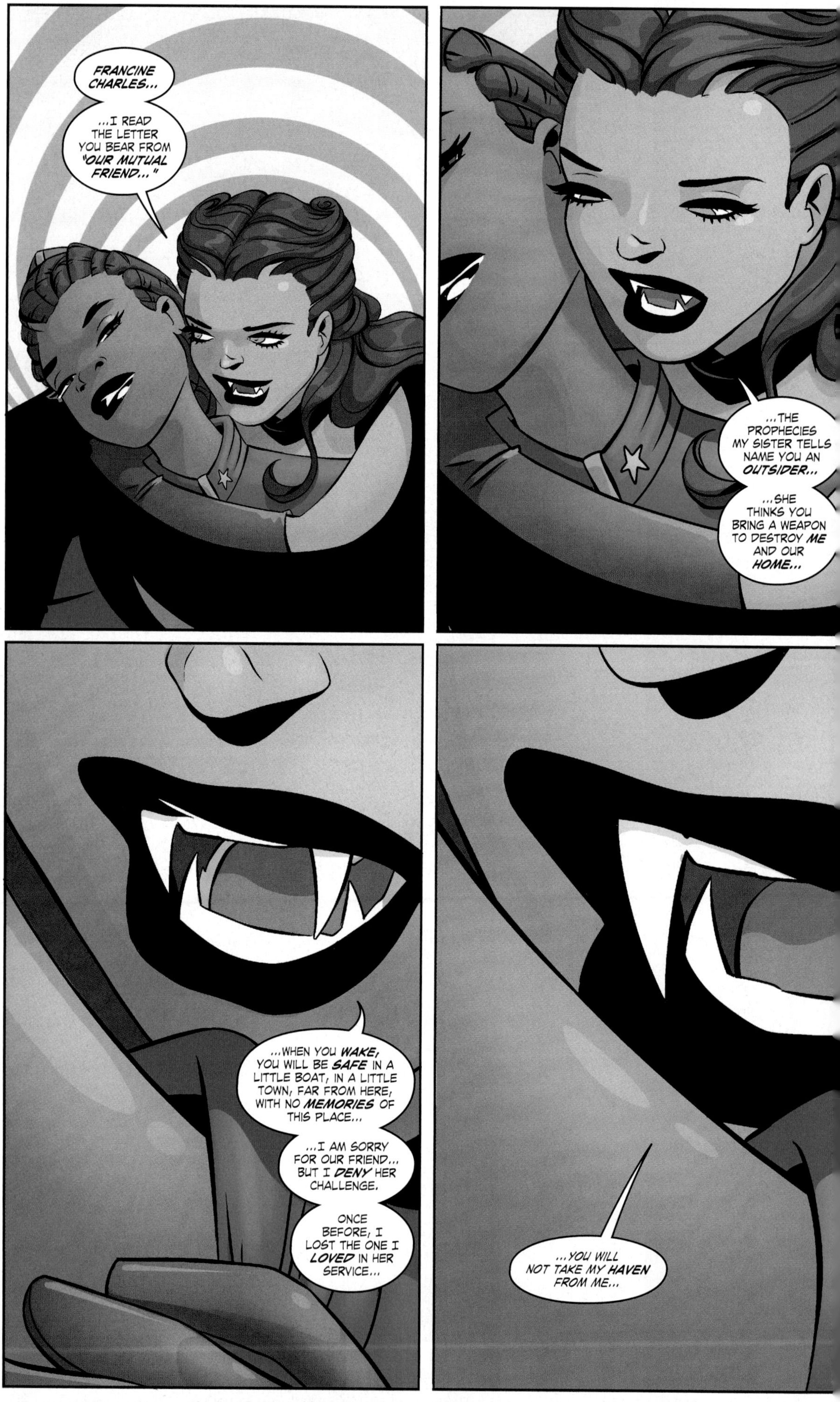
FRANCINE CHARLES...
...I READ THE LETTER YOU BEAR FROM "OUR MUTUAL FRIEND..."
...THE PROPHECIES MY SISTER TELLS NAME YOU AN OUTSIDER...
...SHE THINKS YOU BRING A WEAPON TO DESTROY ME AND OUR HOME...
...WHEN YOU WAKE, YOU WILL BE SAFE IN A LITTLE BOAT, IN A LITTLE TOWN, FAR FROM HERE, WITH NO MEMORIES OF THIS PLACE...
...I AM SORRY FOR OUR FRIEND... BUT I DENY HER CHALLENGE.
ONCE BEFORE, I LOST THE ONE I LOVED IN HER SERVICE...
...YOU WILL NOT TAKE MY HAVEN FROM ME...

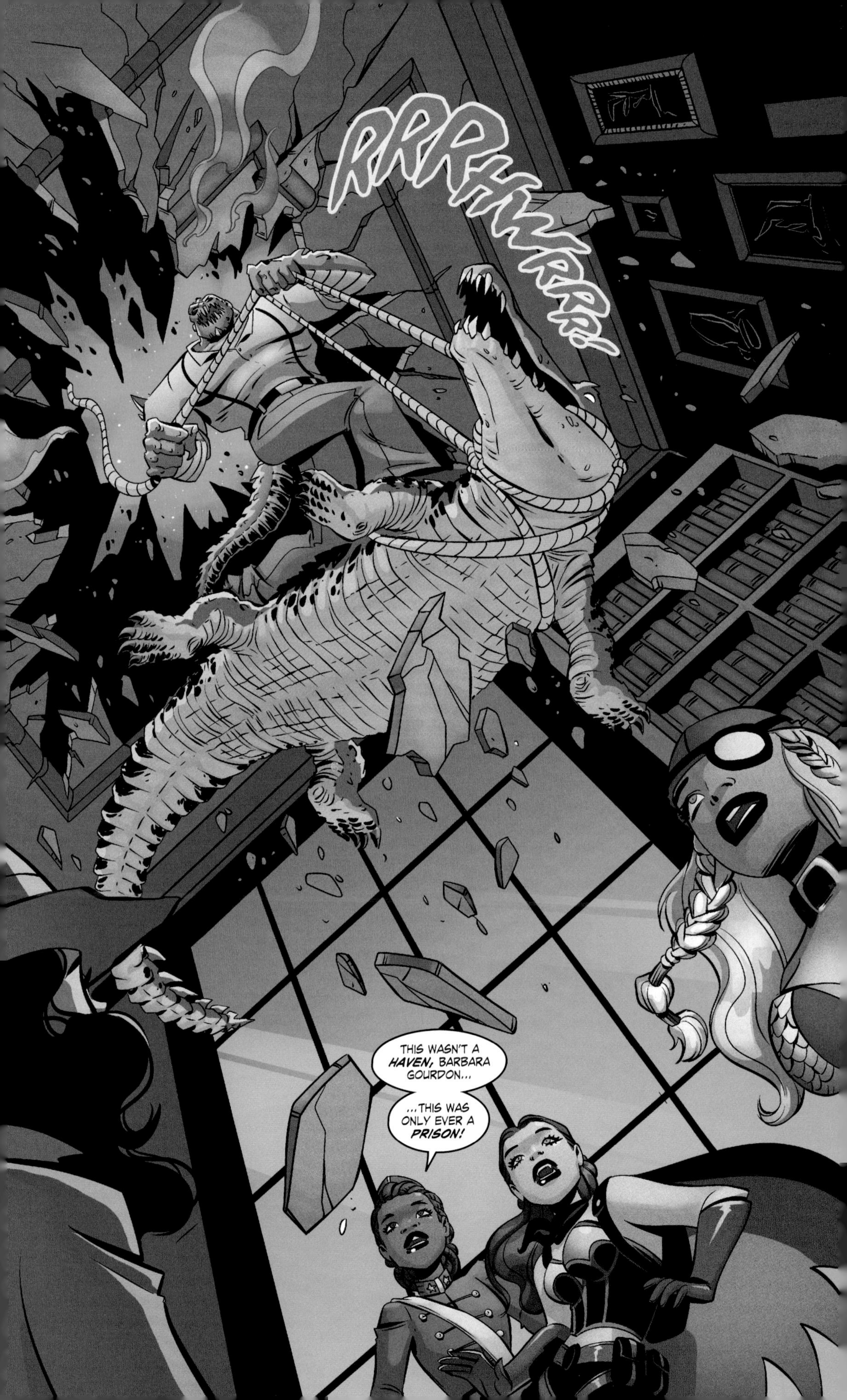
RRRHWRRR!
THIS WASN'T A HAVEN, BARBARA GOURDON...
...THIS WAS ONLY EVER A PRISON!

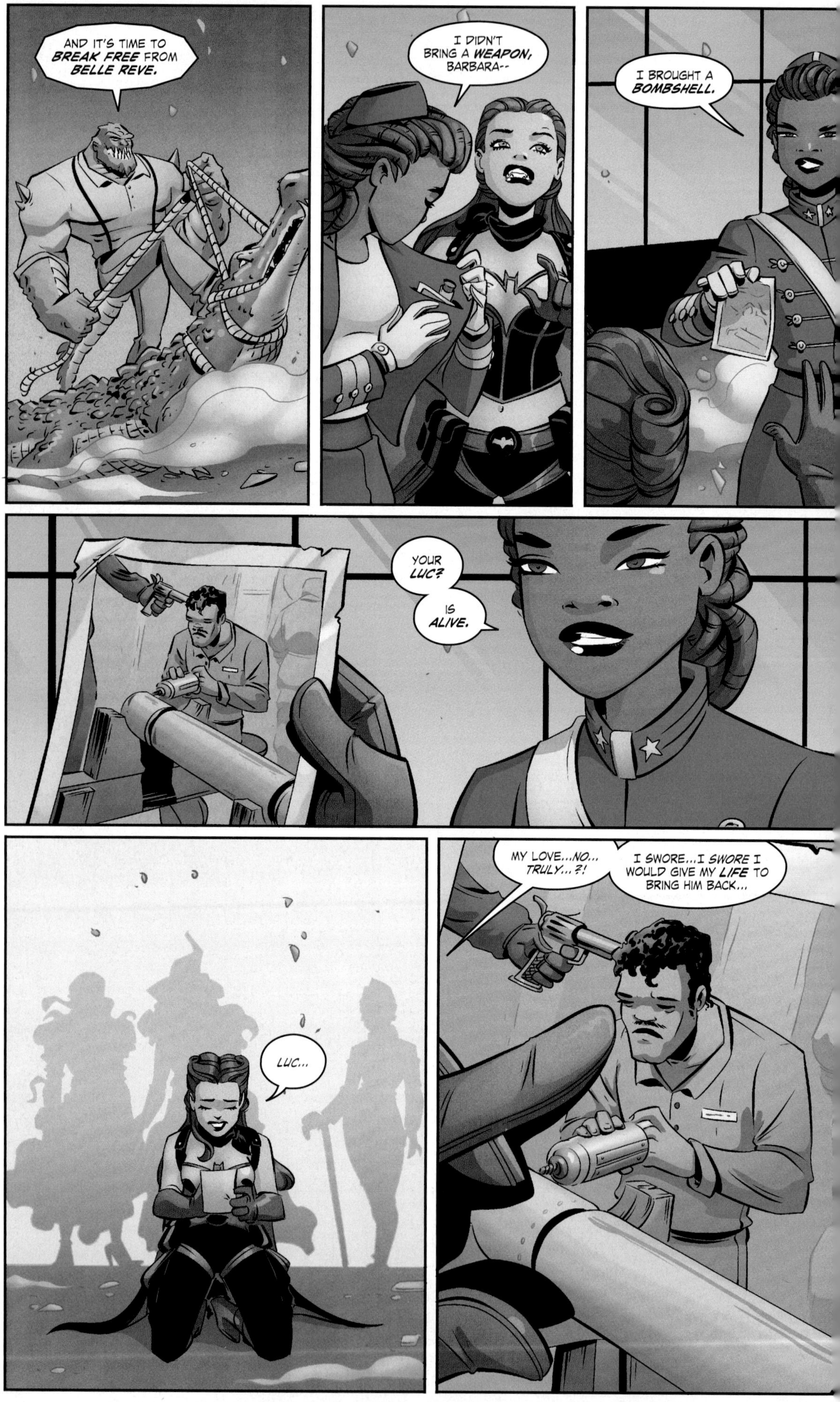
AND IT'S TIME TO BREAK FREE FROM BELLE REVE.
I DIDN'T BRING A WEAPON, BARBARA--
I BROUGHT A BOMBSHELL.
YOUR LUC?
IS ALIVE.
LUC...
MY LOVE...NO... TRULY...?!
I SWORE...I SWORE I WOULD GIVE MY LIFE TO BRING HIM BACK...

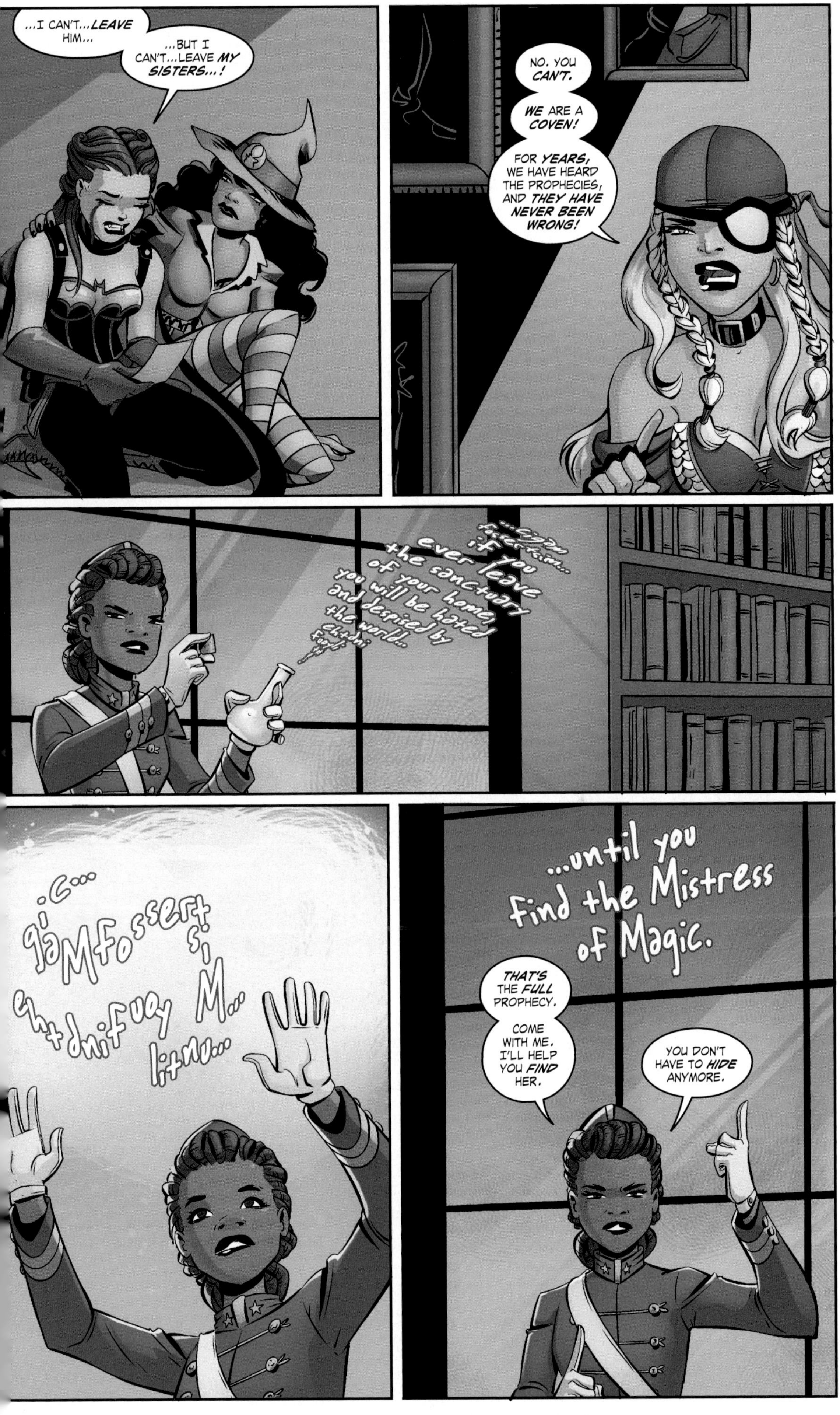

...I CAN'T...LEAVE HIM...
...BUT I CAN'T...LEAVE MY SISTERS...!
NO. YOU CAN'T.
WE ARE A COVEN!
FOR YEARS, WE HAVE HEARD THE PROPHECIES, AND THEY HAVE NEVER BEEN WRONG!
...if you ever leave the sanctuary of your home, you will be hated and despised by the world...
...until you find the Mistress of Magic.
THAT'S THE FULL PROPHECY.
COME WITH ME. I'LL HELP YOU FIND HER.
YOU DON'T HAVE TO HIDE ANYMORE.

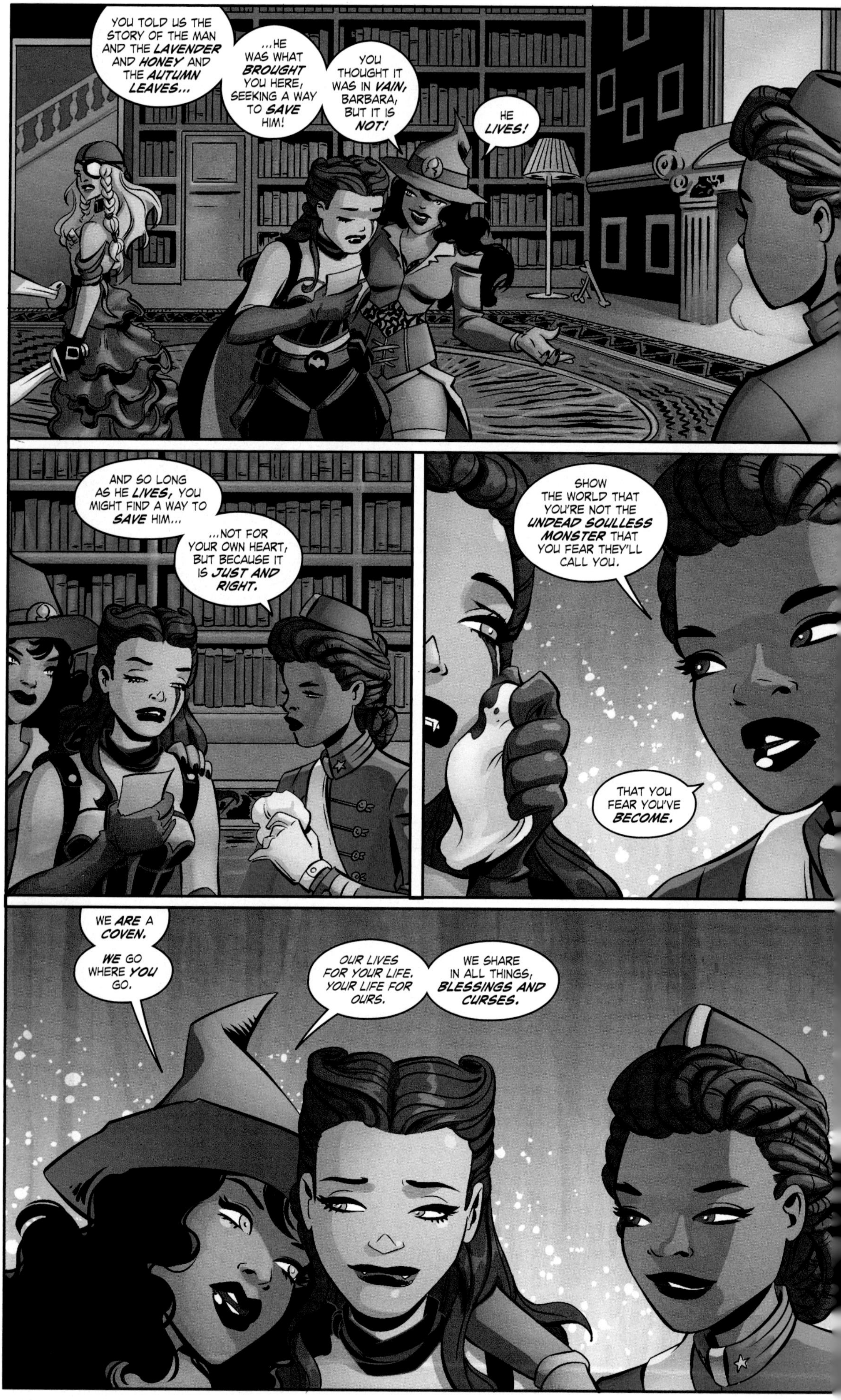
YOU TOLD US THE STORY OF THE MAN AND THE LAVENDER AND HONEY AND THE AUTUMN LEAVES...
...HE WAS WHAT BROUGHT YOU HERE, SEEKING A WAY TO SAVE HIM!
YOU THOUGHT IT WAS IN VAIN, BARBARA, BUT IT IS NOT!
HE LIVES!
AND SO LONG AS HE LIVES, YOU MIGHT FIND A WAY TO SAVE HIM...
...NOT FOR YOUR OWN HEART, BUT BECAUSE IT IS JUST AND RIGHT.
SHOW THE WORLD THAT YOU'RE NOT THE UNDEAD SOULLESS MONSTER THAT YOU FEAR THEY'LL CALL YOU.
THAT YOU FEAR YOU'VE BECOME.
WE ARE A COVEN.
WE GO WHERE YOU GO.
OUR LIVES FOR YOUR LIFE. YOUR LIFE FOR OURS.
WE SHARE IN ALL THINGS, BLESSINGS AND CURSES.

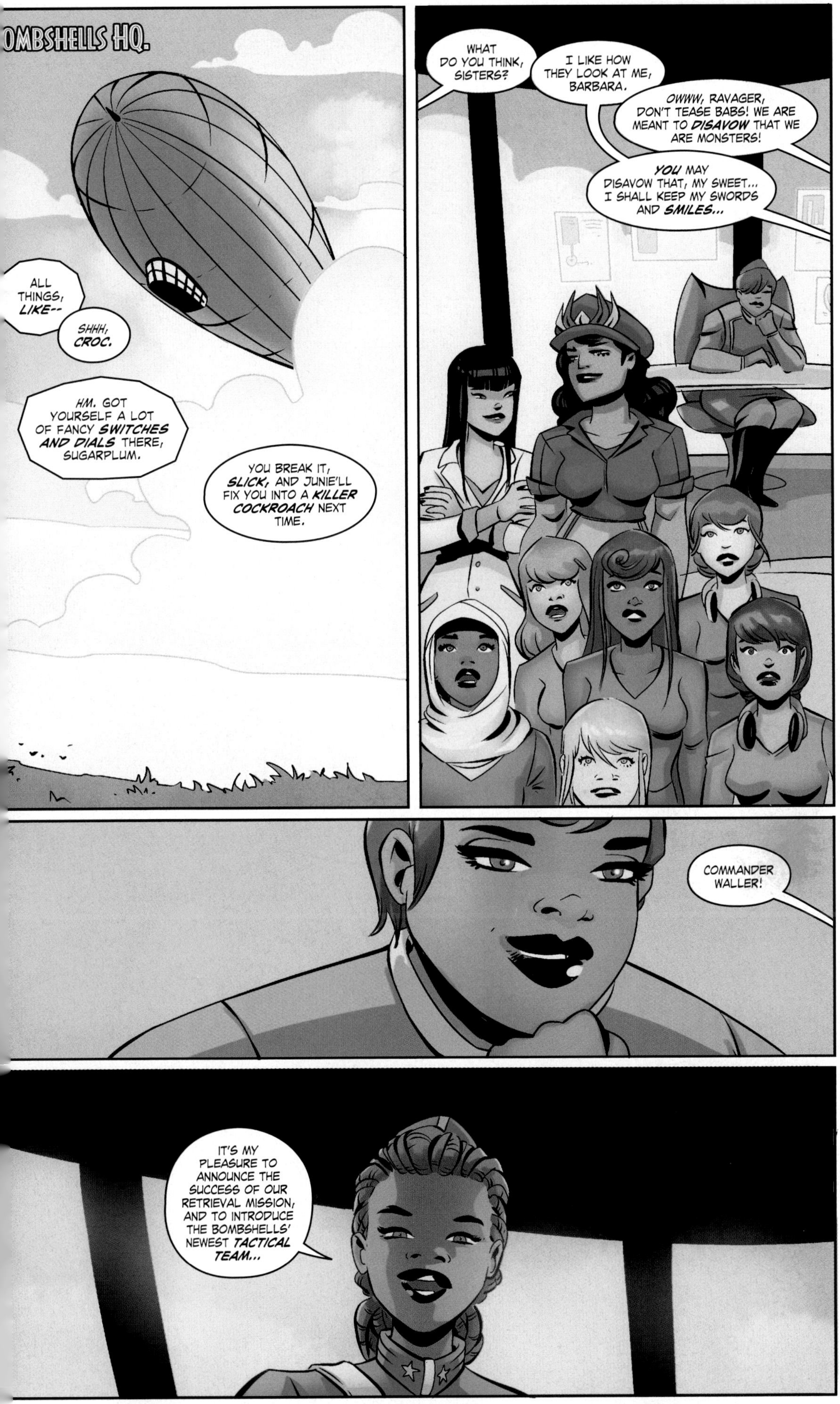
OMBSHELLS HQ.
ALL THINGS, LIKE--
SHHH, CROC.
HM. GOT YOURSELF A LOT OF FANCY SWITCHES AND DIALS THERE, SUGARPLUM.
YOU BREAK IT, SLICK, AND JUNIE'LL FIX YOU INTO A KILLER COCKROACH NEXT TIME.
WHAT DO YOU THINK, SISTERS?
I LIKE HOW THEY LOOK AT ME, BARBARA.
OWWW, RAVAGER, DON'T TEASE BABS! WE ARE MEANT TO DISAVOW THAT WE ARE MONSTERS!
YOU MAY DISAVOW THAT, MY SWEET... I SHALL KEEP MY SWORDS AND SMILES...
COMMANDER WALLER!
IT'S MY PLEASURE TO ANNOUNCE THE SUCCESS OF OUR RETRIEVAL MISSION, AND TO INTRODUCE THE BOMBSHELLS' NEWEST TACTICAL TEAM...

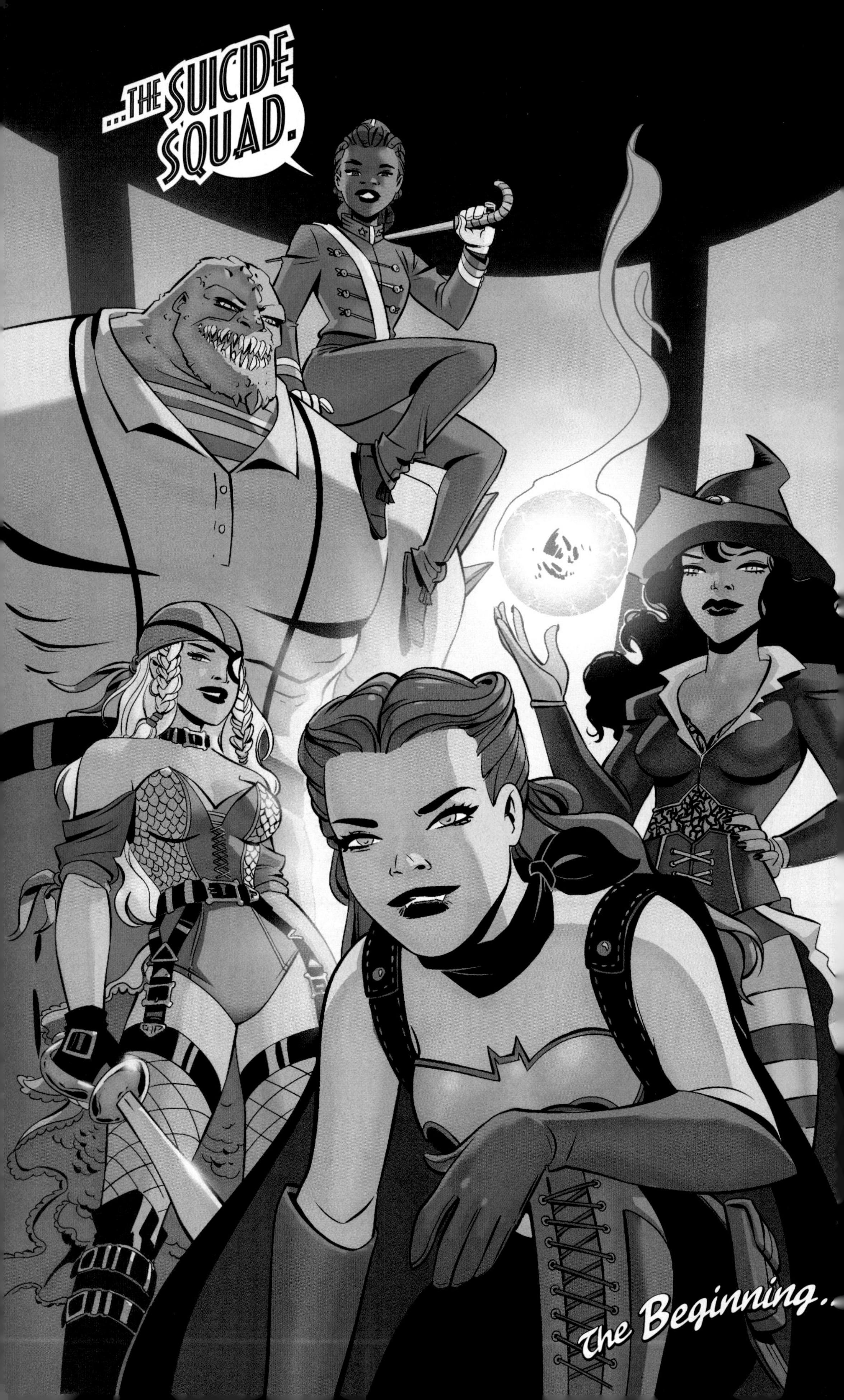
...THE SUICIDE SQUAD.
The Beginning...

DC UNIVERSE REBIRTH

WONDER WOMAN

OL. 1: THE LIES

REG RUCKA
with LIAM SHARP

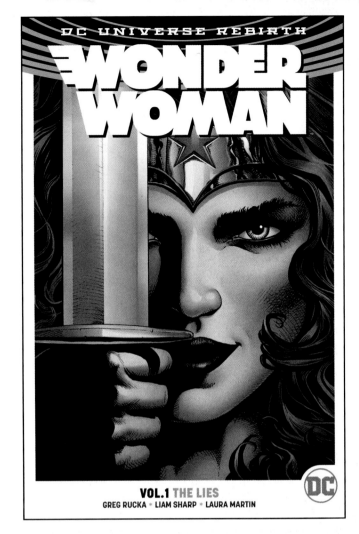

JUSTICE LEAGUE VOL. 1:
THE EXTINCTION MACHINES

SUPERGIRL VOL. 1:
REIGN OF THE SUPERMEN

BATGIRL VOL. 1:
BEYOND BURNSIDE

"A brand-new take on a classic, and it looks absolutely, jaw-droppingly fantastic."
– NEWSARAMA

"A whole lot of excitement and killer art."
– COMIC BOOK RESOURCES

BATGIRL
VOL. 1: BATGIRL OF BURNSIDE
CAMERON STEWART & BRENDEN FLETCHER with BABS TARR

BATGIRL VOL. 2: FAMILY BUSINESS

BATGIRL VOL. 3: MINDFIELDS

BLACK CANARY VOL. 1: KICKING AND SCREAMING

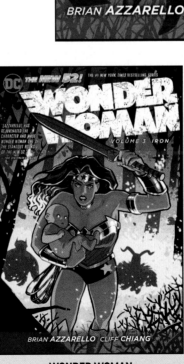

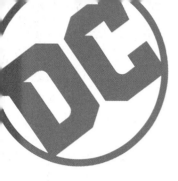

"A smart concept, snappy one-liners and a great twist to match a tag-team of talented artists."
–NEWSARAMA

"Every bit as chaotic and unabashedly fun as one would expect."
–IGN

HARLEY QUINN

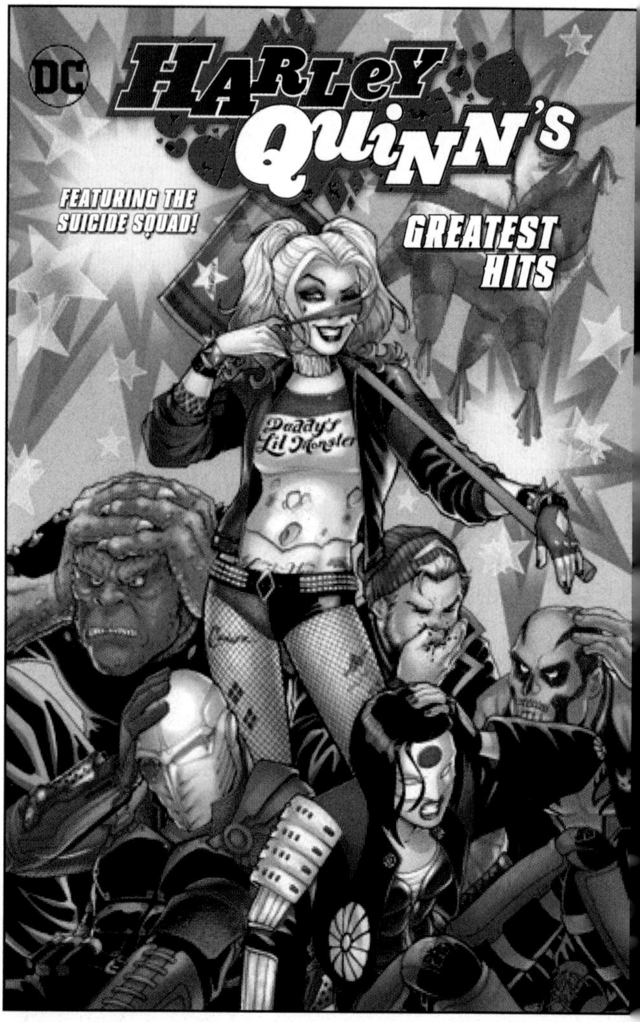

HARLEY QUINN'S
FEATURING THE SUICIDE SQUAD!
GREATEST HITS

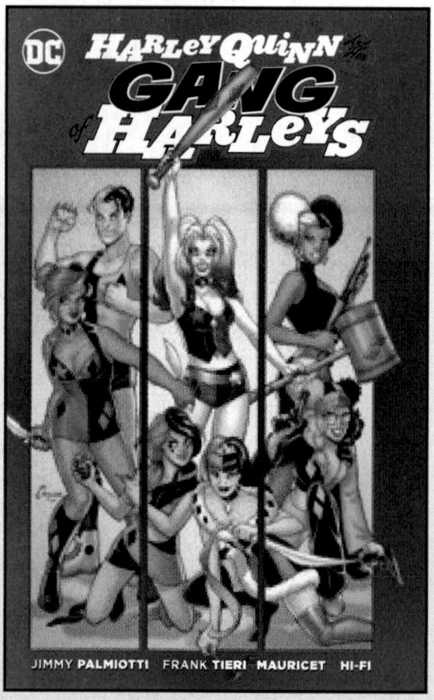

HARLEY QUINN and Her GANG of HARLEYS
JIMMY PALMIOTTI FRANK TIERI MAURICET HI-FI

HARLEY QUINN
AND HER GANG OF HARLEYS

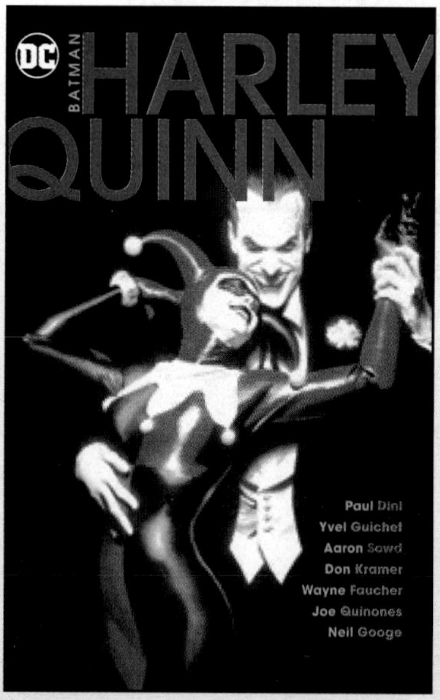

BATMAN HARLEY QUINN
Paul Dini
Yvel Guichet
Aaron Sowd
Don Kramer
Wayne Faucher
Joe Quinones
Neil Googe

BATMAN HARLEY QUINN

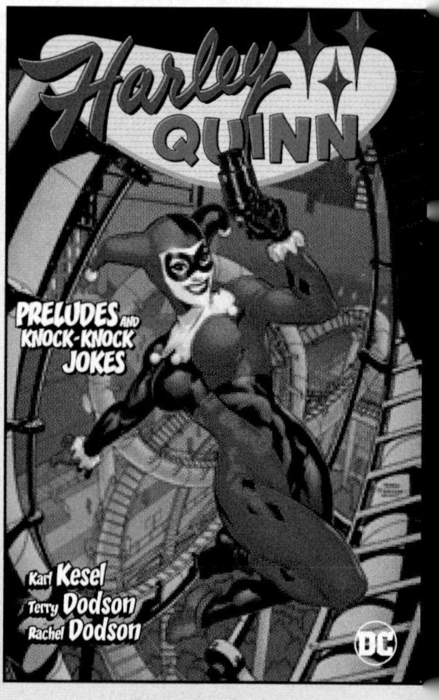

Harley QUINN
PRELUDES AND KNOCK-KNOCK JOKES
Karl Kesel
Terry Dodson
Rachel Dodson

HARLEY QUINN:
PRELUDES AND KNOCK-KNOCK JOKES

Get more DC graphic novels wherever comics and books are sold!